»Faust« ist tolles Zeug und geht über alle
gewöhnlichen Empfindungen hinaus.
— *Goethe to Eckermann, 10 January 1825*

A Companion to Goethe's Faust: Parts I and II

Studies in German Literature, Linguistics, and Culture

Edited by James Hardin
(*South Carolina*)

The Camden House Companions provide well-informed and up-to-date critical commentary on the most significant aspects of major works, periods, or literary figures. The Companions may be read profitably by the reader with a general interest in the subject. For the benefit of student and scholar, quotations are provided in the original language.

A COMPANION TO GOETHE'S
Faust

PARTS I AND II

EDITED BY
PAUL BISHOP

CAMDEN HOUSE

First published 2001 by Camden House.
Reprinted in paperpack 2006.

Camden House is an imprint of Boydell & Brewer Inc.
668 Mt. Hope Avenue, Rochester, NY 14620, USA
www.camden-house.com
and of Boydell & Brewer Limited
PO Box 9, Woodbridge, Suffolk IP12 3DF, UK
www.boydellandbrewer.com

ISBN
Cloth 1–57113–162–0
Paperback 1–57113–335–6

Library of Congress Cataloging-in-Publication Data

A Companion to Goethe's Faust: parts I and II / Edited by Paul Bishop
    p. cm. — (Studies in German literature, linguistics, and culture)
Includes bibliographical references and index.
ISBN 1–57113–162–0 (alk. paper)
    1. Goethe, Johann Wolfgang von, 1749–1832. Faust. I. Bishop, Paul, 1967–
II. Studies in German literature, linguistics, and culture (Unnumbered)

PT1925.C56 2001
832'.6—dc21
                                                                00–052944

A catalogue record for this title is available from the British Library.

This publication is printed on acid-free paper.
Printed in the United States of America.

Contents

Acknowledgments

I AM GRATEFUL TO ALL THE CONTRIBUTORS who agreed to support this project, and have contributed essays to the *Companion*. I am fortunate to work in a Department where *Faust I* is taught at second-year undergraduate level and *Faust II* at Honours; but, in particular, I should like to thank Roger Stephenson for his help throughout the conception and execution of the project, and for his contributions to the Introduction. My editor at Camden House, Jim Hardin, was also immensely supportive throughout the editing process. For her preparation of the index, I am much indebted to Andrea Greengrass. And my thanks are finally due to Meta Jamison, for her technical assistance when editing the contributions.

P. B.
December 2000

Abbreviations

All references to *Faust* are to line numbers, given in parentheses. For reasons of convenience, the text used is from the Hamburger Ausgabe (*Werke*, edited by Erich Trunz, vol. 3 [Hamburg: Wegner, 1949]). Throughout the *Companion*, the following abbreviations are used:

HA   *Werke* [Hamburger Ausgabe]. Ed. Erich Trunz. 14 vols. Hamburg: Wegner, 1948–1964; revised edition, Munich: C.H. Beck, 1972–1988

FA   *Sämtliche Werke* [Frankfurter Ausgabe]. Ed. Dieter Borchmeyer et al. 40 vols. Frankfurt am Main: Deutscher Klassiker Verlag, 1985–1999

GA   *Gedenkausgabe der Werke, Briefe und Gespräche* [Gedenkausgabe]. Ed. Ernst Beutler. 27 vols. Zurich: Artemis-Verlag, 1948–1971

JA   *Sämtliche Werke* [Jubiläumsausgabe]. Ed. Eduard von der Hellen. 41 vols. Stuttgart: Cotta, 1902–1912

WA   *Werke* [Weimarer Ausgabe]. Ed. on behalf of the Grand Duchess Sophie of Sachsen. 134 vols. Weimar: Böhlau, 1887–1919

Introduction: Reading *Faust* Today

Paul Bishop

IN 1999, THE TWO-HUNDRED-AND-FIFTIETH ANNIVERSARY of the birth of Goethe, a computerized analysis of the holdings of the Library of Congress in Washington was undertaken. Peter Dickson's findings, published in the *Washington Post* (12 September 1999), showed that, of the most famous names in history, Goethe was in eighth position, after (in descending order) Jesus, Shakespeare, Lenin, Abraham Lincoln, Napoleon Bonaparte, Karl Marx, and the Virgin Mary. Of those 3,431 books written about him, doubtless a large proportion is about *Faust*.

Two years earlier, in spring 1997, the prestigious German weekly *Die Zeit* conducted a survey among a variety of leading professionals, academics, and intellectuals, to find out which ten books they considered form a canon. In many cases, *Faust* was not only included but featured at the top of the list. The Swiss writer Adolf Muschg, for example, laid great emphasis on the central importance of *Faust*:

> Goethes "Faust" — I und II — ist ein Atlas der europäischen Moderne. Heutige Gymnasiasten werden darin anfangs nur wenige Gegenden wiedererkennen und "besetzen." Das Weitere kann man ihrem Entdeckermut überlassen, es kommt nur darauf an, ihn geweckt zu haben. "Faust" ist ein Stück, das seine Leser ein Leben lang immer neu inszenieren, aber dafür müssen sie ihm einmàl begegnet sein. (*Die Zeit*, Nr 21, 1997)

In the English-speaking world, the status of *Faust* as a canonical work has been most interestingly discussed in recent years by Harold Bloom. His account begins, however, with the statement that "of all the strongest Western writers, Goethe now seems the least available to our sensibility," and he describes *Faust II* as "the countercanonical poem" (203). Yet he goes on to claim that "Goethe's remoteness is part of his enormous value for us now, particularly at a time when French speculators have proclaimed the death of the author and the hegemony of texts. Every Goethe text, however divergent from the others, bears the mark of his unique and overwhelming personality, which cannot be evaded or deconstructed" (204). Yet whilst it might appear from these

remarks that Bloom is keeping company with a conservative critical approach to Goethe, his summary of what he regards as the central message of *Faust* is at odds with much of the criticism on the work:

> [*Faust*] becomes a banquet of sense, though doubtless too replete
> with scarcely healthy viands. As a sexual nightmare or erotic fantasy, it
> has no rival, and one understands why the shocked Coleridge declined
> to translate the poem. It is certainly a work about what, if anything,
> will suffice, and Goethe finds myriad ways of showing us that sexuality
> by itself will not. Even more obsessively, *Faust* teaches us that, with-
> out an active sexuality, absolutely nothing will suffice. (210)

Whereas Bloom concentrates on Goethe's relevance for the present
moment and focuses on one particular issue in *Faust*, the Swiss psy-
chologist C. G. Jung opened up a hugely influential and vaster perspective, albeit at the risk of losing any sense of specificity, when, in his
letter to Max Rychner of 28 February 1932, he wrote:

> *Faust* ist der neueste Pfeiler jener Brücke des Geistes, die sich über
> den Sumpf der Weltgeschichte spannt, anhebend mit dem Gilgamesh-
> Epos, dem *I Ging*, den *Upanishaden*, dem *Tao-te-king*, den Frag-
> menten des Heraklit, und sich fortsetzend im Johannesevangelium,
> den Paulinischen Briefen, im Meister Eckhart und in Dante. [. . .]
> *Faust* ist überweltlich, und darum entrückt er, er ist ebensoviel Zu-
> kunft wie Vergangenheit und darum lebendigste Gegenwart. (121–
> 22)

In the context of the well-attested enduring importance of Goethe's
Faust in general, and the particular urgency of its relevance today, the
purpose of the present volume is threefold. First, it is intended to accompany and assist the reading and interpretation of *Faust* by all those
fascinated by the great poem, especially students, postgraduates, and
academic colleagues. In this sense, then, it is a "companion." Second,
the book offers a variety of essays by leading international experts in the
field of German studies from universities in the United States, the
United Kingdom, Germany, and Italy. Although the contributions
concern themselves with aspects of the work which are, by common
consent, the most important, each author has been able to argue an independent case for the reading of *Faust*, ensuring a plurality, or even a
fruitful tension, of views, standpoints, and interpretations across the
volume as a whole. Finally, it is hoped that the essays contained in the
Companion will stimulate debate on the text, and encourage further research based on a close reading of the original text.

The Composition of *Faust*

The history of the composition of *Faust* is of such complexity that it deserves a book in its own right, and has in fact inspired several, including Eudo C. Mason's detailed study of 1967, John Gearey's study of the composition of *Faust I* (1981), and the data summarized in the chronological summaries appended to the introductions of David Luke's translations. The relationship between the work and the author's life can perhaps best be understood in terms of Goethe's notion of "anticipation." In his conversation with Eckermann of 26 February 1824, Goethe explained how human knowledge is not confined to what we know through actual experience. According to Goethe, our knowledge of fundamental and universal (one might say, archetypal) situations is innate, but the poet in particular possesses the power of projecting into his work by *Antizipation* this image of the world within:

> So konnte ich im "Faust" den düstern Zustand des Lebensüberdrusses im Helden, sowie die Liebesempfindungen Gretchens recht gut durch Antizipation in meiner Macht haben [. . .] Hätte ich nicht die Welt durch Antizipation bereits in mir getragen, ich wäre mit sehenden Augen blind geblieben, und alle Erforschung und Erfahrung wäre nichts gewesen als ein ganz totes vergebliches Bemühen.

So it is by "anticipation" that Goethe can conjure up the depths of the hero's despair and the heights of Gretchen's love out of his own inner consciousness.

Goethe's interest in the Faust legend reached right back to his childhood, when he saw the story performed as a puppet-play in Frankfurt. In his autobiographical work *Dichtung und Wahrheit* (Part II, Book 10) he remembered long after the events:

> Die bedeutende Puppenspielfabel des [Faust] klang und summte gar vieltönig in mir wider. Auch ich hatte mich in allem Wissen umhergetrieben und war früh genug auf die Eitelkeit desselben hingewiesen worden. Ich hatte es auch im Leben auf allerlei Weise versucht, und war immer unbefriedigter und gequälter zurückgekommen. Nun trug ich diese Dinge, sowie manche andre, mit mir herum und ergetzte mich daran in einsamen Stunden, ohne jedoch etwas davon aufzuschreiben. (HA 9, 413–4)

Subsequently, he may have read the later chapbook version of the play by the pseudonymous "Christlich Meynender" (see below), and the trial and execution for infanticide of Susanna Margarethe Brandt in Frankfurt in 1772 may have provided an extra-literary impulse. Much later, in 1783, as *Geheimrat* in the government of Weimar, he signed the death-warrant of a young girl accused of child-murder — to the later consternation of, among others, Thomas Mann (315, 617; see Wilson, 7). Between 1773 and 1775 Goethe began work on the core-scenes of *Faust I*, including the so-called "Gelehrtentragödie" (reflecting his irritation with the university in Leipzig) and the "Gretchentragödie" (reflecting his broken relationship with Friederike Brion). The start on *Faust* was thus probably contemporaneous with his novel, *Die Leiden des jungen Werther* (1774) (Eckermann, 12 February 1829). The sequence of scenes written at this time is known as the "Urfaust," a copy of which was made in 1776 by Luise von Göchhausen, a member of the Weimar court circle. (The copy was subsequently discovered among the papers of one of her descendents and published in 1887 as *Goethes Faust in ursprünglicher Gestalt*.) Compared with the later version of the text, published in volume 7 of his *Schriften* as *Faust, ein Fragment* (1790), the "Urfaust" is, in literary terms, less sophisticated. The scenes entitled "Hexenküche" and "Wald und Höhle" were written during the journey to Italy in 1788, and the positioning of the latter scene in Part One as a whole has provoked much critical discussion.

Thanks to Schiller's chivvying, Goethe returned to his work on *Faust* during the so-called *Balladenjahr* of 1797. His correspondence with Schiller reveals his feelings about the work achieved thus far, and his ambition for the rest of the play. On 22 June 1797, he wrote to Schiller: "Unser Balladenstudium hat mich wieder auf diesen Dunst- und Nebelweg gebracht, und die Umstände raten mir, in mehr als *einem* Sinne, eine Zeitlang darauf herumzuirren"; and on 24 June 1797 he spoke of returning to "diese Symbol-, Ideen- und Nebelwelt." On 27 June 1797 he wrote that the theory of the epic poem, which he and Schiller had discussed in their correspondence and had issued in the essay *Über epische und dramatische Dichtung* (pub. 1827), had helped his work "bei dem Ganzen, das immer ein Fragment bleiben wird." In his letter of 1 July 1797, he described his progress on *Faust* using a strange image. Just as, in *Die Traumdeutung* (1900), Freud speaks of the dream-wish arising from the dense tangle of dream-thoughts "wie der Pilz aus seinem Mycelium" (Freud 1942, 530), Goethe wrote, in strikingly similar terms: "Meinen 'Faust' habe ich, in Absicht auf Schema und Übersicht, in der Geschwindigkeit recht vorgeschoben, doch hat die deutliche Baukunst die Luftphänomene bald wieder verscheucht. Es käme jetzt nur auf einen ruhigen Monat an, so sollte das Werk zu männiglicher Verwunderung und Entsetzen, wie eine große Schwamm-familie, aus der Erde wachsen." The seeming intractability of the material is, however, reflected in further comments in his letters of 1 July, 5 July, 6 December 1797, and 29 April 1798. As well as revising the text and adding the scenes entitled "Studierzimmer," "Vor dem Tor," and "Walpurgisnacht," he prefixed the dedicatory ode ("Zueignung") and the framework (for both Parts) of the "Vorspiel auf dem Theater" and the "Prolog am Himmel." The version that we know today as *Faust: Der Tragödie erster Teil* was completed in 1806 and published in its present form in 1808.

In the meantime, however, he had begun work on Part Two, writing a substantial portion (lines 8489 to 8802) of Act 3, the "Helena" act, in 1800 (in other words, at exactly the same time as he was finishing Part One). This section appeared in print before any other part of *Faust II*, being published in 1827 as *Helena: Klassisch-romantische Phantasmagoria: Zwischenspiel zu Faust* (in volume 4 of the *Ausgabe letzter Hand* of Goethe's works). The title alone, suggesting an accompanying rather than a central function within the economy of the drama, indicates the fluidity of Goethe's conception of the structure of the work, right until its final stages. Yet, for all the intellectual, cultural, and metrical richness and sophistication of *Faust II,* Goethe remained aware of his fundamental debt to the traditional legend. In a letter to Wilhelm von Humboldt of 22 October 1826, Goethe describes "Helena" as "eine meiner ältesten Konzeptionen, sie ruht auf der Puppenspielüberlieferung," although the location of the scene (if the critics' identification is correct) in Mistra, a fortress city not far from Sparta, is an example of the kind of individual and transforming detail Goethe added to the legendary *Stoff.* Whereas Schiller had once encouraged Goethe to carry on his Faustian labors, this role now fell to Eckermann, whose *Gespräche* offer insights into the conditions under which the work continued to develop. By this time, it was clear to Goethe that the text was taking on an ever more complex shape, and his attempts to summarize the action of his rapidly expanding material can be found in the "Paralipomena" (HA 4, 427, 430–33, 438–44; Luke 1994, 241–50). Moreover, Goethe had decided that the completed version would be withheld from his contemporaries by being sealed until after his death. So although Act 1 appeared in volume 12 of the *Ausgabe letzter Hand* in 1828, and, following the completion of the *Klassische Walpurgisnacht* (Act 2) and Act 5 in 1830 and Act 4 in 1831, the text of Part Two in its entirety was only published in volume 41 of the *Ausgabe letzter Hand,* simultaneously volume 1 of the *Nachgelassene Werke* (1832). The completion of what Goethe had, since his diary entry of 11 February 1826, called his "Hauptgeschäft," occurred on 22 July 1831, only shortly before his death; in this respect, however, it is not unique in its importance for Goethe, since the final work on *Wilhelm*

Meisters Wanderjahre, which like *Faust* is described in his diary for 1828–29 as the "Hauptgeschäft," was undertaken in the same period.

In turn, the relationship between the work and its author raises the question of poetic unity. Goethe's own comments on the issue are themselves, as Wilkinson and Willoughby have shown, anything but consistent (95–96). In a conversation with the historian Heinrich Luden on 19 August 1806, for instance, Goethe declared: "Ein höheres Interesse hat doch der Faust, die Idee welche den Dichter beseelt hat, und welche das Einzelne des Gedichtes zum Ganzen verknüpft, für das Einzelne Gesetz ist und dem Einzelnen seine Bedeutung gibt." Yet a couple of decades later, in conversation with Eckermann on 6 May 1827, Goethe denied that there was any central idea in *Faust*:

> Da kommen [die Deutschen] und fragen, welche Idee ich in meinem "Faust" zu verkörpern gesucht. Als ob ich das selber wüßte und aussprechen könnte! — *Vom Himmel durch die Welt zur Hölle*, das wäre zur Not etwas; aber das ist keine Idee, sondern Gang der Handlung. Und ferner, daß der Teufel die Wette verliert, und daß ein aus schweren Verirrungen immerfort zum Besseren aufstrebender Mensch zu *erlösen* sei, das ist zwar ein wirksamer, manches erklärender guter Gedanke, aber es ist keine *Idee*, die dem Ganzen und jeder einzelnen Szene im besonderen zugrunde liege. Es hätte auch in der Tat ein schönes Ding werden müssen, wenn ich ein so reiches, buntes und höchst mannigfaltiges Leben, wie ich es im "Faust" zur Anschauung gebracht, auf die magere Schnur einer einzigen durchgehenden Idee hätte reihen wollen!

Although the reconciliation of these two comments turns on the ideas of inspiration (*Beseelung*) and embodiment (*Verkörperung*), the latter statement should also be seen, however, in the context of the notion of "incommensurability," a central concept mentioned at the end of this conversation — "*je inkommensurabeler und für den Verstand unfaßlicher eine poetische Produktion, desto besser*" — and evoked elsewhere (see 3 January 1830 and 13 February 1831). But for Goethe, the purpose of down-playing the importance of the understanding is not to indulge in irrationalism, but rather, as R. H. Stephenson (1996) has shown, to give the imagination, in its aesthetic modality, its due: "Wenn durch die Phantasie nicht Dinge entständen, die für den Verstand ewig problematisch bleiben, so wäre überhaupt zu der Phantasie nicht viel." Thereby, Goethe added, one had reached the central distinction not just between "poetry" and "prose" but between the poetic and the prosaic in the most generalized sense: "Dies ist es, wodurch sich die Poesie von der Prosa unterscheidet, bei welcher der Verstand immer zu Hause ist und sein mag und soll" (to Eckermann on 5 July 1827). In another conversation with Eckermann, Goethe appears to suggest that his writings, and so also *Faust*, are hermeneutically reserved for a limited readership: "*Meine Sachen können nicht populär werden*; wer daran denkt und dafür strebt, ist in einem Irrtum. Sie sind nicht für die Masse geschrieben, sondern nur für einzelne Menschen, die etwas Ähnliches wollen und suchen und die in ähnlichen Richtungen begriffen sind" (11 October 1828). Rather than composing for an elite, Goethe implies that his writings are aimed at *individuals* (and hence the contrast with the *Masse*), for he knew only too well that such works as *Werther* could be "popular," in the sense of Schiller's "generalisierte Individualität." That said, he was nevertheless prepared on 6 June 1831 to recognize "der Schlüssel zu Fausts Rettung," and to discuss it in somewhat different terms:

> in Faust selber eine immer höhere und reinere Tätigkeit bis ans Ende, und von oben die ihm zu Hülfe kommende ewige Liebe. Es steht dieses mit unserer religiösen Vorstellung durchaus in Harmonie, nach welcher wir nicht bloß durch eigene Kraft selig werden, sondern durch die hinzukommende göttliche Gnade.

Although such an interpretation of the "message" of *Faust* may well be susceptible of "harmonization" with traditional religious (in other words, Christian) beliefs, and although the plot of Part Two, however complex, retains essential elements of the traditional legends, the import of Goethe's *Faust* can be read as an inversion of the Christian original, as a secular or even pagan interpretation of the tradition.

Goethe and the Goddess

Commenting on the importance of eroticism in the second volume of his *History of Sexuality*, Michel Foucault observed that *Faust* exemplified the linkage in Western culture between, on the one hand, pleasure and the access to knowledge, and, on the other, the theme of love for a woman, her virginity, her purity, her fall, and her redemptive power ("un exemple de la manière dont la question du plaisir et celle de l'accès à la connaissance se trouvent liées au thème de l'amour pour la femme, de sa virginité, da sa pureté, de sa chute et de son pouvoir redempteur") (296). His remark on the mythical-legendary *Stoff* of *Faust* might also prompt us to ask: How can a woman ever save a man? For surely only a god can do this. Or a goddess. One way in which to approach Goethe's *Faust*, in order to bring out not only its significance for Goethe's German-speaking contemporaries of the eighteenth and nineteenth centuries but also its relevance for modern, English-speaking readers (an approach that has been used elsewhere, by Patricia

Zecevic, to interpret *Wilhelm Meister* for exactly the same reasons) (Zecevic, 2001), might be to think of the work in terms of the schemata developed by two twentieth-century English poets, Robert Graves (1895–1985) and Ted Hughes (1930–1998). In *The White Goddess: A Historical Grammar of Poetic Myth* (1948; revised 1952 and 1961), Graves elaborated, in considerable detail, his view that the origin of authentic poetic genius lay with the muse. For Graves, the muse was nothing other than the matriarchal lunar deity of primitive times, representing the once-dominant feminine principle that has since been replaced, to catastrophic effect, by masculine rationality and "their new religion of logic" (Graves, 9–10). Since *Faust* offers a veritable compendium of myth, both Christian and pagan, there may well be value in making use of Graves's thesis. Although Goethe claimed (to Eckermann on 21 February 1831) that, without a lifelong preoccupation with the plastic art of Antiquity, the Classical Walpurgisnacht would not have been possible, the forces of primitive paganism first emerge in the witches of the first Walpurgisnacht. Another work, the poem "Die erste Walpurgisnacht," written when Goethe was working on this scene, stages even more clearly a confrontation between paganism and Christianity (Simpson, 147). Moreover, as C. G. Jung argued, Faust's female companions throughout the two parts can be mapped on to an ancient symbolic pattern:

> Schon die Spätantike kannte jene erotische Skala der Vier: Chawwa (Eve), Helena (von Troja), Maria, Sophia; eine Reihe, die sich andeutungsweise im Goetheschen *"Faust"* wiederholt, nämlich in der Gestalt *Gretchens*, als Personifikation einer rein triebmäßigen Beziehung (Eva); der *Helena*, als einer *Anima*-Figur, der *Maria*, als Personifikation der *himmlischen*, das heißt christlich-religiösen Beziehung, und des *Ewig-Weiblichen* (Sophia), als Ausdruck für die alchemistische Sapientia. (Jung 1979, 177–78)

Some thirty years after Graves's study of myth, Ted Hughes proposed a reading of Shakespeare's plays in terms of what he called the "Tragic" or "Mythic Equation." According to this schema, Venus, the great Goddess of sexuality, manifests herself in three different aspects — the Mother, the Sacred Bride, and the Queen of the Underworld (or, to use a different set of categories, as the mother, the wife, and the whore). Opposite her stands Adonis, symbolic of the male order of rationality and realism, who rejects her advances, is killed by her, and miraculously becomes, in turn, the slayer of the Goddess. Bizarre as Hughes's framework sounds, and contentious as it is to Shakespeare scholars, his schema is no more bizarre than what we find in *Faust,* and alerts us to the way in which *Faust* is deeply and perplexingly concerned with male-female relationships and multiple transformations. Indeed, perhaps it is misleading to separate the feminine from disguises *tout court* since, according to Joan Rivière, the very essence of femininity lies in any or all disguise or masquerade (Rivière, 90–101). In *Faust*, we find a seduced virgin who plays a part in killing her mother and murders her child, yet becomes a penitent (Gretchen); a hermaphroditic devil who changes into the guise of a hag, sharing an eye and a tooth with her two ugly, aged sisters (Mephisto/Phorkyas); and an ageing academic who is rejuvenated by a witch's potion and becomes a rake, then an expert in state finances (disguised as Plutus), then a medieval knight, then a military adviser to the Emperor, and finally an ambitious statesman (Faust) — and all in a work that concludes with an invocation of the Eternal Feminine. Arguably the greatest and, in a sense, the most everyday, of Faust's transformations in Part One is his rejuvenation in the *Hexenküche* scene, and Freud pointed out that the fundamental supposition of the Faust tragedy is "die mögliche Rückverwandlung des Forschertriebs in Lebenslust" (Freud 1945, 142). Yet that transformation is accomplished, thanks to the pact with Mephisto, by means of the potion made by the witch, just as, for Freud, therapy seeks to effect a similar transformation through "die Hexe Metapsychologie," by the "white" magic of a change of attitude (Freud 1950, 69; Prokhoris, 2–3, 57).

Although Graves and Hughes offer an account of poetic inspiration without specific reference to Goethe, a recent critical discussion of Goethe's poetry, whilst making reference neither to Graves nor to Hughes, nevertheless shows how a related model of poetic creativity might be applied, via psychoanalytic theory, to Goethe. According to Freud's *Beiträge zur Psychologie des Liebeslebens* (1910), the male child has to renounce his incestual desire for the mother, and his concomitant identification with the father, in order to proceed to full psychosexual maturity. In other words, the ego-drives and the sexual drives of the child are faced with two alternatives: to direct themselves either toward a mother substitute, or toward two women, one of whom is idealized while the other is debased (Freud 1946, 66–77). Drawing on this model, David Wellbery has argued, in connection with Goethe's lyric output, that as the young male cannot love the mother because of the incest taboo, he has to put her image together again and love it in another form (Wellbery, 26). On this (admittedly reductionist) account, the erotic, libidinous nature of artistic energy is nothing other than the imaginary itself, and an analogous view has been advanced by James Simpson, who detects in *Faust I* the presence of an underlying "ur-fantasy" (Simpson, 296). In Jungian terms, such critics are arguing

that the subject, in order to be creative, has to free itself from the
mother in her dual aspects (the Good Mother and the Terrible
Mother). Or in Lacanian terms, the subject must move away from the
imaginary mother in order to accede to the realm of the Symbolic. The
Goethean problematic could thus be seen as formulated in the following lines from a paralipomenon to the "Paria" trilogy: "Vater Vater wo
ist Mutter / Meiner Seelen erste Liebe?" (WA I.5/ii 358). And seen in
this light, it is perhaps significant that, although we learn of the failed
alchemical experiments of Faust's father, that "dunkler Ehrenmann,"
which culminated in the poisoning of thousands (1034–55), we never
hear anything about Faust's mother.

Language in *Faust*

Whilst the richness of the play is truly inexhaustible, it may help the
reader to come to grips with it if, taking a cue from some of the contributions made to this volume, we illustrate the living significance to our
present world of discourse of just a few of its central motifs. In this regard, sexuality informs *Faust* in yet another respect. For, in addition to
being a work of art about the creation of art and the preconditions for
artistic creativity, the work emphasizes the importance of language and
cultural transmission. Thus seen, *Faust* is a text that consciously reflects
on its own medium, language. For within the work, many differing attitudes toward language are expressed, and the theme is especially
prominent in the following episodes.

To begin with, in the opening scene, "Nacht," Faust uses magical
language to conjure up the *Erdgeist*. Underlying magic, and its attempt
to use language to control the world, is the belief in an equivalence
between the structure of language and the structure of the world. By
contrast, the pedant Wagner sees language merely in terms of rhetoric.
Mistaking Faust's dialogue with the *Erdgeist* for the declamation of a
Greek tragedy, Wagner compounds his error by committing himself to
the even more seriously mistaken view that all that matters in language
is the art of declamation: "Allein der Vortrag macht des Redners
Glück" (546). But effective communication, Faust tells Wagner, relies
on something more than words alone, which he calls "urkräftiges Be-
hagen," a primal power, that speaks not just to the understanding of
the listeners but their hearts as well: "Wenn ihr's nicht fühlt, ihr werdet's nicht erjagen" (534). To speak to the heart, one must use the
language of the heart: "Doch werdet ihr nie Herz zu Herzen schaffen,
/ Wenn es euch nicht von Herzen geht" (544–45; cf. 9685–86). Here,
Faust's words echo, and possibly draw on, the distinction in *Über die
neuere deutsche Literatur* (1767) by Johann Gottfried Herder (1744–

1803) between, on the one hand, "everyday" language and "discursive" language, and, on the other, "poetic language" in which, as he put it, thought "cleaves" to the expression (Herder, 403; see Stephenson, 1983, 29–30). In other words, Faust is suggesting that there is a form of communication where "form" and "content" are united in such a way that they become inseparable. Wagner, by contrast, cannot see that the two things might inhere in each other and, according to Faust, this is why all his rhetoric amounts to nothing (554–57).

Because he misunderstands the nature of communication, Wagner despairs of being able to use language properly and, in *Studierzimmer II*, we should not be surprised to see Mephistopheles taking a characteristically cynical view of another character who misunderstands the nature and function of language. Having donned Faust's academic robe, Mephisto encourages the new student to study theology; the reasons he gives are, of course, a satire on that discipline, as well as on the careless use of language in general (Wilkinson 1973). "Haltet euch an Worte!" (1990), Mephisto advises, but the student is concerned that there must be some relationship between language and meaning, between a word and its sense: "Doch ein Begriff muß bei dem Worte sein" (1993). Although Mephisto reassures the student that there *is* a link between a piece of language and a concept, he immediately tells him to ignore it. For it is precisely when the concept is missing, Mephisto says, that language can fill in and smooth over the absence of meaning: "Denn eben wo Begriffe fehlen, / Da stellt ein Wort zur rechten Zeit sich ein" (1995–96). He goes on to consider the power that words did and do exercise upon thinking, thought, and systems of thought, including the construction of the dogmas of faith: "Von einem Wort läßt sich kein Jota rauben" alludes to the Council of Nicaea (CE 325), and the controversy regarding the Trinity between the doctrines of *homoousios* (the view that Christ is of an identical nature as the Father) and of *homoiousios* (the view that Christ is of a similar nature to the Father). In these lines, as Elizabeth Wilkinson pointed out (1973, 152–53), Goethe joins both Herder and Johann Georg Hamann (1730–1788) in their critique of language: are all these intellectual debates no more than a matter of words?

Such a negative and skeptical view of language is voiced elsewhere in the play when, in the opening monologue, Faust says to himself: "Schau alle Wirksamkeit und Samen, / Und tu nicht mehr in Worten kramen" (384–85). A good example of words that have no easily discernible meaning is the Witch's "Hexen-Ein-Mal-Eins"; a striking example, we might say, of mumbo-jumbo (a phrase deriving from African pagan tradition) or hocus-pocus (a parody of the words *hoc est Corpus* in the Latin Mass). In the *Hexenküche* scene, Mephisto satirically attacks the doctrine of the Trinity (2565–66), in words again implying a disjunction between the use of words and their meaning (Wilkinson 1973, 152–53). The power of language is foregrounded in a rather different way by Faust after he has signed the wager with Mephistopheles, when he reflects on the power of the written, as opposed to the spoken, word (1718–29). Faust's speech highlights the power of language to arrest time; his promise, even if only spoken, will be with him forever. Yet it is also the case that although language, when written down, loses something of its essence ("Das Wort erstirbt schon in der Feder"), it can, in its written form, continue to tyrannize us: "Die Herrschaft führen Wachs und Leder."

As against the spectral power of written language to rule our lives, another scene emphasizes the problems involved in linguistic translation. The opening of *Studierzimmer I*, where Faust tries to translate the beginning of the Gospel, re-enacts one of the great cultural achievements of Germany, Luther's translation of the Bible. In 1521, Luther spent ten months in the Wartburg, three of which were spent translating the New Testament, and it was during this period that his legendary confrontation with the devil, in the course of which he threw his ink-well at Lucifer, is alleged to have taken place. For his part, Faust tries to translate New Testament Greek ("das heilige Original") into his beloved native tongue ("In mein geliebtes Deutsch zu übertragen") and, turning to the Gospel according to St. John, encounters the concept of *logos*, a Greek word which could be translated as "statement," "principle," "law," "reason," or "proportion" (Honderich, 511–12). When Faust translates the word variously as "word," "meaning," "power," and finally "deed," we see Goethe typically doing several things at once: linking together the central concepts of his version of the Faust legend; reviving the Christian conception of the divine Logos as the active creative principle, the *logos spermatikos* (cf. 384); engaging again in a polemic against empty words; and, by reiterating the emphasis in *Faust* on deeds, as well as words, stressing the theme of ceaseless activity, the "neue Sphären reiner Tätigkeit" (705) (Wilkinson 1957).

Less explicitly, but no less important, the problematic nature of language reveals itself at work in Faust's seduction of Gretchen. In *Garten*, we see how Faust, having tried to woo Gretchen with jewels, now seduces her with words. From a Lacanian perspective, Faust is giving Gretchen the greatest possible gift, speech; and if we are to believe the Lacanian school, a woman can be captivated by a man's speech, even if she knows it is a seductive ploy (Leader, 52). On this view, the power of language lies precisely in its insufficiency: "Because the object of love can never be fully articulated in language, the man has to keep on speaking because his words can never circumscribe her being" (56). (Especially if the object of love is the Eternal Feminine, it is not surprising that *Faust* turns out to be such a long work.) In the Garden scene, Gretchen herself alludes to the significance of their conversation, with a gesture of modesty and self-deprecation (3077–78). By persisting, however, with his discourse, Faust is able to kiss her hand and, in the next scene, they are kissing and embracing in the summerhouse. Language lacks, and calls forth, the body.

In the scene in Martha's Garden, Faust continues his wooing of Gretchen with a discourse on names and naming (Wilkinson 1974, 126). The scene opens with Gretchen asking Faust to make a promise to her ("Versprich mir, Heinrich!"). What is it she is asking him to promise? That he loves her? That he is telling the truth? That he will answer any question she asks him? Or all of this and more? Equally ambiguous, Faust's reply "Was ich kann!" is both an assent and a limitation. Gretchen then asks Faust about his religious convictions, the occasion for his famous soliloquy "Wer darf ihn nennen?" (3432–58). Why does Gretchen ask this? Does she really want to know if Faust is a Christian? Does she suspect he is not? Does she want to give him an intellectual problem to talk about? Is she trying to find out about the inner life of her lover? Or does she simply want to listen to him talk? Or, once again, all of this, and more? At any rate, Gretchen succeeds in eliciting a lengthy speech from Faust, but his reply, his "credo," must be read in the context of age-old theological debate (Wilkinson 1974, 130–35). As well as echoing the anti-verbalist stance of the *Sturm und Drang*, his answer deploys the rhetorical technique of *enumeratio*, foregrounding in its very structure the homiletic tradition of patristic Christianity whilst, by attempting to seduce Gretchen with the power of rhetoric, alluding to the tradition of religious eroticism (Wilkinson 1957, 229 and 239). As discourse, it offers a perfect example of a highly rhetorical use of language, yet it goes well beyond Wagner's limited ambition for rhetoric. For this consummate linguistic performance, which asserts the power of language at the same time as it ostensibly denies it, equally embodies, as it moves towards the ejaculatory climax (3454), the structure of the sexual act, to which it stands in a relationship of both (for now) substitute and (in retrospect) prelude. So behind the religious rhetoric, there lies the erotic drive of Faust's desire, just as "Dom" is followed by "Walpurgisnacht," and hence, mediated through language, his desire acquires two forms, first verbal, then physical. Before their bodies touch, the lovers have to exchange words.

From discourse, Faust and Gretchen move to intercourse; from text, to sex.

The counterpart to this scene is, in Part Two, Faust's wooing of Helena by teaching her how to speak in classical verse (Wilkinson 1973, 127–28). Variously described by critics as part of Faust's "classical education" (Williams), as an act of "literary seduction and retrieval" (Weisinger), and as a "deconstruct[ion] [of] Classicism" (Phelan), lines 9369 to 9384 of the *Helena* Act are extremely significant. For not only do they recapitulate the earlier debates in Part One — "Das ist gar leicht, es muß von Herzen gehen" (9378) — and echo the substance of the wager — "Die Gegenwart allein — /Ist unser Glück" (9382; cf. 9418) — they also mark the continuing intersection of Goethe's text with the traditional Faust legend, as well as suggesting insights elaborated more recently by psychoanalysis. To begin with, there is the obscure relationship between the Homeric Helen of Troy, such later details of the legend as her birth from an egg — the product of union between Zeus, in the form of a swan, and Leda (recalled by Homunculus [6903–20] and Faust [7271–312, 10047–54]) — and the tree goddess worshipped at Sparta and on Rhodes (Hornblower and Spawforth, 675). Since history and legend are so confusing about the identity of Helena, why should we expect Goethe's text to be any more transparent? Furthermore, in a variant of the legend first recorded by Stesichorus and taken up, in his drama *Helen*, by Euripides, the woman whose beauty the Trojans so admired was not a real woman, but a phantom constructed by the goddess Hera to satisfy Paris, her lover, whilst the real Helen awaited rescue in Egypt by Menelaus, her husband (Hornblower and Spawforth, 675). In Goethe's version, the first time Helena appears, she is nothing but a phantom (6479–565); and, on the second occasion, she disappears again, leaving behind her dress and her veil (9939–44). At first glance, Helena's fluctuating presence seems to confirm Lacan's controversial thesis that *la femme n'existe pas* ("Woman does not exist"), meaning that the ideal image of Woman is structured around nothingness, an absence, or, as he would say, a "lack" (Lacan, 60; Leader, 16). Yet, in this Act, what we have witnessed is precisely the opposite. Faust has shown, through his rhyming verse (just as Goethe has, through his text), how poetry can create, out of the nothingness of language, the words on the page, the presence of aesthetic beauty. Thus seen, the veil of Helena, of which Phorkyas/Mephisto says, "Die Göttin ist's nicht mehr, die du verlorst, / Doch göttlich ist's" (9949–50), is nothing other than the central image of Goethe's lyric output, the "veil of poetry" (*Der Dichtung Schleier* [HA 1, 152]).

Faust Criticism in the Previous Century

In his magisterial survey of *Faust* scholarship, Stuart Atkins ventured the opinion that discussion of *Faust*, up to the middle of the last century or so, seemed to be characterized by "nothing but contradictions" (Atkins 1959, 422). Nothing much, it may sometimes seem, has changed since, despite the appearance of increasingly sophisticated aids to research, such as Henning's *Faust-Bibliographie* (1966–76), whose aim is to encourage scholars to take each others' work into account. For, after all, criticism has contrived to move along more or less the same lines as Atkins discovered over 40 years ago:

> Generous, if not indiscriminate, adduction of information about Goethe's life and world-outlook, about thematic correspondences between *Faust* and other works of his, and about the order of composition of the parts of *Faust*, has tended to prevent a sharp focussing of attention on the text itself. (Atkins 1958, v)

Nevertheless, there has in reality also been considerable development amidst the continuities. Following (or, rather, accompanying) E. M. Butler's monumental three-volume study of various aspects of the Faust legend in the late Forties and early Fifties, the close interpretation of "the text itself," which also characterized Atkins' own work, came very much to the fore: in Barker Fairley's insightful, and still stimulating six essays (1953); in Fritz Strich's study (1964); and in Eudo C. Mason's monograph on the "genesis and purport" of *Faust*, which gave "not only [Mason's] own interpretation of Goethe's *Faust*, but also a representative survey of critical opinion, especially during the last 80 years or so" (vii). If the genetic fallacy still haunted critical approaches to the text, reaching its most recent apogee in John Gearey's study (1981); and if the potentially vicious circle of using Goethe's general (and especially his scientific) thinking to understand *Faust* still underlay the approach of Dorothea Hölscher-Lohmeyer's new version of her 1940 book (1975), then in her hands — as well as those of Alan P. Cottrell (1976), who firmly subordinates external information to "inner relationships" (xi) — critical tact ensures that textual factors are always kept steadily in focus. Greater attention to the structure and form of the text (as distinct, that is, from its background and sources) does, in fact, seem to be the major significant difference that characterizes the literature on *Faust* written in the second half of the twentieth century.

The pioneering, if somewhat diffuse studies of C. G. Jung (and his school) and Wilhelm Emrich have, over time, been refined into precise analyses of the rhetorical and symbolic forms of the play itself. For instance, Paul Requadt's elaboration of L. A. Willoughby's "morphological approach" to *Faust* (1972), like Harold Jantz's study (1978), participates in a marked tendency to trace significant formal relations within the text, illuminated (whilst not dominated) by extra-textual considerations. That approach has been continued in Ehrhard Bahr's and Benjamin Bennett's explorations of "the ironic basis of Goethe's *Faust*" (Bennett, 1976). By the same token, the strategic poise of this dual attitude, seeking to strike a balance between "external" and "internal" approaches, has apparently produced a consensus in the *Faust* criticism of the post-war years. For writers as disparate as Barker Fairley, Harold Jantz, and Elizabeth M. Wilkinson are more or less at one in discerning in the text what they respectively describe as a "sophisticated retrospection," or "symbolic extension," or "diachronic dimension" — precisely and delicately controlled by the dense organisation of the text itself. The text, it is argued, encourages the reader-spectator to "fit in" to the work resonances of the long tradition of Western culture. The learned exegesis of Jochen Schmidt (1999) thus finds its point — like the recent commentaries of Albrecht Schöne (1999), Cyrus Hamlin (2000), and Ulrich Gaier (1999) — *within* "the text itself," now seen as one that accommodates and contains a sustained, albeit ironic, commentary on the cultural history of the West; on *our* cultural history. Jung's insight, expressed in his letter to Max Rychner, that *Faust* is "der neueste Pfeiler jener Brücke des Geistes, die sich über den Sumpf der Weltgeschichte spannt," reveals, with just a little adjustment, why it is, to answer Jantz's central question, "necessary to write yet another book on *Faust*" (1978, ix). As the essays retrospectively collected by Werner Keller (1974 and 1991) clearly demonstrate, *Faust* is a lucid representation of cultural material from every area of Western thought and life, holding it up for our contemplation. So it is no surprise that — as, for instance, in James Simpson's work (1999) — each "new" development in scholarly awareness, from feminism to deconstruction, should open our eyes to its kaleidoscopic deployment of the *Urformen* of Western consciousness. It is to observe more keenly and to understand more clearly just that kaleidoscopic effect that the papers in this collection have been assembled.

A Companion to Goethe's Faust

In "Literary Techniques and Aesthetic Texture in *Faust*," Ritchie Robertson investigates Goethe's use of poetic language in his drama, and he subdivides his study into four sections: dramatic poetry, biblical and literary allusion, liturgy, and complex words. In turn, Robertson examines the metrical forms used, and their significance; the intercultural aspect of Goethe's language; and finally, a selection of the key words that run, like *leitmotifs*, through the text. For example, Mephisto's words to the Student, "So wird's Euch an der Weisheit Brüsten / Mit jedem Tage mehr gelüsten" (1892–93) recall Faust's earlier cry "Wo faß ich dich, unendliche Natur? / Euch Brüste, wo?" (455–56). Likewise, breasts, and their milky product, form part of a nexus of images of organic fluids; in the opening Night scene, Faust desires "daß ich erkenne, was die Welt / Im Innersten zusammenhält, / Schau alle Wirkenskraft und Samen" (382–84). Or, to take a different example, the rhyme pair "Gestalt — Gewalt," which first occurs when the dog transforms itself into Mephisto (1251–52), emerges later in Gretchen's song at the spinning-wheel (3395–97), and is repeated later, in Part Two, in the form of Faust's question before he descends to Persephone to bring back Helen: "Und sollt ich nicht, sehnsüchtigster Gewalt, / Ins Leben ziehn die einzigste Gestalt?" (7438–39). Leaving aside the fact that this rhyme-pair occurs elsewhere in Goethe's works (for example, in "Erlkönig": "'Ich liebe dich, mich reizt deine schöne Gestalt; / Und bist du nicht willig, so brauch' ich Gewalt'") and the further intertextual connotations this implies, the rhyme on "Gewalt" and "Gestalt" brings together, phonetically, two distinct thematic elements of *Faust*: the problem of violence and power, and the desire to structure and give form. Moreover, even such simple lines as Gretchen's "Nach Golde drängt, / Am Golde hängt, / Doch Alles. Ach wir Armen!" can be read in a variety of ways: as a sociological statement; as an anthropological statement; as, in the light of the Satanic properties of gold revealed in the Walpurgisnacht, a religious statement; as a statement of Gretchen's own financial plight; or as an allusion to Virgil (the *auri sacra fames* or "accursed gold-lust drives" of the *Aeneid*, Book 3, line 57) (Gaier, 9–10).

Writing in the historically charged year of 1945, C. G. Jung wrote:

> Faust erreicht nirgends den Charakter der Wirklichkeit: er ist kein wirklicher Mensch, und kann keiner werden (wenigstens nicht im Diesseits), sondern er bleibt die deutsche Idee vom Menschen, und damit eine, wenn auch etwas übertriebene und verzerrte Spiegelung des deutschen Menschen. (Jung 1974, 233).

In "The Character and Characterization of Faust," Martin Swales examines the Faust legend, and the use that Goethe made of it. Behind the (at first blush, German) figure of Johann or Georg Faust, the disreputable fifteenth-century scholar, lies that more universal perennial dissent from the Western Christian tradition dubbed heresy. The story of the first act of "simony," committed in the first century A.D. by Simon Magus of Samaria, is told in the *Acts of the Apostles* (Chapter 8);

but, according to a second or third-century legend, Simon later went to Rome and acquired the name of Faustus, meaning "the favored one" or "the blessed" (*Faustus*, for *faves-tus*, from *favor, favos*, "favorable"). In German, the name "Faust," meaning "clenched fist," may well allude to the Stoic metaphor for "understanding" (Prokhoris, 179). His story became entangled with that of Faustus of Milevis, the late fourth-century propagandist of the heresy of Manichaeism. This Faustus acquired fame in Rome as a famous rhetorician, whose views were combated by St. Augustine (Wills, 34). Subsequently, this figure became associated with an actual historical individual, born circa 1480 in Knittlingen near Bretten in Germany, and this obscure figure, an itinerant scholar, trickster, charlatan, and quack, became crucially fused with the heretical material of the earlier legend. Thus, at the beginning of the sixteenth century, the essential elements of the story as Goethe knew it (from the puppet-play version) were in place. In the chapbook versions, the tale of Faust is a moral lesson, warning against the dangers of necromancy and black magic, whilst at the same time exciting the curiosity (allegedly the vice targeted by the work) of the reader. Above all, Faust began to emerge as a Renaissance figure, associated also with the other face of the era, the Reformation (and, in Germany, Luther in particular); he is inherently a figure of the scientific revolution, for the period of the historical Faust is also the age of Leonardo da Vinci, Christopher Columbus, Machiavelli, Erasmus, Copernicus, and Paracelsus (Edinger, 13). And Faust also comes to stand as a pivotal figure in the change from the Christian era to a period of renewed paganism; or, viewed from a different perspective, from the "age of superstition" to the era of Enlightenment (that "second Renaissance"), of secularism, and "modernity." As Swales points out, the Chapbook version published by Spies in Frankfurt in 1587, mediated the main material of the legend both to Christopher Marlowe and to Goethe. But whereas Marlowe's play is a tragedy of learning, Goethe's *Faust* is much broader, and could well be called a tragedy of being.

One approach to that tragedy is offered by Alberto Destro in "The Guilty Hero, or the Tragic Salvation of Faust." Like Franziska Schößler, who will be discussed below, Destro finds it helpful to compare *Faust II* with Goethe's late novel, *Wilhelm Meisters Wanderjahre*. (The fact that Goethe, in his diary, referred, at different times, to both works as his "Hauptgeschäft" might be taken as a sign of the intimate relation between these two works.) If the sin of the traditional Faust was intellectual curiosity and presumption, then the flaw of Goethe's Faust is much less precise. In one of his last conversations with Eckermann (6 June 1831), Goethe referred to the passage in which the famous lines, "Wer immer strebend sich bemüht, / Den **können** wir erlösen" (11936–37), as being the "key" to Faust's salvation, and it is appropriately the richness of the concept of *Streben* in Goethe's play that lies at the core of Destro's essay. Following Faust's "assumption" in a sumptuous, neo-Baroque apotheosis, Mephistopheles is distracted from his prey by the seductive posteriors of the impudent angels, and the true counterpart in Goethe's version to the famous conclusion of Marlowe's play is not so much the celebrated *Chorus mysticus*, most memorably set to music in Mahler's Eighth Symphony, but the much less mystical, down-to-earth — and earthy — confusion of Mephisto (11753–58, 11796–800). In "The Character and Qualities of Mephistopheles," Osman Durrani examines this figure of the Devil in *Faust*, and offers an explanation of Mephisto's perennially fascinating effect. According to Eckermann's report of a conversation of 3 May 1827, we should regard not only Faust and "das düstere, unbefriedigte Streben der Hauptfigur" but also "den Hohn und die herbe Ironie des Mephistopheles" as, so Goethe is recorded as saying, "Teile meines eigenen Wesens." Certainly there is a psychological dimension to the relationship between Faust and Mephisto; Jung, for example, argued that Mephisto symbolized Faust's "Shadow," an autonomous complex split off from Faust's main personality and hypostatized as the Devil (1974, 242). Far more problematic is the relationship of Mephisto to God, "der Herr," and in part Goethe's play is an exploration of the problem of Evil and the tradition of theodicy. In an early essay "Zum Shäkspeares-Tag" (1771), Goethe de-absolutized Evil and saw it as, in its way, a "necessary evil": "Das, was wir bös nennen, ist nur die andre Seite vom Guten, die so notwendig zu seiner Existenz und in das Ganze gehört, als Zona torrida brennen und Lappland einfrieren muß, daß es einen gemäßigten Himmelsstreich gebe" (HA 12, 227). This is why the Lord tells Mephisto in the "Prolog im Himmel": "Du darfst auch da nur frei erscheinen" (336). For Mephisto's agency is restricted to the phenomenal world, and his freedom is precisely that — mere appearance — and not absolute.

According to Camille Paglia, "*Faust* has a variety of sexual personae, more than any other work of major literature" (254). Although some of these figures are androgynous or bisexual (Mephisto becomes Phorkyas, and at the Carnival the Thin Man, now male greed, was once female avarice), many of them are feminine, forming a pattern of unity and continuity as well as difference and contrast throughout the work. Opposing the more positive feminine figures ("das schönste Bild von einem Weibe" Faust sees in the Witch's mirror [2435], Gretchen, the Mater dolorosa, the Mothers, Helena, Galatea, the Mater gloriosa), there are the more negative aspects of the feminine (illustrated by the witches of the Kitchen Scene and the first Walpurgisnacht, Martha, Gretchen's mother, Lieschen at the well, Lilith, the court ladies, the Sirens, the Lamiae, the Phorcyads, and the Four Grey Women of Midnight). In "Figurations of the Feminine in Goethe's *Faust*," Ellis Dye tackles the difficult question of the function of these female figures and the concept of the Feminine, asking why *das Ewig-Weibliche* does not push, but pull.

A more particular but no less perennial problem for Faust criticism and scholarship has been posed by the three figures who feature in the scene entitled "Finstere Galerie" in Act 1. Although we never actually see them, the Mothers are described to Faust by Mephisto (6214–16, 6218–20, 6222–26), and the entire episode forms a counterpart to the "Hexenküche" scene of Part One (Bub, 779). When asked about the Mothers (10 January 1830), Goethe remained mysterious about them although, as Eckermann mentions, such a coy response was not untypical ("er aber, in seiner gewöhnlichen Art, hüllte sich in Geheimnisse"). In "The Problem of the Mothers," John Williams surveys the critical literature on this problem, investigates the historico-cultural background to these figures, and draws some conclusions about their function within the play. If, to achieve rejuvenation and get Gretchen in Part One, Faust first has to visit the Witch, then the visit to the Mothers, in Part Two, forms the precondition to his first encounter with Helena; while, on the second occasion, he has to descend to Persephone (Goethe's plan to write a dialogue between Faust and the beautiful goddess who languishes in the underworld, discussed with Eckermann on 15 January 1827, remained unexecuted). When, at the beginning of Act 3, we see Helena, the setting, like the metre, is classical; but when the setting moves inside the palace of Menelaus, the buildings, like Faust's costume, are medieval. The significance of this juxtaposition of classical antiquity and early modernity is examined in Anthony Phelan's essay, "The Classical and the Medieval in *Faust*, Part Two." Moreover, the relationship between the classical and the modern was a problem that preoccupied many German eighteenth and nineteenth-century thinkers and writers; Hölderlin, for example, wrote to Casimir Ulrich Böhlendorff on 4 December 1801: "Aber das eigene muß so gut gelernt seyn, wie das Fremde. Deßwegen sind uns die Griechen unentbehrlich. Nur werden wir ihnen gerade in unserm Eigenen, Nationellen nicht nachkommen, weil, wie gesagt, der *freie* Gebrauch des *Eigenen* das schwerste ist" (Hölderlin, 426). Seen in this context, Act III represents a "confrontation between modern and classical" in which "Faust, as representative of the modern intellectual world, is once again" — as in his encounter with Gretchen — "invincible and remains the irresistible vortex whose legacy in *Part Two*, as in *Part One*, is the dead child" (Weisinger, 393).

Helena's opening monologue has strong echoes of an earlier work by Goethe, the opening lines of *Iphigenie auf Tauris* (Weisinger, 389), but there are also connections between *Faust II* and more contemporary works of Goethe. In "Progressive and Restorative Utopia in *Faust II* and *Wilhelm Meisters Wanderjahre*," Franziska Schößler relates the second half of the drama to the major *Wilhelm Meister* novel of the late period, with particular reference to the "historical" panoramas of these two works. By stressing the details of historico-economic significance, she shows how they point to the transformation of a subsistence economy into a capitalist economy of profit-and-loss and the creation of artificial needs. Schößler contrasts the agri-capitalism of the Oheim in the *Wanderjahre* with the carnival masque scene from Part Two and the introduction of paper money, thereby uncovering the radical tendencies of modernization that are thematized in both works. Against such tendencies, Schößler then opposes the notion of the "restorative utopia," which envisages the restitution of such classically-inspired ethical models as the *kalokagathia*, the Greek educational ideal of Goodness and Beauty. Accordingly, Schößler reads Makarie of the *Wanderjahre* as an incarnation of the obsolete model of micro- and macrocosm, against the background of the Marian vision, inspired by Dante, at the end of *Faust II*, with all its neo-Platonic overtones. By the same token, the ideal of the "Schöne-Gute" — developed in the second *Meister* novel through the figures of the beautiful widow, of Susanne in Lenardo's diary (a.k.a. Nachodine), and Makarie — shares a similar conceptual basis with the figure of Helena. The evocation of these restorative utopias, in which Goethe draws on classical notions, is, Schößler argues, far from naïve or simplistic, for an awareness of their anachronistic status is articulated in the form of irony or the apparently esoteric narration. By means of her accomplished analysis, Schößler succeeds in demonstrating the wide-ranging historical dimension of both texts, and in revealing their parallel structures.

Having heard the news that, following the *Trois glorieuses* of the July Revolution, Charles X of France had abdicated, leading to the eventual transferral of monarchical power from the House of Bourbon to its junior, collateral branch, the House of Orléans-Bourbon, on 2 August 1830 Frédéric Soret reportedly visited Goethe, who greeted him with the exclamation: "Der Vulkan ist zum Ausbruch gekommen; alles steht in Flammen, und es ist nicht ferner eine Verhandlung bei geschlossenen Türen!" (Eckermann, 2 August 1830). As it turned out, however, Goethe was not referring to the political events in France, but to the dispute between the French zoologist Georges Cuvier (1769–1832) and the scientist Étienne Geoffroy Saint-Hilaire (1772–1844), whose *Principes de philosophie zoologique* had just been published. Given the long-standing importance to Goethe of science and the significance he attached to his own scientific work (see Stephenson, 1995), it is not surprising that *Faust*, too, reflects this engagement. Taking as his starting-point Faust's desire to know "was die Welt / Im Innersten zusammenhält" (382–83), Peter Smith investigates the presence of scientific themes in Goethe's dramatic poem. Equally, Goethe's claim in "Einwirkung der neueren Philosophie" (1820) that "für Philosophie im eigentlichen Sinne hatte ich kein Organ" (HA 13, 25) should not obscure the fact that he had read widely in Spinoza, Kant, and the German Idealists. In turn, such thinkers as Friedrich Wilhelm Joseph von Schelling (1775–1854) and Georg Wilhelm Friedrich Hegel (1770–1831) sought to align Goethe with their own positions; indeed, Hegel wrote to Goethe on 24 April 1825: "Wenn ich den Gang meiner geistigen Entwicklung übersehe, sehe ich Sie überall darein verflochten und mag mich einen Ihrer Söhne nennen; mein Inneres hat gegen die Abstraktion Nahrung zur widerhaltenden Stärke von Ihnen erhalten und an Ihren Gebilden wie an Fanalen seinen Lauf zurechtgerichtet." In "Goethe's *Faust* and the Philosophers," Cyrus Hamlin examines both the philosophers' response to *Faust*, and the extent to which the work incorporates philosophical themes. In the course of his discussion, the argument of Schiller's *Über die ästhetische Erziehung des Menschen* (1795) emerges as of central importance for understanding the philosophical significance of *Faust*.

In "The Diachronic Solidity of Goethe's *Faust*," Roger Stephenson sums up the significance of *Faust* as a canonical text and as a constituent of world literature. The intellectual framework of his essay is an elaboration of a pair of concepts derived from contemporary linguistics and anthropology: the "diachronic," or the study of linguistic or cultural phenomena through time, as opposed to the "synchronic," the study of the structure of phenomena, independently of their development through time (Wilkinson 1973, 146–47). Thus a diachronic analysis concentrates on the forms of thought that recur, revealing behind what may appear to be time-bound thoughts a historical dimension that could take the form of a perennial problematic or represent a reformulation of a traditional idea. As well as being an exercise in "morphological" analysis (see Willoughby 1970), Stephenson's paper suggests that there is still room — nearly two centuries on — for original and innovative research to be undertaken on this eminently "diachronic" text.

The final two essays reflect on the current attempt to come to terms with *Faust* from a more pragmatic, experiential angle. In "Translating Faust," David Luke offers an unabashedly "personal statement," based on his experience of translating both parts of Goethe's dramatic poem. The range of stanzaic and metrical forms used in *Faust* — blank verse, doggerel (*Knittelvers*), and hymnic structures, as well as, in Part Two, *ottava rima*, *terza rima*, and trimeters (discussed in detail by Ritchie Robertson) — poses a particularly difficult challenge to any translator. The first English translation of *Faust* was published in a review of Part One in the *Monthly Review*, 52 (1810), and in 1822 Shelley made translations of sections of *Faust*. In 1823, Lord Francis Leveson Gower published *Faust: A Drama by Goethe*, and Abraham Hayward offered a prose translation in 1833, while Charles T. Brooks translated Part One using English equivalents of the German versification in 1856. Bayard Taylor's famous verse translation appeared in 1870–1871. Of the twentieth-century versions, those by the poet Louise MacNeice (Parts One and Two, abridged, 1952), Bayard Quincy Morgan (Part One, 1954; Part Two, 1964), Barker Fairley (1970), Philip Wayne (1958–1959), Stuart Atkins (Part One, 1962; Part Two, 1984), Walter Arndt (1976), and, most recently, by John Williams (Part One, 1999), as well as the version by Luke (Part One 1987; Part Two, 1994), offer different attempts to come to terms with Goethe's use of metre. Barker Fairley (1969–70) illuminated the difficulties facing the translator. For many lines from *Faust* have taken on a proverbial status in German, in a manner similar to Shakespeare's *Hamlet* in English, and it is not always possible to find a satisfactory equivalent for them. For example, "Zwei Seelen wohnen, ach! in meiner Brust" (1112) is difficult to translate because, as Fairley pointed out, in English, souls do not dwell in bosoms. According to Elizabeth Wilkinson, there remains, in any case, an untranslatable element in Goethe's poetry, which she locates in "the assimilation of experience into language without the intervention of conceptual thought" (1948–1949, 321).

In the final essay, Robert David MacDonald, a director of the Citizens Company, based in Glasgow, who has produced his own performing version of *Faust*, reflects on the problems of adapting and performing the play, based on his experience of directing the 1985 Glasgow-London production. Goethe himself never lived to see a complete performance of his drama, and although parts of *Faust I* were performed in 1816, 1819, and 1820, Acts 1 to 3 of *Faust II* had to wait until 1849, when they were performed in an adaptation by Karl

Gutzkow (1811–1878), and the whole play was not performed until 1876. In 1895, Henry Irving's London production staged only Part One. As a result, the impact of the work was achieved mainly as a read, not as a performed, text. In terms of its reception, the work was frequently misunderstood by Goethe's contemporaries in terms of a Romantic paradigm. Typical of the backhanded compliments paid to the work are the remarks of the Schlegel brothers; A. W. Schlegel, who wrote in 1811: "Bei solcher Unfähigkeit zur äußern Darstellung ist dennoch aus dem seltsamen Werke erstaunlich viel für die dramatische Kunst, sowohl in der Anlage als Ausführung, zu lernen" (279); and Friedrich Schlegel, in 1815: "Das Mißverhältnis zwischen der Poesie und der Bühne in Deutschland zeigte sich fortdauernd darin, daß nach Klopstock nun auch Goethe manche dramatische Werke hervorbrachte, ohne alle Rücksicht auf die Bühne" (403). In terms of performability, the Schlegels might have had a point in the early nineteenth century, although the work has been performed in Germany very successfully since the 1970s and, as Robert David MacDonald suggests, much can be learnt about the play from its performance.

In 2000, in defiance of Goethe's occasional scepticism about the performability of *Faust* (see, for example, his conversations with Anton Eduard Odyniec of 29 August 1829 and with Friedrich Christoph För-ster of May 1829), the German director Peter Stein was responsible for staging the entire work at the Expo 2000 site in Hanover. Organised to follow up the celebrations of the 250th birthday of Goethe in 1999, this staging was the first unabridged professional production of the entire work (aside, that is, from productions of *Faust I* and *Faust II* at the Goetheanum in Dornach, Switzerland). In total, the play lasted approximately 21 hours, and was performed during a marathon weekend, and over six evenings. Following its premiere on 22 and 23 July 2000 and its run at Hanover (from August to September 2000), the production was staged in Berlin (from October 2000 to July 2001) and in Vienna (August to December 2001). In the Hanover production, two actors, Robert Hunger-Bühler and Johann Adam Oest, played Mephistopheles; Dorothee Hartinger played Gretchen; and in the part of Faust, the thirty-one-year-old Christian Nickel, who was supposed to share the role with Bruno Ganz, not only played his part of the role but also stood in for Ganz, who had fallen, breaking his wrist and pelvis. (This was not the only mishap: in one rehearsal, Stein closed a metal door on one of his fingers, half of which then had to be amputated.)

The press release for the Hanover premiere emphasized the uniqueness of the production: "Fast ein halbes Jahrhundert nach der berühmtesten Faust-Inszenierung durch Gustaf Gründgens bietet sich die

ein- und erstmalige Chance, anläßlich der ersten Weltausstellung in
Deutschland das gesamte Werk in ungekürzter Fassung auf die Bühne
zu bringen [. . .] Dieses gewaltige Theaterstück ist noch nie in seiner
vollständigen Gestalt — von einem Berufstheater — aus einem Guß, in
zeitlichem und örtlichem Zusammenhang gezeigt worden. Auch verfügen wir erst heute über die technischen Möglichkeiten, auf Goethes
wechselnde räumliche Vorschläge einzugehen." In a contribution
written for *Peter Stein inszeniert Faust I und II: Das Programmbuch zur
Inszenierung*, edited by Roswitha Schieb (Cologne: Dumont, 2000),
Stein himself explained how his interest in staging *Faust* had begun:

> Letzten Endes beginnt diese Geschichte Mitte der 50iger Jahre mit
> den Versuchen eines Bildungsbürgerknaben, den *Faust II* zu lesen.
> Ich hatte — damals war das noch Pflicht — den *Faust I* in der Schule
> gelesen und spannend, ja erregend gefunden, doch der zweite Teil
> wurde von den Lehrern als bedeutungsvoll, wichtig, ja besonders
> "goethisch," jedoch als zu schwierig, für Jugendliche ungeeignet, zu
> gewichtig, außer Betracht gelassen. Der Hang zur Besserwisserei,
> sportiver Ehrgeiz, Entzifferungssucht, Lust an Sprache und Sprach-
> witz ließen mich immer wieder den Versuch unternehmen, diesen als
> unbesteigbar verschrieenen Bildungsberg zu bekraxeln. Anreiz waren
> auch die gnadenlosen Verrisse, die das Werk von seinem Erscheinen
> bis ins allerneueste Zeit immer wieder erfahren mußte und die in ihrer
> Gereiztheit die Schwierigkeiten der Interpreten bei der Bewältigung
> ihrer Aufgaben verrieten.

Clearly, the real problem that confronted any staging of the entire
Faust was not Part One, but Part Two. According to Stein, however,
there were at least five compelling reasons for staging *Faust II*. First,
the text was written as drama; second, it has a dramatic structure (a cyclical macrostructure consisting of a series of stage "numbers"); third,
its themes — the relationship of humanity to the future, the predomi-
nance of "virtual reality," the creation of artificial intelligence, the ex-
ploitation of Nature, the increasing pace of life (Goethe's "alles
veloziferisch," Virilio's *esthétique de disparition*) — are all "modern";
fourth, it is presented as a tragedy, even if, in its details, it is a comedy;
and finally, it is a late work: "Goethes Bezugnahme auf sein Jugend-
werk Faust und die Tatsache, daß er als Form wieder das Theater
wählte, gaben ihm die Möglichkeit, all sein Wissen, seine Gedanken
und Vorstellungen als Spielmaterial zu nutzen, es in die Luft zu werfen,
allem und jedem, vor allem sich selbst zu widersprechen und so eine
Frechheit und aggressive Kraft zu entfalten, die Alterswerken norma-
lerweise nicht eigen sind." If, in turn, four major problems stood in the
way of performing Part Two (its length, the space required, the re-

hearsal time required of the actors, and the financial aspect), then the
Expo in Hanover, and the commercial sponsorship associated with the
event, offered a solution to these difficulties.

Using two large stages in Hall 23 of the Hanover Expo, Stein tried
to involve the audience by having the spectators move from one stage
to the other after each interval. In the Carnival Masque scene and at a
banquet set up in the scene in the Great Hall, the members of the
audience themselves became part of the play. Declaring the performance to be "an exhilarating experience," the reviewer for *The Economist*
explained that "a nice air of theatrical communism prevails in that seats
are not assigned" (16 September 2000). According to T. J. Reed, the
production created "its own festive mood" — and if, by the Sunday
evening of the first performance, "people were faster out of their start-
ing blocks ('manners are declining,' said someone behind me, but not
in earnest), that only showed that the *Faust* experience was becoming a
way of life with its own adaptations," and thus also becoming, *pace*
Reed, "a minute equivalent of the way of life" that writing *Faust* was
for Goethe (*The Times Literary Supplement*, 4 August 2000). Writing in
The New York Times, Anne Midgette saw things slightly differently:
"Moving from one space to another creates a kind of theatrical democ-
racy: no-one is guaranteed a better seat than anyone else. An unfortu-
nate by-product of this concept, at least during the première, was a
kind of cattle-stampede effect every time the doors opened, as elegantly
clad, presumably sophisticated men and women practically mowed each
other down in their efforts to get a good spot" (6 August 2000). In
sum, however, she concluded: "However flawed the production, there
is something undeniably exhilarating about experiencing this whole text
in two days." Writing in *The Guardian*, Michael Billington wrote:
"The German critics accuse Stein of destructive fidelity to Goethe's
text. But what I saw in his production was not pedagogic subservience
but a total realisation of the multiple levels of Goethe's work" (2 September 2000).

This remark highlights the fact that, if foreign theater critics and
Auslandsgermanisten broadly welcomed the performance, many German-speaking critics were much harsher in their judgments. Reviewing
the production for the *Neue Zürcher Zeitung*, Barbara Villiger Heilig
made the apposite remark: "Peter Stein nahm schon vor der Premiere
den Kritikern jeglichen Wind aus den Segeln, indem er öffentlich er-
klärte, sie würden seine Inszenierung garantiert verreissen. Schade, dass
er einigermassen Recht behalten musste." For it was not just the conservative German *Frankfurter Allgemeine Zeitung* that sharply criticized
Stein's production ("Immer wieder zeigt Stein, wie schön er Massen

choreografieren kann, wie er Spaziergänge und Polonaisen und Paraden in den Griff bekommt, aber wenn es darauf ankommt, eine Welt sich um Personen drehen zu lassen, dann müsste unter der Pappe dieser Welt auch irgendetwas lodern, was zu uns herüberbrennt"). For instance, in the Berlin *Tagesspiegel*, under the headline "Peter Stein bezwingt auf der Expo in 22 Stunden die deutsche Riesendichtung. Umsonst," Rüdiger Schaper disagreed strongly with the production values of the performance: "In selbstzerstörerischem Hass auf das Regietheater, das Stein auf hervorragende Weise mit begründet hat, wurde der weltberühmte Theatermann zum Renegaten, zum Eiferer. Der anti-zeitgenössische Faust, das Klassische schlechthin, schwebte ihm vor: nichts Geringeres, als Goethe noch einmal zu erschaffen, so wie der Mensch die Schöpfung imitiert — und usurpiert." Concluding his piece, this reviewer claimed: "Man spürt die Enge der thüringischen Residenz. Man ahnt ein Lebenswerk, das Goethesche Lebensdrama: einen Kosmos zu erschaffen in einem Provinzkaff, in einer Welt ohne gültige Religion, schon abgeschnitten von den Quellen der Antike und der Weisheit des Mittelalters. Tragischer Irrtum: Stein glättet, harmonisiert, überpinselt, was Goethe als wilde, an Stilen überbordende, heillose Collage hinterließ. Faust II — kein Stück, ein Steinbruch" (25 July 2000). Above all, Stein's fidelity to the text of the play, his refusal to cut any lines or to try, in the staging, to "update" the work, led Reinhard Wengierek, the critic of the German daily newspaper *Die Welt*, to write: "'Am Anfang war die Tat!,' weiß Faust. Stein weiß es besser: Am Anfang war das Wort! Das ist sein Dogma, Textfrömmigkeit seine Ideologie. Die Vernichtung des Rotstiftes mag unser Sitzfleisch qüalen. Unsere Seele beglückt es mit einer Flut sonst selten oder nie gehörter Verse. Bewahrt uns vor Vergröberung, Verniedlichung, Verballhornung, Verbiegung aus dem eitlen Geist aktueller Moden. Stein spielt Goethe-Museum. Faust in der Vitrine" (25 July 2000). If Georg Dierz's review in the *Süddeutsche Zeitung* found much to complain about in the logistics of the performance from the spectator's point of view — "Der Dichter hat ein Leben lang daran geschrieben, der Regisseur hat ein Jahr lang daran geprobt, jetzt wird ein Wochenende lang gesessen und gestanden [. . .] Wenn da die Kaffeemaschine nicht richtig funktioniert, ist da schon mal kein gutes Omen" — his colleague, C. Bernd Sucher, was even more critical about what Stein had put on the stage: "Die Szenen ermüden, weil sie vom Zusachauer nichts anderes fordern als hörige Gefolgschaft [. . .] Dem Zuschauer bleibt nicht die geringste Möglichkeit, selber zu Worten Räume, Farben und Gebärden zu imaginieren [. . .] Abstraktion ist [Steins] Sache nicht. Vor lauter Vergnügen am Ausmalen vergisst er, dass im Zentrum des Faust nicht Maschinen stehen, nicht Kostüme, Rüstungen und Holzspielzeuge, sondern Menschen" (24 July 2000; 25 July 2000). And a reader's letter to the same newspaper, published a few days later, went even further, maintaining that Stein's "Mammutinszenierung [...] passt in unsere Protzgesellschaft, die mit Gigantismus ihre Brutalitäten zuzudecken versucht," and in turn condemning Goethe as "ein schon zu seiner Zeit reaktionärer und moralisch diskreditierter Schriftsteller, der noch kürzlich als vorbildlicher deutscher Dichter gefeiert wurde, just in jenem Jahr, in dem Deutschland in die Liga der Kriegsaggressoren zurückkehrte," *Faust* as "ein Drama, das mit seiner Glorifizierung des männlichen Raub- und Beziehungsmörders als Nationalkunstwerk der Deutschen fungiert," and "ein irres Budget, um dieses Werk in voller Länge zur Aufführung zu bringen" (31 July 2000). In its own way, this letter demonstrates the apparent confusion in the minds of many of the professional reviewers as to which they disliked most: Stein's production, Goethe's play, Goethe himself, or German culture *tout court*.

Moreover, the discrepancy between the more generous attitude of foreign critics to Stein's production and the highly negative opinions on it of the German-speaking reviewers does much to substantiate Goethe's suspicion of contemporary criticism ("Es versteckt sich hinter jenem Gerede mehr böser Wille gegen mich, als Sie wissen," he told Eckermann on 14 March 1830), as well as to demonstrate the continuing power of *Faust* to fascinate — and, above all, to provoke. According to Peter Stein: "Beim Faust geht es um die Tragödie des modernen Menschen. Ich will ihn darstellen und begreifen. Die Interpretation muss das Publikum leisten" (in *Spiegel Online*, 19 July 2000). Likewise, this *Companion to Goethe's Faust: Parts I and II* is a further set of responses to that fascination and that provocation, and another set of attempts to make sense of the work. In another conversation with Eckermann on 29 January 1827, Goethe is reported to have said of *Faust* that "alles [ist] sinnlich und wird, auf dem Theater gedacht, jedem gut in die Augen fallen. Und mehr habe ich nicht gewollt." That at the same time Goethe intended — and achieved — much else and much more is demonstrated by the breadth and variety of essays in this volume.

INTRODUCTION: READING FAUST TODAY xli

Works Cited

Atkins, Stuart. Goethe's Faust: A Literary Analysis. Cambridge, MA: Harvard UP, 1958.

———. "Faustforschung und Faustdeutung seit 1945." Euphorion. 53 (1959). 422–40.

Bennett, Benjamin. "'Vorspiel auf dem Theater': The Ironic Basis of Goethe's Faust." German Quarterly. 49 (1976). 438–55.

Bloom, Harold. The Western Canon: The Books and School of the Ages. New York: Harcourt Brace & Company, 1994.

Bub, Douglas F. "The 'Hexenküche' and the 'Mothers' in Goethe's Faust." Modern Language Notes. Vol. 83, No. 5 (October, 1968). 775–79.

Butler, E. M. The Myth of the Magus. Cambridge: Cambridge UP, 1948.

———. Ritual Magic. Cambridge: Cambridge UP, 1949.

———. The Fortunes of Faust. Cambridge: Cambridge UP, 1952.

Cottrell, Alan P. Goethe's "Faust": Seven Essays. Chapel Hill: U of North Carolina P, 1976.

Edinger, Edward F. Goethe's Faust: Notes for a Jungian Commentary. Toronto: Inner City Books, 1990.

Fairley, Barker. Goethe's "Faust": Six Essays. Oxford: Clarendon P, 1953.

———. "On Translating Faust." German Life and Letters. 26 (1969–1970). 54–62.

Foucault, Michel. Histoire de la sexualité. Vol. 2. L'usage des plaisirs. Paris: Gallimard, 1984.

Freud, Sigmund. Die Traumdeutung. In Gesammelte Werke. Vols. 2/3. Frankfurt am Main: Fischer, 1942.

———. "Eine Kindheitserinnerung des Leonardo da Vinci." In Werke aus den Jahren 1909–1913. Gesammelte Werke. Vol. 8. Frankfurt am Main: Fischer, 1945. 127–211.

———. "Die endliche und die unendliche Analyse." In Werke aus den Jahren 1932–1939. Gesammelte Werke. Vol. 16. Frankfurt am Main: Fischer, 1950. 59–99.

———. "Über einen besonderen Typus der Objektwahl beim Manne." ["Beiträge zur Psychologie des Liebeslebens," 1] In Werke aus der Jahren 1909–1913. Gesammelte Werke. Vol. 8. Frankfurt am Main: Fischer, 1945. 66–77.

Gaier, Ulrich. Goethe: Faust-Dichtungen. Vol. 2. Kommentar I. Stuttgart: Reclam, 1999.

Gearey, John. *Goethe's Faust: The Making of Part One*. New Haven: Yale UP, 1981.

Graves, Robert. *The White Goddess: A Historical Grammar of Poetic Myth*. London and Boston: Faber and Faber, 1961.

Hamlin, Cyrus, ed. *Faust: A Tragedy. Interpretative Notes, Contexts, Modern Criticism*. 2nd ed. New York: W. W. Norton, 2000.

Henning, Hans. *Faust-Bibliographie*. 5 vols. Berlin: Aufbau-Verlag, 1966–1976.

Herder, Gottfried. *Frühe Schriften*. Ed. Ulrich Gaier. *Werke in zehn Bänden*. Vol. 1. Frankfurt am Main: Deutscher Klassiker Verlag, 1985.

Hölderlin, Friedrich. *Sämtliche Werke*. Ed. Friedrich Beissner. Vol. 6. Stuttgart: W. Kohlhammer Verlag, 1954.

Hölscher-Lohmeyer, Dorothea. *Faust und die Welt: der zweite Teil der Dichtung. Eine Anleitung zum Lesen des Textes*. Munich: Beck, 1975.

Honderich, Ted, ed. *The Oxford Companion to Philosophy*. Oxford and New York: Oxford UP, 1995.

Hornblower, Simon, and Antony Spawforth, eds. *The Oxford Classical Dictionary*. 3rd ed. Oxford and New York: Oxford UP, 1996.

Hughes, Ted. *Shakespeare and the Goddess of Complete Being*. London and Boston: Faber and Faber, 1992.

Jantz, Harold. *The Form of Faust: The Work of Art and its Intrinsic Structures*. Baltimore and London: The Johns Hopkins UP, 1978.

Jung, C. G. "Nach der Katastrophe." In *Zivilisation im Übergang. Gesammelte Werke*. Vol. 10. Olten und Freiburg im Breisgau: Walter-Verlag, 1974. 219–44.

———. *Die Psychologie der Übertragung*. In *Praxis der Psychotherapie: Beiträge zum Problem der Psychotherapie und zur Psychologie der Übertragung. Gesammelte Werke*. Vol. 16. 2nd ed. Olten und Freiburg im Breisgau: Walter-Verlag, 1979. 168–319.

———. *Briefe*. Ed. Aniela Jaffé and Gerhard Adler. Vol. 1. Olten und Freiburg im Breisgau: Walter-Verlag, 1972.

Keller, Werner, ed. *Aufsätze zu Goethes Faust I*. Darmstadt: Wissenschaftliche Buchgesellschaft, 1974.

———, ed. *Aufsätze zu Goethes Faust II*. Darmstadt: Wissenschaftliche Buchgesellschaft, 1991.

Lacan, Jacques. *Télévision*. Paris: Seuil, 1973.

Leader, Darian. *Why Do Women Write More Letters Than They Post?* London and Boston: Faber and Faber, 1996.

Luke, David, trans. *Goethe: Selected Poetry*. Harmondsworth: Penguin, 1964.

————, trans. *Goethe: Selected Poetry*. London: Libris, 1999.

————, trans. *Faust: Part One*. Oxford and New York: Oxford UP, 1987.

————, trans. *Faust: Part Two*. Oxford and New York: Oxford UP, 1994.

Mann, Thomas. "Goethe als Repräsentant des bürgerlichen Zeitalters" [1932]; "Über Goethe's 'Faust.'" [1939] *Reden und Aufsätze*. Vol. 1. *Gesammelte Werke*. Vol. 9. 2nd ed. Frankfurt am Main: Fischer, 1974. 297–332, 581–621.

Mason, Eudo C. *Goethe's Faust: Its Genesis and Purport*. Berkeley and Los Angeles: U of California P, 1967.

Paglia, Camille. *Sexual Personae: Art and Decadence from Nefertiti to Emily Dickinson*. New Haven: Yale UP, 1990.

Phelan, Anthony. "Deconstructing Classicism: Goethe's *Helena* and the Need to Rhyme." In *New Ways in Germanistik*. Ed. Richard Sheppard. New York, Oxford, Munich: Berg, 1990. 192–210.

Prokhoris, Sabine. *The Witch's Kitchen: Freud, Faust, and the Transference*. Trans. G. M. Goshgarian. Ithaca and London: Cornell UP, 1995.

Requadt, Paul. *Goethes "Faust I": Leitmotivik und Architektur*. Munich: W. Fink, 1972.

Rivière, Joan. "Womanliness as a masquerade." [1929] In *The Inner World and Joan Rivière: Collected Papers 1920–1958*. Ed. Athol Hughes. London and New York: Karnac Books, 1991. 90–101.

Schmidt, Jochen. *Goethes Faust, Erster und Zweiter Teil: Grundlagen, Werk, Wirkung*. Munich: Beck, 1999.

Schöne, Albrecht, ed. *Faust. Kommentare*. Frankfurt am Main: Deutscher Klassiker Verlag, 1994. [FA 7.2]

Simpson, James. *Goethe and Patriarchy: Faust and the Fates of Desire*. Oxford: Legenda, 1998.

Stephenson, R. H. *Goethe's Wisdom Literature: A Study of Aesthetic Transmutation*. Bern, Frankfurt am Main, New York: Peter Lang, 1983.

————. *Goethe's Conception of Knowledge and Science*. Edinburgh: Edinburgh UP, 1995.

————. "Goethe's Prose Style: Making Sense of Sense." *Publications of the English Goethe Society*. NS 66 (1996). 33–41.

Strich, Fritz. *Goethes Faust*. Bern, Munich: Francke, 1964.

Weisinger, Kenneth D. "Discourse Wars: Literary Seduction and Retrieval in *Faust II*." In *Cabinet of Muses: Essays on Classical and Comparative Literature in Honor of Thomas G. Rosenmeyer*. Ed. Mark Griffith and Donald J. Mastronade. Atlanta, Georgia: Scholars Press, 1990. 387–402.

Wilkinson, Elizabeth M. "Goethe's Poetry." *German Life and Letters.* 2 (1948–1949). 316–29.

———. "The Theological Basis of Faust's Credo." *German Life and Letters.* 10 (1957). 229–39.

———. "Goethe's *Faust*: Tragedy in the Diachronic Mode." *Publications of the English Goethe Society.* NS 42 (1973). 116–74.

———, and L. A. Willoughby. *Goethe: Poet and Thinker.* London: Edward Arnold, 1962.

Williams, John R. "Faust's Classical Education: Goethe's Allegorical Treatment of Faust and Helen of Troy." *Journal of European Studies.* 13 (1983). 27–41.

Wills, Garry. *Saint Augustine.* London: Weidenfeld & Nicolson, 1999.

Wilson, Daniel M. *Das Goethe-Tabu: Protest und Menschenrechte im klassischen Weimar.* Munich: Deutscher Taschenbuch Verlag, 1999.

Zecevic, Patricia. *The Female Voice in López de Úbeda's "La Pícara Justina" and Goethe's "Wilhelm Meister"* (Frankfurt am Main: Lang, forthcoming [2001]).

Literary Techniques and Aesthetic Texture in *Faust*

Ritchie Robertson

Dramatic Poetry

*F*AUST IS A DRAMATIC POEM, and to appreciate it one needs to understand its poetic language. The reader without German need not despair, for the many translations include some masterpieces — here I would single out those by David Luke — which provide real access to the poem. This essay, however, is written for the reader who knows German, or at least enough German to tackle Goethe's text with a translation to hand.

Such a reader will soon notice the variety of Goethe's dramatic poetry. In some poetic dramas, especially those committed to a high or dignified style, all the characters speak a broadly homogeneous language, which only incidentally, and through nuance, serves the expression of individuality. That is the case in Racine, in Schiller, and in Goethe's own neoclassical dramas *Iphigenie auf Tauris* and *Torquato Tasso. Faust,* however, is quite differently conceived. Each of the main characters is a distinct person inhabiting a distinct world which in turn expresses his or her individuality. "Die Natur bildet den Menschen," wrote Goethe in 1775, "er bildet sich um, und diese Umbildung ist doch wieder natürlich; er, der sich in die große weite Welt gesetzt sieht, umzäunt, ummauert sich eine kleine drein, und staffirt sie aus nach seinem Bilde" ("Anteile an Lavaters *Physiognomischen Fragmenten*" [WA I.37, 329–30]). Hence Part One repeatedly emphasizes the "world" that a character inhabits. Looking round his Gothic study, Faust laments: "Das ist deine Welt! das heißt eine Welt!" (409). He imagines Gretchen, whose domestic peace he has disrupted, "Umfangen in der kleinen Welt" (3355). And since the characters inhabit different worlds, they often fail to understand one another. Barker Fairley pointed out how often in *Faust* apparent dialogues are really competing monologues: "It is a case of people not quite talking to one another" (Fairley, 24). Thus Faust's discourses are lost on his pedantic assistant,

Wagner; the profession of faith that Gretchen extorts from him clearly
goes over her head; and in his many conversations with Mephisto,
Faust is slow to register that he has thrown in his lot with a devil,
showing considerable obtuseness even in the recognition scene "Trüber
Tag. Feld." With these different worlds of consciousness side by side in
the play, Goethe's dramatic verse assumes an extraordinary variety and
flexibility, which is sustained in Part Two. Here we move further from
familiar drama of human interaction into pageantry, mystery, allegory,
and a vast display of what the aged Goethe, in his letter to Sulpiz Boisserée of 24 November 1831, called "ernst gemeinte Scherze." But in
both parts, as Eckermann noted (13 February 1831), the separate
scenes are "little world-circles, each existing alone" ("für sich besteh-
ende Weltenkreise"), each with its own atmosphere conveyed through
poetic language.

Lack of space requires me to concentrate mainly on the dramatic
poetry of Part One. I shall briefly survey the main metrical forms
Goethe uses, keeping to a minimum the counting of syllables, and
aiming to bring out how meter expresses character and mood. I shall
then show, with some reference to Part Two, how Goethe's language
was enriched by the Bible, by his study of world literature, and by the
language of the liturgy. Finally, returning to Part One, I shall look
closely at the poetic deployment of some key words, aiming to show
how Goethe exploits the tension and instability in the range of meanings they can have, and thus poetically suggests yet further implications
which hover on the edge of the text.

The staple meter of both parts of *Faust* is madrigal verse ("Madri-
galvers"), which, according to the invaluable study of *Faust's* meters by
Markus Ciupke, accounts for 2642 lines out of 4612 in Part One and
for 2127 out of 7498 in Part Two. As its name suggests, madrigal verse
originated as a song meter; it was also used in the eighteenth century
for chatty verse-narratives such as fables. It is largely iambic, with a
varying number of stressed syllables, usually four to six, but sometimes
fewer; additional unstressed syllables can be inserted, and many varia-
tions on the iambic pattern are possible. Thus a line can acquire an energetic start from an initial trochee:

> Wenn ihr's nicht fühlt, ihr werdet's nicht erjagen (534);

haste can be suggested by dactyls:

> Stürzen wir uns in das Rauschen der Zeit (1754);

and solemn emphasis can be supplied by a spondee:

> Zwei Seelen wohnen, ach! in meiner Brust (1112).

Madrigal verse is the *lingua franca* of *Faust*. It is used especially for conversation, even when the characters talk past each other. It is flexible in line-length, permitting even such short lines as "So tausendfach" (2025) and "Mein Bruder ist Soldat" (3120). It is flexible also in its rhymes, permitting couplets ("Paarreim"), alternating rhymes ("Kreuzreim," abab), and "embracing rhymes" ("umarmender Reim" or "Blockreim," abba). It is the medium in which the Lord converses with Mephisto, and Faust with Wagner, Mephisto and Gretchen. To see its dramatic potential, consider the following exchange:

DER HERR.   Hast du mir weiter nichts zu sagen?
            Kommst du nur immer anzuklagen?
            Ist auf der Erde ewig dir nichts recht?

MEPHISTO.   Nein, Herr! ich find' es dort, wie immer, herzlich schlecht.
            Die Menschen dauern mich in ihren Jammertagen,
            Ich mag sogar die armen selbst nicht plagen.

DER HERR.   Kennst du den Faust?

MEPHISTO.   Den Doktor?

DER HERR.   Meinen Knecht!
                        (293–9)

The Lord's first words are dignified, reserved, impatient and gruff. In each of his three lines, the first few words are lightly stressed, preparing for an irritated emphasis on "weiter," "immer," and "ewig" — three words which themselves form a crescendo by stating Mephisto's constant dissatisfaction ever more strongly. The first two lines have four beats, the third has five, and Mephisto outdoes his master by replying with a six-beat line which, moreover, starts with an emphatic, defiant spondee ("Nein, Herr!") and ends by answering the Lord's rhyme with a word that is antithetical in meaning ("schlecht" to "recht"). His following couplet, however, proves to be embraced by a "Blockreim." Its last line is an antilobe, that is, a line divided among more than one speaker, which quickens the dramatic tempo (there are several antilobes later in the fight scene with Valentin [3708ff.]). The line ends with the description of Faust as "Meinen Knecht!" uttered firmly by the Lord, whose laconic, almost military manner suggests the habit of command, in extreme contrast to Mephisto's almost unstoppable loquacity.

When our attention moves from heaven to earth, we find ourselves listening to the first of Faust's great monologues. Several of these deserve separate discussion. The first, delivered in his study, includes some of the most famous lines in a play which, like *Hamlet*, is full of quotations, and moreover introduces the atmosphere of sixteenth-century Germany in which the Faust legend originated:

> Habe nun, ach! Philosophie,
> Juristerei und Medizin,
> Und leider auch Theologie
> Durchaus studiert, mit heißem Bemühn.
> Da steh' ich nun, ich armer Tor,
> Und bin so klug als wie zuvor! —
>
> (354–59)

Goethe found verse like this in the work of the Nuremberg shoemaker-poet Hans Sachs (1494–1576). As early as the seventeenth century, conscientious metrists dismissed such rough verse as "Knittelvers" (literally "cudgel verse"), but Goethe adopted it for his early comic plays (e.g. *Hanswursts Hochzeit*, 1773–1775) and used it in a tribute to its master, "Hans Sachsens poetische Sendung" (1776). "Knittelvers" has four (occasionally five) beats and a varying number of unstressed syllables; it can begin with a trochee ("Habe," "Durchaus") or an iamb ("Und leider auch"); and it is most often a sequence of rhyming couplets. It sounds rough, blunt, even naive; it is often used to address the audience directly. Goethe uses it for the Student who has his leg pulled by Mephisto, for Gretchen on her first appearances, and for her brother Valentin. But it was a bold stroke to adapt "Knittelvers" to express Faust's frustration at having traversed the whole circle of scholarship without having learnt anything worth knowing. Great poets, said Heine in *Ideen: Das Buch Le Grand*, express despair through a comic mask, as Shakespeare does with the Fool in *King Lear;* and "den großen Denkerschmerz, der seine eigne Nichtigkeit begreift, wagt Goethe nur in den Knittelversen eines Puppenspiels auszusprechen" (Heine, 282).

If the study of poetry really were a matter of counting syllables, one might discern no great difference between the "Knittelvers" of Faust's opening monologue and the language of his Easter monologue in "Vor dem Tor":

> Vom Eise befreit sind Strom und Bäche
> Durch des Frühlings holden, belebenden Blick;
> Im Tale grünet Hoffnungsglück;
> Der alte Winter, in seiner Schwäche,
> Zog sich in rauhe Berge zurück.
> Von dorther sendet er, fliehend, nur
> Ohnmächtige Schauer körnigen Eises

> In Streifen über die grünende Flur;
> Aber die Sonne duldet kein Weißes [. . .].
>
> (903–11)

Here again the fluency comes from the varying number of unstressed syllables, the liberty of beginning a line with a trochee or an iamb, and the movable rhymes. These lines, however, differ from "Knittelvers" in their lyrical profusion of adjectives, their colors (green, white), their discreet vowel-patterning ("Vom E̲i̲se befr̲e̲it") and alliteration ("belebenden Blick"), and in the personification of natural phenomena: winter, now old and feeble, retreats to the mountains before the gaze of the spring and the refusal of the sun to tolerate any snow or hail. A purist would query some of the rhymes: the impure rhyme of "Blick" with "Glück" is common enough to pass, but "Eises" does not properly rhyme with "Weißes." Elsewhere Goethe notoriously rhymed words that were pronounced similarly in Frankfurt and Leipzig, and may not have seemed provincial in the eighteenth century, but sound incongruous now: "Buch" with "genug" (419, 421), "nach" with "Tag" (698, 701), and "neige" with "Schmerzensreiche" (3587–88).

Faust again evokes nature lyrically in his monologue in "Wald und Höhle" (3217–50). Here the meter is blank verse, the iambic pentameter familiar from Shakespeare and from Lessing's famous play *Nathan der Weise* (1779), and developed into a subtle instrument of lyrical and psychological exploration by Goethe himself in the neoclassical plays, *Iphigenie* and *Tasso,* which he composed in the same years as this passage. Why the passage should thank the Earth Spirit for giving Faust what he asked for, when we have already seen the Earth Spirit dismissing Faust scornfully, and why it should blame the Earth Spirit for saddling him with Mephisto who, as the "Prolog" tells us, is the emissary of the Lord — these much-discussed enigmas need not concern us here (see Mason, 110–78; Zimmermann, 261–64). The lines reveal a contemplative Faust whom we have not seen before, except very briefly when he summoned up the Macrocosm:

> Du führst die Reihe der Lebendigen
> Vor mir vorbei, und lehrst mich meine Brüder
> Im stillen Busch, in Luft und Wasser kennen.
> Und wenn der Sturm im Walde braust und knarrt,
> Die Riesenfichte stürzend Nachbaräste
> Und Nachbarstämme quetschend niederstreift,
> Und ihrem Fall dumpf hohl der Hügel donnert,
> Dann führst du mich zur sichern Höhle, zeigst

Mich dann mir selbst, und meiner eignen Brust
Geheime tiefe Wunder öffnen sich.

(3225–34)

In this quotation, natural violence is framed within peaceful contemplation, enhanced by the regularity of the meter. In the first and last few lines, the adjectives are all static ("still," "sicher," "geheim," "tief"). Faust is a passive onlooker; none of the verbs has him as its subject. Only in the central passage do violent, onomatopoeic verbs convey how the huge fir tree is blown down by the gale; the three successive stresses in "Fall dumpf hohl" themselves enact, as Ciupke finely observes, the crashing of the tree-trunk (Ciupke, 73).

A more familiar Faust appears in "Marthens Garten," explaining his religious creed to Gretchen, who, not being entirely naive, is suspicious of his orthodoxy. Here Faust turns to "free rhythms" ("freie Rhythmen"), a verse-form pioneered in the 1750s by Klopstock to express an ecstatic devotion to God, and adopted by Goethe in such famous early hymnic poems as "Prometheus" and "Ganymed." Free rhythms are normally unrhymed; Faust here uses rhymes (3432–33, 3435–36) only to underline the futility of theistic or atheistic affirmation, and goes on to express, in a series of short lines varying in length and stress, his sense that divinity is present and active around and within us. The loose meter and lack of rhyme are compensated by intricate verbal repetition — "Der Allumfasser, / Der Allerhalter, / Faßt und erhält er nicht / Dich, mich, sich selbst?" (3438–41) — and sound-patterning — "Und steigen freundlich blickend / Ewige Sterne nicht herauf!" (3444–45). The excited mood is heightened by exclamations and rhetorical questions.

One last illustration of Faust's metrical versatility, and also of Goethe's response to poetic tradition, comes from Part Two. In the opening scene, "Anmutige Gegend," Faust, having been cast into a therapeutic sleep by kindly spirits, wakes and delivers a monologue in iambic pentameter and *terza rima* modeled on Dante's *Divine Comedy*. Before writing this scene in 1826, Goethe had been studying Dante in the new German translation by Karl Streckfuss. Its setting recalls the Earthly Paradise which Dante's Pilgrim enters in *Purgatorio* xxviii, before drinking from the river Lethe and being led through it by Matilda to meet Beatrice (Hirdt, 76–77). The rhyme-scheme *terza rima* (ababcbcdcdede, etc.) creates a continuity which can only be ended by a final and all the more emphatic "Kreuzreim." While Dante's cantos often end in a rather understated way, Goethe uses all the available emphasis to end this scene. Having contemplated the natural energies embodied in the waterfall, Faust considers how it nevertheless refracts the sunlight:

> Allein wie herrlich, diesem Sturm ersprießend,
> Wölbt sich des bunten Bogens Wechseldauer,
> Bald rein gezeichnet, bald in Luft zerfließend,
> Umher verbreitend duftig kühle Schauer.
> *Der* spiegelt ab das menschliche Bestreben.
> Ihm sinne nach, und du begreifst genauer:
> Am farbigen Abglanz haben wir das Leben.
>
> (4721–27)

Here we see Goethe moving from the evocation of nature via his studies of light and color to the didacticism that so pleased his Victorian admirers. The continuous tercets are well suited for meditation. The regularity of the pentameters is broken only by the initial trochee "Wölbt sich," underlining the activity of the refracted light and alliterating significantly with "Wechsel." The tercets then reach a powerful closure by rhyming two of the poem's key words, "(Be)streben" and "Leben." The last word picks up the opening line of this soliloquy: "Des Lebens Pulse schlagen frisch lebendig" (4679), a line which is, strictly speaking, tautological; but if Shakespeare can get away with pleonasm in writing about "a strange invisible perfume" (*Antony and Cleopatra*, Act 2, Scene 2, line 219), Goethe's example further confirms that great poetry can override the ordinary rules of expression.

Of the other major characters, Mephisto is remarkable for his ability to adapt to whomever he is talking to. He picks up the "Knittelvers" used by the Student; he adopts the madrigal verse and the coarse humor of the drinkers in "Auerbachs Keller"; and he uses the full flexibility of madrigal verse in his tense, spiky, competitive, only superficially companionable exchanges with Faust. When luring Faust back to Gretchen in the "Wald und Höhle" scene, he modifies madrigal verse to represent Gretchen's yearning in a brilliant imitation of love-poetry:

> Die Zeit wird ihr erbärmlich lang;
> Sie steht am Fenster, sieht die Wolken ziehn
> Über die alte Stadtmauer hin.
> Wenn ich ein Vöglein wär'! so geht ihr Gesang
> Tage lang, halbe Nächte lang.
>
> (3315–19)

With its two dactyls ("Über die," "Stadtmauer") and the emphasis on "hin" required by the rhyme with "ziehn," the third line has a slow, dragging motion which expresses Gretchen's absorption in Faust and her weariness in waiting for him. The following line becomes irregular by incorporating the song-line "Wenn ich ein Vöglein wär," and the last is again slowed by the leisurely opening trochee ("Tage") and the internal rhyme on "lang."

Here Mephisto acts, in keeping with the dialectical scheme of *Faust*, as the unwitting agent of life, tempting Faust away from sterile melancholy and back into involvement with others. Often his language is bracing and vigorous, as when he urges Faust to leave his study:

> Drum frisch! Laß alles Sinnen sein,
> Und grad' mit in die Welt hinein!
> Ich sag' es dir: ein Kerl, der spekuliert,
> Ist wie ein Tier, auf dürrer Heide
> Von einem bösen Geist im Kreis herumgeführt,
> Und rings umher liegt schöne grüne Weide.
>
> (1828–33)

In comparing Faust's studious seclusion to bewitchment by an evil spirit, Mephisto is bold to the point of insolence. For he is himself an evil spirit who proposes to lead Faust on a futile and circular journey. Moreover, his simile illustrates his constant tendency — appropriate to the Spirit of Negation — to reduce and degrade. In his study, Faust was at least using his reason, the highest human faculty, yet Mephisto compares him to an animal, and offers as an alternative only sensual satisfaction.

Faust himself calls Mephisto an animal, or worse — "Untier" — in the scene "Trüber Tag. Feld," where the two come most directly into conflict. This scene is written in prose, as other scenes ("Auerbachs Keller," "Kerker") originally were, and may have been written as early as 1772. Faust's furious rhetoric, typical of the Sturm und Drang of the 1770s, rebounds against Mephisto's indifference, shown first by his "Sie ist die erste nicht" and then by his cool "Endigst du?" ("Have you finished yet?"), and is revealed as the bombast of a guilt-stricken and powerless man. He has no reply to Mephisto's irritated reproach: "Wer war's, der sie ins Verderben stürzte? Ich oder du?" But the vigorous prose brings out, not only Faust's moral desperation, but also the wider implications of the confrontation. Faust equates Mephisto with the serpent of Eden, and seems to see in him a fiendish monster with bared teeth: "Fletsche deine gefräßigen Zähne mir nicht so entgegen!" — while Mephisto acutely observes in Faust the tendency of all tyrants (that is, irresponsible and self-willed rulers) to discharge their own frustrations onto others. Faust has not quite attained insight, either into his own faults or into the fatal consequences of allying himself with the devil. Only the "Kerker" scene will bring him as close as possible to understanding that he has done something wrong that can never be put right in this world.

Gretchen, his victim, has already widened her powers of expression. Although she first speaks in the homely simplicity of "Knittelvers" (and returns to it in the scene "Am Brunnen"), with Faust she uses madrigal verse, implying a greater sophistication that will help to betray her. Her depth of feeling is conveyed first by her folk-song "Es war ein König in Thule," whose theme of loyalty ironically fails to predict her own fate, and later by her monologue at the spinning-wheel. Although its loosely iambic four-beat lines, arranged in quatrains, resemble a folk-song meter, and although it has been set to music by Schubert and many others, this monologue is not sung by Gretchen but recited, following the rhythm of the spinning-wheel. With its mounting passion, it prepares us for the free meters into which she breaks when her situation becomes desperate and her feelings unbearable. While in her address to the Virgin Mary ("Zwinger") her utterances are still shaped partly by liturgical rhythms, partly by those of folk-song, her agony in the Cathedral scene, where she comes close to fainting, is conveyed by free rhythms, speeded by enjambements:

> Mir wird so eng!
> Die Mauernpfeiler
> Befangen mich!
> Das Gewölbe
> Drängt mich! — Luft!

(3816–20)

The "Kerker" scene shows Gretchen at her lowest and her highest points. Having borne and drowned her child, and been driven mad by guilt, betrayal, social ostracism, and (no doubt) official brutality, she nevertheless resists the invitation to flee with Mephisto, whose evil nature she has already recognized, and throws herself on the divine mercy. The scene is hard to match anywhere in world literature. Shakespeare's mad Ophelia arouses pity, but Gretchen passes through utter distress to tragic heroism by rejecting Faust for the God who, according to the harsh version of Christianity purveyed by the Evil Spirit in the "Dom" scene, must already have condemned her. No wonder that Goethe, having originally written the scene in prose, felt obliged to versify it in order to reduce "die unmittelbare Wirkung des ungeheuern Stoffes" (see his letter to Schiller of 5 May 1798). After her song, which reveals her identification with her dead child, Gretchen speaks in rhyming lines of irregular length, varying from five beats to one — "O weh! deine Lippen sind kalt, / Sind stumm" (4493–94). The basically iambic pattern lets the ebb and flow of emotion be expressed through variation with dactyls — "Niemand wird sonst bei mir liegen!" (4528) —, amphibrachs — "Sie winkt nicht, sie nickt nicht, der Kopf ist ihr schwer" (4570), — and trochees — "Lagert euch umher, mich zu bewahren!" (4609). As Gretchen obsessively re-lives their love-affair, her flight, infanticide and arrest, and anticipates her imminent execution, Faust is reduced to uttering single lines which gradually cease to rhyme with anything Gretchen says ("Der Tag graut! Liebchen! Liebchen!" [4579] finds no rhyme).

Throughout Part One, Gretchen, for all her simplicity, shows a greater range of expression than Faust. She speaks, recites, sings and prays. Faust never sings. Even Mephisto, in "Auerbachs Keller," sings the Song of the Flea, thus satisfying the coarse tastes of the drinkers who have previously been singing about a poisoned rat. The supernatural beings either sing, or speak in song-like meters. The opening praise of the universe uttered by the archangels is modeled on versified psalms. The choruses who celebrate Easter utter basically dactylic verses, modeled on medieval Latin hymns, with prominent "gleitende Reime," that is, rhymes extending over more than one syllable:

> Tätig ihn Preisenden,
> Liebe Beweisenden,
> Brüderlich Speisenden [. . .]
>
> (801–03)

A similar meter, the adonic, is used by the spirits who sing Faust to sleep by evoking a beautiful Mediterranean landscape:

> [. . .] Decken die Laube,
> Wo sich fürs Leben,
> Tief in Gedanken,
> Liebende geben.
>
> (1466–69)

Biblical and Literary Allusion

Goethe's intimacy with the Bible is obvious, especially in his earlier works (see Durrani; Kaiser). It pervades the texture of *Faust*. Thus when Faust calls himself "Ebenbild der Gottheit" (516, 614), he is recalling how God made Man in His own image and likeness (Genesis 1:26); when he tells Wagner not to be a "schellenlauter Tor" (549), he echoes the "tinkling cymbal" ("klingende Schelle" in Luther's translation) of I Corinthians 13:1; and his visionary "Feuerwagen" (702) suggests the fiery chariot which carries Elijah up to heaven (2 Kings 2:11). From many possibilities, I will single out three striking allusions.

As a young man Goethe studied the Old Testament intently with the aid of such Hebrew as he knew and of the new historical approach to its composition and context (HA 9, 508–12). In particular, he attempted a new translation of the Song of Songs, which he considered "die herrlichste Sammlung liebes Lieder die Gott erschaffen hat" (see his letter to Merck of 7 October 1775), and this lyricism helped to inspire Gretchen's poetry of yearning (see Pniower; Simpson). The phrase which the Authorized Version renders "my bowels were moved for him" (Song of Solomon 5:4) was translated by Goethe as "mich überliefs," which appears in *Faust* as Gretchen's exclamation "Mich überläuft's!" (3187). The cynical Mephisto adapts the Song ("Thy two breasts are like two young roes that are twins, which feed among the lilies" [4:5]) in telling Faust:

> Ich hab' Euch oft beneidet
> Ums Zwillingspaar, das unter Rosen weidet
>
> (3336–37).

When Goethe was completing *Faust: Der Tragödie erster Teil*, he decided to frame the drama in a heavenly prologue which he modeled on the Book of Job. The scene's core is contained in Job 2:1:

> Again there was a day when the sons of God came to present themselves before the Lord, and Satan came also among them to present himself before the Lord.

The subsequent dialogue, in which the Lord calls Job "my servant" and Satan undertakes to destroy his piety, forms a template for the conversation between the Lord and Mephisto, in which Mephisto engages in a one-sided wager that he will divert Faust from his divinely appointed path. Ironically, the analogy with Job rebounds on Mephisto; for much later, when angels descend to carry off Faust's immortal part and frustrate his hopes, the roses they throw bring him out in sores which he himself compares to Job's —

> Wie wird mir! — Hiobsartig, Beul' an Beule
> Der ganze Kerl
>
> (11809–10).

The parts of the Bible that Goethe especially draws on, the Song of Solomon and the Book of Job, are those which have traditionally seemed most incongruous within the Old Testament canon. Thus Goethe foregrounds those parts of the Bible which orthodox commentators have preferred to marginalize. In dealing with the New Testament he does something similar, for in "Bergschluchten" two female penitents from the Gospels, the sinful woman of Luke 7 and the Samaritan woman of John 4, are placed alongside Mary of Egypt, who figures in the saints' legends collected by the Jesuits. Here Goethe is implicitly questioning the special status of the sacred text.

Goethe draws not only on the Bible but also on his wide reading in world literature. Ernst Robert Curtius called *Faust* "a 'restitution of all things' (Acts 3:21) in the continuity of the world's literature" (Curtius, 189). Sometimes mythical figures appear conscious of their literary status: thus Helena, on first appearing, mentions her posthumous reputation, and the witch Erichtho introduces the "Klassische Walpurgisnacht" by assuring us that despite the libels of later poets (Lucan and Dante) she is "Nicht so abscheulich, wie die leidigen Dichter mich / Im Übermaß verlästern . . ." (7007–08) (see Dante's *Inferno*, ix. 23). (Erichtho first appears in Book 7 of the epic *Pharsalia* by Lucan (39–65 A.D.) as a Thessalian witch consulted by Pompey before the battle of Pharsalia.)

Goethe's interest, however, extended far beyond Europe. The conversation in the "Vorspiel auf dem Theater" among Director, Poet, and Clown is modeled on the dialogue between dramatist and actress that opens the Indian play *Sakuntala* by Kalidasa (c. 400 A.D.), which Goethe knew in the translation that Georg Forster had made from an English version. Although Goethe's fascination with the Muslim world found expression mainly in his *West-östlicher Divan* (1819), at least one scholar has detected many echoes of the *Arabian Nights* in *Faust II*, though her case often seems overstated (see Mommsen).

The most varied literary allusions come in the third act of Part Two, a version of which was published separately in 1827 as *Helena: Zwischenspiel zu Faust*. The literary references are part of Goethe's project, which he described to an admirer, the scholar Carl Jacob Ludwig Iken, in a letter of 27 September 1827 as follows: "Es ist Zeit, daß der leidenschaftliche Zwiespalt zwischen Klassikern und Romantikern sich endlich versöhne." The act accordingly moves from classical verseforms to those of modern Europe: Goethe, like his contemporaries, regarded Romantic literature as a continuation of medieval poetry, and had already displayed this conception in the masque entitled "Die romantische Poesie" which he composed for the Duchess Louise of Weimar in 1810 (Sengle, 279–80). At the outset, Helena speaks in iambic trimeters, a verse-form drawn from Greek tragedy —

> Bewundert viel und viel gescholten, Helena,
> Vom Strande komm' ich, wo wir erst gelandet sind
> (8488–99)

and the Chorus replies in irregular meters which range from two
stresses to five. Mephisto, appearing in the guise of Phorkyas, moves
from iambic trimeters to trochaic tetrameters, lines with eight feet of
which the last is catalectic (that is, consisting only of one syllable):

Tritt hervor aus flüchtigen Wolken, hohe Sonne dieses Tags,
Die verschleiert schon entzückte, blendend nun im Glanze herrscht.

(8909–10)

Goethe's classical meters are far from mechanical: both Helena's and
Phorkyas's diction allows for extra syllables (as in "flüchtigen" above)
which make for a quicker, lighter delivery. According to Kurt May's
reckoning, 118 out of 484 lines contain a foot with an extra syllable
(May, 161–62). These additions often draw attention to emotionally
charged words, as in the line "Denn Ruf und Schicksal bestimmten
fürwahr die Unsterblichen / Zweideutig mir" (8531–32), where, from
"bestimmten" onward, we practically have three amphibrachs.

After the transformation scene, Faust appears in medieval armor and
speaks in blank verse, the staple meter of Northern European languages
from Shakespeare onwards. A new and distinctively "Romantic" note is
introduced by Lynkeus, the lynx-eyed watchman who apologizes for
neglecting his duty in short trochaic quatrains:

Laß mich knieen, laß mich schauen,
Laß mich sterben, laß mich leben,
Denn schon bin ich hingegeben
Dieser gottgegebnen Frauen.

Harrend auf des Morgens Wonne,
Östlich spähend ihren Lauf,
Ging auf einmal mir die Sonne
Wunderbar im Süden auf.

(9218–25)

Here we have a familiar lyric form, anticipated especially in the trochaic
four-line stanzas (redondillas) found in Calderón and other classical
Spanish writers, and used especially for the subject of love (Atkins, 91).
We also recognize the hyperbolic homage characteristic of Petrarchan
poetry (see Forster). Helena's beauty eclipses the sun; later she darts arrows of love at all who see her (9260–63) and the glow of her cheeks
turns rubies pale (9311–12).

As ancient meters yield to modern verse-forms, the reconciliation of
Classicism and Romanticism is achieved in the justly famous and
touching scene where Helena, having noticed an unfamiliar symmetry
in Faust's language, learns to speak in rhyme:

FAUST.   Nun schaut der Geist nicht vorwärts, nicht zurück,
           Die Gegenwart allein —

HELENA.   ist unser Glück.

FAUST.   Schatz ist sie, Hochgewinn, Besitz und Pfand;
           Bestätigung, wer gibt sie?

HELENA.   Meine Hand.
                                          (9381–84)

Many strands of meaning come together in this passage. First, since we are inquiring into Goethe's use of world literature, we may notice that it unites not only Helena and Faust, Classicism and Romanticism, but also East and West. For the story of rhyme being invented to express the harmony of two lovers is an Eastern one, which Goethe found in the works of the Orientalist Joseph von Hammer-Purgstall (1774–1856) and adapted for one of the poems in his *West-östlicher Divan*:

> *Behramgur*, sagt man, hat den Reim erfunden,
> Er sprach entzückt aus reiner Seele Drang;
> *Dilaram* schnell, die Freundin seiner Stunden,
> Erwiderte mit gleichem Wort und Klang.
>
>   (HA 2, 79)

Next, this exchange signifies Helena's full development into an individual. When she first appeared, she spoke of herself in her social roles: "Komm' ich als Gattin? komm' ich eine Königin?" (8527) (for more examples, see May, 166–67). By now, however, the encounter with Faust has brought her into full presence as an individual. Her presence is registered in language, as a recent subtle reading of the rhyming episode has brought out (Phelan, 206). But it is not only a linguistic creation, for the interchange between Faust and Helena ends by embodying their union in a handclasp ("Meine Hand"). And this gesture evokes reminiscences. It reminds us how often in Goethe — the dramatist of the embodied self — emotional contact is rendered in touch rather than words. Lotte takes Werther's hand in the moment of emotional communion indicated by the name "Klopstock!" (HA 6, 27); at the end of *Iphigenie* the friendship between Greeks and "barbarians" is sealed by a handshake ("reiche mir [. . .] deine Rechte" [HA 5, 67]); *Tasso* ends with a wordless embrace. But within the architectonics of *Faust*, the true alliance of Faust and Helena recalls by contrast the deceitful wager between Faust and Mephisto, which was sealed by the two parties placing their hands on top of each other with the words "Schlag auf Schlag!" (1698).

One further example of Goethe's homage to world literature deserves attention: the evocation of Arcadia that ends the scene "Innerer Burghof." Ancient pastoral poetry, in which happy shepherds sing of love, was reshaped by Virgil in his Eclogues and situated in Arcadia, a valley of the Peloponnese — the "Nichtinsel" (9512) where Faust establishes his realm jointly with Helena. Mythical and natural motifs from Virgil — Apollo, Pan, nymphs and shepherds, goats cropping the bushes — all reappear in the leisurely quatrains (9506–73) which return to the flexible madrigal verse of Part One (see Curtius, 183–202; Rüdiger, 188–94; and Flavell). Faust's monologue culminates in the reconciliation of culture and nature, thrones and bowers:

> Gelockt, auf sel'gem Grund zu wohnen,
> Du flüchtetest ins heiterste Geschick!
> Zur Laube wandeln sich die Thronen,
> Arkadisch frei sei unser Glück!
>
> (9570–53)

We might be tempted to read these lines as expressing the supreme moment of happiness that Faust told Mephisto he could never experience (1688–1700). But we should notice that Faust uses the subjunctive mood ("sei"), not stating a fact but voicing a desire, Later, when he does speak of "den höchsten Augenblick" (11586), it is with reference to the free society of the future which he hopes to found on land reclaimed from the sea. In Arcadia, likewise, Faust's happiness depends on the future, for there is another Virgilian allusion in his phrase "das holde Kind" (9555), anticipating the birth of his son Euphorion, but also recalling Virgil's Fourth Eclogue and the "child, under whom the iron brood shall first cease, and a golden race spring up throughout the world" (Virgil, 29). This passage, probably intended as a hyperbolic compliment to one of Virgil's patrons, has often been construed as an unwitting prophecy of the birth of Christ. In *Faust*, the child Euphorion overreaches himself and dies, disrupting the idyll and confirming that earthly happiness can only be short-lived.

Liturgy

As we move through *Faust*, we find that scenes focused on Faust himself, or on Faust and one interlocutor (Wagner, Mephisto, Gretchen), alternate with crowd and ceremonial scenes. First we have the crowd enjoying Easter Sunday in "Vor dem Tor." Later we have a church service ("Dom") and its antithesis, the witches' celebration of Walpurgisnacht. In Part Two ceremonial scenes predominate: the masque of Plutus in Act 1, the Classical Walpurgisnacht culminating in the trium-

phal pageant of Galatea, Faust's wooing and wedding of Helena in
Act 3, and finally Faust's heavenly apotheosis. The appreciation of the
Helena episode offered in 1828 by Thomas Carlyle — still an out-
standing essay in the sympathetic interpretation of an enigmatic text —
applies to much of Part Two:

> In fact, the style of *Helena* is altogether new; quiet, simple, joyful;
> passing by a short gradation from Classic dignity into Romantic
> pomp; it has everywhere a full and sunny tone of colouring; resembles
> not a tragedy, but a gay gorgeous mask. (Carlyle, 124)

For his dramatic spectacles, Goethe drew especially on Calderón, a
dramatist whom he ranked alongside Shakespeare (see his conversation
with Eckermann of 28 March 1827). Calderón's Baroque theatre specialized in visual displays, such as sudden transformations of scenery,
the appearance of armies on the stage (as in "Innerer Burghof"), and
the use of stage machinery like the cloud effect at the beginning of
Act 4 and the opening of Hell-mouth on the stage in Act 5.

For now, however, I want to concentrate on how Goethe increases
his range of poetic forms by exploiting the Roman Catholic liturgy. In
the "Dom" scene we hear the "Dies irae," traditionally used in requiem
masses, and composed by the Franciscan Thomas of Celano (c.1200–
c.1255). It warns of the Day of Judgement (the "day of wrath") when
the divine judge shall discern and punish any secret sins. The stanzas
Goethe chooses to quote present Christianity as harshly retributive; he
omits the long sequence of verses invoking the divine mercy. No wonder Gretchen faints.

Gretchen's prayer to the Virgin in "Zwinger" seems to have been
suggested by a thirteenth-century hymn which also forms part of the
Catholic liturgy and is uncertainly ascribed to the Franciscan poet Jaco-
pone da Todi (1230–1306). It begins:

> Stabat mater dolorosa
> Juxta crucem lacrimosa
>   Dum pendebat filius.
>
> Cujus animam gementem,
> Contristantem et dolentem,
>   Pertransivit gladius.

[The sorrowful mother was standing weeping beside the Cross while
her Son was hanging on it. Through her lamenting, anguished and
sorrowing soul the sword had passed. (Brittain, 246)]

Gretchen is about to be a mother; her child will die, at her own hand; she too will feel intense sorrow. To complicate yet further the pattern of resemblances and divergences, we have the figure of Frau Marthe, her accommodating neighbor, whose Christian name is that of another Mary's sister (Luke 10:38–42) and whose surname, "Schwerdtlein" (2899), recalls the image of the sword piercing the Virgin's soul (Luke 2:35). Comic pastiche is suggested when we encounter Marthe lamenting the death of her husband, mainly because she has no death certificate. One should neither ignore nor over-interpret these similarities; but they give Frau Marthe a semi-comic place in the sequence of real and mythical female figures leading from the witches in Part One via Helena and the sea-nymph Galatea up to the appearance of the Virgin Mary at the end of Part Two (for the parallels between Galatea and the Virgin Mary, see Hamlin).

The final scene, "Bergschluchten," purporting to depict Faust's ascent to heaven, has particularly puzzled commentators. The Christian imagery, with saints, hermits, angels, and the Virgin Mary, comes strangely from someone who described himself (to Lavater, on 29 July 1782) as "kein Widerkrist, kein Unkrist aber doch ein dezidierter Nichtkrist." Goethe's belief in immortality, in the survival of a personal essence or entelechy, draws on Aristotle and Leibniz rather than Christian sources. The thought behind "Bergschluchten" is deeply eclectic, and its imagery is no less original (see Schmidt; and Bremer). Just as Goethe, in the "Klassische Walpurgisnacht," made free use of Greek mythology to express the variety of natural forces, so here he makes analogous use of Christian mythology to express man's aspirations to the transcendent. His imagery derives from Renaissance painting, from Dante, and from the account of the angelic hierarchies provided by Dionysius the Areopagite, a fifth-century Neoplatonic writer to whom Dante pays tribute in *Paradiso* x. 115–17 and xxviii. 130–2 (and whose influence is discussed by Patrides).

The scene shows Goethe's empathy with the spirit of Counter-Reformation Catholicism, not only in the visual similarity between Faust's ascent and the illusionistic perspectives of a Baroque church ceiling, but in the verse, the keynote being set by the bold dactylic meters of the Chorus and the Pater Ecstaticus:

> Ewiger Wonnebrand,
> Glühendes Liebeband,
> Siedender Schmerz der Brust,
> Schäumende Gotteslust [. . .]
>
> (11854–57)

These lines gain added vitality from a residual uncertainty about how to read them. Dactyls usually tail off into two unstressed syllables, but these end with a syllable ("brand," "band," etc.) which demands more emphasis both by its semantic content and its accumulation of consonants. Precedents for this meter have been found in medieval and Renaissance Latin hymns (see Ciupke, 195). A different kind of dactylic verse, interspersed with iambs, is used later by the chorus of Younger Angels:

> Nebelnd um Felsenhöh'
> Spür' ich soeben,
> Regend sich in der Näh',
> Ein Geisterleben.
>
> (11966–66)

Here the initially dactylic pattern is disturbed by the need to stress "in" and "Geist-."

The metrical variety continues. A simpler, trochaic meter is used by the Doctor Marianus in his invocation to the Virgin, underlining the direct intensity of his emotion. The three female penitents speak in trochaic tetrameters —

> Bei der Liebe, die den Füßen
> Deines gottverklärten Sohnes [. . .]
>
> (12037–38)

in which the initial stress starts each line with a quiet energy that builds up to their final chorus (12061–68). And after that the penitent formerly named Gretchen repeats not only the meter but also the very words of her earlier prayer to the Virgin, except that now "Schmerz" has been transformed into "Glück" (12072). Finally the Chorus Mysticus, a choir without visible singers, which one imagines filling the heavens, again exploits the resources of the dactyl: "Alles Vergängliche" (12104) can be read as a slow and solemn dactyl, but "Das Ewig-Weibliche" needs a stress on the second syllable which decelerates it further, giving us an emphatic amphibrach ("Das Ewig-") which rises to freedom in the increasingly light syllables of the closing dactyl ("Weibliche").

Complex Words

Any reader of *Faust* notices that a rather small number of key words keeps recurring: "Herz," "Sinn," "Kraft," "Geist," "Tat," "Wort," "Liebe," "schaffen," "wirken." Such recurring words enrich poetic drama by thickening its texture. Their connotations change subtly in different contexts; and when one remembers the same word from different passages, one discerns new relationships, new implications. Long ago the American New Critics and their British counterparts showed us how to read Shakespeare with attention to what William Empson called "complex words." Empson's reflections on the word "honest" in *Othello,* Cleanth Brooks's study of the word "man" in *Macbeth,* disclose an exploration that Shakespeare was semi-consciously conducting as part of his creative activity (Empson; Brooks). In Goethe's case, although his recorded statements are valuable evidence for the meaning of *Faust,* they are not themselves its meaning; the text is not simply a poetic restatement of convictions formulated in prose, but restlessly explores the implications and limitations of these convictions. External evidence for Goethe's intentions must not be used to petrify the live process of debate going on within the text.

I want now to examine certain complex words in Part One of *Faust.* These are words with a range of meaning and with tensions among their various meanings, tensions which are enacted both in the dramatic structure of the play and on the micro-level of its poetic texture. From numerous possibilities I have selected "Gott," "Geist," "Brust," "Busen," and "Leib."

The Prologue in Heaven presents us with a divine being who, however, is never called God, but "the Lord," as in the Old Testament. Mephisto calls him "Lord" to his face and refers to him behind his back as "the Old Man" ("der Alte"). The ordinary Christian term "Gott" is used by Faust when he prepares to translate St. John's Gospel ("Die Liebe Gottes" [1185]); and otherwise, only by Gretchen ("Glaubst du an Gott?" [3426]), by Faust replying to her in the scene "Marthens Garten," and again at the end where Gretchen appeals to the "Gericht Gottes." Elsewhere, Mephisto speaks circumspectly of "ein Gott" (1781, 2441), or (mocking Faust) "einer Gottheit" (3285). Faust himself, contemplating the sign of the Macrocosm, asks: "Bin ich ein Gott? Mir wird so licht!" (439). He often uses the word in the plural to denote a state of being to which he vainly aspires (652, 3242): "Götterleben" (620), "Götterwonne" (706), "Götterhöhe" (713). Clearly Faust has no actual belief in a single Supreme Being, even though he unwittingly serves that Being; his self-description as "der Gottverhaßte" may be taken as a bitter metaphor (3256). Faust considers himself to be the "Ebenbild der Gottheit" (516, 614), the image of God, not simply as a human being created by God, but as an exceptional being whose powers exceed those of the angels ("Ich, mehr als Cherub" [618]). He wishes to transcend human limits, to become a god, to cast off what is earthly ("abgestreift den Erdensohn" [617]), an ambition duly mocked

by Mephisto (3266, 3290). The Earth Spirit derides his pretensions to
be an "Übermensch" (490).

The vainglorious character of such ambitions is intimated by Mephisto when he writes in the Student's album the words in which the
Biblical serpent tempted Eve to eat the forbidden fruit: "Eritis sicut
Deus, scientes bonum et malum" (2048) — "ye shall be as God,
knowing good and evil." The intellectual ambitions shown by the Student must lead eventually to Faust's overweening desire for "Gottähn-
lichkeit" (2050). When Faust utters his despairing curse upon the three
cardinal virtues, the spirits proclaim him a demi-god:

> Weh! weh!
> Du hast sie zerstört,
> Die schöne Welt,
> Mit mächtiger Faust;
> Sie stürzt, sie zerfällt!
> Ein Halbgott hat sie zerschlagen!
>
> (1607–12)

Here we are reminded that Faust is a symbolic figure, signifying by his
intellectual drive the Enlightenment's rejection of the Christian cosmos
still inhabited by Gretchen. The spirits, later described by Mephisto as
his lesser servants, flatter Faust's vanity by punning on his name and
calling him a demi-god. Their hint is developed by Mephisto when he
compares Faust specifically to the demi-god Prometheus, punished for
his excesses by having a vulture devour his liver daily:

> Hör auf, mit deinem Gram zu spielen,
> Der, wie ein Geier, dir am Leben frißt.
>
> (1635–36)

What does Faust understand by becoming a god? His exclamation "Mir
wird so licht!" (439) suggests radiance; it implies substituting spiritual
existence for physical life. He also senses a frustrated divinity within
himself:

> Der Gott, der mir im Busen wohnt,
> Kann tief mein Innerstes erregen;
> Der über allen meinen Kräften thront,
> Er kann nach außen nichts bewegen.
>
> (1566–69)

Both these suggestions — spiritual existence and inner powers — are
developed by Goethe's uses of "Geist," a word whose semantic range
makes it notoriously hard to translate. At one extreme it means

"mind," though with suggestions of energy and emotion that distinguish it from "Verstand" (intellect, understanding) or "Vernunft" (reason). Faust often uses the word in this sense, e.g. "des Geistes Flügeln" (1090), "Des Geistes Flutstrom" (698). At the other extreme, "Geist" means a supernatural being that does not need physical embodiment: the Spirit of the Earth ("Erdgeist"), the crowds of spirits that attend Mephisto, and the spirits of the air whose existence is to Wagner unquestionable (1130) and to Faust a matter of hypothesis ("O gibt es Geister in der Luft [. . .]" [1118]). In the early modern period, when Faust is supposed to live, the widespread belief in an invisible world of spirits found learned support in Neoplatonic writings; and Goethe knew not only these but probably also the more recent account of the spiritual realm by the seer Emanuel Swedenborg (see Jantz 1951, 27–35 and 63).

Beside these two meanings of "Geist," the subjective and the supernatural, there are other meanings which mediate between them. The Earth Spirit is a distinct being, but also a force of nature. He represents the creative and destructive energies that animate the physical universe. As such, the Spirit is not simply external: Faust, himself a natural being, feels his heart, senses and emotions powerfully stirred by the approach of the Earth Spirit. Later, when Faust begins translating St. John's Gospel, he needs to be "inspired by the Spirit," "vom Geiste recht erleuchtet" (1228), and this implies the Holy Spirit. The Holy Spirit is personified — "Mir hilft der Geist!" (1236) — but it works through Faust's own mental and emotional powers and is thus not sharply distinct from the subjective sense of "Geist."

Despite these mediations, the complexity of the word "Geist" lies in its range from the subjective to the supernatural. Its use implies the question whether the restless human spirit ("eines Menschen Geist, in seinem hohen Streben" [1676]) can aspire to enter the "Geisterwelt" (443). Can man's inner, mental, emotional powers carry him beyond human limits?

The mark of human limitation is the body. Spirits are disembodied; Mephisto merely assumes such human forms as suit his needs — a wandering scholar, a nobleman — though like the traditional devil he always seems to be lame (cf. 2184, 2499). To be human is to be embodied. The human spirit needs material embodiment, just as light, according to Mephisto, needs material objects ("Körper" [1354–58]) in order to exist at all.

Goethe frequently uses two words which have literal, corporeal and also mental meanings: "Busen" and "Brust." These have to cover a semantic range for which in English there are three words: "bosom," "breast," and "chest." The "Busen" is especially the seat of the emotions, be they fearful (411), ecstatic (3287), melancholy (3654), or passionate: "Mein Busen fängt mir an zu brennen!" says Faust, enraptured by the Witch's picture of a beautiful woman (2461). "Busen" can imply both physical and emotional intimacy, as when Gretchen wishes to lie on Faust's "Busen" (4465), or when she exclaims "Mein Busen drängt / Sich nach ihm hin" (3406–07); this is a milder version of the *Urfaust*'s rawly physical and passionate "Mein Schoos! Gott! drängt / Sich nach ihm hin."

The word "Brust," which in the plural also means a woman's breasts, juxtaposes the emotional and the physical yet more sharply. It can again be the seat of emotions, Faust's "tiefbewegte Brust" (307; cf. 3233, 3247). It is narrowly physical when Gretchen asks for her child (or her baby sister?) to be buried "mir an die rechte Brust" (4528). It can connote the physical intimacy between the lovers (1682, 3346); Faust, in an outburst of fetishism, tells Mephisto to bring "ein Halstuch von ihrer Brust" (2661); and we have a glimpse of the lovers' amorous play when Faust, seeing a vision of Gretchen, exclaims: "Das ist die Brust, die Gretchen mir geboten" (4197). But since the breast is what the mother offers the child, Faust is also revealing the male fantasy of being a child again, and he repeats this fantasy in relation to Mother Nature, into whose "tiefe Brust" he acquires insight (3223). His longing for contact with Nature is most ardently expressed in some lines of almost Shakespearean richness early in the play:

> Wo fass' ich dich, unendliche Natur?
> Euch Brüste, wo? Ihr Quellen alles Lebens,
> An denen Himmel und Erde hängt,
> Dahin die welke Brust sich drängt —
> Ihr quellt, ihr tränkt, und schmacht' ich so vergebens?
>
> (455–59)

Mother Nature's breasts are an overflowing source of life (as the polyptoton of "Quellen" and "quellt" conveys), sustaining heaven and earth; these briefly seem like twins, being suckled side by side, till the singular verb "hängt" unifies them into a single cosmos. The withered breast ("welke Brust") suggests Faust's own emotional desiccation and hints at a constant process of renewal in which the male breast, full of lofty aspirations but without its own source of life, has to be repeatedly nourished by the milk-filled breasts of feminine Nature.

Together, "Busen" and "Brust" convey a complex understanding of bodily existence. Mental life — the thoughts and feelings within one's bosom — is continuous with physical life; lovers embracing communicate at once emotionally and physically; and the polyvalence of "breast(s)" says much about the interdependence of men and women and the shared humanity of both. The man with lofty thoughts in his breast was nourished at his mother's breasts and seeks sustenance at the breast of his lover.

For the body itself, Goethe uses the word "Leib." "Körper" is used only by Mephisto, referring to material objects in general (1354–58). "Leib" is used casually in numerous set phrases (2603, 3277, 3419, 3754) which nevertheless recall and confirm that human life has to be embodied. The word acquires more prominence when Goethe exploits its rhyme with "Weib" (2436/8, 2603–04, 3327/9). Faust's sensual desire, his physical appetite, are thrust on the reader's attention. But there are significant shifts of tone. His carnal appetite is brutally evident when he reproaches Mephisto:

> Bring die Begier zu ihrem süßen Leib
> Nicht wieder vor die halb verrückten Sinnen! (3328–29)

But the same phrase acquires passionate lyricism when Faust, rapt by his Walpurgisnacht vision, says:

> Das ist die Brust, die Gretchen mir geboten,
> Das ist der süße Leib, den ich genoß. (4197–98)

And carnality is connected with incarnation, as Faust has earlier acknowledged:

> Ich bin ihr nah', und wär' ich noch so fern,
> Ich kann sie nie vergessen, nie verlieren;
> Ja, ich beneide schon den Leib des Herrn,
> Wenn ihre Lippen ihn indes berühren. (3332–35).

Superficially, this is a libertine jest. Looked at more closely, it expresses two understandings of the Eucharist. Gretchen presumably accepts the Church's teaching on the sacrament and believes that in swallowing the Host she is making contact with Christ's body beneath the accidental guise of bread. Thus for her the miracle of incarnation is repeated whenever she receives communion. Goethe himself was more skeptical. Even when he took communion as a young man, he described its purpose as remembrance — "mich an des Herren Leiden und Tod zu erinnern" (he wrote in his letter to Susanna von Klettenberg of 26 August 1770). Faust's relation to Gretchen is similarly one of intense remembrance, and though he can and does forget her, he remembers her vividly at the Walpurgisnacht in a visionary premonition of her death.

In its texture, then, *Faust* shows us a profound and subtle meditation on what it is to be human, to be incarnate. Faust may fantasize
about becoming a disembodied spirit, but the play in fact leads him
from the merely intellectual existence of a scholar to a richer experience
of human life as lived in and through his body. By its complex words,
the play discourages us from a dualistic view of spirit and body. Mephisto may be a spirit assuming a temporary embodiment, but to be
human means not just being in a body but being a body. At the end of
Part Two, when Faust, "das edle Glied / Der Geisterwelt" (11934–
35), does enter the spiritual world, the angels proclaim the indissoluble
unity of spirit and matter:

> Wenn starke Geisteskraft
> Die Elemente
> An sich herangerafft,
> Kein Engel trennte
> Geeinte Zwienatur
> Der innigen beiden,
> Die ewige Liebe nur
> Vermag's zu scheiden.
>
> (11958–65)

Not only are these themes woven into the texture of the play; they
are visible also in its structure. Faust's opening monologue is delivered
on Easter Eve. He is prevented from suicide by the choruses on Easter
Sunday. Just as he imagined that in summoning up spirits he was becoming a god, so he conceives death as being swept up in a fiery chariot to higher spheres of "Götterwonne" and "Götterhöhe" (706, 713).
By contrast, the choruses tell of another person who, according to
Christian belief, really did die but overcame human limitations and rose
from the grave to immortal life. These Easter choruses are not simply
decorative. They round off a long scene of some 450 lines in which
Faust has repeatedly tried to transcend ordinary human life: by becoming a god, by summoning up spirits and treating them as equals, and
then by planning suicide in the hope of thus attaining a higher existence. All these aspirations are implicitly rebuked by contrast with the
death and resurrection of Christ. Beyond that, the question as to how
we are to interpret the juxtaposition is left open. Faust cannot share the
chorus's faith, but their songs reanimate memories of his childhood,
stir his emotions, and make him want to go on living. Different readers
will see different kinds and degrees of irony in the paradoxical couplet:

O tönet fort, ihr süßen Himmelslieder!
Die Träne quillt, die Erde hat mich wieder!
(783–84)

We may find in it an anticipation of Zarathustra's injunction: "Ich beschwöre euch, meine Brüder, *bleibt der Erde treu* und glaubt denen nicht, welche euch von überirdischen Hoffnungen reden!" (Nietzsche, 280). But we should also note how Faust's unrealistic ambitions correspond to those that later kill his son Euphorion. Though warned that his strength, like that of the giant Antaeus, depends on staying in touch with the solid ground (9611), Euphorion insists on attempting ever loftier flights, and eventually crashes to the ground like Icarus. Thus he repeats, with fatal consequences, the attempt to transcend earthly life from which Faust was dissuaded by the Easter choruses, a parallel pointed out by Jantz (1978, 35). Even in his apotheosis, Faust does not discard his body, but acquires a purified body. The whole poem recalls a letter of Goethe's (to Lavater of 28 October 1779) about a friend's efforts to interest him in the secrets of the Book of Revelation: "ich bin ein sehr irdischer Mensch [. . .] Ich dencke auch aus der Wahrheit zu seyn, aber aus der Wahrheit der fünf Sinne und Gott habe Geduld mit mir wie bisher."

Works Cited

Atkins, Stuart. "Goethe, Calderon, and *Faust: Der Tragödie Zweiter Teil*." *Germanic Review*. 28 (1953). 83–98.

Bremer, Dieter. "'Wenn starke Geisteskraft [. . .]': Traditionsvermittlungen in der Schlußszene von Goethes *Faust*." *Goethe-Jahrbuch*. 112 (1995). 287–307.

Brittain, Frederick. (Ed.) *The Penguin Book of Latin Verse*. Harmondsworth: Penguin, 1962.

Brooks, Cleanth. "The Naked Babe and the Cloak of Manliness." *The Well Wrought Urn*. New York: Reynal and Hitchcock, 1947. 21–46.

Carlyle, Thomas. *Critical and Miscellaneous Essays*. Vol. 1. London: Chapman and Hall, 1888.

Ciupke, Markus. *Des Geklimpers vielverworrner Töne Rausch: Die metrische Gestaltung von Goethe's "Faust."* Göttingen: Wallstein, 1994.

Curtius, Ernst Robert. *European Literature and the Latin Middle Ages*. Trans. Willard Trask. New York: Pantheon, 1953.

Durrani, Osman. *Faust and the Bible: A Study of Goethe's Use of Scriptural Allusions and Christian Religious Motifs in "Faust I" and "II."* Berne, Frankfurt am Main, Las Vegas: Peter Lang, 1977.

Empson, William. *The Structure of Complex Words.* London: Chatto and Windus, 1951.

Fairley, Barker. *Goethe's "Faust": Six Essays.* Oxford: Clarendon Press, 1953.

Flavell, M. Kay. "'Arkadisch frei sei unser Glück.' The Myth of the Golden Age in Eighteenth-Century Germany." *Publications of the English Goethe Society.* NS 43 (1972–1973). 1–27.

Forster, Leonard. *The Icy Fire: Five Studies in European Petrarchism.* Cambridge: Cambridge UP, 1969.

Hamlin, Cyrus. "Tracking the Eternal-Feminine in Goethe's *Faust II*." In *Interpreting Goethe's Faust Today.* Ed. Jane K. Brown et al. Columbia, SC: Camden House, 1994. 142–55.

Heine, Heinrich. *Sämtliche Schriften.* Ed. Klaus Briegleb. Vol. 2. Munich: Hanser, 1968.

Hirdt, Willi. "Goethe und Dante." *Deutsches Dante-Jahrbuch.* 68/69 (1993/1994). 31–80.

Jantz, Harold. *Goethe's Faust as a Renaissance Man: Parallels and Prototypes.* Princeton, NJ: Princeton UP, 1951.

———. *The Form of Faust: The Work of Art and its Intrinsic Structures.* Baltimore and London: Johns Hopkins UP, 1978.

Kaiser, Gerhard. "Goethe's Faust und die Bibel." *Deutsche Vierteljahrsschrift für Literaturwissenschaft und Geistesgechichte.* 58 (1984). 391–413.

Mason, Eudo C. *Goethe's "Faust": Its Genesis and Purport.* Berkeley and Los Angeles: U of California P, 1967.

May, Kurt. *"Faust II" in der Sprachform gedeutet.* Munich: Hanser, 1962.

Mommsen, Katharina. *Natur- und Fabelreich in "Faust II."* Berlin: de Gruyter, 1968.

Nietzsche, Friedrich. *Also sprach Zarathustra. Werke in drei Bänden.* Ed. Karl Schlechta. Vol. 2. Munich: Hanser, 1956.

Patrides, C. A. *Premises and Motifs in Renaissance Thought and Literature.* Princeton, NJ: Princeton UP, 1982.

Phelan, Anthony. "Deconstructing Classicism — Goethe's *Helena* and the Need to Rhyme." In *New Ways in Germanistik.* Ed. Richard Sheppard. New York, Oxford, Munich: Berg, 1990. 192–210.

Pniower, Otto. "Goethes Faust und das Hohe Lied." *Goethe-Jahrbuch.* 13 (1982). 181–98.

Rüdiger, Horst, "Weltliteratur in Goethes *Helena.*" *Jahrbuch der Deutschen Schiller-Gesellschaft.* 8 (1964). 172–97.

Schmidt, Jochen. "Die 'katholische Mythologie' und ihre mystische Entmythologisierung in der Schluß-Szene des Faust II." *Jahrbuch der Deutschen Schillergesellschaft.* 34 (1990). 230–56.

Sengle, Friedrich. *Das Genie und sein Fürst: Die Geschichte der Lebensgemeinschaft Goethes mit dem Herzog Carl August.* Stuttgart and Weimar: Metzler, 1993.

Simpson, James. *Goethe and Patriarchy: Faust and the Fates of Desire.* Oxford: Legenda, 1998.

Virgil. *Eclogues, Georgics, Aeneid I–VI.* Trans. H. Rushton Fairclough. [Loeb Classical Library.] Cambridge, MA and London: Harvard UP, 1935.

Zimmermann, Rolf Christian. *Das Weltbild des jungen Goethe.* Vol. 2. Munich: Fink, 1979.

The Character and Characterization of Faust

Martin Swales

GOETHE DID NOT INVENT THE FAUST FIGURE. There was a real Faust, who was born some time around 1480 in South Germany. He seems to have made a living as a wandering scholar who practised medicine, probably also hypnosis. He cast horoscopes and no doubt dabbled in alchemy and magic of various kinds. He was also a show-man, a flamboyant, clever and a somewhat dubious character. One way and another he was manifestly the kind of person to whom legends readily attached themselves. His significance lay not simply in what he said or did or was but also in the kind of stories to which he gave rise. In his more-than-individual, symbolic function he clearly embodies the emergent energies, the restiveness of early modern culture.

It is important to stress this matter of the two-fold significance of the original, real-life Faust figure because, as we shall see, it becomes a central ingredient not only in the transmission of the legend but also in Goethe's incomparable treatment of that legend. Put most simply: the character of Faust is one that represents more than personal energies and gifts and aspirations, one that has, by that token, broader cultural and philosophical implications — and at the same time the figure is in-dividuated, particular, specified. Goethe understood this supremely well; his Faust is a force, a corpus of energies, a complex living principle; but he also recognizably and necessarily is a person who does certain things. As far as I am aware, no creative writer has surpassed Goethe in the breadth and range of his understanding of the Faust figure.

What were the particular forms of the narrative that Goethe inher-ited? In 1587 a popular tale entitled the *Historia von D. Johann Fau-sten* appeared at the Frankfurt am Main book fair, published under the imprint of Johann Spies. The work (or *Volksbuch* as it is often called) recounts how Faust, an overweening intellectual and speculator of the elements and necromancer, sells his soul to the Devil in exchange for twenty-four years of service, by virtue of which he gains access to all manner of erotic, social, and cosmological adventures. At the end of the allotted time he dies gruesomely, and his soul is forfeit. The story — no doubt because it concerned itself with a figure who, as we

have seen, was known to and firmly anchored in the popular imagination — caught on rapidly. It was translated into various languages, one
being English; and it came to the attention of Christopher Marlowe. It
also provided the stuff of popular adaptations for the theatre, and particularly for puppet shows. It was in these forms that the legend caught
the interest of the very young Goethe. Subsequently he became acquainted with the 1587 story, albeit in a somewhat later version.

If we look at the *Faust* material that came down to Goethe, we can,
I think, register an important creative disturbance at the heart of the
legend, and it has centrally to do with the issue of character on which I
have already commented. The 1587 *Volksbuch* is a work of firm didactic
purpose; moralizing commentary abounds. But, like all cautionary tales,
it cannot abstain entirely from taking an interest in the forms of the
wrongdoing that it so resolutely condemns. There is, then, an implicit
acknowledgment of the intensity of Faust's desire to know and understand the universe. The *Volksbuch* is aware of the energies of modern,
secular scientific culture. Moreover, at the end of the tale, as the moment of reckoning comes ever closer, we hear intimations of a theo-
logical-cum-philosophical issue. The *Volksbuch* is a deeply Lutheran
work and it is therefore not surprising that it is touched by the paradox
that sin and abjection may be the precondition for salvation. It is by no
stretch of the imagination a neglected masterpiece; but it has a richness
of intimation that, one suspects, served to inspire Christopher Marlowe. His *Tragical Historie of Dr. Faustus* captures magnificently the
titanism of the human will to ask questions whatever the cost. And it
also engages with that sense of sin that has to do not with a particular
act of transgression but rather with an omnipresent psychological and
socio-cultural sense of the monstrosity of having abolished the divinity.
Both the *Volksbuch* and Marlowe's tragedy invest the Faust figure with
general symbolic significance. And that symbolic significance is an unsettling and troubling one, for it is compounded of both greatness and
depravity. Both texts are, however, unable to solve a key artistic and
human dilemma posed by the legend: the titanic Faustian quest entails
not just knowing but also doing. And the doings of the Faust figures in
both the 1587 tale and Marlowe's play tend to be trivial, because they
are utterly episodic. That episodic mode derives, of course, from the
Devil's magic which, by definition, makes any wish instantly fulfilla-
ble — and disposable. This possibility of profuse and varied incident is,
at one level, artistically attractive — and it was vigorously exploited in
the puppet-play versions of *Faust*. But the danger is that it all too easily
slithers into banality.

Let me recapitulate the nexus of concerns I have described as the creative disturbance at the heart of the legend that Goethe inherited. Tantalizingly he only came across Marlowe's play late in life, when his own understanding of the *Faust* project was fully formed. But, even without Marlowe, he knew that at the heart of the Faust narrative was the story of an overreacher whose energies and aspirations were compounded of both sublimity and depravity; the story of a supremely active self whose activity tended to descend into episodic triviality. It is the measure of Goethe's genius that he realized that his central task was to sustain and explore these paradoxes and dilemmas — and not to resolve them.

I want to begin, before I come to a detailed discussion of Goethe's great text, by sketching in the principal changes he made to the *Faust* material. There are five strands we should note. And the first four have centrally to do with the generality of the Faust figure; while the fifth embodies his specificity. Firstly: Goethe transforms the value-scheme of the story from the traditional, theologically and morally grounded opposition between good and evil, right and wrong, obedience and disobedience to a primarily secular, existentially defined scheme that pits energy against sloth, drive against apathy, activity against inactivity. Second: he justifies Faust and the energetic principle that he enshrines — while counting the cost of that energy. Third: he transforms the traditional twenty-four-year pact between Faust and Mephisto, the devil figure, into an open-ended bet on experience. Faust does not believe that there can ever be a moment in his life when he will be completely fulfilled, when there will be no reaching beyond the present moment in quest of other, as yet unexplored realms of activity. Mephisto undertakes to provide that moment, to put an end to the Faustian energy, to his "Streben." Fourth: Goethe, in keeping with that predominant secularization of the value-scheme to which I have referred, finds a way to re-configure the devil figure. Mephisto's aim, as we have seen, is to switch off the dynamo that drives Faust. And to this end, he adopts a two-fold strategy. One is (true to his traditional role) that of the salesman, the purveyor, by magical means, of instant gratification; and the other is that of the cynic who appeals to Faust's discontent by demonstrating that no individual experience ever keeps its promise, and that, by extension, all experience is interchangeable and worthless. What Goethe achieves here, at a stroke, is an insight into the whole problem of the triviality of what the titanic spirit can actually experience in the world. And he also understands that he must define a yardstick by which we can distinguish triviality from substance. Hence, and this is the fifth departure from the tradition, and the one which grounds his whole treatment of the story in moral specificity, he creates the Gretchen figure. In the depiction of the love between Faust and Gretchen he takes us into a realm of intense human substance and once-and-for-all finality; and for this there is no equivalent anywhere in the earlier *Faust* material. Of course, in one of the most famous lines in German literature, Mephisto converts even this experience, this woman, into mere episode — "Sie ist die Erste nicht." But the play knows better than that. Episodes are not given but made; made in the attitude of the human agent to the experience in question. The overreaching energy of Faust makes an episode of every experience. That is the source of his splendid existential intensity — and of his moral depravity. Luminously, Goethe holds the great creative disturbance of the *Faust* legend in perfect, complex focus.

I want now to pursue these issues in the drama itself; and I want to concentrate on the issue of characterization — particularly (but not exclusively) on the characterization of Faust himself. As we shall discover, the definition of his character shifts constantly for reasons that are embedded deep in Goethe's understanding of the legend. One is that Goethe constantly re-worked the *Faust* material. There is the *Urfaust* of the 1770s, *Faust, ein Fragment* of 1790; *Faust I* of 1808; and *Faust II* of 1832. In other words, this project is one that obsessed him throughout his creative lifetime. And it is, on that account, hardly surprising that the central figure changes and grows with Goethe's own creative progress. Moreover, Goethe's constant re-working of the *Faust* material was more than simply a private obsession on his part, an inability (as we might put it) to get it right the first, second, or third time. Rather, the rewriting process has to do with the energy of the project itself. The matter can, I think, be best explained if we return for a moment to the transformation of the 24-year, fixed-term pact into an open-ended wager. In the new configuration of the contract between Faust and his devilish antagonist, everything depends on what Faust makes of his experience, on what he says to any given, passing moment. There is no other arbitration at work. And this imparts an immense dynamic to the whole story: it is about ongoing, and changing processes of understanding and signification and evaluation. And this is the measure of the text's understanding of the flux and dynamism of modern culture. In other words, Faust is a figure who constantly re-writes his selfhood; and the play in which he figures necessarily re-writes and re-configures the definition of that selfhood. His character is not a given, not a stable, known, once-and-for-all quantity. It is something ceaselessly in process.

What, then, are the levels and frameworks of character definition at work in Goethe's *Faust*? I want to begin with two levels that are meta-individual, that define Faust as representative of a certain kind of generality. One has to do with the sense in which *Faust* is a philosophical drama; within this framework of signification Faust stands for humankind, for the glories and disasters of this uniquely self-conscious species. And the other derives from Goethe's wish to write the historico-cultural drama of modernity. Within this context Faust embodies the kind of human subjectivity that is enshrined at the heart of modern culture; and it is a subjectivity that is radically individualist, secular, and scientific in its temper. Time and time again Faust interacts with other characters, and they (particularly Mephisto and to a certain extent Gretchen as well) change their character-configuration in accordance with Faust's changing persona. But they are less protean and volatile than he is. To say this is not, of course, to offer some uncritical worship of Faust. There has been plenty of that — particularly within Germany. Hans Schwerte's study *Faust und das Faustische* surveys a particular form of — frequently ideologically motivated — misuse of the Faust character. In view of that often unedifying story it is perhaps tempting to abstain from generalizations and symbolizations of the Faust figure, to content oneself with Faust without invoking "das Faustische." But this is, in the last analysis, wrong, I believe — precisely because Goethe's great drama puts before us a figure who is both individuated and generalized. The richness and range of the definition of the figure has to do with the scale of Goethe's creative commitment to the *Faust* story and to its protagonist, and not with any form of hero-worship.

Let us consider now the philosophical framework for and definition of the Faust figure. *Faust I* begins with three prefatory statements, which frame the action proper, and which precede the subtitle "Der Tragödie erster Teil." And all three of them, in their different ways, create a conceptually differentiated framework within which we are to hear the resonances of Faust's story; and each of them provides a generalizing context for the Faust figure. The first statement is a poem, "Zueignung," in which the poet addresses the characters — "Gestalten" — of his imagination. They are hovering, unstable entities who return to haunt him and ask again to be captured and expressed by the creative faculty. The poet turns to the memories evoked by these figures and finds that the past overlays the present. The poem ends:

> Was ich besitze, seh' ich wie im Weiten,
> Und was verschwand, wird mir zu Wirklichkeiten.

At one level, of course, this is unmistakably the voice of the poet speaking qua poet, the poet who finds present immediacy displaced by the products of an earlier phase of his imagination's working. At another level, however, the poem speaks more generally of processes that we can all understand because they are powerfully embedded in our self-consciousness. Frequently we find that the immediate, palpable present is supplanted by pictures located in the mind's eye — pictures of past experience, of alternative experience, of possible future experience. In other words: we do not indwell simply, integrally, instinctually in the present, because the mind constantly transgresses the particularity of immediate experiential contexts. And, as we shall see, precisely this ability will be at the very heart of the Faustian personality. He is, in particularly energetic and vivid and problematic form, what we all are.

The second prefatory statement, the "Vorspiel auf dem Theater," is a discussion that takes place in, and is also about, the theatre. Three figures express different concerns — the theatre manager, the comic figure, and the poet. At issue is the ability of fiction to represent human behavior — and to speak to human onlookers. I do not have the space to comment in detail on the "Vorspiel" here; but one point in particular needs stressing. The theatre is both the medium of Goethe's *Faust*; and it is also one of its governing metaphors. In English it is intriguing that the verb "to act" has two meanings: to carry out various deeds, and to perform a role. Perhaps that double meaning can help us to focus one of the key intimations of *Faust* as a work both sited in and reflecting on the theatre: because of the human dimension of self-consciousness, the individual subject is constantly aware of "acting" in both senses of the word. We are, in other words, both on stage and in the audience; we are, in our lives, both doers and onlookers at our doing. The theatre in this context provides a central existential metaphor, because, of all the literary forms, it has an intense physical liveliness, and it also makes us spectators at that intense physicality. We will recall these issues when we consider the two souls within Faust's breast. Once again, the key point I am after has to do with the generality of Faust: he is, in exceptional and radical form, what humankind is.

The third — and most weighty — prefatory statement is the "Prolog im Himmel." Goethe draws on a number of traditions here, on the world theatre of medieval mystery plays and Baroque drama; and also on biblical sources — particularly on the Book of Job which opens with a meeting of the Heavenly Host, and which brings together the Lord and the Devil. The result of their meeting is that the Lord gives the tempter permission to conduct an experiment whose aim is to destroy Job's faith in God. The constellation as between God and His adversary, in Goethe's Prologue, is similar, although, as we have already had occasion to note, the underlying value-scheme has moved beyond any traditional definitions of a theologically validated universe. What is at stake is the nature and destiny of secular humanity. The archangels sing in praise of the ongoing energies of creation, encompassing both the old (Ptolemaic) cosmology of the harmony of the crystalline spheres ("Brudersphären Wettgesang") and the new (Copernican) cosmology of an earth rotating about the sun. Mephisto then appears and brings a discordant note into the chorus of glory by pointing out how bad things are "bei uns." And by this little phrase he means not Hell, but the human sphere: "Ich sehe nur, wie sich die Menschen plagen" (280). Mephisto goes on to portray the disquiet of the human creature, endowed with enough self-consciousness to be unquiet, but not enough to find perfect clarity. The Lord mentions Faust in this context as His servant; but Mephisto offers a portrait of Faust as the supremely unquiet — and by that token undeferential — spirit:

> Vom Himmel fordert er die schönsten Sterne
> Und von der Erde jede höchste Lust,
> Und alle Näh' und alle Ferne
> Befriedigt nicht die tiefbewegte Brust.

(304–7)

The central point we need to note here is two-fold: first, that Faust is the test case in respect of humankind. He is exemplary; not in the sense that he is perfect, but rather in that he abundantly embodies and expresses the being of "der Mensch." And second: he is representative of humanity precisely by virtue of being discontented. His self-consciousness makes him restless and questing, caught between "Nah" and "Ferne" (we remember the opening poem "Zueignung"). Yet that condition is one of being "halb bewußt"; hence it cannot come to rest in stability of being and cognition — nor can it revert to unreflectivity.

It is on this state of being that the Lord and Mephisto engage in a wager, one that prefigures that between Faust and Mephisto. Because the contract is a wager and not a pact, the arbitration on the human condition, and on Faust as its most evident test-case, is left open. The Lord claims that such discontent is service in His cause — confused, uncomprehending service, but service nonetheless — because discontent is the mainspring of activity, and the Lord abhors sluggishness and quiescence: "Des Menschen Tätigkeit kann allzu leicht erschlaffen" (340). This, as we have already noted, is at the heart of the transformed value scheme that sustains Goethe's version of the *Faust* story. Mephisto enters into the wager with the Lord, convinced of his ability, as antagonist of the divine will, to quench the discontent, the will to activity that is at the heart of Faust's — and humankind's — being in the world. How Mephisto intends to proceed we do not yet know. All we know from the Prologue is the Lord's view of Mephisto's role, which is that ultimately, although he (Mephisto) sees himself as descended from the serpent in the Garden of Eden and by that token as able to lead mankind away from God's purposes, he, in the grand scheme of things, cannot win, because he is bound to function as an irritant to Faust, ensuring that he does not ever come to rest. As we shall see when we move into the action of *Faust* proper, Mephisto is by no means as unresourceful as the Lord implies.

I have spent time and space on the "Prolog im Himmel" not only because of its manifest importance as a contextualizing statement but also because it so powerfully generalizes the Faust figure within a philosophically conceived narrative. Time and time again the Lord and Mephisto debate the state of mankind; and time and time again Faust is invoked as the exemplar of the human species. Viewed under this aspect, *Faust* emerges as a sustained rumination on the relationship between mind and matter in human experience.

The action begins with Faust alone in his study. And, as befits somebody who is a supremely self-conscious spirit, he is soliloquizing, debating with himself. He oscillates between the need to consider and to analyze experience on the one hand, and the craving for immediacy and physicality of experience on the other. Hence, when he studies the sign of the macrocosm, he feels himself vouchsafed a perspective of divine contemplation: "Bin ich ein Gott? mir wird so licht!" (439). Yet almost immediately that dimension of transcendental abstraction is rejected as pure "Schauspiel" (we recall the metaphor of the theatre from the "Vorspiel auf dem Theater") in the name of the sensuous imperative:

> Welch Schauspiel! Aber ach! ein Schauspiel nur!
> Wo fass' ich dich, unendliche Natur?
> Euch Brüste, wo?
>
> (454–56)

The oscillations of Faust's moods, intensified by the brief meeting with Wagner, that epitome of intellectual triviality, bring him to the point of suicide, but he stays his hand as the songs of Easter remind him of his childhood. Easter, in so far as it has any meaning for Faust, is a phase of secular regeneration, having essentially to do with the natural cycle of the seasons and with the coming of spring. The "Osterspaziergang" provides Faust with images of mankind liberated from winter. And he summarizes the happiness felt by the village people:

> Hier ist des Volkes wahrer Himmel,
> Zufrieden jauchzet groß und klein.
> "Hier bin ich Mensch, hier darf ich's sein!"
>
> (938–40)

This is a rare moment when Faust feels sympathy with common humanity. But when he expresses that kinship, crucially he does so not as a sentiment uttered with the force of his own convictions but as a quotation, as an example of what the common people feel at springtime. (The matter of the "quotational mode" will preoccupy us again at the very end of the drama.) Later, in the course of the Easter Walk, Faust, in conversation with Wagner, speaks of the eternal discontent that plagues him, and he does so in terms of explicit generality:

> Was man nicht weiß, das eben brauchte man,
> Und was man weiß, kann man nicht brauchen.
>
> (1066–67)

The "man" is, of course, part of Faust's function as spokesman of humanity. Admittedly, a few lines later, in the famous declaration of the presence of the "two souls" within him, he speaks in the first person. But this is because he is emphasizing the contrast between himself and Wagner:

> Zwei Seelen wohnen, ach! in meiner Brust,
> Die eine will sich von der andern trennen;
> Die eine hält, in derber Liebeslust,
> Sich an die Welt mit klammernden Organen;
> Die andre hebt gewaltsam sich vom Dust
> Zu den Gefilden hoher Ahnen.
>
> (1112–17)

The force of this self-definition takes us back to the "Prolog im Himmel," to the notion of the unquiet self as the paradigmatically human self — but it is, of course, a disquiet to which Wagner is largely impervious. (And that imperviousness diminishes him.)

It is that self that is at issue in the two great "Studierzimmer" scenes which bring Faust and Mephisto together, and which culminate in the wager. Faust, throughout these scenes, is close to despair, and he enters into the wager in the spirit of sheer disbelief that anybody could think human beings might ever find satisfaction. Witness the vitriolic ferocity of the speech in which he curses all forms of human achievement and comfort:

> Fluch sei dem Balsamsaft der Trauben!
> Fluch jener höchsten Liebeshuld!
> Fluch sei der Hoffnung! Fluch dem Glauben,
> Und Fluch vor allen der Geduld!
>
> (1603–06)

Mephisto's introduction of himself as contractual partner is utterly in the spirit of the traditional devil of the *Faust* legend: "Ich gebe dir, was noch kein Mensch gesehn" (1674). Faust is scornful of the Devil's blandishments and lists a series of wishes, all of which have to do with an acceleration of experience:

> Zeig mir die Frucht, die fault, eh' man sie bricht,
> Und Bäume, die sich täglich neu begrünen!
>
> (1686–87)

What is at stake here is Faust's wish to close the gap between the actuality of experience on the one hand and the known patterns and processes of matter on the other, to find fruit and trees that act out, in forms of exemplary material concentration, what the mind knows to be the totality of the fruit's and tree's existence on earth. Mephisto appears not to understand, and instead speaks of simple pleasures, of times "Wo wir was Guts in Ruhe schmausen mögen" (1691). Faust immediately picks up and disputes that disarming phrase "in Ruhe" —

> Werd' ich beruhigt je mich auf ein Faulbett legen,
> So sei es gleich um mich getan!
>
> (1692–93)

And he then formulates the terms of the wager:

> Werd' ich zum Augenblicke sagen:
> Verweile doch! du bist so schön!
> Dann magst du mich in Fesseln schlagen,
> Dann will ich gern zugrunde gehn!
>
> (1699–1702)

Mephisto agrees. And behind this wager of course, and known to only one of the parties to the contract, we hear the wager from the "Prolog im Himmel." At stake is energy, drive, activity versus sloth, quiescence, inactivity; at stake is the nature and specification of the human species on earth. We remember that, in the Prologue, Mephisto offered no definition of his strategy; rather, he was content to allow the Lord to decree the terms of his own ineffectualness. But now, in the confrontation with Faust, we begin to see him come into focus. At one level, Mephisto will offer pleasure; and this is the obvious salesman's pitch. But at the end of his dialogue with Faust, and before the entry of the Schüler, Mephisto has a soliloquy. Faust, as we have already noted, is the great soliloquizer. Mephisto for the most part is seen in interaction and debate; hence, his soliloquies, when they occur, are particularly important. What he expresses here is an experiential possibility that has nothing to do with any attempt to pleasure Faust into inactivity:

> Ihm hat das Schicksal einen Geist gegeben,
> Der ungebändigt immer vorwärts dringt,
> Und dessen übereiltes Streben
> Der Erde Freuden überspringt.
> Den schlepp' ich durch das wilde Leben,
> Durch flache Unbedeutenheit,
> Er soll mir zappeln, starren, kleben,
> Und seiner Unersättlichkeit
> Soll Speis' und Trank vor gier'gen Lippen schweben;
> Er wird Erquickung sich umsonst erflehn,
> Und hätt' er sich auch nicht dem Teufel übergeben,
> Er müßte doch zugrunde gehn!
>
> (1856–67)

What Mephisto recognizes here — and it is truly the source of his engagement with the Faustian principle — is that the latter's "Streben," his propensity to devalue each particular available earthly experience in the name of the potentiality of what might be, could so easily be transformed into a doctrine of cynicism, whereby nothing is worth striving for, nothing is worth the candle. In other words, Mephisto understands the potential nihilism at the heart of Faust's energy. And, once the battle is joined at this level, the issues are incalculably weighty — and it is impossible to be certain as to the outcome.

I must, for reasons of space, bring this phase of the argument about the characterization of Faust to a close. And I want to do so by summarizing the key issue and by anticipating certain of the conclusions Goethe draws. I have endeavored to focus on that definition of Faust's character that sees him as the all-important test case in a philosophical wager about the nature and value of human being in the world. Faust is concerned to achieve a fusion of the energy and vitality of living, of linear experientiality, on the one hand and the synchronic overview afforded by the mind's reflectivity on the other. That quest cannot be brought to a triumphant conclusion. But the aspiration that it enshrines can unleash prodigious energies. However — and this is Mephisto's hope — it could also unleash brutal nihilism. Time and again, in Faust's experience, the interplay between the two irreconcilable souls produces both dynamic elation and eroding despair. We have already had occasion to discuss the despair. It is, however, important not to undervalue the moments of delight, for they too, in Goethe's vision, are part of the perennial endowment of humanity. A key moment in this context is the opening of Part Two, where Faust rejoices not only at the physical glory of natural processes but also at the ability of the human mind to picture, to reflect and reflect on that power. Here Faust speaks for and to humanity at large:

> Allein wie herrlich, diesem Sturm erprießend,
> Wölbt sich des bunten Bogens Wechseldauer,
> Bald rein gezeichnet, bald in Luft zerfließend,
> Umher verbreitend duftig kühle Schauer.
> *Der* spiegelt ab das menschliche Bestreben.
> Ihm sinne nach, und du begreifst genauer:
> Am farbigen Abglanz haben wir das Leben.
>
> (4721–27)

The rainbow is an event that wonderfully conjoins mind and matter, permanence and flux; and hence, for Faust, it symbolizes human being in the world and knowing of the world. The interplay of pronouns in this speech — from "du" to "wir" — says it all: Faust expresses here the elation — both physical and mental — of being alive, and he speaks in our name. Yet that elation never becomes a securely possessed, permanent condition. When, just before the meeting with Sorge, Faust reflects on the beauty of the reintegration with humankind that would come from his abjuring of magic, that image stays precisely as an image, a quotational moment, and no more:

> Könnt' ich Magie von meinem Pfad entfernen,
> Die Zaubersprüche ganz und gar verlernen,
> Stünd' ich, Natur, vor dir ein Mann allein,
> Da wär's der Mühe wert, ein Mensch zu sein!
>
> (11403–7)

The vision of human solidarity is held in the unreality of the subjunctive mode. We are reminded of that moment from the Easter walk where once again human solidarity was at issue, but that declaration of human solidarity was quoted — rather than affirmed — by Faust:

> Zufrieden jauchzet groß und klein.
> "Hier bin ich Mensch, hier darf ich's sein!"
>
> (939–40)

It is highly significant that at the moment of his death Faust again speaks of notions of human community — and he does so in the quotational mode. He envisages a human society living on land reclaimed from the sea, a group of people made strenuous by the need to wrest the basis of their everyday existence from the elements. Faust takes delight in the notion of teeming humanity, of a "Gewimmel" (the same word is used in the Easter walk); but the delight is in the conjectural mode:

> Solch ein Gewimmel möcht' ich sehn,
> Auf freiem Grund mit freiem Volke stehn.
> Zum Augenblicke dürft' ich sagen:
> "Verweile doch, du bist so schön!
> Es kann die Spur von meinen Erdetagen
> Nicht in Äonen untergehen." —
> Im Vorgefühl von solchem hohen Glück
> Genieß' ich jetzt den höchsten Augenblick.
>
> (11579–86)

Even the present moment of bliss has an all-important dimension of futurity. However much Faust speaks here of his own selfhood, he also invokes the generality of mankind:

> Das ist der Weisheit letzter Schluß:
> Nur der verdient sich Freiheit wie das Leben,
> Der täglich sie erobern muß.
>
> (11574–76)

And even this generalizing moment postulates fulfilment not in the here and now but in the conditional. Mephisto does not hear the conditional. He rejoices, as the two-fold strategist (both salesman and cynic) that he is, at his two-fold victory. He rejoices that Faust has spoken the words of contentment and has, therefore, lost the wager. But he also rejoices over Faust's corpse at the sheer nullity of all experience. In German "Streben" and "Sterben" are separated only by a slight transposition of two letters. Because everything is finite and has to die, nothing, for Mephisto, is ultimately worth the effort:

> "Da ists vorbei!" Was ist daran zu lesen?
> Es ist so gut, als wär' es nicht gewesen,
> Und treibt sich doch im Kreis, als wenn es wäre.
> Ich liebte mir dafür das Ewig-Leere.
>
> (11600–603)

Mephisto could be right, of course. He is not; in Goethe's last-minute, cliff-hanging arbitration Faust is saved. But it is very last-ditch. (And one whole tract of that last ditch is being dug in the closing scene of Faust's life.)

Why, then, does Mephisto lose? One answer has to do with the limitations of his totalizing cynicism. It is an attitude more easily tenable in respect of other people's than one's own experience. Mephisto sees Faust's death as the Q.E.D. of ultimate nullity. But he is, unfortunately and unexpectedly, excited by the physical beauty of the angels — particularly by their bottoms. Even the cynic can be overtaken by lust, it seems, can be distracted from pure negativity by a glimpse of something pleasurable. And the other answer has to do with Faust himself. The opening of the "Prolog im Himmel," as we noted, contains a celebration of the ongoing energies of the created world. And the closing phase of the drama echoes that validation:

> Das Ewig-Weibliche
> Zieht uns hinan.
>
> (12110–11)

This is the answer to Mephisto's "das Ewig-Leere." And ultimately, although it is often a close call, Faust does share in that affirmation which is potently in evidence at the beginning and end of the play. Remarkably, for this intensely secular drama, there is a whiff of theologically-tinged affirmation to be sensed. In Genesis, when God finishes the creation, He sees that it is good. And Faust too glimpses that goodness. On those grounds he can be justified. But it is in essence a secular validation, as we have seen. Goethe knew, however, that in order to remain within the dimension of the sayable and picturable, he would have to borrow from Christian iconography — hence the interceding, mediating role of Gretchen at the end. He said to Eckermann on 6 June 1831:

> Daß der Schluß, wo es mit der geretteten Seele nach oben geht, sehr schwer zu machen war und daß ich, bei so übersinnlichen, kaum zu ahnenden Dingen, mich sehr leicht im Vagen hätte verlieren können, wenn ich nicht meinen poetischen Intentionen durch die scharf umrissenen christlich-kirchlichen Figuren und Vorstellungen, eine wohltätig beschränkende Form und Festigkeit gegeben hätte.

In terms, then, that borrow — rather than fully subscribe to — instances of Christian redemption (and we have had occasion to notice how important the quotational mode is throughout Goethe's great drama), Faust is saved. But the victory is a close-run thing. The negativity that Mephisto embodies is not easily banished — neither from the philosophical stratum of the play (which we have just been considering) nor from its cultural-historical argument, to which I now turn.

I want to stress at the outset that this concern also depends upon and contributes to the definition of Faust's character in general terms. At one level of generality Faust stands for "der Mensch," as we have seen. At another he stands for modern man, for a way of life and form of subjectivity that is consistently expressive of modern culture. Let us begin by summarizing what we learn of Faust from the opening two scenes of the drama (that is, before the first meeting with Mephisto): three things emerge with great force. First: he is an intense individualist, he believes in the authority of his own experience, his own judgements, and is not beholden to received wisdom, to dogma, to shared institutional assumptions. Moreover we have no sense of his functioning within any kind of communal context; he is very much man alone, and emphatically, assertively so. Second: he is a radically secular spirit. When the sound of Easter bells and music prevents him from taking his own life, it is not the Christian faith that speaks to him but rather the corporate energies of nature, manifested in the advent of spring. As he says in one of the most famous lines in German literature (and *Faust* is full of them), "die Botschaft hör' ich wohl, allein mir fehlt der Glaube" (765). Third: he is recognizably a scientific spirit. Admittedly he is still drawn to magic arts, to forms of alchemy and necromancy. But the essential thrust of what he is after is:

> Daß ich erkenne, was die Welt
> Im Innersten zusammenhält.
>
> (382–83)

That is recognizably the aspiration of a mind utterly committed to understanding the totality of material processes in the spirit of modern scientific inquiry. In all these three senses, then, Faust functions in Goethe's great drama as a figure representative of the cultural temper of modernity. And I want to suggest that that definition of his character transfers itself to and informs the characterization of the figures with whom he interacts.

In what sense can Mephisto be seen as a figure expressive of modernity? Let us recall our understanding of the devil figure within the philosophical framework of the drama. We noted that Mephisto employs two strategies to quench the Faustian drive. One is by making experience instantly available. The other is by the constant, drip-drip-drip erosion of the value of any human experience in the name of sophisticatedly reductive cynicism. Both these aims are bound up with his traditional endowment as tempter figure: he has magic powers at his disposal. In early versions of the legend, Mephisto's supernatural powers are often of the magic-carpet kind. But that is much less in evidence in Goethe's treatment of the story. Rather, Mephisto's magic provides essentially for an acceleration of experience. And that accords with his two roles: acceleration produces both the seductive discourse of the salesman, promising immediate gratification, and the dissolving scepticism of the cynic, who knows that swiftness of experience may well breed contempt for experience. Viewed under this aspect, Mephisto is the supreme representative of specifically modern nihilism. At the end of the drama, as we have seen, he is defeated. But the brutal disparagement of experience that he expresses unforgettably in such lines as "Das ist der Lauf der Welt" (3204) or "Sie ist die Erste nicht" (Trüber Tag. Feld) will not be easily or readily removed from modernity's love affair with speed.

The characterization of Gretchen partakes too of Goethe's reckoning with modernity. The story of her love for Faust is wonderfully realized in terms of individual psychology (and I shall return to this aspect later). But one can also understand it as a meeting of pre-modern and modern worlds. Gretchen is inseparable from the communal dimension that has shaped her life hitherto, from the interlocking structures of family, school, church, and village. And one feels the full weight of the cultural differences between her and Faust in the famous scene of the "Gretchen-Frage." The term itself is still current in the German language, and it means the decisive, the make-or-break question. The question is: "wie hast du's mit der Religion?" (3415). It is her way of asking what Faust believes in, what he lives for and by. His response is an impassioned declaration of a kind of pantheism — to the effect that God is everywhere, unnameable but knowable in intense experience. Yet behind his fine words we hear what Gretchen clearly senses — that he does not believe in God in terms of any traditional confessional affiliation. Moreover, she is right to fear Mephisto because, as we have seen, he represents the negativity at the heart of the culture that Faust enshrines. Gretchen's words may be naive; but the concerns that animate them are entirely legitimate.

Mention of Gretchen's words brings me to another aspect of her characterization; and it is one that shows Goethe at the height of his creative powers. Faust, as we have already had occasion to note, is a great soliloquizer. He is so because he is an acutely self-aware spirit who is constantly engaged in debate with himself. And moreover, as an intellectual who has studied widely, he is endowed with the cognitive and linguistic equipment to explain himself to himself. But Gretchen is in an entirely different position. She comes from modest circumstances;

and she has received little education. Hence she is neither cognitively nor linguistically equipped to negotiate an experience that challenges her to the depths of her being. Put simply: she desperately needs to soliloquize; but how is she to do it? How is Goethe to find words for her that will not sound forced or sentimental? His solution is masterly. On three particular occasions when Gretchen soliloquizes, two conditions (and they have to do with the conditions of and on her being) have to be met. One is that she has to be doing something; her hands need to be active. On one occasion, she is undressing and getting ready for bed; on another, she is working at the spinning wheel; on another she is putting flowers in a vase before an image of the Virgin Mary. In such moments we sense that the activity of the hands imparts rhythms of security which can help the mind to think. And when she thinks and expresses her thoughts — and this is the second condition for Gretchen's soliloquizing mode — she has to borrow the discourse of her inwardness from established sources: from the folk song ("Es war ein König in Thule"), from the work song ("Meine Ruh' ist hin"), from the prayer ("Ach neige"). With this wonderfully expressive and unsentimental characterization Goethe inaugurates a whole line of realistic social dramas which go through the nineteenth and twentieth centuries (Büchner, Hebbel, Ibsen, Chekhov, Brecht). Within the *Faust* drama the characterization of Gretchen allows us to hear her as a representative figure, representative of a pre-modern world that Faust ultimately destroys. Goethe asks us, then, to understand, and to count the cost of, modernity. The reckoning he offers is sternly impressive. He makes us register the strength, dignity, and cohesion of the pre-modern world — and also its narrowness and limitation. One thinks particularly of the Valentin action, of the scene at the well where Lieschen, in spiteful conversation with Gretchen, rejoices at the misfortune of a village girl who has got herself pregnant.

The role of Faust as exemplar and spokesman of modernity continues into the Part Two of the drama. Part Two has less of the urgent narrative pulse of Part One. Rather, we find ourselves entering an allegorical drama in which the various possible modes of modernity are set out before us. In Act 1 we see Faust and Mephisto coming to the aid of the collapsing finances of the Holy Roman Empire by the injection of modern, speculative economics; they bring paper money into circulation. In Act 2 we glimpse modern philosophy in the Baccalaureus figure who espouses Fichte's doctrines of radical subjectivism — and also modern science, because Wagner, Faust's pupil in Part One, has now become an experimenter in his laboratory and contrives to make artificial life by producing a little man, Homunculus, who lives in a protective glass housing. We as modern readers tend to hear this sequence both in its early nineteenth-century context (where it is contemporary with that other great legend that explores the dangers of scientific experiment, *Frankenstein*) and as prefigurative of our contemporary (that is, early third-millennium) anxieties about genetic engineering, cloning. The Homunculus figure speaks urgently of and to the modern world; but he also has antiquarian longings in him and is deeply attracted to the ancient world. The extended "Klassische Walpurgisnacht" to which he leads us contrasts powerfully with the (Northern) "Walpurgisnacht" of Part One. Both sequences express the cultural — and cultic — imaginings that have animated and animate the two great centres of European creativity. The ancient world, centred in the southeastern Mediterranean, has an affirmatory relationship to bodiliness, to physical nature. The governing metaphors of the "Klassische Walpurgisnacht" are of fluidity, are positively (that is, both manifestly and assentingly) erotic, and pave the way for the meeting of Faust and Helena. It is a realm in which Mephisto is uneasy at the unashamed (that is, unguilty) sensuousness that is everywhere in evidence. As Homunculus puts it:

> Nordwestlich, Satan, ist dein Lustrevier,
> Südöstlich diesmal aber segeln wir —
>
> (6950–51).

The "Walpurgisnacht" of Part One is phallic, violent, perverse, and takes Faust away from Gretchen. It is Mephisto's true home because it is the site of that European modernity that is spectacularly disturbed in its relationship to nature and that is, in consequence, deeply disturbed in its relationship to human carnality. (Mephisto, significantly, appears in Part Two in the supremely ugly guise of Phorkyas.) The obscenity of the northern "Walpurgisnacht" is poles apart from the relaxed physicality of its classical counterpart. Once again, as in Part One, Goethe asks us to count the cost of modernity.

In Act 3 of Part Two Helena appears. At one level, Goethe is here fulfilling one of the demands of the traditional *Faust* material — that Faust should manage to raise from the dead the most beautiful woman of all time. At another, he engages with a key issue of his own (modern, that is, nineteenth-century) culture: namely its love affair with the Ancient World. The European nineteenth century witnessed an extraordinary flowering of archaeology as scholars and visionaries such as Schliemann set about uncovering the material traces of ancient civilization. The Helena who appears in Act 3 is an icon from the ancient world, cherished by the modern (that is, nineteenth-century) world; and she also seems to have more than a hint of postmodern self-awareness about her. She knows that she is a figure of legend, and the twice repeated "viel" of her opening line — "Bewundert viel und viel gescholten, Helena" (8488) — has everything to do with her existence as an utterly "texted" creature. The coming together of Faust and Helena is a meeting conducted in and through cultural mediation: Faust teaches Helena how to rhyme. Ancient verse derived its structure and rhythmic force from its metricality. What Faust can teach Helena is the modern musicality of rhyme. Helena is an adept pupil; the rhymes soon come thick and fast as both internal and end rhymes; and Helena's wonderful, breathless "da bin ich" becomes Faust's philosophical category of "Dasein":

> HELENA. Ich fühle mich so fern und doch so nah,
> Und sage nur zu gern: Da bin ich! da!
>
> FAUST. Ich atme kaum, mir zittert, stockt das Wort;
> Es ist ein Traum, verschwunden Tag und Ort.
>
> HELENA. Ich scheine mir verlebt und doch so neu,
> In dich verwebt, dem Unbekannten treu.
>
> FAUST. Durchgrüble nicht das einzigste Geschick!
> Dasein ist Pflicht, und wär's ein Augenblick.
>   (9411–18)

It is a delicious scene, a unique moment (caught in the extraordinary superlative of "einzigst") in which at the grand representative level ancient and modern meet; yet Goethe's verse also injects a note of charm, of linguistic and erotic excitement into the high cultural allegory.

The product of Faust and Helena's union is Euphorion, the spirit of modern poetry. Euphorion's representativeness works at many levels: he incorporates that headlong energy that early nineteenth-century European culture associated especially with Byron. But the immortal longings that lead to his death embody both older intertexts (Icarus/ Dedalus) and also a modern (that is, prefiguratively Wagnerian) love death. Moreover, the whole sequence in which he appears is (as Goethe's text makes clear) intended to be expressed throughout by both word and music. Thereby Goethe acknowledges the particular contribution that opera was to make to modern drama, most particularly in the European nineteenth century. Once again, the mode of his drama incarnates its representative historicity.

Act 4 shows us how Faust, acutely aware of the struggle between pre-Revolutionary and post-Revolutionary forces, is perfectly capable of allowing his self-interest to dictate his allegiances. He sides with the

Kaiser rather than with the Gegen-Kaiser; and thereby he, the scientific, bourgeois, mercantile expression of the new age, kow-tows to the old order in quest of the two things that it still has to offer — the aesthetics of rank (aristocratic titles), and land. In the closing phases of Goethe's drama it is the landowner and imperialist entrepreneur who comes to the fore. Faust is concerned not just to own the land he has acquired but to transform it — and to reclaim new land from the sea for human habitation. As Philemon and Baucis register, he brings about an elemental reconfiguration of the familiar world. Land is transformed into water (by the creation of canals); and water is transformed into land by drainage and a system of dikes. The old woman can only conclude:

> Wohl! ein Wunder ist's gewesen!
> Läßt mich heut noch nicht in Ruh;
> Denn es ging das ganze Wesen
> Nicht mit rechten Dingen zu.
>
> (11111–14)

Faust is the spirit of the modern trinity of "Krieg, Handel und Piraterie" (11188), and the mistrust with which the old people respond to his projects of modernization is equalled by the fury with which he resents their presence on territory for which he has great plans. The bell of their little chapel on the dunes drives him to distraction — "Das Glöcklein läutet, und ich wüte" (11258). He orders Mephisto to evict them. The latter is happy to exceed the brief given him by his master, and the old people are destroyed in the fire that consumes their home. But the initial impetus to proceed against them is Faust's. True to his role as modern capitalist, he who believes so passionately in land ownership is somewhat cavalier in his relationship to other people's land ownership. Like the culture he represents, Faust is both in love with and destructive of the land. (One of the central paradoxes of modern culture — that it rapturously sings the praises of that natural realm that it so heedlessly destroys — is captured wonderfully in the songs of Lynkeus the watchman.) Goethe sustains the paradox to the end. In the final speech before his death one hears Faust's delight in his ability to challenge and reshape nature, to be a creator, and, by that token, a kind of divinity in his own right:

> Grün das Gefilde, fruchtbar; Mensch und Herde
> Sogleich behaglich auf der neusten Erde.
>
> (11565–66)

And Faust imagines a whole community that would share his energy, his commitment to dynamic living, that would be "nicht sicher zwar,

doch tätig-frei," that would know it exists only by virtue of its own capacity for "Gemeindrang" and "kühn-emsige Völkerschaft" (11564,
11568). Faust echoes here the Archangels' vision of the ceaseless self-
regeneration of the created world in the "Prolog im Himmel." He
aligns himself with the principle of energy rather than contentment.
This, as we have already noted, is central to the philosophical import of
the drama. We also need to register, however, the cultural-historical
force of Faust's last words. They are sustained not only by a belief in
existential intensity but also by a sense of communal living "auf der
neusten Erde" (11566). The new community, on the new earth, has, as
it were, no God-given right to live where it does; rather, it makes that
right for itself. Marxist critics have seen this vision as the prefiguration
of a classless society; bourgeois critics have tended to stress the promise
of a strenuous, enterprising community. In any event, Faust's last
words have a force that conjoins the philosophical statement of the
drama with its cultural-historical concern to understand the temper of
modernity.

Inevitably, because of the nature of its concerns, *Faust II* moves
into the realm of allegory. John Williams speaks of the Faust of the second part as being "far removed from the psychologically differentiated
and motivated personality of the first part" (Williams, 39). Goethe himself, in a remark to Eckermann of 17 February 1831, defined the difference between the forms of characterization in the two parts of his
drama as follows:

> Der erste Teil ist fast ganz subjektiv; es ist alles aus einem befan-
> generen, leidenschaftlicheren Individuum hervorgegangen, welches
> Halbdunkel den Menschen auch so wohltun mag. Im zweiten Teile
> aber ist fast gar nichts Subjektives, es erscheint hier eine höhere, bre-
> itere, hellere, leidenschaftslosere Welt, und wer sich nicht etwas um-
> getan und einiges erlebt hat, wird nichts damit anzufangen wissen.

That distinction is echoed by Gert Mattenklott, who describes the
protagonist of *Faust II* in the following terms: "kein individueller Held
[. . .] sondern ein Name für verschiedene historische Kräfte und Anteile
von Wesenheiten" (Mattenklott, 468). Clearly, the force of those ar-
guments is ungainsayable. And they are part of a long tradition that has
sought to hear the symbolic richness, the generality of philosophical
statement and concern as the chief glory of Goethe's *Faust* drama. But
there is a danger to this train of thought, which is that it tends to
overlook moments of specificity where the drama insists on the presence of experiential particularity. This is a vital dimension of the play
because it emphasises that cognitive principles and historical energies

entail deeds. When Faust translates the first line of St. John's Gospel, he transforms it into "Im Anfang war die Tat!" (1237). The Lord in the Prologue warns against the slackening of "des Menschen Tätigkeit" (340). Faust's last vision is of a community that is "tätig-frei" (11564). The last three lines of the play rhyme the notion of energetic flow — "Zieht uns hinan" — with the finitude of deeds — "Hier ist's getan" (12109–11). In other words, the notion of deeds done is central to the play's import. And we must never forget that Goethe's *Faust* is a play, a piece of theatre. In the theatre activity entails temporal and spatial specificity. The theatrical illusion is present to us because it is physically incarnated on stage. Moreover, supremely in the theatre, words are deeds, they are events just as much as the moments of physical interaction. *Faust* is neither a philosophical tract nor a poem; it is a drama. And it is a drama because it entails, as an essential dimension of its theme, the dimension of present enactment.

I want just to note briefly a few key moments where the issue of word and deed as specificity comes powerfully into focus. As anybody who has worked on Faust's opening monologue with an actor will know, one of the first aspects that needs to be registered is the violent swings of mood and pace. The specificity of the opening moment of the play, then, is one of psychological disquiet. The whole of the Faust/Gretchen action is shot through with moments of intense theatrical specificity. One thinks of the brutal command of male desire — "Hör, du mußt mir die Dirne schaffen! (2619). Or of Gretchen's excitement at finding the casket of jewels — "Was mag wohl drinne sein?" (2785). Or of her sense of her own feminine beauty:

> Wenn nur die Ohrring' meine wären!
> Man sieht doch gleich ganz anders drein.
>
> (2796–97)

I have already commented on the subtlety and resonance of Goethe's characterization of Gretchen — the hands at work, the borrowed forms of discursive self-analysis. But there are also countless details of portraiture that bring the character into tinglingly specified life. In the double wooing scene one notes, for example, a hint of socially derived tension; Gretchen corrects Faust's grandiose reaction to her description of the reality of family life:

FAUST.   Du hast gewiß das reinste Glück empfunden.

MARGARETE. Doch auch gewiß gar manche schwere Stunden.
           Des Kleinen Wiege stand zu Nacht
           An meinem Bett; es durfte kaum sich regen,

> War ich erwacht;
> Bald mußt' ichs tränken, bald es zu mir legen,
> Bald, wenn's nicht schwieg, vom Bett aufstehn
> Und tänzelnd in der Kammer auf und nieder gehn,
> Und früh am Tage schon am Waschtrog stehn;
> Dann auf dem Markt und an dem Herde sorgen,
> Und immer fort wie heut so morgen.
> Da geht's, mein Herr, nicht immer mutig zu;
> Doch schmeckt dafür das Essen, schmeckt die Ruh.
>
> (3136–48)

The "mein Herr" in the penultimate line speaks volumes in terms of both gender and class. Men tend to talk of the pure joy of rearing children because they rarely have a great deal to do with it. And this "Herr" is not just a man; as Gretchen instantly recognizes, he is educated and of a higher class. He is, therefore, utterly unfamiliar with forms of household drudgery. At the same time, of course, Gretchen is excited by the differences between them — and ashamed of her own ignorance:

> Du lieber Gott! was so ein Mann
> Nicht alles, alles denken kann!
> Beschämt nur steh' ich vor ihm da,
> Und sag' zu allen Sachen ja.
>
> (3211–14)

The scene of the "Gretchen-Frage" is masterly in the precise psychology of the interplay between the two figures. It is, for example, noteworthy that Gretchen begins by addressing Faust by name — "Versprich mir, Heinrich!" (3414), and he, in his attempts to allay her anxieties, patronizes her — as we note from the forms of address which he uses — "mein Kind," "mein Liebchen," "du holdes Angesicht," "liebs Kind," "liebe Puppe," "du ahnungsvoller Engel," "Liebchen."

I could continue to add to the details of the argument, but I think that there is no need. The point I am after is a simple — but also a weighty — one. It is that the Faustian principle of activity does not simply remain a principle; rather, it is enacted in the play by means of particular actions, of specific things said and done. In the introductory section to this chapter I made the point that Goethe managed, with consummate skill, to solve the problem posed by the necessarily episodic structure of Faust's experience. Part of his solution is to create a female character who is no mere episode: Gretchen comes alive before us. And that is why Mephisto's (in every sense) throwaway line — "Sie ist die Erste nicht" (Trüber Tag. Feld) — is so monstrous. In any good performance of the play, we have the powerful sense that Gretchen is particular, is special; and the destruction of her is morally outrageous. She is destroyed not by a principle, not by an idea, but by a person. And, in the lacerating close of Part One the name of that person "Heinrich, Heinrich" is screamed through the deepening darkness. Names, it seems, can have everything to do with the specification of experience.

Of course, as we have seen and as Goethe himself saw, *Faust II* moves away from much of the social and psychological specificity of Part One. But it is important to recognize that this dimension is never entirely silenced. The whole sequence of the eviction of Philemon and Baucis towards the end of the drama is a case in point (and the moral issue is as grave as it was in respect of Gretchen). As the text makes abundantly clear, Faust's decision to proceed against the old people has primarily to do with personal vanity and greed:

> Vor Augen ist mein Reich unendlich,
> Im Rücken neckt mich der Verdruß,
> Erinnert mich durch neidische Laute:
> Mein Hochbesitz, er ist nicht rein!
>
> (11153–56)

It is important that we register this voice of monstrous individuated will in Faust. Goethe constantly insists that the activity principle depends on a psychological disposition that begets deeds, and deeds have immediate consequences in the world of finite human interaction, for good and for ill. His death speech is, as we have seen, sustained by a vision of a new community that will come into being. Yet we feel that Faust's primary motives have less to do with altruism than with an unadorned self-assertion, a will to some kind of personal immortality:

> Es kann die Spur von meinen Erdetagen
> Nicht in Äonen untergehn. —
>
> (11583–84)

The figure who speaks these words is old, frail, blind, on the very point of death. But what we hear, undiminished by physical dereliction, is the will to self-assertion.

I want to draw my argument to a close. I have sought to illuminate Faust (and the other figures in the drama) in terms of an understanding that is both generalizing and specifying. Faust is a figure who exists with extraordinary intensity in a number of realms, realms that interact with and on occasion contradict each other, that are constantly in debate and contestation. And that debate provides the permanently shifting framework that focuses and re-focuses the definition of Faust's character. The upshot is a drama that asks us, as spectators, to attend to and to respond to a number of different kinds of theatre, a world theater of the human self, an allegorical summation of the European past and present, a theatre of highly specific socio-psychological realism. All of which may sound like a tall order. But I believe that we can respond to that challenge, not least because theatre allows us to inhabit an immediate and palpable presence that is also supremely knowing and self-aware. And that self-awareness generates the philosophical profundity of the work. Philosophically minded critics have explicated that profundity by, for example, making links between Goethe's *Faust* and Hegel's *Phänomenologie des Geistes*. But Hegel's phenomenology does not have, nor does it need, characters. Whereas a play does. The ideas of the theatre text have to be refracted through the obdurate materiality of recognizable human creatures who will be impersonated on the stage by men and women of particular shapes, sizes, ages. And I believe that Goethe understood this in an immediate and profound way. In his *Farbenlehre* he constantly insisted (in rebuttal of Newton's optics) that color was not so much a property of white light as the result of what happened when white light interacted with material phenomena — such as dust, water, vegetation. Color came into being, then, for Goethe, as an event in the world. Similarly, he knew that any drama had to incarnate what it wanted to say in that particular fictional palpability that is theatre performance. A distinguished critic, writing on *Faust II*, comments on the frequent stage directions, but argues that they are primarily metaphors and should not lead us to believe that the work is genuinely intended for theatrical performance (Lange, 288). I beg to disagree. Of course the stage directions are not precise indications of the one and only way that the piece can be staged. But they do remind us unremittingly that the text before us needs to be made palpable illusion before it achieves its full expressivity.

One final reflection. No doubt all great dramas inhabit at one and the same time realms of generality and specificity. This is manifestly true of Oedipus, Antigone, Hamlet, Phèdre. But I believe that the interplay between the two categories of statement is most vividly in evidence in Goethe's *Faust* project. In Faust's utterances, there is an intense rhetoric of generality, but there is also one of specificity. The very terms of the wager conjoin both the whole of humankind and the particular self which has to do the experiencing:

> Und was der ganzen Menschheit zugeteilt ist,
> Will ich in meinem innern Selbst genießen.
>
> (1770–71)

And, as we have seen, the arbitration in respect of the wager is not outward and public but inward and specific. Everything depends on what this one person says of and makes of his experience. Paradoxically, Faust's very subjectivity makes him representative of human generality in the modern world, which is why so many of the moments when he speaks of the beauty of human solidarity — "Hier bin ich Mensch, hier darf ich's sein!" (940) — are (as we have noted) quotational.

In this richness of characterological statement, in this ceaseless interplay of particularized and symbolic discourses, Goethe's *Faust* speaks, I venture to suggest, with incomparable force to the cultural and theoretical framework in which we find ourselves at present. On the one hand, many literary critics and theoreticians tell us that character no longer exists in works of literature; that literary texts give us only notations of selfhood, nouns, pronouns, lexemes, in a universe of textual, and only textual, signification. On the other hand (and in part in reaction against that anti-characterological orthodoxy) John Sutherland, a distinguished commentator on English literature, has produced volumes directed to the enterprise of treating literary characters as knowable people (*Is Heathcliff a Murderer?* [Oxford, 1996]; and *Can Jane Eyre be happy?* [Oxford, 1997]). Perhaps it is the case that, as modern readers, we are aware of both claims. And if that is so, then Goethe's *Faust*, like no other work of modern European drama known to me, can help us to explore the various forms of signification that are at issue — in the work itself, of course, but also conceivably in our lives as well.

Works Cited

Ahrens, Hans. *Kommentar zu Goethes "Faust I."* Heidelberg: Winter, 1982.

Anglet, Andreas. "*Faust*-Rezeption." *Goethe Handbuch.* Vol. 2 *Dramen.* Ed. Theo Buck. Stuttgart and Weimar: Metzler, 1997. 478–513.

Atkins, Stuart. *Goethe's "Faust": A Literary Analysis.* Cambridge and London: Harvard UP, 1958.

Beddow, Michael. *Goethe: "Faust I."* London: Grant and Cutler, 1986.

Bennett, Benjamin. *Goethe's Theory of Poetry: "Faust" and the Regeneration of Language.* Ithaca and London: Cornell UP, 1986.

Binder, Alwin. *Das Vorspiel auf dem Theater: Poetologische und geschichtsphilo-sophische Aspekte in Goethes "Faust"-Vorspiel.* Bonn: Bouvier, 1969.

Binswanger, Hans Christoph. *Money and Magic: A Critique of the Modern Economy in the Light of Goethe's "Faust."* Trans. J. H. Harrison. Chicago: Chicago UP, 1994.

Boyle, Nicholas. *Goethe, Faust Part One.* Cambridge: Cambridge UP, 1987.

Brown, Jane K. *Goethe's "Faust": The German Tragedy.* Ithaca and London: Cornell UP, 1986.

Emrich, Wilhelm. *Die Symbolik von "Faust II."* Königstein Ts.: Athenäum, 1964 (5th edition).

Friedrich, T., and L. J. Scheithauer. *Kommentar zu Goethes "Faust."* Stuttgart: Reclam, 1973.

Gaier, Ulrich. *Goethes "Faust" Dichtungen: Ein Kommentar.* Vol. 1. *"Ur-faust."* Stuttgart: Reclam, 1989.

Gearey, John. *Goethe's "Faust": The Making of Part One.* New Haven: Yale UP, 1981.

Hamm, Heinz. *Goethes "Faust": Werkgeschichte und Textanalyse.* Berlin: Volk und Wissen, 1978.

Hesse-Belasi, Gabriele. *Signifikationsprozesse in Goethes "Faust Zweiter Teil."* Frankfurt am Main: Lang, 1992.

Jantz, Harold. *The Form of "Faust": The Work of Art and its Intrinsic Struc-tures.* Baltimore: Johns Hopkins UP, 1978.

Kaufmann, Hans. *Goethes "Faust" oder Stirb und Werde.* Berlin and Weimar: Aufbau, 1991.

Keller, Werner. *"Faust. Eine Tragödie* (1808)." In *Goethes Dramen: Neue In-terpretationen.* Ed. Walter Hinderer. Stuttgart: Reclam, 1980. 244–80.

——, ed. *Aufsätze zu Goethes "Faust I."* Darmstadt: Wissenschaftliche Buchgesellschaft, 1974.

——, ed. *Aufsätze zu Goethes "Faust II."* Darmstadt: Wissenschaftliche Buchgesellschaft, 1991.

Kommerell, Max. *"Faust II:* Zum Verständnis der Form." In *Geist und Buch-stabe der Dichtung.* Frankfurt am Main: Klostermann, 1944. 9–74.

Lange, Victor. "Faust. Der Tragödie zweiter Teil (1832)." In *Goethes Dra-men: Neue Interpretationen.* Ed. Walter Hinderer. Stuttgart: Reclam, 1980. 281–312.

Lohmeyer, Dorothea. *Faust und die Welt: Der zweite Teil der Dichtung.* Mu-nich: Beck, 1975.

Mahal, Günther. *Faust: Die Spuren eines geheimnisvollen Lebens.* Berne: Scherz, 1980.

Mahl, Bernd. "Die Bühnenegeschichte von Goethes *Faust.*" *Goethe Handbuch.* Vol. 2. *Dramen.* Ed. Theo Buck. Stuttgart and Weimar: Metzler, 1997. 522–38.

Mason, Eudo. *Goethe's "Faust": Its Genesis and Purport.* Berkeley: University of California Press, 1967.

Mattenklott, Gert. *"Faust II."* *Goethe Handbuch.* Vol. 2. *Dramen.* Ed. Theo Buck. Stuttgart and Weimar: Metzler, 1997. 391–477.

Matussek, Peter. *Naturbild und Diskursgeschichte: "Faust"-Studie zur Rekonstruktion ästhetischer Theorie.* Stuttgart: Metzler, 1992.

———. *"Faust I."* *Goethe Handbuch.* Vol. 2. *Dramen.* Ed. Theo Buck. Stuttgart and Weimar: Metzler, 1997. 352–90.

May, Kurt. *"Faust II Teil" in der Sprachform gedeutet.* 2nd ed. Munich: Hanser, 1962.

Meyer, Herman. *Diese sehr ernsten Scherze: Eine Studie zu "Faust II."* Heidelberg: Stiehm, 1970.

Requadt, Paul. *Goethes "Faust I": Leitmotivik und Architektur.* Munich: Fink, 1972.

Schlaffer, Heinz. *"Faust Zweiter Teil": Die Allegorie des 19. Jahrhunderts.* Stuttgart: Metzler, 1981.

Schmidt, Jochen. *Goethe's "Faust" Erster und zweiter Teil.* Munich: Beck, 1999.

Scholz, Rüdiger. *Die beschädigte Seele des großen Mannes: Goethes "Faust" und die bürgerliche Gesellschaft.* Rheinfelden: Schäuble, 1982.

Scholz, Rüdiger. *Goethes "Faust": ein einführender Forschungsbericht.* Rheinfelden: Schäuble, 1984.

Schwerte, Hans. *Faust und das Faustische: Ein Kapitel deutscher Ideologie.* Stuttgart: Klett, 1962.

Smeed, John W. *Faust in Literature.* London: Oxford UP, 1975.

Wieland, Renate. *Schein, Kritik, Utopie: Zu Goethe und Hegel.* Munich: Text und Kritik, 1992.

Wilkinson, Elizabeth M. "Goethe's *Faust*: Tragedy in the Diachronic Mode." *Publications of the English Goethe Society*, 42 (1971–72). 116–74.

Williams, John R. *Goethe's "Faust."* London: Allen and Unwin, 1987.

Zabka, Thomas. *"Faust II" — Das Klassische und das Romantische: Goethes "Eingriff in die neueste Literatur."* Tübingen: Niemeyer, 1993.

The Guilty Hero,
or the Tragic Salvation of Faust

Alberto Destro

D ESPITE THE ENORMOUSLY LONG LIST of critical publications on
Faust, there is still ample room for discussion of the extent to
which Goethe himself identifies with Faust, or in some way "lies behind" him, or is actually offering him as an exemplary or positive hero.
That Goethe does not identify with his hero has been the assumption
of the best critics for some time (see Erich Trunz [in HA 3, 494];
Keller, 318). It is an issue of major importance and, once clarified, an
entire, interminable era of Faustian studies (analyzed by Wilhelm Böhm
and "Hans Schwerte" [alias Hans Ernst Schneider, see König et al.])
may finally be put behind us. On this view, the term "Faustian" was
made into an ideological absolute, no longer applied to the character
Goethe created, but — in its most extreme usage — to a hypostasis of
"German man," endowed with a civilizing mission of an inexorable,
fatal clarity. Already modified by a number of scholars in the 1920s and
1930s, with the end of the Second World War this interpretation
seemed to have been definitively removed from the roll call of acceptable critical hypotheses. However formulated, it took for granted the
author's identification with his main character, a hero not only in a
formal or rhetorical sense as protagonist of the work of fiction, but the
exemplary figure of an extraordinary man, the name for a higher destiny. This distortion of the sense of Goethe's play entailed an "Enttragi-
sierung der Tragödie Goethes" (Schwerte, 9), the elimination of a
tragic significance that is plainly put to rights in Schwerte's title. A
character in some ways exemplary (not just in a paradigmatic, or typical, sense, but put forward as an example *ad imitandum*) necessarily
implied quite a considerable amount of empathetic identification with
his author, at least equal to that demanded from the reader. But is this
really the case with *Faust*, and in particular *Faust II*, which forms the
focus of this essay?

An examination of Faust the hero without bias in his favor leads us
in quite a different direction, revealing a significant epic distance between the author and his creation. That distance is, I suggest, best ap-

preciated by a review of the text from a primarily moral perspective. Leaving aside the particular usage of the notion of morality as found in, for example, Nietzsche, I shall employ a common-sense version of the criterion of moral judgment, and see how it works in the case of Faust.

The crisis at the start of the drama as a whole appears quite understandable from this perspective. Having devoted the whole of his life to study, and mastered whatever the culture of his time could offer, Faust then discovers, at the end of a life of sacrifice, renunciation, and contempt for "success," the vanity of his efforts. The contrast in this respect with Wagner, who has interpreted science solely as a means to gain an academic *cursus honorum*, is clear. All scientific knowledge taken together does not provide true insight into what holds the cosmos together, into what is behind creation. From the perspective of morality, Faust's despair, born of authentic disappointment, deserves every respect, despite our awareness of the charlatanism of at least a part of the "science," in particular the medical science, of the time, as revealed in the scene *Vor dem Tor* (1030 ff.). But when Faust tries to get out of the crisis by falling back on magic, driving himself beyond the limits of the human, this is no longer the case. An impatience born of desperation may be understandable, but is none the more morally acceptable for that. Into this fracture in Faust's moral fiber steps Mephistopheles and, after the odd skirmish, he is able to bring Faust over to his side, marked by his signing the famous wager. From this moment on, all of Faust's behavior appears morally problematic. Not always guilty, certainly, but all too often so. What is the nature of this guilt?

His guilt lies first of all in his choosing the ambiguous instrument of magic and the aid of the devil to reach where human powers alone would be inadequate. Only an aristocratic sense of his own (intellectual) nobility leads Faust to reject the grosser aspects of Mephistopheles' powers, as in the scenes *Auerbachs Keller* and *Hexenküche*. Later, his guilt lies in the magically rejuvenated middle-aged scholar's brutally sensuous determination to seduce the young and innocent Gretchen. But this latter instance requires qualification, inasmuch as, in the eyes of Goethe the realist, sensuality is inseparable from love. Sensuality can be (as in Faust's case) the first expression of love, as well as an essential component (again the case with Faust, but all the more so for Gretchen, whose awakening senses offer a thematic basis for our reading of *Faust*). Faust's guilt is much more serious where he shows awareness of the devastating effects his passion will have on Gretchen's little world, whose peace is shattered. In his great soliloquy at the end of *Wald und Höhle*, Faust says that he "has had to undermine" her

peace (3360); and, in addition, he abandons Gretchen as the catastrophe strikes. His desertion is, of course, also due to the influence of
Mephistopheles, who involves him in the Walpurgis Night adventure,
but desertion it is, and Faust does not appear to offer much resistance
to Mephisto's temptations. It is true that his responsibility for the
purely physical seduction is arguably mitigated, quite soon afterwards,
by his actually falling in love, which appears to occur almost as the outcome of an extraneous and higher power: "Armsel'ger Faust! Ich kenne
dich nicht mehr," says Mephisto (2720). And the guilt associated with
his desertion is further mitigated by his decision, led back to the
thought of Gretchen by one of the visions of the night of the Witches'
Sabbath, to demand of Mephistopheles a liberating intervention. That
said, however, it is undeniable that our problematic "hero" is several
times stained by very serious moral blemishes.

Things are, from a moral standpoint, no better in Part Two, where
all the actions in public of Faust/Mephistopheles — the court has difficulty telling the difference between the two, merging together as they
do in the exercise of their magical powers, so that it might not be far
from the truth to talk, at least in terms of outward appearances, of a
single person with a dual identity — seem to be based on the dubious
morality of illusion. The instrument through which they save the Empire's finances in Act 1 (paper money, backed up only by hidden treasures whose whereabouts are unknown) is just as illusory as the military
interventions that decide the battle in Act 4. Furthermore, the successes
of the reclamation pursued by Faust in Act 5 will prove in the long run
to be illusory, at least in Mephistopheles' nihilistic interpretation:

> Du bist doch nur für uns bemüht
> Mit deinen Dämmen, deinen Buhnen;
> Denn du bereitest schon Neptunen,
> Dem Wasserteufel, großen Schmaus.
> In jeder Art seid ihr verloren;—
> Die Elemente sind mit uns verschworen,
> Und auf Vernichtung läuft's hinaus.
>
> (11544–50)

Faust continues to believe in magic (until, that is, the *Mitternacht*
scene), his inborn impatience leading him to make use of it to gain all
his ends at once, disdaining the humble, obscure application of mere
human effort. (In Part One his response to Mephisto's depiction of a
"green," organic way of life [2351–61] was: "Das bin ich nicht ge-
wohnt, ich kann mich nicht bequemen, / Den Spaten in die Hand zu
nehmen" [2362–63].) Hence his complete acceptance of magical illu-

sion for almost the entire duration of the play cannot, morally speaking, be compensated for by the partial and momentary recognition of this error, after the burning of Philemon and Baucis's hut:

> Könnt' ich Magie von meinem Pfad entfernen,
> Die Zaubersprüche ganz und gar verlernen,
> Stünd' ich, Natur, vor dir ein Mann allein,
> Da wär's der Mühe wert, ein Mensch zu sein.
>
> (11404–7)

It is only a tragic irony, almost a kind of retaliation, that the act that Faust has welcomed as the supreme fulfillment of his life, the construction of the new land reclamation canal, is in fact the digging of his own grave (yet again the work of the magic forces of the Lemures), and is an illusion. But Act 5 exposes layers of guilt in Faust that go well beyond his devotion to magic. The wealth of which he appears to be the owner does not derive from the feudal property on the coast the Emperor gave him (in its turn, moreover, given in recognition of the dubious magic assistance in battle), but of piracy and hence undoubted immorality. In addition, intent on his magnificent plans of reclamation (positive enough in itself), Faust does not — even at the very end — scruple over the means:

> Wie es auch möglich sei,
> Arbeiter schaffe Meng' auf Menge,
> Ermuntere durch Genuß und Strenge,
> Bezahle, locke, presse bei!
>
> (11551–54)

In his absolute determination to carry out his program (formulated in the quotation *after* the killing of Philemon, Baucis, and the wayfarer), an accident like that of the burned-down hut is shown to be, of course, not expressly desired, but yet almost taken for granted, a tragic mischance that cannot be allowed to get in his way. There can be no doubt that Act 5 reveals a quickening in the pace of the intensity of Faust's guilt, as he passes from the immorality of illusory magic to the more substantial crimes of piracy and murder, from which he does not seem willing (by contrast with similar misdeeds in Part One) to dissociate himself with any firmness.

Behind Faust's most significant positive action, the conquest of new fertile land by the sea, there is apparently no real desire to do good, but only selfishness. It is self-fulfillment, the affirmation of his own creativity, the expression of his own desire to make a mark, that Faust has at heart, as in his revealing words at the start of Act 4: "Da wagt mein

Geist, sich selbst zu überfliegen; / Hier möcht' ich kämpfen, dies möcht' ich besiegen" (10220–1). The fleeting remark at the end of his life, "Auf freiem Grund mit freiem Volke stehn" (11580) cannot be meant as the decisive reason for what he has done. On the contrary, the land having by now been largely reclaimed, its being put to good use appears a kind of crowning achievement, a further necessary improvement that will cover its conqueror in glory. Virgin lands make sense if they are cultivated, but the settlers are practically an appendix to the colonizing enterprise, not its main purpose. And the vision of a people that, resembling the Faust who has opened up the new settlement for them, will never be able to rest in secure possession of it, but will have to conquer the certainty of the future day by day, appears almost a projection of Faust's personality, its continuation in collective form, and thus in the last analysis an ultimate glorification of egotism. At the center of our attention, then, remains Faust's persona, solidly there, enveloped in a brilliant but radical egocentricity.

By this time it will be obvious that, in Goethe's eyes, Faust's character is, from an ordinary moral point of view, highly problematic, and that the road critics have taken in the pursuit of his positive moral substance in reality leads nowhere. Faust surely cannot be considered a moral hero, and insistence on continuing inquiry in this direction represents a failure to understand his ultimate salvation. The salvation of Faust the magician, the robber, the instigator of murderers, sounds like a mockery of any kind of ethical judgment on him. Very different, at the end of the Part One, was the case of Gretchen, who was "gerettet" (4611), precisely thanks to her recognition of her own moral guilt (which, despite the wildness of the language, clearly emerges) and her consequent acceptance of expiation.

In reality, the law Faust obeys is not that of morality in its everyday meaning, which from Moses to Kant was rooted in our relation of responsibility to others, but rather the immoral "morality" of the Superman, for whom the supreme law is self-realization. Hence the exceptional emphasis given throughout the play to the concept of action, and the characterization of Faust (the Faust renewed by the wager with the devil: previously, we are to given to imagine, all his vital energies were fulfilled in extremely intensive studies) as *Tatenmensch*, driven by an insatiable *Tatendrang* (it is no coincidence that these terms recur very frequently in the critical literature). From the perspective of this law of self-realization, the play throws up further moral dilemmas.

The first legitimation of Faust as a man of action originates in his own words in the draft of the translation of the beginning of St. John's Gospel, where for *logos* understood as "Wort" is substituted first "Sinn" (meaning "will, intention"), then afterwards "Kraft," and the final substitution is the only term Faust fully accepts, "Tat" (1224–37). Action is therefore the be-all and end-all, the driving force of the world. It goes without saying that this affirmation, making use of the enormous emotional weight attached in the Christian world to this foundation text, the Gospel, he is claiming to translate, is not an expression of cosmological ambitions, but expresses rather the point which Faust's own self-consciousness makes basic to his psychological sense of identity, at least from the moment (376–37) he gave up pursuing his studies to the exclusion of all else. From this moment he is to be understood primarily as a being who acts (Destro, 1997). And his history becomes a series of actions, deriving from an anxious desire to experience "life" (understood also as erotic experience), which issues in an insistent restlessness, leading him first into "the provincial little world" that forms the background to his involvement with Gretchen, then into the "great world" of politics in the imperial court, and then to beyond the bounds of the temporal scheme of myth, ending up as the emblematic capitalist, presented as reclaimer of land from the sea. In a story in which heaven and earth have had a hand, Faust emerges as seducer, dueler, a courtier expert in magic, an organizer of entertainment (heavy with esoteric meaning), the intrepid hero of myth who goes down into the depths of Mother Earth and on to Hades, the feudal conqueror, the lover of Helen, the general, the businessman-engineer and the businessman-cum-pirate. It would be hard to find another work in world literature in which, though often compressed in short stylized formulas of the highest quality, the main character engages in a comparable wealth or variety of action. If Faust is to be judged according to criteria of an activism obeying an inner dynamic, it must be admitted he is obedient to this law, the basis of his being, to an exemplary extent. There is a limit to it, however, and it goes by the name of Mephistopheles.

Mephistopheles is the demon spirit who "stets das Böse will" (1336), and this evil is nihilism, the negation of life and hence of all creation. His ideal is "das Ewig-Leere," eternal emptiness (11603): it is no coincidence that these are the last words he utters in the full exercise of his powers, before being changed into the traditional "poor devil" inevitably fooled by the divine powers in the scene following, *Grablegung*. Significantly, it is not Mephistopheles who urges Faust on to criminal action, but Faust himself takes the initiative, ordering him to make things work out so that Gretchen shares his bed the first night they meet. Mephistopheles naturally piles on the difficulties, emphasizing the girl's innocence, and knowing full well that this can only further whet Faust's appetite. In the same way, later on, when Faust finds himself driven on not merely by sensuality but by a much more complex and profound feeling of love, Mephistopheles does everything in his power to lead him back to the preferred terrain of orgiastic eroticism. This is one meaning of the extremely lengthy *excursus* of the *Walpurgisnacht*, an exceptionally subtle indirect recommendation of that eroticism which will continue to play a major role in the genuine love-story of Faust and Gretchen, right up to and including the scene in the prison. And again, it is Mephistopheles who guides the hand of Faust in the murder of Valentin. But, overall, the devil does not instigate criminal actions directly, restricting himself rather to stressing the morally problematic aspects of what Faust himself promotes (especially in Part One). His main characteristic, both in Part One and still more markedly in Part Two, is nevertheless to fuel Faust's incessant urge to action, though usually in an illusory or magical sense. Faust acts, but he acts through Mephistopheles, who knows only the tools of illusion, and hence of deception.

To understand the essence of Faust, it is important to grasp that, both subjectively and objectively, he is characterized as a man of action, but his acts reveal themselves to be either immoral through his own will (the seduction of Gretchen), or immoral through the influence of Mephistopheles, who goes beyond Faust's real intentions (from the murder of Valentin to that of Philemon and Baucis); or else unreal, because reflecting the deceptions of magic (all of Faust's public interventions in Part Two). Yet however unreal these actions of Faust (or the Faust/Mephistopheles duo) may be, one cannot fail to notice that they turn out to be very effective, if only temporarily, because on another level the workings of illusion reveal themselves to be merely ephemeral. For example, the paper money straightens out the finances of the Empire, but for how long, if no one is able to bring to light the treasures that are its collateral? The magic creatures win the battle, but what will happen the next time the imperial forces have to fight? The forces of the devil carry out the work of land reclamation and subtract the land from the waves, but will not the whole enterprise turn out to be an enormous disaster in the end, as Mephistopheles himself forecasts or hopes? Indeed, it might turn out of be of central importance that we realize their unreal character. Mephistopheles' nihilism makes him incapable of acting in directly positive ways, and hence all his actions are, even if they serve their purpose for the moment, merely apparent. But this nihilism of action — not so much in the sense of a nihilistic purpose to the action, as much as nihilism in the action itself— throws discredit on Faust himself. Faust is a man of action, but of unreal, or illusory actions. His personality, based as it was on "Tat," appears to be threatened in its very substance by this illusory nothing that is its action.

All of this might seem to be a problem of the individual psychology of Faust the character, almost made absolute as a real person. But this would be a very naive and reductive reading of the problem. An adequate analysis of the problem should, rather, attempt to understand, via the clarification of the main features of his fictive character, the relation the author has toward it, and hence the function of meaning that he has attributed to the character himself within the figurative framework (in other words, the play itself) in which he acts.

Following Jochen Schmidt's admirable analysis of the upward dynamic of Faust's entelechy in the Beyond in the portrayal of *Berg-schluchten* (1990), I should like to emphasize that Faust's activism is by no means an isolated case within the framework of the Enlightenment culture in which Goethe was rooted. On the contrary, without ignoring certain other more remote influences, including patristic literature, especially his extensive knowledge of Origen (whose theory of apocatastasis or the final reintegration of all creatures in God plays an important part in the form and imagery of the salvation of Faust), very close, precise textual parallels can be shown to exist between, on the one hand, the image of paradise in the last scene of the play and, on the other, key formulations of the early Enlightenment. Such parallels point to a wide-ranging and widely shared affinity between Goethe, his *Faust*, and that cultural moment. Schmidt quotes two passages to illustrate this point, one from Joseph Addison's "The Spectator" (a magazine Goethe knew and liked, to the extent of recommending it to his sister) of 7 July 1711, and the other from Leibniz's *Principes de la nature et de la Grâce fondés en raison* (1714) (Schmidt, 253). In his article, Addison speculated about the motives of "an infinitely wise Being" and wondered:

> How can we find that Wisdom, which shines through all his Works, in the Formation of Man, without looking on this World, as only a Nursery for the next, and believing that the several Generations of rational Creatures, which rise up and disappear in such quick Successions, are only to receive their first Rudiments of Existence here, and afterwards to be transplanted into a more friendly Climate, where they may spread and flourish to all Eternity? There is not, in my Opinion, a more pleasing and triumphant Consideration in Religion than this of the perpetual Progress which the Soul makes towards the Perfection of its Nature, without ever arriving at a Period in it. To look upon the Soul as going on from Strength to Strength, to consider that she is to shine for ever with new Accessions of Glory, and brighten to all Eter-

nity; that she will be still adding Virtue to Virtue, and Knowledge to Knowledge; carries in it something wonderfully agreeable to that Ambition which is natural to the Mind of Man. Nay, it must be a Prospect pleasing to God himself, to see his Creation for ever beautifying in his Eyes, and drawing nearer to him, by greater degrees of Resemblance. (Addison, 108)

Similarly, the passage from Leibniz (the final section of his *Principles of Nature and of Grace, founded on Reason*) runs as follows:

Ainsi notre bonheur ne consistera jamais, et ne doit point consister dans une pleine jouissance, où il n'y auroit plus rien à désirer, et qui rendroit notre esprit stupide; mais dans un progrès perpétuel à de nouveaux plaisirs, et de nouvelles perfections. (Leibniz, 1959, 718)

[Thus our happiness will never consist, and ought not to consist, in a complete enjoyment, in which there would be nothing left to desire, and which would make our mind stupid, but in a perpetual progress to new pleasures and new perfections. (Leibniz, 1934, 31)]

Both these passages are of such a close affinity with Goethe's vision of the *progressum ad infinitum* that still stretches forward in the future life, that they provide clear evidence of the roots of Goethe's writing in eighteenth-century culture in general and in the Enlightenment in particular. For Schmidt, Goethe's application in Act 5 of these forms of the infinite, metaphysical perfectibility of the human soul to the historical conditions of the nineteenth century, is an "ironic" engagement with these notions. Yet to call it "ironic" seems reductive here, given the fact that it can be interpreted only as an expression of the playful aspect (albeit in a sublimely serious game) of the portrayal of paradise in the *Bergschluchten* scene. What Goethe actually expresses in this scene is his own version of the myth of the eternal ascending evolution of the entelechy. This notion was explored elsewhere by Goethe in, for example, his letter to Zelter of 19 March 1827 ("Die entelechische Monade muß sich nur in rastsloser Tätigkeit erhalten; wird ihr diese zur anderen Natur, so kann es ihr in Ewigkeit nicht an Beschäftigung fehlen"), and in his conversation with Eckermann of 4 February 1829, where Goethe's faith in the survival of the soul is derived from precisely the "concept of activity" that characterizes Faust. Yet in the drama, this myth acquires the contours of a historical vision that is dramatically pessimistic and perhaps even tragic.

If it is easy to see the texts of Addison and Leibniz as examples of the myth-making of Enlightenment optimism in its still ideal and pure phase, prior to the inevitable contamination of historical praxis, what meaning will they have for a Goethe who, for decades, has been trying to work out his own answer to the drama of the French Revolution, and to the problems of incipient capitalist industrialization? Any answer must take into account the problematic, even negative, examination of the entrepreneurial spirit as it appears in Act 5, where its potentially criminal nature is exposed (Lukács). Goethe's ironic vision of the world of modern finance in Act 1 was, in a similar way, appreciably problematic. The optimistic mythologizing that emerges from the pages of Addison and Leibniz appears, at first blush, remote from the perspective of the mature Goethe, who surveys the actual paths taken by History.

To the gloomy picture of the representative moments of socioeconomic modernity to which *Faust* bears witness — for example, in the spheres of politics (10156–59) and capitalist entrepreneurship (11336–37) — it is useful to add the results of Giuliano Baioni's wideranging study of Goethe's reflections on the problem of revolution (the key to Goethe's historical and political thinking). In particular, if we focus on Baioni's bitter diagnosis of *Wilhelm Meisters Wanderjahre*, an outline of great, though almost spectral, clarity emerges. Rightly, Baioni takes a structuring element of the late novel to be the ideology of *Entsagung*, a type of renunciation that finds an outlet in the communitarian utopia, in the subordination of the individual to society, and in the criterion of utilitarianism. Hence the *Wanderjahre*, a novel whose fundamental pessimism Baioni does not try to conceal, can be read as Goethe's attempt to extricate himself from and get beyond the ideological crisis into which he had been thrown by the explosion of the French Revolution. The excesses of the Terror especially were seen by Goethe to be the emergence into the light of day of the chaotic and destructive forces that lie in the depths of the human heart. For Goethe, such forces can only be neutralized by and in society, through the rule of law, the harmony of class relations (however unequal), and a hierarchical structure, ensuring to every class its own adequate role.

Comparison with the *Wanderjahre*, whose final revisions coincide with the final phase of work on *Faust II* (the second, definitive version of the novel appeared in 1829), is illuminating for an understanding of the play. If we ask how far Goethe identifies with the hero of the *Wanderjahre*, a clearer picture of *Faust* emerges. For Goethe clearly approves of the process that leads Wilhelm to develop the ideology of renunciation and utility. Wilhelm acquires the features of a positive model, and his experience is repeatable or, at least, it seems to be. It by no means detracts from the exemplary character of Wilhelm's inner (and also biographical) experience that his insights are bought at a high price and cost Goethe a great deal: the equivalent of the modification, over several decades, of his demand for totality and an openness to whatever humanity had to offer, because his pessimistic diagnosis of contemporary history made it impossible to cultivate such ideals without adjustment to the imperatives of the modern world. According to this view, one arrives at renunciation through necessity, not through free choice. Now in this respect Faust emerges as a kind of anti-Meister. For what in Wilhelm appears as the renunciation of individual egoism, the subordination of the individual to the collective, and a sense of responsibility towards the group, is in Faust, *mutatis mutandis*, an insatiable thirst, egocentricity taken to solipsistic lengths, and submission to his own individual daemon. Right to the end, Faust is the incarnation of the inspired genius of the German *Sturm und Drang*. Goethe's entire classical and post-classical development, especially after the French Revolution, is occupied by the portrayal of the difficult, painful overcoming of this egocentric model. So for any critic, a central problem is to show how *Faust II* functions as part of a poetic search by its author, which at the same time, in the *Wanderjahre*, finds its complementary antithesis, marked with the bitterest of attitudes, and a sorrowful exemplarity.

The dialectical link connecting Faust to Wilhelm has been recognized by such critics as Hans Joachim Schrimpf (1956). Yet it would be a mistake to think, as both Schrimpf and Baioni do, of the problem of development of Goethe's thinking in this connection simply in the light of the *Faust-Wanderjahre* sequence and on the basis of the genesis of these two works (*Faust* originates as far back as the Frankfurt years, while the *Wanderjahre* originated in the nucleus of short stories with which Goethe was occupied from 1807). Such a line of argument assumes a clarity of inspiration and unity of purpose from the first plan of the works onwards that is absent from these two late masterpieces, subject as they were to much, often radical, re-working and re-thinking. Rather, these two works might best be regarded as parallel, albeit divergent, outcomes of a single line of meditation on the great problems of the epoch; as evidence, that is, of an awareness of the political and industrial revolutions. Faust, the character, would thus be the problematic (because rooted in a complex relation to history) embodiment of an answer to the problems of the time which, in Wilhelm, who subordinates the individual to the community, can be seen in its regrettable and at the same time positive features. If there is a relationship of sequential movement the two works, I do not see how it could be otherwise than from *Wanderjahre* to *Faust*, and not — as is generally and tacitly assumed — vice versa.

There are at least two reasons for such a conclusion. First, there is the definitive character, richly documented in the biographies of the author, that Goethe wished to give his play, which was actually sealed by the author and consigned to posterity: *Faust II,* as the last words of the venerable poet and made accessible only to future generations, was thus effectively removed from discussion by contemporaries, as the disconcerted reactions when the play appeared in print confirm. According to the author, his last work is *Faust* and not *Wilhelm Meister,* as his word on the completion of Part Two to Eckermann on 6 June 1831 suggest: "Mein ferneres Leben [. . .] kann ich nunmehr als ein reines Geschenk ansehen, und es ist jetzt im Grunde ganz einerlei, ob und was ich noch etwa tue." But examination of Goethe's basic line of development over his last few decades, the period of his great and dramatic coming-to-terms with the history of his revolutionary age, reveals, to my mind at least, the gradual emergence of an increasingly bitter pessimism, held in check with increasing difficulty by an immense self-discipline, identifiable not so much in the conduct of his life (as seen, for instance, in his formal manner that so irritated some of his contemporaries) as in the strenuous struggle to find something positive to oppose to the destructive forces of the historical scene in general and, in particular, the anarchic chaos to which all revolutionary activity seemed to amount. There is something almost sublime in the attempt of the old Goethe, despite the pitiless diagnosis of the present and of the dangers that threatened, to find intimations of human salvation (orderly, organic, and constructive). And that salvation can only be expressed as the utopian content of the last novel, almost an inheritance left by one who has painfully understood much, and who, by the chance of birth, still has in front of him the chance to operate in History. This is the route that leads up to the *Wanderjahre,* and *Faust II* marks a further step in this development.

Faust appears to place himself in diametrical opposition to any possible *Entsagung,* and he certainly never betrays the slightest concern over social usefulness. He acts *in,* but not *for,* society; and so his actions (as we saw, largely illusory anyway) are aimed at his own success. Thus Faust operates at the court to create a position of prestige for himself; then he fights to gain the favor of the Emperor and to obtain land; and finally he proceeds to the great work of land reclamation as the supreme affirmation of his "will to power." Goethe's last hero, as a protagonist of the life of social relations, is, then, a negative hero.

At the same time, it should not be forgotten that *Faust II* is filled to overflowing with historical references, and that among its aims is the display of a kind of *summa* of over two thousand years of Western (not just German) history, right up to and including the developments of his own day with the emergence of an aggressive and unscrupulous capitalism. This aim is pursued by means of carefully worked-out anachronisms recast into a coherent poetical display to whose understanding the poet directs us with a pedagogical clarity, underlining in Act 1 of Part Two the equation poetry-allegory, in the words of the Boy Charioteer: "Wir sind Allegorien," and "Bin die Verschwendung, die Poesie" (5531, 5573) (Emrich, 169–76). We therefore have to draw the conclusion that the asocial character of Faust is in keeping with the historical diagnosis that the author has entrusted to the play — a diagnosis that is singularly gloomy, with no way out. In society, Faust finds merely occasions (one is tempted to say materials) for his own self-realization, which in the end will also be revealed to be illusory, just as the public actions of Faust/Mephistopheles are. There is not even the suggestion of a utopian opening towards a possible, humanly acceptable historical outcome, as there is in the novel of the same period. Faust ends tragically, just as the subtitle the author insisted upon indicates. The poet's last word, in respect of Faust, seems to be a desperate withdrawal from even the utopian gleam of hope opened up by the novel.

Decades before, beginning with *Die Leiden des jungen Werthers* (1774), the main lines of Goethe's socio-political thinking had been based on the concept of a balanced relation between the bourgeoisie and the nobility. On this model was then superimposed, with infinitely greater anxiety and sometimes almost with a kind of breathless desperation, the battle to create barriers against the chaos revealed by the Revolution, a battle which, after *Die Wahlverwandtschaften* (1809), tends to be transferred wholly to within the bourgeois world. If this barrier is to be found in the heroic choice of "renunciation" and social utility, as Giuliano Baioni has suggested, *Faust* has all the appearance of a confession of pessimism with regard to that painful utopia. High and noble though the communitarian ideal might be, what History actually seems to be preparing is a world of egoism and oppression.

This bleak outlook, however, would appear to conflict with the ending of Part Two and therefore with the whole of the play, if we take the "ending" to be both the concluding scenes together (*Grablegung* and *Bergschluchten*), both of which take place beyond Faust's earthly existence and share a primarily "metaphysical" character. Just as Faust's actual history starts after the two initial prologues, the *Vorspiel auf dem Theater* and the *Prolog im Himmel*, so it ends with the last scene on earth (in other words, in the real world), where he actually dies. What follows is certainly important, just as the prologues were important, but it is of an entirely different nature from the drama of his life. The structure of *Faust* is analogous to that of certain medieval mystery plays, or of an important tradition in Baroque theater (for which Calderón is held to be the model); or else, closer to Goethe, of those shoddy products of popular (especially Viennese) theater, the magical *Besserungsstücke*, in which an action or principle in a supernatural world of fairies and spirits is carried out or verified on the earth, thus providing the substance of the farcical plot that follows. Often this train of events is set off by a bet between the gods, or a rivalry that can only be resolved through a conflict between their respective followers on earth. In the end, a sudden, rapid and decisive reappearance of the magical creatures sanctions the demonstration of what, in the prologue in the upper world, had been put forward as the object of contention. The history of these *Zauberstücke*, in which the supernatural world guaranteed order and therefore happiness on earth, consists of a progressive devitalization of the cardboard figures of fairies and magicians. They are treated disrespectfully and teased, at first tentatively and then increasingly openly, until the last text of some literary substance, the *Lumpazivagabundus* of 1833 by Johann Nestroy (1801–62), in which the author, at the end of an incredibly artificial and outlandish happy ending, forgets to call the gods back on to the stage, even though they had been the ones to start the ball rolling. Thus the events will terminate in the only place that really exists, in the real world, in the earthly home of their human protagonists.

So can *Faust* be summed up as a colossal *Besserungsstück*? To pose the question in this form points to the contrast between the richness and complexity of Goethe's text with the mass of "low" cultural products assembled to satisfy the hunger for novelty of the popular Viennese stage. And yet it is hard completely to eliminate the urge to compare them, bearing in mind the comparative unimportance of the metaphysical framework in the action of the scenes of *Faust*: the spectator is made to forget that the outcome of the unequal initial bet between God and Mephistopheles can never be in doubt: "Es irrt der Mensch, solang' er strebt" (317). And the comparison could be taken as far as the continued existence of the divine protagonist of the *Prolog* in the heavenly episode of the *Bergschluchten*, in which although God no longer appears, room is left for a divine and theologically original role for Mary as the personification of the Feminine Divine. But there the parallel ends, since the ending of *Faust* is far removed from the need for the reconciliatory blandishments of the spectator watching the happy ending of the magic comedies. On the contrary, the ending of *Faust II* proves to be so extraordinarily incongruous, bearing in mind Faust's

immoral behavior, that it raises a large number of problems of interpretation. For this reason, the final scene has sometimes has been clas-
sified quite dismissively as one of the "serious jokes" with which the
author brings his last work to an end, with an evident overestimation of
the noun and a concomitant neglect of the adjective. In reality the
function of this mystical and metaphysical finale is far from being artificial and decorative, despite the obvious relish for literary play, evidenced in the pastiche of Catholicism.

To clarify further the complex set of problems around the function
of Faust the character, we need to recall the very close affinity Jochen
Schmidt finds between the destiny of the soul of Faust and typical Enlightenment ideas (themselves indebted to a tradition of Christian es-
chatological thinking as ancient as it is unorthodox), in which the basic
optimism of that ideology was revealed. Goethe has recourse to these
images of infinite perfectibility (in which the glorification of the eternal
essence of Faust consists), not at the start of a phase of cultural expansion, and projected towards a radiant future, like the early Enlightenment positions of Addison and Leibniz, but at the end of a life that
finds itself faced with such historical phenomena as revolution and industrialism, which are experienced as negative or, at the very least, extremely problematic. Indeed, Goethe appears to find it so difficult to
come to terms with these problems that he has to fall back on the utopian vision of the *Wanderjahre*. And yet — and this is the real problem
for criticism — Goethe proceeds to glorify precisely his problematic
hero, Faust, despite all the historical pessimism of which he may be
seen to be the expression. Nor does it help to reduce the complex vision of *Bergschluchten* to a trifle, a mere literary game, for these ironic
elements are transcended by the seriousness and coherence of its presentation, the wealth and enormous range of subtle cultural references,
and the mystical hymnic tonality itself.

We must never lose sight of the historical pessimism that is a feature
of all of the later Goethe's thinking, and forms the explicit object of
Baioni's analysis. This pessimism appears in *Faust II* in the most extreme terms, in the sense that it is no longer presented, as it was earlier,
in terms of the relation between the aristocracy and the bourgeoisie,
nor in the more recent ones of the relation between the individual and
bourgeois civil society; but rather in a form in which one side actually
eliminates the other of the relation. So society in *Faust* no longer exists,
except as the area in which the sole actor, Faust himself, exercises his
self-expression. Faust has no responsibilities towards society, but only
towards his own ego (or what amounts to the same thing, his daemon).

For his part, Goethe repeatedly attributed a special kind of "responsibility" (obviously not moral in the usual sense) to exceptional personalities. For example, in the case of Newton, Goethe made the distinction between a particular pair of opposites: "good will" (*guter Wille*), characterizing the moral action of ordinary humanity; and "determined will" (*entschiedenes Wollen*) that, as an unrestrainable natural force, guides the actions of the exceptional individual (*Materialien zur Geschichte der Farbenlehre*, HA 14, 173); and apropos of Napoleon, Riemer recorded the following remark made in February 1807: "Außerordentliche Menschen, wie Napoleon, treten aus der Moralität heraus. Sie wirken zuletzt wie physische Ursachen, wie Feuer und Wasser" (Herwig, 2, 190).

In *Faust*, the protagonist on whose shoulders so much pessimism falls is saved, undergoing a metaphysical apotheosis, the poetical seriousness of which cannot be doubted. The glorification of Faust is real, but we may ask ourselves whether he is supposed to be an example to all humans, representing a common destiny. And the answer sounds slightly paradoxical. The underlining of "Streben" as the pre-eminent characteristic of Faust's personality and the precondition of his salvation — to the point that his salvation itself consists in rendering eternal that ascending "Streben" — would seem to be the destiny of the few, and certainly not of all. Furthermore, various (and unclarified) remarks by Goethe lead us to think of a differentiation in the metaphysical destiny of single individuals, in accordance with their nature. For example, Goethe told Eckermann on 1 September 1829: "Wir sind nicht auf gleiche Weise unsterblich." In the great panorama of the drama we meet at least one other example of death that shows no trace of the infinite ascension of the glorification of Faust. These are the choral singers who, as handmaids, accompany Helen to her destiny. They appear superficial, voluble, and incapable of responding to life in any other vein than in the light play of the senses, as well as incapable of realizing the depth of tragedy of the beauty that condemns Helen (of whose loveliness they never tire of singing, as if it were the supreme divine gift) to be always the arouser and victim of male sexual longing. Even discounting an amused one-sidedness in the words of Mephistopheles, who repeatedly mocks them, it has to be recognized that there is a good deal of truth in his diagnosis. At the end of Act 3, after their mistress Helen has left the world of the living to follow Euphorion into Hades, and after the leader of the choral singers, Panthalis, has in her turn chosen to follow her, the other members of the chorus also find their the last hour has come, though this simply means that they return to nature as nymphs and dryads (9985–10038). Not for them the sad eternity of Hades (in which nevertheless a shadowy individuality is preserved), nor the even less likely "Christian" salvation Faust will receive. For the handmaids, whose personality appeared so superficial, living just for the moment and its pleasures, destiny reserved a natural, pre-human future. But this makes Faust's destiny *post mortem* stand out all the more prominently, in that it sees the central core of his personality as residing in that ceaseless dynamic activity that projects him up into the highest of metaphysical heavens.

Moreover, the cause of Faust's salvation is seen *only* in this aspect of his personality. *"Wer immer strebend sich bemüht, / Den können wir erlösen"* are the angels' words (11936–37). No link at all is made between Faust's concrete actions and his salvation. Faust is glorified, not for what he has done, but for what he has been, for his personality. Or to put it another way: his actions are measured, not according to moral criteria (in other words, of responsibility toward others), but only according to the criterion of how far he corresponds to the law of his actual character, the "Streben," to the terms of which every evaluation and every moral judgment about him is reduced. Faust is destined to glorification in any case, whatever he has done, simply because of the fact that he has been faithful to his own nature: "Fausts 'Sünde' besteht nicht im getanen Bösen oder im unterlassenen Guten, — seine spezifische Verfehlung läge allein in der Trägheit, im Selbstverlust an den ohne Tatendrang durchlebten Augenblick" (Keller, 329).

In addition, another essential point to emphasize is the rigorous individualism of the upward-moving salvation of Goethe's paradise. Faust's soul rises, and in so doing is purified and perfected: but it affects himself, exclusively. There is no choral or community side to it at all (unless, that is, we count the verses sung by the groups of the blessed who sing, aria-like, of certain, neo-Catholic scenes of Heaven, describing the ascending path of the newly blessed one and, with the last words of the "Selige Knaben," hoping for the further ascent of Faust himself in future). It could be argued that the soul of Faust is only concerned about its own perfection. Other souls (among which *in primis* Gretchen's) are concerned for Faust, and pray for him, whereas Faust himself seems to proceed directly on his journey to individual salvation, unconcerned with anything outside this goal. This tightly-focussed resolution is expressed in the clearest possible way, not through Faust's own words (we have, after all, just witnessed his death) but through — his silence. In the two final scenes of the great drama, the protagonist is given no further lines, even if he still holds the center of the stage. Everyone talks about him, but he says nothing, signifying the break, of a considerably paradoxical nature, with every social or even interpersonal connection of a soul involved in a process of individual purification.

The crucial feature of this process of salvation is the downward movement of divine love which, in the form of "Das Ewig-Weibliche," "zieht uns hinan" (11210–1). At this juncture, the interpretative problem of providing an adequate definition of the nature of this "love," and in particular its relation to the universally metamorphosizing "Eros" of the end of Act 2 (cf. 8479–80), emerges in one obvious respect. This "love" coincides lexically, but certainly not semantically, with a Christian conception of love (and from what has been said so far, the extent of the gap that separates this Heaven of Goethe's from a Christian "Heaven," however interpreted, is easily appreciated). Goethe's love seems to be a force rather than a relationship between people. The personal dimension seems to fade or actually disappear (as it clearly does in the case of the Greek concept of "Eros," and less clearly, in what might be termed a circumstantial way, in the case of the celestial love personified in the "Goddess" Mary of the Heaven in which Faust ascends), conferring something impersonal, necessary, or even automatic on the process of salvation of Faust's soul, not least because of the lack of any connection with his moral conduct when alive.

To summarize: The events of Faust's life sum up some of the essential stages of the whole of Western history and, in so doing, he is characterized negatively, both for the illusory nature of his actions and for his final guilt. Nonetheless, his soul is saved on account of its faithfulness to itself, through an elusive principle of love — a combination of a cosmogonic idea (Eros), a feeling of love (Gretchen), and a divine creative force. As the protagonist of the entire history of the West right up to the turning point of industrialism, Faust is saved in ways and for reasons that are completely individual *and at the same time* above the personal or divine and cosmic. All this looks like a renunciation of History as a meta-individual dimension by a Goethe at the end of his life — an extreme profession of pessimism about our ability to understand or recover History, a kind of desperate backward somersault from the splendid attempt of the *Wanderjahre* to outline a possible historical space tailored to the needs of humanity, falling back on mere individual destiny that is, or may be, a destiny of salvation, of eternal fulfillment. This fulfillment is one that takes place outside of History, and it would seem (remembering Faust's guilt) in spite of History.

"Tragedy," therefore, *Faust* certainly is, but in a very special sense. That much became clearer to Goethe while he was engaged in the writing: in *Faust I*, the term still largely obeyed the dictates of traditional definition, even if the hypothesis of the final salvation of the main character, in contrast to the traditional myth, had flashed through Goethe's mind at a very early stage. Abeken reports the words of Wieland in 1809, according to whom Goethe, in his very first years at Weimar, had declared that, in contrast to the general expectations of a Mephistopheles who would "den Faust holen," the opposite would happen: "Umgekehrt: Faust holt den Teufel" (Herwig, 1, 395). And the logic that led, despite Faust's guilt in Part One, to a metaphysical "happy ending" drove Schelling in 1802 to suggest that Faust would be "in höhere Sphären erhaben vollendet" (Gräf, 139). "Tragedy" it also is because the final salvation paradoxically covers up a failure, Faust's inability to establish a relation with others that does not function as, or is not subordinated to, his own egocentricity. *Faust* as a tragedy of the impossibility of acting on history (that is, *for* history, *for* the civilized community) — this seems to be the final outcome of a line of thought that looks back on at least six decades of a very long life. The price of salvation in *Faust* appears to be not, as in the *Wanderjahre*, the elimination of individual happiness, but the elimination of the social dimension. At the end of his colossal *Besserungsstück*, a truly tragic, paradoxical salvation seems to be the last word of the grand old man of Weimar.

Translated by Charles Hindley.

Works Cited

Addison, Joseph [et al.]. *The Spectator.* Vol. 1. London: Dent, 1907.

Baioni, Giuliano. *Classicismo e rivoluzione: Goethe e la Rivoluzione Francese.* [1969] Naples: Guida, 1998.

Böhm, Wilhelm. *Faust, der Nichtfaustische.* Halle an der Saale: M. Niemeyer, 1933.

Destro, Alberto. "L'eroe colpevole o la salvezza tragica di Faust." *Studia theodisca.* 3 (1996). 109–26.

———. "Faust, Johannes und die Geschichte." *Studi Germanici.* Vol. 35, No. 1 (1997). 7–23.

Emrich, Wilhelm. *Die Symbolik von Faust II: Sinn und Vorformen.* [1943] Frankfurt am Main: Athenäum, 1964.

Gräf, Hans Gerhard, ed. *Goethe über seine Dichtungen: Versuch einer Sammlung aller Äusserungen des Dichters über seine poetischen Werke. Zweither Theil: Die Dramatischen Dichtungen.* Vol. 2. Frankfurt am Main: Literarische Anstalt, 1904.

Herwig, Wolfgang, ed. *Goethes Gespräche: Eine Sammlung zeitgenössischer Berichte aus seinem Umgang auf Grund der Ausgabe und des Nachlasses von Flodoard Freiherr von Biedermann*. 6 vols. Zurich: Artemis, 1965–1987.

Keller, Werner. "Größe und Elend, Schuld und Gnade: Fausts Ende in wiederholter Spiegelung." *Aufsätze zu Goethes "Faust II."* Ed. Werner Keller. Darmstadt: Wissenschaftliche Buchgesellschaft, 1991. 316–44.

König, Helmut, Wolfgang Kuhlmann, and Klaus Schwabe. *Vertuschte Vergangenheit: Der Fall Schwerte und die NS-Vergangenheit der deutschen Hochschulen*. Munich: C. H. Beck, 1997.

Leibniz, Gottfried Wilhelm. *Opera philosophica*. Ed. Johann Eduard Erdmann and Renate Vollbrecht. Aalen: Scientia, 1959.

———. *Philosophical Writings*. Trans. Mary Morris. London/New York: Dent/Dutton, 1934.

Lukács, Georg. *Goethe and his Time*. Trans. Robert Anchor. London: The Merlin Press, 1968.

Schmidt, Jochen. "Die 'katholische Mythologie' und ihre mystische Entmythologisierung in der Schluß-Szene des 'Faust II.'" *Jahrbuch der Deutschen Schillergesellschaft*. 34 (1990). 230–56.

Schrimpf, Hans Joachim. *Das Weltbild des späten Goethe*. Stuttgart: Klett, 1956.

Schwerte, Hans. *Faust und das Faustische: Ein Kapitel deutscher Ideologie*. Stuttgart: E. Klett, 1962.

The Character and Qualities of Mephistopheles

Osman Durrani

The Early History of the Devil

THE DEVIL HAS MANY FACES. In traditional depictions, he appears as a horse, a dog, a cat, an ape, a toad, a raven, a vulture, "aber auch als ein anständig gekleideter Mann oder als ein schöner Soldat." Shape-shifting is his speciality. His lineaments do not conform to a type or gender. "Manchmal ist er ein großer, dunkel gekleideter Mann von häßlichem Aussehen; manchmal hat er ein weibliches, manchmal ein betont männliches Gesicht" (Colpe, 68). The character he manifests is no less diverse and elusive than his outward appearance.

He makes his literary début in the Old Testament, initially as the successful tempter in Genesis. In the later Book of Job, Satan bets that he will be able to turn a righteous man away from his maker, on condition that his victim is afflicted with personal misfortune to a sufficient degree. Satan loses his wager and the celestial super-powers do not re-assemble to discuss the outcome. Instead, the initial debate gives way to a lyrical evocation of Job's proverbial, long-suffering patience. Job submits to the Lord's authority as revealed to him by the Voice in the Whirlwind and is rewarded for maintaining his faith regardless of his personal tribulations (Job 38–40). Theologians see in this episode a justification of the presence of evil and an answer to the much debated question of why an almighty God should have created the imperfect world we inhabit. "Theodicy" is the name given to the process of re-solving the paradox of an evil world generated by a supposedly benign, all-powerful creator (Hick, 3–20).

The devil plays a more active and diverse role in the New Testa-ment, not least because Christ relies on a worthy opponent in order to accomplish his mission. *Nullus diabolus nullus redemptor*: without the devil there is no need for a Saviour (Russell 1986, 33; Roskoff, I, 208–11). Here we find him intervening in the affairs of men as the "Prince of this World" (John 12:31, 14:30, 16:11), and tempting them with the promise of untold riches: "All these I will give you, if you will only fall down and do me homage," said to the Saviour in his mortal guise (Matthew 4:9). It is a short step to the notion of a powerful, malignant spirit who interacts freely with human beings and lures them into wrong-doing, offering limitless gifts as bribes and sweeteners.

It was not until the sixteenth century that the devil as a complex character entered literary culture. There are several reasons why a revival of interest in the demonic occurred at this point in time. New translations of the Bible gave the scriptures greater vividness and more direct appeal than they had possessed in the Latin texts. The bestsellers of the day were concerned with the persecution of witches (Sprenger and Kramer, *Malleus maleficarum*, 1485) and the exposure of vice (Brant, *Das Narrenschiff*, 1494), both subjects in which the devil had a hand. The sudden decline in the influence of the medieval church led people to seek a more immediate relationship with their maker, which was patently open to disruption by evil forces. For many, it made sense to view the recently abandoned Catholic faith as the devil's construct, which explains why Faust's adversary often acts like a monk in the early versions of the story. It is now appreciated that witch trials and exorcism rituals were an important part of the cultural background to the literature of the period (Roskoff, II, 293–314; Baron, 129–46; Schöne, 186).

Martin Luther accepted the physical intervention of the devil as a fact. His table talk, letters and sermons frequently return to the misdeeds of the Evil One, which had a grim reality. In his imaginings, the devil would rattle around behind his stove, pelt the roof with nuts, roll casks down the stairway, appear as a serpent or a star, and even lodge himself in his bowels, where he would grunt like a pig and emit terrible stenches (Oberman, 232–34). Graphic accounts of Luther's mental and physical torments fuelled public interest in the nature and qualities of the great adversary and generated a rapid increase in the number of books and treatises published on the subject. Many *Teufelsbücher* stress the hierarchical organisation of Hell. Just as there were many different ranks among the angels ("cherubim," "seraphim," "thrones"), various classes of devil were envisaged, each responsible for a distinctive portfolio of transgressions. The *Eheteufel* would specialise in the disruption of fond relations between husband and wife, encouraging deceit, adultery, and promiscuity. Another such spirit, graphically evoked by Andreas Musculus (*Vom Hosen Teuffel*, 1555), would encourage fashion-conscious young men to spend inordinate sums on silken leggings. There were cohorts of distinct devils, eager to encourage gluttony, dancing, swearing and other putative vices (Roos, 78–89; Mahal, 342).

What is interesting and relevant to Goethe is that the devils were now proving themselves to be up to date; they were interested in contemporary vices; they homed in on vulnerable individuals; they were indisputably "homocentric" (Russell 1986, 63). With multifarious interests and contradictory qualities, they were modern emblems of the human vices they effectively mimicked.

It is in this context that we encounter the name of Mephistopheles, or Mephostophilis, or other recorded permutations of an outlandish-sounding name whose meaning has never been satisfactorily resolved. "No friend of Faust" or "No friend of light" are explanations that have been put forward (White, 95–110, esp. 104–5). More important is the fact that Mephistopheles is associated with one victim (Faust), and one vice only — the pursuit of knowledge, especially such knowledge as was derived from classical antiquity. It is for this reason that his name "sounds Greek" to modern ears and has an academic ring to it. Those ignorant of the classics have no such aspirations and are invulnerable to his attentions. The seeker of knowledge, the scholar, the professor is his favourite victim. Souls are in peril when scholars turn away from the Bible and look to Plato and Aristotle, Lucretius and Epicure for moral guidance; no less so when distracted by Homer and Plautus from the study of the Church Fathers.

The salient qualities of the spirit who figures as Mephostophilis in the anonymous chapbook (*Historia von D. Johann Fausten*, 1587) result from this combination of factors. Faustus is a lecturer at the University of Wittenberg, the same institution in which Luther taught. He is a figure in whom the forward-looking virtues of Paracelsus, Leonardo, and Columbus mingle with the vices of a loud-mouthed town-crier and cheapskate apothecary (Brown, 72; Keller, 260–64). Faustus summons an evil spirit (as distinct from *the* devil himself) for a variety of incongruous purposes: to resolve academic debate about the universe, to act as companion on his travels, and also to fulfil his mundane personal lusts. The *Historia* is more of a ponderous sermon than a fast-moving narrative. Presumably, the sixteenth-century author, working within the relatively liberal intellectual climate of Frankfurt (Baron, 26–91), intended it to be both. Mephostophilis is invested from the outset with a multi-layered function. He is, simultaneously, an example of gross depravity and a morally aware theologian; he distracts Faustus by offering him shallow pleasures, and yet, when asked, warns him about the magnitude of God's wrath and shows a desperately keen awareness of the need to repent. A few years on, Christopher Marlowe, using an English translation of the German original, pursued the same line when he had him implore his victim in piteously self-condemnatory terms:

Think'st thou that I, who saw the face of God,
And tasted the eternal joys of heaven,
Am not tormented with ten thousand hells
In being deprived of everlasting bliss!

(Doctor Faustus 3: 78–81)

The spirit who simultaneously assists and deceives survives in Goethe. Mephistopheles stimulates and corrupts by turn, and intrigues us with his inconsistent stratagems. His kaleidoscopic brilliance prevents him from forfeiting our sympathy. In his dual role, he looks back to the doctrinal preoccupations of the Christian Middle Ages as well as forward to the self-destructive obsessions of modernity.

Goethe and the Problem of Evil

It is not immediately obvious why Goethe, in his own words a "decided non-Christian" (letter to Lavater, 29 July 1782), should have chosen to take up, as his life's work, what was by then a relatively obscure story about the temptations of a scholar by an emissary from Hell. *Faust* remains something of an oddity in his oeuvre, which tends to focus on modern individuals; compare Werther's hyper-sensitive *Weltschmerz* and the marital difficulties of the couple in *Die Walhverwandtschaften*, or on historical or mythological figures such as Torquato Tasso and Iphigenia. Its status as a tragedy is controversial. But the main question raised by the play's antecedents is why Goethe, a thoroughly secular thinker from an early age, should have wished to depict the quest for a man's immortal soul by evil forces in which he himself no longer believed.

Goethe is quite clear on this point. From his earliest essays, he maintains that good and evil are not to be thought of as irreconcilable opposites, but as two sides of the same coin: "das, was wir bös nennen, ist nur die andre Seite vom Guten" ("Zum Shäkspeares-Tag"; HA 12, 227). Life itself, far from being static, is a continuous process of expansion and contraction, of interdependent diastolic and systolic pressures, a pattern with great importance for *Faust*. Elsewhere, Goethe calls it simply "die ewige Formel des Lebens" (WA 2.1, 15; Requadt, 60–62). It is hard to see how, given his refusal to countenance a battle between opposing good and evil forces, Goethe could stage a fight for the doctor's soul as previous authors had done. Does such a contest ever take place? This is no idle question, and it is rendered acute by the lines addressed by the Lord in the "Prologue in Heaven" to his putative adversary:

> Ich habe deinesgleichen nie gehaßt.
> Von allen Geistern, die verneinen,
> Ist mir der Schalk am wenigsten zur Last.
> Des Menschen Tätigkeit kann allzuleicht erschlaffen,
> Er liebt sich bald die unbedingte Ruh;
> Drum geb' ich gern ihm den Gesellen zu,
> Der reizt und wirkt und muß als Teufel schaffen.—
>
> (337–43)

The dialogue between supposedly antithetical entities presents both parties in a radically unfamiliar light. Mephisto's first words (280, 283–84, 296–98) contain evidence of compassion and could, were he, as a mere "rogue," able to rise above the suspicion of hypocrisy, be read as attempting to address the issue of theodicy (Michelsen, 249–55). Also, the Lord is tolerant to the point of indifference when it comes to evaluating the role played by evil in human life. Far from being an impediment to goodness, evil is a stimulant that prevents human creativity from atrophying. The moral position of this "Herr," far removed from that of the rigorous defenders of morality, goes hand in hand with the liberal moral climate of the Enlightenment (Durrani, 26–31). From a structural point of view the Lord's assertion that Faust will not be "drawn away from the primal fount" appears, puzzlingly, to disenfranchise Faust's antagonist before the play has properly begun and to anticipate an ending that will, come what may, relieve the devil of his prize:

> Zieh diesen Geist von seinem Urquell ab,
> Und führ' ihn, kannst du ihn erfassen,
> Auf deinem Wege mit herab,
> Und steh beschämt, wenn du bekennen mußt:
> Ein guter Mensch in seinem dunklen Drange
> Ist sich des rechten Weges wohl bewußt.
>
> (324–29)

These lines were written in 1797, by which time Goethe appears to have made up his mind that the devil was to be worsted — an ending more in keeping with medieval morality plays, in which sinners are regularly saved (Russell 1986, 64), than with the stark pessimism of the chapbook. That he should have spelled out the conclusion before the curtain went up on Faust could be seen as a flaw. But I argue that the work has gained rather than lost in scope as a consequence. A view of the world emerges that is much more modern than that found in the confrontational tragedies of the past. True, we are told what the outcome will be — but Brecht uses a similar strategy to underpin his epic theatre and justifies it on the grounds that it produces a high level of concentration on what actually takes place on stage. "Spannung auf den Ausgang" comes to be replaced by "Spannung auf den Gang" (Brecht, 20). By revealing that he will be thwarted, attention is focused more relentlessly on Mephistopheles, and readers and audiences are directly confronted with urgent questions about his role and identity. Because entrapment in error is an essential consequence of man's obligation to strive, the autonomous status of evil must be negated. Given Goethe's holistic perception of life, Mephistopheles can do little more than mirror, somewhat darkly at times, Faust's many-layered, ever-restless personality. This he does by shifting in and out of subsidiary roles such as servant, accomplice, tutor, and commentator. His instability becomes his prime quality. He offers Faust an invitation to face the multiplicity of reality, embodying, through constant metamorphosis, the "principle of the real" (Brown, 68). His apparent love-hate relationship with words, which he defines with a disdain that verges on affection (1995–2000), is a telling symptom in one who restlessly shifts his position, making more promises than he is ever able to keep.

A play about Faust that lacked a devil would be a contradiction in terms. Yet Goethe did not find the introduction of Mephistopheles easy, and repeatedly postponed writing the scenes in which he was to present his mission-statement. Mephisto's antics in Auerbachs Keller and in the Hexenküche scenes, as well as his role in engineering the wooing and undoing of Gretchen, were committed to paper some time before the scenes in which he reveals himself to his victim. For reasons already outlined, it is convenient to see in him a companion figure or "alter ego" to the doctor whose latent amoral and selfish desires he embodies. What is less easy to describe is his brief, and it is because this deviates in key respects from the traditional diabolical enterprise of moral corruption that Goethe postponed completing these preliminaries until the remainder of *Faust I* was almost finished. There remains a disharmony in the clash between Mephisto's medieval role as Faust's tempter and his modern one as Faust's psychological double, which, like much else in the composition, is ultimately not fully resolvable (Gaier, 168).

The Pact Scenes

Evil can take many forms, and the dog, though popularly seen as man's best friend, can be one of them and is often employed as such in literature. Goethe's Mephistopheles is first glimpsed, on Easter Sunday evening, in the guise of a black hound, a form in which he mimics that of a loyal companion, but also represents the accursed beast frequently treated in the Bible (Deuteronomy 23:18) as an image of evil (Woods, 228–46). It is a fittingly duplicitous disguise, one of many adopted by Mephistopheles, whose partiality to role-play was signalled in the Prologue. Shape-shifting into wild animals is a common myth that indicates, among other things, the devil's multiple spheres of interest (Russell 1972, 275). The hocus-pocus in which he engages while revealing himself to the doctor, and his apparent reluctance to confront the pivotal question of a compact, are the first of many puzzles. Passing through various forms, including hippopotamus (1254) and elephant (1311), he addresses Faust in the more familiar likeness of a student. This gives the doctor an opportunity to interrogate him in Socratic mode as to his provenance and pedigree, and to recognise his destructive designs on mankind (1379–82).

It is here that the seeming contradictions of the Prologue reassert themselves. Far from concealing his intentions, Mephistopheles makes no secret of his commitment to evil, and reveals not only his clandestine ambitions, but also the apparent lack of success which "invariably" wrecks his endeavours (1335–36). So striking is this impromptu admission of ineffectiveness, so closely does it echo the confident pronouncement of the Lord in the Prologue, that many critics consider it inappropriate in one whose aim is to subvert his victim. It renders the play undramatic by anticipating its conclusion, and, worse still, "demephistophelises" (Seidlin, 171) Faust's foe by making him little more than the mouthpiece of the Lord. The problem can be resolved, up to a point, by adopting Seidlin's explanation that by "good," Mephistopheles can only be referring to what he himself, *qua* devil, considers to be "good," i.e. that which good folk call "evil" (Seidlin, 173; Keller, 296–97). Yet Faust himself does not seem to take the words in this sense. He immediately picks up the point about Mephisto's lack of success as agent of corruption and seizes the opportunity to suggest a pact between them (1414–15), showing himself to be more receptive to the "Romantic," self-ironizing streak in his adversary than many critics have been. Milton's picture of the Fiend had been no less contradictory (Russell 1986, 109; compare *Paradise Lost* I, 217–18)

If the first "Study" scene presents a perplexing picture of a devil who is ready to deny his diabolical qualities, the second, confusingly also headed "Study," does little to resolve the paradox. But here, the two roles are reversed. Faust is the one who despairs (1591–1606), and in his now melancholy frame of mind readily gives in to Mephisto's offer of magical assistance. Quite what this might involve is never made clear — Mephistopheles seems willing to offer just about anything and Faust shows little interest in specifics — until, almost as an afterthought, the pact is followed by a separate wager, in which Faust utters an impassioned, defiant promise never to be lulled into tranquillity. Nothing that Mephistopheles can offer will ever provide him with lasting satisfaction. The consequences of this attitude for Faust's afterlife — so important in earlier descriptions of the pact — are deliberately ignored (1660).

How much, if any, of this goes into the unseen pact cannot be determined (Hucke, 165–66). But a number of further incidents suggest that, here again, Goethe was not motivated to make Mephistopheles pursue his traditional aims with any consistency. A devil who dares to rear his head in the age of Enlightenment must remain something of a clown, especially when aware of his limitations, as this one is (1641); and the inconsistencies are sanctioned by the source material. Thus we find Mephistopheles, as soon as the deal is done, encouraging his reluctant prey to enjoy himself (1764), only to change tack unexpectedly and pour scorn on his suddenly awakened resolve to "sample the highs and lows of life" (1770–80). Their roles are imperceptibly reversed. Faust now craves a life of wild debauchery, Mephistopheles counsels restraint. Needless to say, when Faust does ask for time to stand still (3194), indeed, to repeat itself (2599), something he explicitly vowed never to do (1699–1702), Mephistopheles does not bother to step forward and claim his reward.

In what has been said about the author's reluctance to accept the dichotomous opposition of good and evil we have the beginnings of an explanation for Mephisto's ambiguity. Faust has been seeing things from an all-too-human perspective. As the Earth Spirit reminded him, he was insensitive to the connections between despair and delight, between sensual pleasure and spiritual achievement. Mephistopheles has close links with the Earth Spirit in Faust's mind (3217–19), and it has been argued that he gradually came to supersede the Earth Spirit when Goethe revised his text in the 1790s (Mason, 110–78). Part of his role is to provide an interface between the oppositions to which that "great" Spirit made reference. In the roles of sophist and freethinker, no less then when acting the gentleman, conjuror and buffoon, he points to options and interesting possibilities rather than to certainties.

For this reason alone, it would be idle to speculate, as many have done, whether or not the meeting with Margarete (the "Gretchen" of the later scenes) is deliberately contrived by him or a product of chance that reduces the devil's hold over Faust. Contemporary critics incline to the view that the encounter was not fortuitous (Schöne, in FA 7.2, 288). Mephistopheles encourages and discourages the ensuing courtship by turns, aware that Faust needs no devil to engineer the girl's degradation. He comes into his own as a go-between, a facilitator and spin-doctor. By his own admission unused to the ways of the world (2058), his victim must accept instruction in power dressing (1535–43) and drug-taking (2519–21) before being let loose on the streets. Faust's progress in wooing Gretchen is watched over, useful advice is proffered (2648–52; 2674), and his little triumphs with the girl trigger pride and joy in the cold heart of the Fiend (3543). The word "spy" (3521) provides a convenient label for his reactive role as a self-gratifying voyeur (Bennett, 83–111).

The Witches' Sabbath

The high point in the devil's calendar is the Witches' Sabbath, when Hell is let loose on earth for one night of unbridled revelry. Faust is guided towards Mount Brocken, a traditional haunt of sorcerers and spooks, for the festival of St. Walpurga's Night (*Walpurgisnacht*). An epiphany of wickedness may be anticipated here. Yet when Goethe came to write the definitive version of his Walpurgis Night scene, a change of plan occurred. Much of the vigor of his attacks on the seductive power of money and sex, already committed to paper in draft form, had dispersed, and Faust and Mephistopheles never get close to Satan. There are a few lingering hints that they are pressing forward towards the hub of these infernal operations (4116–17), but the centre is not attained. Paradoxically, Mephistopheles seems intent on frustrating Faust's ambition to participate:

FAUST.   Doch droben möcht' ich lieber sein!
                Schon seh' ich Glut und Wirbelrauch.
                Dort strömt die Menge zu dem Bösen;
                Da muß sich manches Rätsel lösen.

MEPHISTOPHELES. Doch manches Rätsel knüpft sich auch.
                Laß du die große Welt nur sausen,
                Wir wollen hier im Stillen hausen.

                                                (4037–43)

Nowhere in the entire play does Mephistopheles betray his traditional ideals more conspicuously than here, where there is a chance to ascend effortlessly towards the very presence of the Evil One. Instead of confronting Satan, Faust gets no further than a group of miserable old had-beens grouped around the embers of a dying camp-fire, a free-market witch (Trödelhexe) and some dubious dancers. There follows a brief, harrowing vision of his beloved (4183–205), and the intermezzo

"Walpurgisnachtstraum," which is satirical in its import, but may have little direct connection with the story of Faust.

Although we know approximately what Goethe omitted, there are various opinions as to why he did so. Fragments of a perverse "Sermon on the Mount" have survived, delivered by Satan to his new recruits. The fragmentary leftovers ("paralipomena") are omitted from most editions and translations (for an expurgated, and for a complete, version of the extant material, see WA 1.14, 296–311 and FA 7.1, 552–59). One of the satanic "beatitudes" (addressed to the males in his audience) will suffice to sum up the devil's reliance on gold and sex:

> *Satan rechts gewendet.*
> Euch giebt es zwey Dinge
> So herrlich und groß
> Das glänzende Gold
> Und der weibliche Schoos.
> Das eine verschaffet
> Das andre verschlingt
> Drum glücklich wer beyde
> Zusammen erringt.
>
> (WA 1.14, 306)

Goethe's reasons for excising this material can only be guessed at; but two considerations will have weighed on his mind. A personal reluctance to encourage belief in the autonomous existence of evil, in a manner propagated by the most bigoted of Hell-fire preachers, must have been one. But another concern will have been his opinion that the true evil in life is found not in what Christians call "sin," but in half-heartedness, shallow mediocrity, and untalented dilettantism. For this reason, the Brocken is populated not by demons and sinners familiar from Christian iconography, but by samples of old-fashioned, reactive or half-baked values: military men, upstarts, court favorites, fawning ministers of state, best-selling authors, and other museum-pieces of self-righteousness and subservience. Many of these may be read as lampoons of the poet's contemporaries (Morris, 696–700). The witches' world is decidedly "royalist" (*monarchisch*) in outlook, as Goethe observed to Eckermann (21 February 1831). It represents a pre-revolutionary devotion to the Establishment. This could be another reason for Mephisto's failure to accompany Faust into the presence of a devil who recognises that the world is held together, not by kings and princes, but by greed and lust. It is hard to disagree with Michelsen's view that the self-styled "Geist des Widerspruchs" (4030) is a master of self-contradiction (Michelsen, 247). By and by, Mephistopheles is manoeuvred into a defence of the status quo, as happens when he fails to accede to Faust's wishes (4042–43), and then himself "auf einmal sehr alt erscheint" (4092, stage direction).

Albrecht Schöne and other critics regret the removal of the "Black Mass" from the final version of *Faust*, claiming that references elsewhere in the play to gold, and to the witch's potion, are rendered less meaningful in the absence of this "key" scene. Even the Prologue in Heaven can benefit from being read in the context of the deleted "Satan Scene," the more so as parts of the two scenes were originally written on the same folio sheet. The frenetic, hysterical goings-on on the Brocken anticipate aspects of Gretchen's trial on charges of infanticide and, most probably, witchcraft (Schöne 1982, 163–64, 177–95, 205–30). But what remains of the Walpurgis theme suffices as an indication of the cultural environment of Gretchen, whose mother and friends are, as far as we can deduce from the scenes in which they appear or are alluded to, subject to intense forms of medieval superstition and bigotry (Fairley, 66–86). Such is Mephisto's particular province. Its dimensions are so clearly revealed in the history of the young girl's rejection by her greedy, self-righteous companions (represented by the terrifying but unseen presence of her mother no less than by Marthe, Lieschen, and Valentin) that the explicit sermon of a satanic overlord is redundant in the completed work.

Mephistopheles in Classical Antiquity

Mephisto's association with role-play and change is yet more pronounced in Part Two. Here we find him adopting the masks of astrologer, miser, inventor of paper currency in Act 1, before transforming himself more radically into a female Phorcyad in his subsequent travels through classical antiquity. He now appears to detach himself more definitively from Faust than he had in earlier parts of the drama. Yet it is important to note that his association with Faust continues, even when they are separated from one another and engaged in seemingly unrelated activities.

Mephistopheles appeared in Part One, sporadically, as the physical embodiment of threadbare attitudes and vices characteristic of a northern European, Germanic-Christian world. He specialized in the negative dimension of knowledge (sophistry), of wealth (theft), and of sensuality (seduction). Only occasionally was Faust able to stand back and express a reluctance to commit various kinds of crime and an awareness of a positive element in Gretchen's devotion. In Part Two, when Faust embarks on a voyage of discovery that takes him back in time to the roots of classical antiquity and to a meeting with Helen of

Troy, Mephistopheles again functions as a negative alter ego to his companion in an altered context.

The first major development for which he assumes responsibility is the "invention" of paper money (6119–30). Opinions vary as to whether this marks a return to a grandiose, and positive "Faustian" project, or another diabolical temptation (FA 7.2, 455–57). The words with which he recommends this innovation to the Emperor are seductive and the virtues of paper money remain suspect. Its value and purpose are to circumvent traditional financial instruments, such as bartering, in favour of new trading derivatives that bring rapid results, such as the public auction (6125). Here we have an early indication of the role that Mephistopheles will adopt in the "große Welt" of Part Two, where he regularly supports the questionable side of technological progress and social engineering. A comprehensive investigation of the negative, mercantile aspects of the world that unfolds in Part Two is provided by Schlaffer (1981).

The attempt to generate the images of Helen and Paris by magical means fits in with a fast-track approach to the absorption of cultural data. In the unproductive environment of the Emperor's court, peopled by shadowy dandies, courtesans and hangers-on, Faust is persuaded to demonstrate the shades of the ancient paragons of beauty to an inquisitive crowd of voyeurs. Mephistopheles is involved behind the scenes, as the "prompter" (6399, stage direction) who puts words into the mouth of the astrologer. No one at court is prepared to learn about antiquity by diligent self-application; people want a spectacle, a happening, and they want it without further ado. This is Mephisto's speciality: he produces quick fixes, fraudulent options, and phantasmagorical solutions to the perennial pursuit of knowledge, beauty, and financial stability. The seemingly sublime figures he generates are the products of a virtual reality. Their insubstantiality is signalled explicitly by the "explosion" (stage direction preceding 6563) that occurs when the viewer attempts to make actual physical contact with one of the moving images.

No sooner is the Emperor's court left behind than the focus shifts to the stagnant late mediaeval world from which Faust had previously struggled to escape. But it is a world already racked by a longing for a better understanding of life-enhancing harmony and of how to salvage or recreate the legacy of antiquity, an unresolved problem that had both political and artistic ramifications in Goethe's age. Here, it seems that Mephisto's powers will finally be shown to be limited. The synthetic man, Homunculus, a product of some diabolical cloning process, does not fit in with the sombre, Mephistophelian view of the world,

but himself longs for liberation and for a natural union with the re-
splendent Galatea, which he eventually achieves unaided by Mephistopheles. But the devil is not inactive in the Arcadian world of
harmony that unfolds in the third act of Part Two. He is not a complete stranger to beauty (8912). He adopts a female role, that of Phorcyas, the ugly sister and co-member of the three Graiae (the "grey
ones") who preside over human destiny.

Act 3 depicts Faust's pursuit of Helen, the epitome of feminine
loveliness; and Mephistopheles cannot appear in her presence as a post-
classical, Nordic phenomenon. When he becomes Phorcyas, he sheds
his guise more completely than anywhere else in the play, aligning his
gender with Helen's, and laying aside his "evil" qualities in exchange
for a mask of utter ugliness. It was Goethe's view that classical antiquity
was indifferent to evil in the Christian sense, but instead venerated
beauty as the supreme virtue. Phorcyas can therefore be imagined as
continuing the Mephistophelian mission of negativity on a classical
plane by embodying an array of aesthetically reprehensible qualities.

It is frequently assumed that apart from appearing as the uncouth
antithesis of Helen of Troy, Phorcyas's role is severely limited. The import of Act 3 is taken to lie in Faust's union with the timeless nonpareil
of beauty and in his consequent self-delivery from the restrictive world
which he had inhabited in Part One. Yet his attempts to achieve lasting
harmony come to nought. Helen herself decides that a synthesis of
happiness and beauty cannot be permanent (9940). Despite its promise
of fulfilment, Act 3 again results in failure. Phorcyas is given, if not the
last word, then at least the ultimate non-verbal commentary on the renewed thwarting of Faust. She rises to a gigantic height before remov-
ing her mask, veil, and stilts, and revealing her true identity. This,
Goethe adds in a sly metatextual aside, will suffice as a commentary on
the preceding act, should any such commentary be required. The indications are that Mephistopheles/Phorcyas was no less involved here
than in the preceding scenes. Hence the dissolution of the Arcadian
idyll, the failure of Faust to establish a permanent liaison with the antique heroine, the collapse of his daringly engineered synthesis of ancient and modern art. Even the Greek ideal is shot through with the
ambivalence and instability that we have come to associate with Mephisto's empire.

Mephistopheles in Modernity

The reception accorded to Mephistopheles by readers, critics and
scholars has been subject to surprising fluctuations over the years. The
initial response was enthusiastic. Madame de Staël was one of his first

admirers, and in *De l'Allemagne* (1810), her celebrated book on German culture, she waxed enthusiastic not only about his qualities but also about the function she imputed to him: "The devil is the hero of the piece" (Staël II, 177). The first productions, staged in several German theaters to honor the poet on his eightieth birthday, were interrupted by the loud applause of students who responded with cheers to Mephisto's caustic comments about the greed of the Church and the ineptitude of politicians. Repeatedly, these early productions had to be censored.

The powerful and yet ambivalent symbol of self-determination appealed to a Romantic generation intent on achieving progress on a broad range of fronts. But the Romantics soon had their day, and later critics, themselves restricted by *Gründerzeit* and other "Establishment" parameters, attempted to render Mephisto's role consistent with an ethos of restless striving in the face of temptation. In this context, Mephistopheles figured as the representative of evil, however much this may have run counter to Goethe's artistic intentions and to his publicly professed creed. He was seen, by turn, as a provider of temptations which the ever-restless Faust managed to overcome, or as epitomizing Faust's own ruthless and selfish qualities, which he simultaneously nurtures and exemplifies. Two representative examples must suffice: Rickert's positivistic approach was informed by hopes of recovery from the humiliation sustained by Germany in the First World War, Böhm's cautionary reading by concern that Germany had over-reached herself by embracing the flattering image of her "Faustian" destiny. The involvement of Faust and Mephistopheles in a process of ethnic cleansing, albeit under the cloak of public usefulness (*Faust II*, Act 5), points back to the "cultural imperialism" of the past (Schlaffer, 121) as well as forward to the Holocaust and beyond.

Goethe's intention was not to reawaken interest in the magical spooks and delusions that previous, benighted generations may have been deluded into taking at face value. The often confusing juxtapositions of supposedly "supernatural" and "all-too-human" elements serve a different purpose: that of recording the high points and plumbing the depths of human nature in so far as this can be achieved through the enhancing but distorting mirror of poetry. Mephisto's apparent preoccupation with envy, deceit, and deviousness conceals an ability to give sharper definition to Faust's qualities through negation, critique and parody. This he does, from the moment of their first encounter until the bell finally tolls for Faust in Part Two, regularly evincing a strongly progressive streak, as Karl Marx recognised in frequent quotations and allusions (Prawer, 23–63). His lasting legacy is to have given inspiration to the man/devil encounters in world literature (most notably, in Feodor Dostoyevsky's *The Brothers Karamazov*, Thomas Mann's *Doctor Faustus*, and Mikhail Bulgakov's *The Master and Margarita*).

The emblematic function of Mephistopheles has had a consequence that reflects the preoccupations of his Lutheran creator in a remarkable way. These literary representations dispose us to associate great wickedness with great intelligence. Just as Faustus is drawn to evil through scholarship, by his restless dissatisfaction with an epistemology he has already mastered, the great evil-doers of this century tend to be portrayed as hyper-intelligent. Serial killers like John Doe (*Seven*), power-crazy madmen like Hugo Drax and Ernst Stavro Blofeld in James Bond movies, hubristic Nazi henchmen such as Hermann Karnau in Marcel Beyer's *Flughunde* or Amon Goeth in *Schindler's List* are Mephistophelian clones by dint of their sophisticated brainpower. This literary and cinematic cliché has produced a powerful association in the public mind between knowledge and evil, which lives on in public protests against scientific research, as exemplified by genetic engineering. It might be salutary to remember that the overwhelming majority of apprehended serial killers (Fritz Haarmann, Peter Sutcliffe), no less than the National Socialist leadership, were not distinguished by exceptional levels of intellect. Their destructive obsessions had less to do with a surfeit of academic scholarship than with a penchant for *unreflecting* brutality.

From among the array of interpretations that Mephistopheles has received over two centuries of criticism, I shall conclude by examining two examples which proceed from concerns germane to the current generation: gender and progress.

A recent paper by Silke Falkner puts forward the startling opinion that Faust's salvation is owed, in part at least, to Mephisto's surrender to homosexual desire. The conventional view of the burial scene, in which Mephistopheles shows physical interest in a group of male angels, is that it serves to emphasize his perversion (Rickert, 470) while providing Faust's immortal spirit with a chance to make an escape. Falkner puts a new interpretation on this scene by showing that Mephistopheles has always remained surprisingly coy and generally restrained in his sexual exploits. A few ribald jokes and longing glances are all he permits himself, until the penultimate scene. Here, he belatedly experiences the full force of love and is consumed by a fire more potent than the flames of Hell (11753–55). It is his first experience of love (11783), and it is homoerotic in nature. In a technical sense, Faust is saved because Mephistopheles has succumbed to love in this form, when he should be devoting his energies to ensnaring Faust's soul. Since it was the Lord's plan to save Faust, Mephisto's feelings are not, as Rickert and many others maintain, a perversion, but an unalienable part of the divine plan, a gift of God, no less. Falkner concludes from this, somewhat grandiosely, that by "allowing Mephisto an opportunity for salvation via homosexual love, Goethe has redeemed homosexuality not only for his contemporaries but for readers of all generations" (Falkner, 155). Faust's burial remains a controversial scene, in which Mephistopheles is perhaps doing no more than returning to his old attacks on the Church, which tolerates misrepresentations of asexual angels in human effigy and thus endows pure spirits with a specifically male sexual identity. Sodomy was numbered among the qualities with which the devil tempts humankind and was frequently cited as a feature of satanic cults (Schöne, 129–31, esp. notes 42 and 47). But Falkner's views do draw attention to a crucial element in Goethe's depiction of the devil: that his all-too-human traits place him firmly within our world, whose qualities he must reflect to the widest extent that can be achieved. That these qualities are all potentially productive is a major contention of the playwright.

The question of Mephisto's attitude to time has recently been much debated. Peter Matussek speaks for many when he portrays Faust as suspended between the Lord's abhorrence of stagnation and the devil's inconstant, mindless commitment to speed (Matussek, 381). The gifts he provides for his master lose their value as they become "exchangeable objects" (Keller, 307). For an up-to-the-minute response to the way in which Mephistopheles exerts his influence over Faust, we turn, in conclusion, to a publication commemorating the 250th anniversary of the poet's birth in August 1999. Manfred Osten unravels the satanic import of the tempter's mission thus: to speed up Faust's journey through life, to accelerate his experiences, thereby rendering them fragmentary and shallow. The yoke to which Faust submits is speed, considered by Goethe to be "das größte Unheil unserer Zeit," for which he combined *volocitas* and *Lucifer* to coin the term *velociferisch* (WA 1.42/ii, 171). Faust's initial desire to know more than he ought is symptomatic of the modern strategy of accumulating greater quantities of knowledge than our intellect can handle. His subsequent race through life, involving flight, short-term solutions to perennial, intractable problems, paper money and fleeting entertainment, reveal a sinister presence behind the scenes: Mephistopheles as Lord of the global village, master of virtual reality. In this reading, we are all victims of his stratagems; a fact highlighted by those modern Germans who, with Sten Nadolny and Günter Grass, advocate "Langsamkeit" as the most apposite response to today's obsessions with speed: Nadolny's novel *Die Entdeckung der Langsamkeit* was well received on its appearance in

1983, while Grass has recently suggested that the study of *Langsamkeit* might be incorporated into school curricula (see "Der lernende Lehrer" in *Die Zeit*, 21/1999). The magic of Mephistopheles is revealed to be an acceleration of time and motion, as his predecessor patiently explains to the astonished Duke of Vanholt in Marlowe's *Tragical History*. The fresh grapes that the Duchess was able to enjoy in mid-winter were not generated by magic but flown in from overseas "by means of a swift spirit that I have, I had them brought hither, as ye see" (*Doctor Faustus* 11: 22–23). The results are inevitably short-lived. The lost comedies of Terence and Plautus, which the doctor claimed he could restore, would only last for a few hours before disappearing again (Hucke, 19–20). There could be no more apt deconstruction of Mephisthophelian magic than as a relentless, unreflective obsession with haste, nor any more compelling evidence of its equal relevance to past and present.

Works Cited

Baron, Frank. *Faustus on Trial: The Origins of Johann Spies's "Historia" in an Age of Witch Hunting*. Tübingen: Niemeyer, 1992.

Bennett, Benjamin. *Goethe's Theory of Poetry. Faust and the Regeneration of Language*. Ithaca: Cornell UP, 1986.

Böhm, Wilhelm. *Goethes Faust in neuer Deutung*, Cologne: Seemann, 1949.

Brecht, Bertolt. "Das moderne Theater ist das epische Theater. Anmerkungen zur Oper *Aufstieg und Fall der Stadt Mahagonny*," in: Bertolt Brecht, *Schriften zum Theater: Über eine nicht-aristotelische Dramatik*. Frankfurt: Suhrkamp, 1969. 7–28.

Brown, Jane K. *Goethe's* Faust: *The German Tragedy*. Ithaca: Cornell UP, 1986.

Butler, E. M. *The Myth of the Magus*. Cambridge: Cambridge UP, 1948.

Colpe, Carsten. "Aus der Geschichte des Teufels im Abendland." In Carsten Colpe and Wilhelm Schmidt-Biggemann, eds., *Das Böse: Eine historische Phänomenologie des Unerklärlichen*. Frankfurt: Suhrkamp, 1993. 63–89.

Durrani, Osman. *Faust and the Bible: A Study of Goethe's use of Scriptural Allusions and Christian Religious Motifs in* Faust I *and* II. Berne: Lang, 1976.

Fairley, Barker. *Goethe's Faust: Six Essays*. Oxford: Clarendon, 1953.

Falkner, Silke R. "'Love only succors / Those who can love': Mephisto's Desiring Gaze in Goethe's *Faust*." In Christoph Lorey and John L. Plews, eds., *Queering the Canon: Defying Sights in German Literature and Culture*. Columbia, S.C.: Camden House, 1998. 142–58.

Gaier, Ulrich. *Goethe's Faust-Dichtungen: Ein Kommentar. Band I: Urfaust.* Stuttgart: Reclam, 1989.

Hick, John. *Evil and the God of Love.* London: Macmillan, 1966.

Hucke, Karl-Heinz. *Figuren der Unruhe: Faustdichtungen.* Tübingen: Niemeyer, 1992.

Keller, Werner. "Faust. Eine Tragödie." In Walter Hinderer, ed., *Goethes Dramen.* Stuttgart: Reclam, 1992. 258–329.

Mahal, Günther. *Faust: Die Spuren eines geheimnisvollen Lebens.* Reinbek bei Hamburg: Rowohlt, 1995.

Marlowe, Christopher. *Doctor Faustus.* Ed. Roma Gill. London: Black, 1989.

Mason, Eudo C. *Goethe's Faust: Its Genesis and Purport.* Berkeley: U of California P, 1967.

Matussek, Peter. "Faust I." In *Goethe-Handbuch. Band 2: Dramen.* Ed. Theo Buck. Stuttgart: Metzler, 1997. 352–90.

Michelsen, Peter. "Mephistos 'eigentliches Element.' Vom Bösen in Goethe's 'Faust.'" In Carsten Colpe and Wilhelm Schmidt-Biggemann, eds., *Das Böse: Eine historische Phänomenologie des Unerklärlichen.* Frankfurt: Suhrkamp, 1993. 229–55.

Morris, Max. "Die Walpurgisnacht." *Euphorion* 6 (1899). 683–716.

Oberman, Heiko A. *Luther: Mensch zwischen Gott und Teufel.* Berlin: Severin und Siedler, 1983.

Osten, Manfred. "Die beschleunigte Zeit. 'Alles veloziferisch' — Anmerkungen zur Modernität Goethes." In *Die Zeit*, 26 August 1999 (35/1999). 33–34.

Prawer, Siegbert. "Mephisto and Old Nick. Refractions of Goethe in the Writings of Karl Marx." *Publications of the English Goethe Society* 45 (1974–75). 23–63.

Requadt, Paul. *Goethe's "Faust I": Leitmotivik und Architektur.* Munich: Fink, 1972.

Roskoff, Gustav. *Geschichte des Teufels.* 2 vols. Leipzig: Brockhaus, 1869.

Rickert, Heinrich. *Goethe's Faust: Die dramatische Einheit der Dichtung.* Tübingen: Mohr, 1932.

Roos, Keith L. *The Devil in 16th Century German Literature: The Teufelsbücher.* Berne: Lang, 1972.

Russell, Jeffrey Burton. *Witchcraft in the Middle Ages.* Ithaca: Cornell UP, 1972.

———. *The Life of Lucifer: The Devil in the Middle Ages.* Ithaca: Cornell UP, 1984.

————. *Mephistopheles: The Devil in the Modern World*. Ithaca: Cornell UP, 1986.

Schlaffer, Heinz. *Faust Zweiter Teil: Die Allegorie des 19. Jahrhunderts*. Stuttgart: Metzler, 1981.

Schöne, Albrecht. *Götterzeichen, Liebeszauber, Satanskult: Neue Einblicke in alte Goethetexte*. Munich: Beck, 1982.

————, ed. *Goethe: Faust*. Volume I: Texte; Volume II: Kommentare. Frankfurt: Deutscher Klassiker Verlag, 1994. [FA 7.1 and 7.2]

Seidlin, Oskar. "Das Etwas und das Nichts. Versuch zur Neu-Interpretation einer Faust-Stelle." *Germanic Review* 19 (1944). 170–75.

Staël-Holstein, Germaine de. *De l'Allemagne*. 3 vols. London: Murray, 1813.

White, Ann. *Names and Nomenclature in Goethe's "Faust."* London: Institute of Germanic Studies, 1980.

Woods, Barbara. "The Devil in Dog Form." Dissertation, U of California, 1955.

Zabka, Thomas. "Dialectik des Bösen: Warum es in Goethes 'Walpurgisnacht' keinen Satan gibt." *Deutsche Vierteljahrsschrift für Literaturwissenschaft und Geistesgeschichte* 72 (1998). 201–206.

Figurations of the Feminine in Goethe's *Faust*

Ellis Dye

T HE LAST WORDS of Goethe's *Faust*, sung by a Chorus mysticus, are: "Das Ewig-Weibliche / Zieht uns hinan." These words raise many questions: Is there such an essence as "das Ewig-Weibliche"? If so, what is it? Who can apprehend it, and in what way — a man through observation or a woman through self-reflection, or perhaps someone of either sex, by any of a variety of imaginative or introspective techniques? Must it be made visible by some example such as Iphigenie's "reine Menschlichkeit"? What does the verb "hinanziehen" mean and what is its link with its subject? Does the Eternal Womanly necessarily, as a manifestation of its essence, draw us "hinan" (and does "hinan" imply "onward" as well as "upward")? Or does it merely attract or "pull" accidentally from time to time, depending on circumstances? Is it capable of pulling us *downward*, as the mermaid pulls the fisherman down into her deep heaven in the ballad "Der Fischer? "Es ist unglaublich, wie der Umgang der Weiber herabzieht," said Goethe in a moment of pique over the influence of Caroline Jagemann on the Weimar theatre (in a conversation with Kanzler von Müller of 14 December 1808). Henriette Herwig has lately returned the favor with her title "Das ewig *Männliche* zieht uns hinab" (my emphasis).

Why does the Eternal Feminine pull instead of push? (The fisherman's wife of the fairy tale pushes; Adelheid von Walldorf in *Götz von Berlichingen* both pulls *and* pushes.) Does "das Ewig-Weibliche" pull from the outside like a magnet or does it mark the unfolding of an immanent form? Can members of either sex and all sexual orientations freely strive to emulate "das Ewig-Weibliche"? Or is it not a matter of emulation but only one of attraction, that is, do we desire it in the way that King Thoas desires Iphigenie (his political need for a son and successor aside)? The words of the Mater gloriosa to Margarete in the scene "Bergschluchten," "wenn er dich ahnet, folgt er nach" would allow either possibility.

On whom does "das Ewig-Weibliche" exert its influence — on everybody, just on men (Arens 1989, 1052), or just on the members of the chorus? Is gender not the issue, but only an example of the polarity of complementary "Grundverhaltensweisen" of human beings (Schöne, 817)? Should we read "uns" as *not* referring to the members of the chorus, since organized singers only give voice to someone else's words? Who is the author of these words, and why did he or she compose them? Although composed in another time and place, are they a fitting response to the situation in which they are sung, and in that context "motivated" anyway? Might "uns" refer only to a small group of initiates — not necessarily men or members of the chorus, but just those persons who are peculiarly receptive to the allure of "das Ewig-Weibliche" or who are within its reach by virtue of having unceasingly "striven?" What is the importance of the fact that "we" don't draw ourselves "hinan," but are borne onward or upward by an agency that is not ourselves? What is the role of language in all of these paradigms, including the broad term "weiblich," which encompasses both "womanly" and "feminine" in English?

It may be possible to discern in *Faust* a gender-specific implied consciousness or "author's voice" — according to such evidence as the roles and behavior of the *dramatis personae*, the implied audience, and the way in which the audience is addressed. "One can read [. . .] *Faust* as the projection of a male point of view of the world in which the male's ceaseless striving and erring is sanctioned by divine authority" (Schweitzer, 136). According to Arens, the world of *Faust* is "[eine] wesentlich männliche Welt" (1989, 1052). This view would be meaningful, however, only if we knew what the nature of male or female consciousness is, and if we knew whether Arens means that *Faust depicts* a masculine world or whether it *speaks from* or *to* a masculine world. We no longer assume that there is such an essence as the masculine or feminine *per se*. Rather, it is widely agreed that gender is constructed and largely a matter of culture — constructed differently at different times and in different places. Even women writers have employed and continue to employ "masculine" patterns of thought. How might the facts of socialization interface with the fact that life and a world are given to all of us, which implies not only that there is in all of us a receptivity and openness that is usually associated with the feminine but that we are defined by reception? Are not all creatures existentially feminine — receivers or receptacles of being?

The task of appreciating the feminine in *Faust* is all the more difficult and interesting not only because, like most dramas, it has no denominated narrator or even one otherwise identified by gender, but also because of Goethe's complex, ambiguous estimation and manipulation of the meaning of gender differences throughout his writings — affected and enriched, perhaps, by his own fragile and ambiguous sexuality. Whether or not one gives any credence to the ill-supported claim of Hugo Pruys's meretricious book that Goethe was a closet homosexual or to Eissler's primitive psychoanalytic portrait of him as sexually conflicted and retarded, such hermaphroditic figures as Homunculus, Knabe Lenker, Euphorion, and even Mephistopheles (8029) in *Faust* alone, along with Mignon, Therese, and the beautiful Amazon — even Mariane in her officer's uniform — in *Wilhelm Meisters Lehrjahre* make up a diverse, problematic display of androgyny, not to mention the ways in which Wilhelm Meister and Eduard in *Die Wahlverwandtschaften* are implicitly feminized (for example, in the words, "Empfänglich, wie er war," which are applied verbatim both to Eduard and to Wilhelm [HA 6, 250; HA 8, 229]). William Larrett has discovered a symbol of wholeness in the androgynous figures in the *Lehrjahre*, an idea given support by our knowledge of Goethe's fascination with alchemy and its pictorial representations of the "tincture" or the philosophers' stone as a hermaphrodite and symbol of "geeinte Zwienatur" as well as by the plenitude implicit in every "polarity," including the opposition between Faust's longing and insufficiency, and the "Fülle" he associates with Gretchen (2693–94). Schiller — who thought himself a manlier man than Goethe — wrote to Christian Gottfried Körner on 2 February 1789: "Ich betrachte ihn wie eine stolze Prüde, der man ein Kind machen muß, um sie vor der Welt zu demüthigen." (Writing to Goethe on 18 November 1796, Schiller reversed the sexual metaphor in reporting to Goethe the injury caused by the *Xenien* to his good name in Copenhagen: "Mir wird bei allen Urteilen dieser Art [. . .] die miserable Rolle des Verführten zuteil, Sie haben doch noch den Trost des Verführers.") When they became better acquainted, Schiller urged Goethe to provide more philosophical structure for the "Geburten" of his imagination, in particular *Wilhelm Meisters Lehrjahre*. Goethe, however, kept his own counsel and sent Book 8 to the publisher Unger without letting Schiller see revised copy. Although no author's work is the unmediated expression of his or her nature or situation, Goethe's life invites consideration as a background for his virtuosic treatment of gender and the ambiguities of gender. Biography is never irrelevant.

"Wenn ein Gott sich erst sechs Tage plagt, / Und selbst am Ende Bravo sagt, / Da muß es was Gescheites werden" (2441–43), concedes Mephistopheles in response to Faust's enthusiasm for the female figure in the magic mirror in "Hexenküche." Margarete, to whom Faust is then led, is the most appealing representative of the feminine in the drama and Goethe's primary innovation in the history of the *Faust* theme. Many readers and especially the adapters of Goethe's play for opera — above all, Gounod — have tended to view her as its heroine, and Faust as a mere accessory of her tragedy. The "perfect sacrificial victim," Margarete is characterized by "a simplicity and innocence that do not know their own holy worth, and a meekness and lowliness that are the highest gifts of a lovingly bountiful Nature" (Burke, 145 and 147). Her youth magnifies the tragedy of her victimhood. Matussek finds that nobody has yet shown why Margarete's fate deserves to be called "tragic," quoting Nietzsche's ridicule of the idea that there is any tragedy in the seduction of "eine kleine Nähterin" by "ein grosser Gelehrter aller vier Fakultäten," who — such is the scholar's impotence — could not have succeeded without the assistance of the devil (377). Gretchen is "über vierzehn Jahr doch alt" (2627), older than Juliet and certifiably nubile, but without experience that would enable her to see "was er an mir find't" (3216). She is also honest (it distresses her to deceive her mother), sensitive (she abhors Mephistopheles [3469–99]), independent of mind ("Doch — alles, was dazu mich trieb, / Gott! war so gut! ach war so lieb!" [3585–86]), and unsentimentally maternal as she cares for her baby sister during the long convalescence of her mother. "It is a touching story of her life as a surrogate mother, a time of work-roughened hands, nights of broken sleep, nursing a sick child, soothing a fretful one, and — a fine naturalistic touch — rising early to do the inevitable laundry. There is little romanticism in her account of a girlhood overburdened by maternal responsibility, but it is clear that the hard months of caring for the child were the richest of her otherwise dreary life" (Guenther, 79–80).

In the quality of maternity Margarete possesses the most estimable attribute of women in Goethe's writings. Werther's Lotte is also introduced as the mother to her younger siblings, and Ottilie, a "scheinbare Mutter" is so adorable to the young architect in *Die Wahlverwandtschaften* that he transforms her, in his mind and in the creche tableau he sets up as her background and context, into the mother of God (HA 6, 403). It was strong affection for the maternal that inspired the young Goethe's self-anointing invocation to the "Genius unsers Vaterlands" to let a German youth go forth and find a maiden, "the second mother of her family," who would give truth and living beauty to his songs (MA 1.2, 350–51). That Margarete is only a "second mother" when Faust meets her is noteworthy because the surrogate mothers in Goethe are obvious stand-ins for the Virgin Mary, because the loss of her virginity is a crucial factor in Gretchen's tragedy, and because allegory, the dominant mode of signification in *Faust*, implicitly valorizes representation in the form of surrogateness (while symbolism is a paradox in which uniqueness and representation coincide). It is as a Madonna that the artist's beloved in "Künstlers Morgenlied" and that the woman living with her off-stage husband in a hut made of stones from an ancient temple of Venus of the free-rhythmic "Der Wandrer" are perceived and saluted: "Gott segne dich, junge Frau, / Und den säugenden Knaben / An deiner Brust!" In the inset novella "Sankt Joseph der Zweite" of *Wilhelm Meisters Wanderjahre*, a new Holy Family, the Madonna in the middle, is presented to the reverent spectator, Wilhelm. Among other embodiments of the maternal in *Faust* are "the Mothers" (see John Williams's chapter in this volume), Galatea, as an image of her own mother, Venus-Aphrodite (8386), Helen, and the Virgin herself, in sadness and in glory. Matussek sees Gretchen as nothing but a sex object to Faust and notes not only that Faust never addresses her by name until she is in prison but that the epithets: "Dirne" (2619), "Geschöpfchen" (2644), "Puppe" (3476) are as impersonal and as diminishing as those employed by Mephistopheles, who calls her an "unschuldig Ding" (2624). Mephistopheles, however, exposes the bravado in Faust's posturing by likening him to "Hans Liederlich" (2628) and a "Franzos" (2645), and Faust goes on to reproach himself for denying Margarete's personhood in the scene "Abend" (2722–24), where her tidy room and the chair in which her grandfather probably dispensed Christmas presents remind him that she has feelings and a history. That he could have been so callous as to ignore this nearly causes him to suffer a crisis of identity: "Armsel'ger Faust! ich kenne dich nicht mehr" (2720).

Margarete is soon aware that what Faust wants of her is sex, yet she is eager to deserve his respect. It is important that the audience both sympathize with this desire and see Faust's attraction to her as neither wholly unworthy nor unreciprocated. It is excessively cynical to say that the goblet which the King in Thule tosses into the sea "ist kostbar auch als Symbol der Treue, der Tugend also, an der Faust es fehlen lassen wird, die er aber vortäuschen muß, um Margaretes Intimität zu erobern" (Matussek, 367). Much is missed if Faust is seen as nothing more than a Lovelace and Margaret as only another case of "verführte Unschuld." Still, Faust does exploit and sacrifice her, however "unavoidably" (3072, 3363). Precisely her self-sacrificing love for him leads to her pregnancy and her real, tragic maternity, as she is driven to distraction by her conscience and the persecution of self-righteous townspeople, murders her child while in the throes of psychosis, and is executed — after a desperate, aimless flight that is grotesquely anticipated

in the song "Es war eine Ratt im Kellernest." Margarete's problem —
not unlike that of Faust himself! — is "Lieb im Leibe," a condition of
the heart, from which no one can flee.

When Matussek observes that Gretchen owes something to
Friederike Brion, whom "G[oethe] liebte [. . .] um ihrer Naivität wil-
len" (355), he concedes that she represents a type. Yet his recom-
mended approach to Gretchen would enact "ein situationsnahes
Nachvollziehen ihrer individuellen Psychodynamik" and show "die Bedeutung beschämender Ereignisse für die Auslösung einer wahnhaften
Persönlichkeitsspaltung" (378). One can say in favor of this individual-
ized, psychological approach that it recognizes Margarete as a person
and does not skate glibly over the personal dimensions of her tragedy.
Nevertheless, Requadt is right: "Da Gretchen nicht eigentlich Indivi-
duum ist, entzieht sie sich letzlich auch der psychologischen Analyse"
(236). In the genre of world theater, to which Jane Brown has convincingly assigned *Faust*, there is not "necessarily much concern with
psychological analysis or even consistency" (Brown 1986, 21; cf. 93).
In his review of Calderón's *Die Tochter in der Luft* in *Über Kunst und
Altertum*, Goethe himself observed "daß menschliche Zustände, Ge-
fühle, Ereignisse in ursprünglicher Natürlichkeit sich nicht [. . .] aufs
Theater bringen lassen, sie müssen schon verarbeitet, zubereitet, subli-
miert sein" (GA 14, 846). This is not to say that a historicized psychology — one aware of its own historicity — would be irrelevant to an
understanding of literature. Literary characters are, after all, fictional
human beings, and should be representable in the language employed
in our efforts to understand real human beings. The problem, perhaps
more with illusionist than with non-illusionist theater, rests in the widespread and abiding supposition that we may gain possession of time-
lessly reliable techniques for understanding individuals. But would
anyone today be enlightened by Ernst Feise's diagnosis of Werther as a
"nervöser Charakter"? Neither can Margarete be fruitfully diagnosed in
the terms of the dominant psychology of the last half-century. Like
other "naive" female characters such as Werther's Lotte or the old
Anne Margret in Brentano's *Geschichte vom braven Kasperl und dem
schönen Annerl*, Margarete is a kind of "noble savage" and the product
of the ideological conflict that made the primitive admirable and naiveté in women endearing.

To acknowledge that Margarete represents a type is not to suggest
that she is less fully "realized" than characters in other literary works.
She is one of the most sympathetic young women in world literature
and her tragedy is one of the most moving. She is more attractive and
more convincing than any of the women in *Wilhelm Meisters Lehr-*

jahre — even than the coquettish but charming Philine. Nor must we diminish Faust's affair with Margarete as being only a dalliance and a stage in *his* biography, for she remains present to the reader as an ideal and icon of exploited and abused womanhood, and returns, exhibiting her abiding significance, at the beginning of Part Two, Act 4 and at the play's end. In telling the story of Margarete, Goethe both expressed indignation at society's cruelty toward unwed mothers — he had direct knowledge of the case of the infanticide Susanna Margaretha Brandt — and confessed his own guilt for having "sacrificed" Friederike Brion, a confession given dramatic form in the series of "faithless lovers": Weislingen, Clavigo, Fernando (in *Stella*), and Faust.

Goethe at the same time employs traditional representations of the feminine, and activates in the reader or spectator a complex, sometimes contradictory range of feelings toward them. While in *Faust* woman is as she is seen and made use of by a man, what is also made available for inspection and criticism is the man himself as a viewer and consumer of the feminine — a connoisseur, judge, and executioner of woman. Goethe's detachment from his male protagonists is evident in the ironic treatment of Wilhelm Meister in the *Lehrjahre* and from Wilhelm as a spectator in his description as "der beschauende Wandrer" in the *Wanderjahre* (HA 8,15). Titles such as "Der Wandrer," "Torquato Tasso," "Faust" (or, for that matter, "Iphigenie auf Tauris") do not so much invite us to adopt the protagonist's point of view — and, in so doing, forget him as we internalize his experience — as make the character available as a subject of contemplation and judgment. Thanks to Stuart Atkins and Jane Brown (18–19, passim), we understand Goethe's use of the traditions of "world theater" and need no longer mistake him for an inept or careless practitioner of neo-Aristotelian tragic theory, striving with incomplete success to make the reader or viewer identify and suffer with his characters.

There is no grid with enough dimensions to chart the variety of figurations of the feminine in *Faust*, whether in moral valence, in real, communicated vitality or any other coordinates. They extend from authentic characters in the play or in plays within the play — *dramatis personae* such as Margarete or Frau Marthe Schwerdtlein or Lieschen or even the flirtatious girls in "Outside the Gates of Town" — to historical, mythological, and legendary figures (the Graces, Fates, Furies and *Gärtnerinnen* in the masque, the prophetess Erichtho, Oreas, Manto the seer, the Sirens, Sphinxes, Lamias, Phorkyads and Cabiri, the Dorids and Nereids, including Galatea, in the *Klassische Walpurgisnacht*, Helena, the penitent women of Act 5). They also extend to visions and characters in dreams (the beautiful woman in the mirror, Leda in Faust's dream); to offstage acquaintances of the characters who appear on stage (Bärbel who is pregnant, forsaken and the subject of Lieschen's gossip; Gretchen's mother). They include, too, personifications in soliloquies ("unendliche Natur," in the scene "Nacht"; "Mutter Nacht" [1351; 8812]), and allegories in multiple telescoped frames; or caricatures who make but one cameo appearance (for instance, the women at the Emperor's court). Helena, Sorge and Eilebeute are all characters in the play (but the first is "round," while the latter two, as allegories, are not even flat, but mere ciphers), whereas Fear, Hope, Victoria and "Geiz" (as Avaritia, she was once female but is now, as "der Geiz," "männlichen Geschlechts" and played in the masquerade by Mephistopheles [5665]) are only allegories in the pageant within the play. In one respect, the Mater dolorosa and the Juno-, Leda- and Helena-like cloud formations (10050) function only as physical props — meaningful *Requisiten*. In another, both the Mater dolorosa and the Mater gloriosa are icons; they embody what they represent. Margarete is both a character and a symbol — of the "mediated Absolute," "the embodiment of transcendence in the world, of the Absolute in nature, of the ideal in the real" (Brown 1986, 90 and 100). One author ranks Gretchen's mother, whom we never see but only hear about, as "the first in a long line of negative feminine figures *in the play*" (Anchor, 30; my emphasis): Jantz lists as negative portrayals of women "the witches in kitchen and on the Brocken, Martha, the "virtuous" Lieschen, Lilith, the ladies at court, the Sirens, Lamias, and Phorkyads, the Trojan girls of the chorus, Eilbeute [*sic*], and others — some of them committed to active evil, a few, like the Sirens, ambiguous, the rest merely limited and negative" (39).

Undeniably, some of the females in *Faust* are admirable and others patently reprehensible, contemptible or unpalatable. However, it is necessary not only to classify the female figures as either positive or negative but to acknowledge such differences in reality or tangibleness as that between the silent, phantom Helena of Act 1 and the Helena of Act 3, who worries about her angry first husband's intentions and then, in a *hieros gamos* with a difference, marries the medieval Faust and bears him a son — although, of course, even the latter is less "real" than either Margarete or Frau Marthe. Helena's son Euphorion, a fiction within several fictional frames, is at once a reincarnation of Boy-Charioteer, a "new" Icarus, and a monument to Lord Byron. Among the grotesque or less appealing females are the earthy and lusty witches of "Hexenküche" and "Walpurgisnacht" (Medusa and Baubo, a personification of the female vulva, who told the mournful Demeter di-

verting jokes) and the classical "witches" in the "Klassische Walpurgisnacht" (sirens, Lamias [7235]). To the numerous "negative" portraits
of women also belong the chorus of Trojan women, the types and allegories of the pageant, the enumerated but nameless women in "Hell
erleuchtete Säle" and "Rittersaal" (naturally, the six lustful ladies who
judge Paris, in a witty reversal of the classical judgment *by* Paris, are not
as critical as are their husbands), the ominous Sorge of Act 5 — and
Frau Marthe Schwerdtlein. One could extract from *Faust* a female
rogues' gallery, but no woman in the play exhibits the culpability, indeed the criminality, of its protagonist. Of all the females in *Faust*, only
Margarete, Marthe, and, less tangibly, Helena and Baucis achieve a
presence that might be thought of as three-dimensional reality, although Lieschen, several witches, many allegorical figures, the captive
Trojan women, Phorkyas, and the Mater gloriosa all have speaking
parts. It is one manifestation of the drama's playfulness that Mephistopheles, as Phorkyas, becomes Helena's foil as the ugliest female of
them all, a transformation sometimes explained as showing that *Faust I*
is concerned with the morally good, while *Faust II* revolves around
what is aesthetically beautiful. This distinction overlooks the Emperor's
political problems in Act 4, Faust's struggle with Sorge, his destruction
of Philemon and Baucis and their visitor, and the *caritas* that is manifested by Margarete and the Mater gloriosa in the final scene, "Bergschluchten."

Consider Frau Marthe Schwerdtlein, whose eager opportunism
contrasts with Gretchen's unselfish innocence. As part of the conventional quartet of a high and a low pairs of lovers, such as occur in several of Shakespeare's plays, Mozart's operas and in Lessing's *Minna von
Barnhelm* (where the witty Franziska and Paul Werner are contrasted as
figures of fun with the charming but serious Minna and the too rigid
Major von Tellheim, and where much of the comedy resides in the fact
that the women are the clever ones and the aggressors), Frau Marthe is
an implement of comic relief and provides a means of bringing Faust
and Gretchen together. As Matussek notes, Faust's dancing with the
young witch and Mephisto's with the old is "eine Kontrastspiegelung,
die ihrerseits die Choreographie der *Garten*-Szene spiegelt" (369). As
the go-between, not unlike Juliet's nurse, who helps Mephisto "couple" Gretchen with Faust, Marthe is a parody on woman as mediatrix
and has even been seen as a succubus for wanting to marry the devil
(Röllike, 68). For this matron — more in need than in heat — any
husband would suffice. She wants desperately to catch a man, and she
imagines this to be the aim of any woman. The limits of her devotion
to her dearly departed first husband are indicated in the couplet "Viel-

leicht ist er gar tot! — O Pein! — / Hätt' ich nur einen Totenschein!"
(2871–72). It is not out of the question that she would give to her
own daughter, if she had one, the same advice that is given by the scur-
rilous mother at the pageant in *Faust II*: "Heute sind die Narren los, /
Liebchen, öffne deinen Schoß, / Bleibt wohl einer hangen" (5196–
98). Her advice to Gretchen about the second box of jewels, "Das muß
Sie nicht der Mutter sagen; / Tät's wieder gleich zur Beichte tragen"
(2879–80), is expressed in frank, un-selfrighteous acceptance of human
weakness and a woman's need to be practical. In a different world, Frau
Marthe would be a different woman, but here, in a sixteenth-century,
provincial European town and in an eighteenth-century comedy, her
husband gone and, now she hears, dead, she must be the harridan that
she is. She is not cynical, however, and, as sexist conventions require,
she is certainly no match for that urbane cynic, Mephistopheles (neither
she nor the witch of "Hexenküche" catches Mephisto's jokes and eva-
sions). Rather, she combines naiveté and a peasant simplicity with a
precarious emotionalism. Her tears on hearing of her dying husband's
alleged plea for forgiveness are sincere (stage direction, 2959), and so is
her reaction to Valentin's bitterness. When he denounces with his dying breath the sister who has disgraced him, Frau Marthe is honestly
shocked: "Befehlt Eure Seele Gott zu Gnaden! / Wollt Ihr noch
Lästrung auf Euch laden?" — which elicits the harsh, self-righteous
epithet, "Du schändlich kupplerisches Weib!" (3764–65, 67).

Granted that Marthe is a foil to Margarete, what do the two have in
common that makes comparison possible? When in *My Fair Lady* Professor Higgins asks, "Why can't a woman be more like a man?" he has
something in mind that women share and that tries a man's patience.
With Frau Marthe in view, we might risk the claim that what this is —
that what unites women across all other boundaries than that of gender — is powerlessness and a paradoxical greater ability, developed in
too frequent submission to the stronger opposite sex, to accept the
givenness of things. Woman's weakness is her strength. In her resilient
practicality, Frau Marthe is not far removed from Gretchen or from
Werther's Lotte, whose equanimity in caring for a dying friend amazes
Werther (HA 6, 83) and who, like the young mother of the children in
Werther's "automatic drawing," can watch the leaves fall, untroubled
by any other thought, or so Werther supposes, than that winter is
coming (HA 6, 17). What the leading females in *Faust* most exhibit,
however, is the power of love.

Helen of Troy, the most beautiful woman ever (8519), has been a
scandal for millennia, and is announced as such in the opening lines in
Act 3 of *Faust II*: "Bewundert viel und viel gescholten, Helena"

(8488). In *Laokoon* (Chapter 21), Lessing notes the inability of verbal art to represent Helen's beauty and finds that Homer wisely showed it *indirectly*, through its effect on the men of Troy. As Faust's paramour, Helen was a primary attraction of the *Wanderbühnen* and the puppet theaters — the heathen *femme fetale* and paragon of "sweet sensuality" that Nietzsche, in *Die Geburt der Tragödie* (1872), holds up as an "exuberant, triumphant" contrast to the "disincarnate spirituality" worshipped by Christians (section 3). Helen is the disreputable and available beauty and the "*Schutzheilige*" of every adulteress and, indeed, any woman with any kind of checkered past, including also the prematurely deflowered Gretchen and all of the penitent women introduced at the end of *Faust*. In the usual Romantic dialectic (for example, in Eichendorff's "Das Marmorbild"), Helen, or one of her effigies, is the antipode to the Virgin Mary (or one of *her* effigies), and contests with her for the soul of the male protagonist (in Wagner's *Tannhäuser* the dying Elisabeth wins out over Venus). In *Faust*, Helena and Margarete complement one another, although they are explicitly linked only at the beginning of Act 4, where the evaporated Helena takes her leave from Faust and "strives" eastward, yielding the field to an image of Gretchen, who, as "Seelenschönheit" rises into the ether, drawing upward with her the best part of Faust's innermost self.

Although she can turn heads and even paralyze with her beauty (6568), Goethe's Helen is not a "Teufels-Liebchen" (6201) or a Medusa, but a persecuted and anxious refugee, unsure of her own history (8874–75) and in danger of being sacrificed by her husband Menelaus and the Greeks (8528–29). Among Goethe's female characters, not the Helen of *Faust*, but Adelheid von Walldorf — a vamp at the court of Bamberg and the opposite of Götz's sister Maria, who is betrothed to Weislingen — comes closest to being a daughter of the traditional chapbook Helen, especially in the first, unpublished version of Goethe's tragedy — the *Geschichte Gottfriedens von Berlichingen mit der eisernen Hand dramatisiert* (1771). Adelheid is condemned to death by a secret court for adultery and for having *sucked* [not *drawn*] her husband and his page into death — "durch geheime verzehrende Mittel zum Tode gesaugt" (HA 4, 517). Although she admonishes her to appeal to the heavenly avenger to accept her death as retribution for her crimes, even her executioner is temporarily in thrall to Adelheid's beauty. Like the hunter sent to dispatch Snow White, he thinks in passing of deceiving his commissioners and sparing her. Or perhaps he is more like Mortimer in Schiller's *Maria Stuart*, who would rescue Mary *for himself*, and who, denied this prize, enjoys a vicarious sexual satisfaction as he imagines the ax slicing through Mary's "blinding white neck" (Act 3, Scene 6) — much as Faust imagines the sword having sliced through the neck of Gretchen in his vision during "Walpurgisnacht" (4203–05). If Frau Marthe's weakness is her strength, Adelheid's strength is her weakness, in that she is unable to control the effect of her own powerful sexuality on the quick excitability of men.

Sacrificing women is the way to restore a broken world. Western culture's "radikale Verteufelung oder Dämonisierung der Frau, des weiblichen Schoßes, der weiblichen Geschlechtlichkeit" (Schwerte, 139) forms a tradition that is redolent of misogyny, making woman — at once the "Devil's gateway" and the "Bride of Christ" (Bloch, 65–91), "niedrig und göttlich, [. . .] Heilige und Hure" (Moog-Grünewald, 254) — both threat and scapegoat for the crimes and misfortunes of men as well as the site of displaced male guilt. This tradition is expressed in the wresting of the souls of witches from the claws of the devil "durch Darangabe des Leibes" in the words of Thomas Mann's loathsome Privatdozent Schleppfuß (*Doktor Faustus*, chapter 13), but the aura of witchcraft hovers even around those not charged with this crime — in German literature, for example, in addition to Adelheid, around Agnes Bernauer, Emilia Galotti — "eine Rose gebrochen, ehe der Sturm sie entblättert" — and Brentano's Lore Lay, who herself begs the bishop to condemn her to a fiery death at the stake. Woyzeck's execution of yet another Marie in Büchner's play and Berg's opera, the self-sacrifice of Klara Anton in Hebbel's *Maria Magdalena* are further tokens of this paradigm. Ciphers of woman as vile sexuality, at once an attraction and an abomination to self-righteous males, are, in a succession of names in "L" and "M," Lulu (in Wedekind's *Die Büchse der Pandora* [1904], G. W. Pabst's movie of the same name, and Alban Berg's opera *Lulu* [1937]), Lola Lola in *Der blaue Engel* (she is "die Künstlerin Fröhlich" in *Professor Unrath*), Lola in *Damn Yankees*, and Lolita in the Nabokov novel — also Lorelei Lee, the Marilyn Monroe character in *Gentlemen Prefer Blondes*, Mary Stuart, Millwood, Marwood, Lady Milford, Margarete and Anna Mahr in Hauptmann's *Einsame Menschen*. Marie Antoinette was demonized as a *femme fatale* in hundreds of caricatures prior to her execution in 1793 (Saint-Armand, passim). Not all of the named females fall victim to the dagger, sword or guillotine, but Margarete in *Faust* is among those who do.

The female characters, deities, and allegories in *Faust* constitute a colorful panoply of signification, but each is also a bearer of a broad, general meaning, which resides not in *what* the feminine or a given female character signifies but *in her function as signifier,* and in the fact that her meaning reflects an implied male consciousness and culture —

in short, that she is a sex object. The male figures in Goethe's play, its protagonist in particular, also function as signifiers, and have been studied even more than have the women, but the implied gender of those addressed informs the meaning of characters of either sex. That being said, what do the woman, the female figures, and the feminine (abstractly considered) *as signifiers* represent in *Faust*?

Harold Jantz, conceding some merit to "the conventional interpretation" of the Eternal-Womanly as "the representation of divine grace and love" (44), expands its meaning to include fertility and creativity while noting that "the original meaning of the word *natura* was birth" (33). The picture can be further broadened to include physicality, eros, domesticity, and divinity; also fluidity, agency, origin and destiny). Yet Jantz considers neither the extent to which the meaning of the feminine derives from its meaning *to a man* — in the first instance, to the protagonist of Goethe's drama — nor the importance of sinfulness and repentance as elements of its meaning. Nor does the appeal to traditional notions of tragedy suffice, according to which Margarete's downfall results from the perversion of her natural motherliness (a reading which also yields a seemingly symmetrical interpretation of the life of Faust as man whose laudable "dunkler Drang" intermittently goes astray — but note the difference in valence between Gretchen's instinctive maternity and Faust's manly groping for the right way).

Margarete is a Madonna, indeed a *mater dolorosa*, but this does not explain why she, the other penitents, and the Virgin Mary are peculiarly suited to lead us onward. Nor does the point that all three have lost a child make an infanticide into the sister of the Virgin Mary or of the mythical Helen, who has lost her son Euphorion (Jantz, 36–37). Why her moral ambiguity as both saint and sinner qualifies her as a mediatrix may be suggested by Goethe's trilogy "Paria," where the son of a Brahmana, distraught over her unjust execution by her now remorseful husband, seeks to reattach his mother's head, but in his haste attaches it to the body of an adulteress instead. The Brahmana is now a hybrid ("das Höchste dem Niedrigsten eingeimpft" [FA I. 22. 61]), and will link class opposites and mediate between them, which also may help explain the penitent women as not just symbols of "human fallibility" (Jantz, 45), but as figures anchored both in the profane and the divine. There is something deeply, ideologically Christian about this Indian legend of "Paria," with its implicit assumption that a mediator must combine in its being the mutually exclusive essences of the contraries — divinity and humanity, purity and sinfulness. The priestess not only reaches out to both, she *is* both, and can serve for this reason as a

conduit and a bridge across the divide. The death and resurrection of
Jesus Christ, at once God and man, exemplifies the alchemical paradigm of dying and becoming, while woman, as "Geburt und Grab," is
the vessel of transmutation. She corresponds to the sepulcher, the
"Stätte der Verwesung" and "wohlverwahrte Kristallretorte, worin der
Stoff seiner letzten Wandlung und Läuterung entgegengezwängt wird"
(as Naphta, the Nietzschean nihilist, claims in "Ein Soldat und brav" in
Der Zauberberg). This is why, in the creation of Homunculus, she can
be supplanted by a "Kristallretorte" in the laboratory, in which human
spermatozoa die, putrefy and re-emerge as something new and "geläu-
tert." Goethe elsewhere represents his own consciousness as an alembic
in which inherited material is preserved, transmuted and re-presented
(HA 13, 38). *Mutatis mutandis,* Galatea on her "Muschel," "dem ur-
alten Sinnbild des weiblichen Schoßes" (Schöne, 566) — Galatea, who
is "der Mutter Bild" (8386) and a personification of "das lebenzeugen-
de Wasser" (Hölscher-Lohmeyer, 115–116; Jantz, 37; Brown 1986,
181, n. 6) — can receive and join Homunculus, who "möchte gern
entstehn" (8246) in a *hieros gamos* which anticipates the marriage of
Faust to the timeless and ageless mythical Helen (7426–34). The "marriage" of Homunculus and Galatea reproduces an ancient paradigm.
"Zu den Grundanschauungen der antiken Mysterien [. . .] gehört eben
die Identität von Hochzeit und Tod einerseits, von Geburt und ewi-
gem Hervortreten des Lebens aus dem Tode andererseits," observes
Karl Kerényi (172). No matter (*pace* Hamlin, 146) that Galatea does
not seem to notice Homunculus as he dissolves into the sea. Topical
schemata, not the categories of psychological realism, are the tools employed in the non-illusionist drama of Goethe's *Faust*. At several removes but exemplifying the same paradigm, Margarete, under the
guidance of the Mater gloriosa, is the means of the dead Faust's transformation.

Goethe selects mothers, not virgins, as symbols and vessels of
transmutation, the paradoxical exception being the Virgin Mother herself, who, although she has known no man, *has* known conception and
tragedy and is as much a receptacle (of a divine *Eingießung*) and a vehicle as any other mother figure. *Faust* assigns special status to fallen
women, who are allied with Eve, the "Urmutter" and primal female
sinner, and who (symbolically conflated with the Virgin Mary) will lead
"us" to a new being in nothingness, an encompassing, obliterating
brilliance that is equivalent to darkness, total bliss! "Denn alles muß in
Nichts zerfallen, / Wenn es im Sein beharren will" (Goethe, "Eins und
alles"). As Busch puts it, "Die Transzendenz ist gegenüber der Dingwelt etwas, was keine Dinge enthält, und damit vom Standort der

Dingwelt aus ein raum- und zeitloses *Nichts* wie das Nirwana" (73). While the supernatural status of her impregnator indemnifies the Virgin from the charge that she is a common adulteress like the penitent women of "Mountain Gorges" — a sinner in God with God in her — she, like them, was betrothed to another man. It is worth noting that the German for "*immaculate* conception" is immaculate *reception* — "unbefleckte Empfängnis." Impregnation, whether by a man or by the Holy Spirit and whether or not it is thought to maculate the recipient, involves a transaction between a giver and a receiver.

As long ago as Gottfried's *Tristan* (viz. Isolde's self-diagnosis that "la-meir" — a synthesis of *la mer*, *l'amour*, and *la mort* — is what ails her), the association of woman with water is a commonplace in, for example, verses by Brentano, Mörike, and the last song of Müller's and Schubert's "Die schöne Müllerin," where the brook sings a lullaby to the miller boy who lies at rest in her bed: "Sollst liegen bei mir, / Bis das Meer will trinken die Bächlein aus." Similarly the Nymphs in "Am untern Peneios" sing to Faust: "Am besten geschäh' dir / Du legtest dich nieder, / Erholtest im Kühlen / Ermüdete Glieder, / Genössest der immer / Dich meidenden Ruh; / Wir säuseln, wir rieseln, / Wir flüstern dir zu" (7263–70). Although he does not accept this invitation, Faust's desire from the beginning is to immerse himself in a liquid opposite — "in deinem Tau gesund mich baden" — as he puts it in his apostrophe to the moonlight in the early scene "Nacht" (397). Contemplating suicide, he sees himself "ins hohe Meer [. . .] hinausgewiesen" (699), even at the risk of flowing into nothingness (719). In our oscillation between self-assertion and self-surrender — what Goethe familiarly defined as "sich verselbsten" versus "sich entselbstigen" (HA 9, 353) — the force to which the autonomous self longs to surrender itself is, of course, female. It is "das Ewig-Weibliche," the paradigmatic agent of engulfment throughout the long history of Western culture. Woman is the agent and vessel of mixing and mingling, the universal solvent — the *menstruum universale*, the maternal *Wunderschoß* (8665). As "Schoß der alten Nacht" (8649), she dissolves form and identity — in the dissolution of selfhood in darkness, and in the mixing of ashes in fire. She answers to man's desire to undo "Spezifikation" — to his longing for a uniform darkness devoid of "Körper" (1354–58) and for a night into which the bodies of lovers evaporate, "daß ich luftig mit dir inniger mich mische und dann ewig die Brautnacht währt" (Novalis, *Hymnen an die Nacht*, 1st hymn). The blessed longing depicted in the *Divan* poem, "Selige Sehnsucht," is a longing for perfection ("Vollendung") in self-sacrifice ("Selbstopfer" — two titles considered for the poem but abandoned by Goethe) — a longing for death, not for self-preservation. This is why such agents of engulfment as the Phorkyads (7969–8033) live "versenkt in Einsamkeit und stillste Nacht" (8000). These associations are variously personified by such minatory "women" as sirens, the Lorelei, mermaids, and the Charybdis. In a paralipomenon to *Faust,* Satan instructs: "Euch giebt es zwey Dinge / So herrlich und groß / Das glänzende Gold / Und der weibliche Schoos. / Das eine verschaffet / Das andre verschlingt" (FA 1.7.1, 553). (There may be an allusion here to the myth of the "vagina dentata," which overdetermines the idea of incorporation by combining the concept of engulfment by the enveloping womb with the idea of oral devouring.) In fact, if the Earth Spirit's words "Geburt und Grab, / Ein ewiges Meer" (504–05) is a self-reference, we might even ponder whether this Spirit of the *Earth* is not female — a possibility masked by the gender of the noun *Geist* (instead of Bruno's *anima terrae* — i.e., like "Geiz" instead of Avaritia, "männlichen Geschlechts") but plausible in its semiotic context. What Faust seeks in every immersion is transmutation, metamorphosis, which is also the goal of the igneous Homunculus in his marriage with the aqueous Galatea.

Woman is liquid not only by virtue of the facts of human reproduction and her metonymic identity with amniotic fluid, nor even only because of her association with the sea. Just as significant is her essential formlessness and lack of structure. In the traditional marriage topos (as in Goethe's "Amyntas," where, however, the host is an apple tree, instead of an elm) woman is always the ivy, never the elm, always the parasite in need of support, always pliant and malleable, parasitic and destructive, a limp vine waiting to be borne erect and take shape. Not stiffened by false dignity or by inflated notions of class or honor, she is authorized by her powerlessness and second-class status even to cheat in pursuit of her purposes. "Curiosity, mendacious deception, susceptibility to seduction, lust" are the qualities that Nietzsche assigns to the feminine in section 9 of *Die Geburt der Tragödie,* where he contrasts the "Aryan" myth of Prometheus with the "Semitic" one of Eve. (Prometheus wrests fire away from Zeus, while Eve, through cunning and deceit, persuades Adam to taste of the fruit of the tree of knowledge of good and evil.) He cites with obvious relish the Hexenmeister in "Walpurgisnacht" on the difference between men and women. Woman gets a head-start in the pursuit of sin, but, as the antiphonal chorus replies, a man vaults to the goal in one lusty leap (3978–85).

Lacking a defining moral code, woman is a vacuum waiting to be filled and ready to devour any male who dares to plumb her cavernous non-being. The world of the Mothers in *Faust II* is more formless even than the unfathomable ocean, where Faust might at least see waves and an occasional dolphin (6239–44) and in whose boundless "Nichts" and liquidity (6246, 6248) he may hope to find "das All." Underway, he will be propelled back and forth by loneliness (6226–27), just as his pact with the devil and his pursuit of Margarete were motivated by loneliness (6235–38). The Mothers, who are beyond time and space, are as unrepresentable as the celestial void into which Faust is carried at the play's end. Since, however, the females in *Faust* all signify the same thing, so that Gretchen is identified with Helena and she, in turn, with Galatea (and with Galatea's mother Aphrodite); since all of them are stand-ins for the Virgin Mary; since, further, these women are the metaphorical equivalents of moonlight and water, including the baptismal water of death and rebirth, surrogation itself stands out as an important concept, legitimating surrogate maternity and with it all other forms of representation. And in valorizing representation, the system of correspondences in *Faust* denies the uniqueness of character and even the concept of character, as Max Kommerell notes: "Haben Faust und Mephisto ihre Einheit in Sprechton und Denkform: Urbilder von Tätigkeiten, die sich manchmal [. . .] fast bis zur Figur verdichten, bald bis zur Chiffre zurückweichen, so fällt damit ein uns geläufiger Grundbegriff des Dramas hin: der Charakter" (29).

Acknowledging that woman is a link in a chain of signifiers in *Faust* is, however, not the end of the story. In the first place, according to the paradigm of dying and becoming, death may be followed by, or may coincide with, rebirth, and "das Ewig-Weibliche" may, after all, guide Faust to new spheres of "reiner Tätigkeit" (705). Second, as we have noted, the male protagonist is no less a signifier, therefore no less a mediator and no more a unique individual, than the female figures with whom he interacts. Finally, *Faust* is full of metaphorical reversals. For example, it is only consistent with the picture of woman as receptacle that Faust's self-annihilating fantasies on Easter morning and again in "Wald und Höhle" are couched in terms of a fluid *masculine* element flowing into a solid female opposite. In raising the poison to his lips, Faust seeks translation to a higher sphere — death here and re-emergence there — but the nothingness he is willing to risk "flowing" into (719) has to be a *female something* — perhaps an "ewig verschlingendes, ewig wiederkäuendes Ungeheuer" (Werther's conception of *Nature* after he has become despondent, but consistent with the conception of "das weibliche Schoß" in *Faust*).

Implicit in the *fließen* metaphor is a dissolution of male identity and the metonymic equation of a man with seminal fluid. Deliquescence and flowing are prominent metaphors in the writings of Gottfried

Arnold (see Zimmermann 1: 189) and favorites of Arnold's eager student, the young Goethe. Faust's self-reproach in Margarete's bedroom
is stated in terms of fluid imagery: "Mich drang's, so grade zu genießen, / Und fühle mich in Liebestraum zerfließen" (2722–23). And in
"Wald und Höhle," Mephisto ridicules Faust's fantasy of "swelling to
the level of a divinity, probing the marrow of the earth and then flowing over into everything" (3285–89): "Verschwunden ganz der Erdensohn" (3290). Similarly, as Thales observes of Homunculus breaking
his glass on Galatea's Muschelwagen, "Jetzt flammt es, nun blitzt es,
ergießet sich schon" (8473). Homunculus's "desire assumes obvious
sexual implications when [he] shatters his glass against the shell and
dissipates himself orgasmically into the ocean" (Hamlin, 146). There is
no need to postulate as signifieds "eine ejaculation praecox" (Zabka,
148, n. 66), masturbation, or single-sex models of procreation
(Niekerk, 6; Matussek, 386; Scholz, 91; Bennett, 92).

Günter Grass's *Katz und Maus* may add to our understanding of
what the act of masturbation — or, for that matter, sexual penetra-
tion — as a signifier represents. When Joachim Mahlke masturbates and
ejaculates into the sea, he metonymically replicates the act of Homunculus "pouring himself" into the sea, which is in turn a re-enactment of
the siring of Venus (Brown 1986, 209). In Grass's novel the sea is
identified with the Virgin Mary, at whose lower parts Mahlke aims his
prayer and whom he imagines himself impregnating when he aims his
tank gun at the photograph she holds in front of her abdomen as a target. This matches the "todbringende Hochzeit" of the torpedo penetrating the ship's belly, with the tale of which duel beneath the sea the
submarine commander had bedazzled the assembly in the school
auditorium and aroused Mahlke's ambition to earn the Iron Cross.
Similarly, when he pours himself into the sea Homunculus mirrors
Faust spilling over "liebewonniglich" into "everything" (3289). In-
jected with love, the female *Nichts/alles* is a grave — like the laboratory
receptacle in which, according to the recipe of Paracelsus (Gray, 205–
06), the implanted male seed dies and putrefies and is reborn as Homunculus. At work here is Goethe's idea of polarity — an asymmetrical
and reversible polarity, like sex, in which one pole serves the other, but
in which, in a typically provocative Goethean paradox, the patient as receptacle is simultaneously an agent of transformation. A dramatic text is
not merely a succession of representations, but an occasion for dialogue
with the reader or audience. Satire, with which *Faust* is saturated, is inherently dialogic. Even Mephisto's trifling with Frau Marthe or his advice to the freshman in the second "Study" scene and his remarks to
the same young man as Baccalaureus in "Hochgewölbtes Gotisches

Zimmer" implies a conversation with the reader or audience, who are expected to understand his double entendres, whether his interlocutors understand them or not. That woman is portrayed as an object of desire and a means of Faust's salvation does not mean that the play simply endorses the instrumentalization of the feminine — any more than it endorses the forcible expropriation of someone else's homestead (Philemon and Baucis) or the judicial murder of infanticides.

The meaning of the feminine in *Faust* is central to an understanding of the terms of Faust's wager with Mephistopheles. It is no accident that temporal metaphors dominate Faust's projection of the outcome if he loses the wager: "Die Uhr mag stehen, der Zeiger fallen, / Es sei die Zeit für mich vorbei!" (1705–06). Time is constitutive of being, so if Mephisto succeeds in making Faust bid the moment to stay, time will in fact end for him and the clock stop. The fatal words would be a performative, bringing about the state they summon: "Werd' ich zum Augenblicke sagen: / Verweile doch! du bist so schön! / Dann magst du mich in Fesseln schlagen, / Dann will ich gern zugrunde gehn! / Dann mag die Totenglocke schallen, / Dann bist du deines Dienstes frei, / Die Uhr mag stehn [. . .] !" (1699–1706). Faust wants not just for the moment to "tarry a while" (Brown 1986, 80), he wants it to become eternal, wants time to stop absolutely. Mephistopheles will win the wager if he can bring Faust to a moment of ecstasy — a paradoxical term in that "ecstasy" means standing out — outside of selfhood, outside of time. Faust's wager amounts to a tautology. If he loves ecstatically, so that time stops, he will lose both the wager and his life, which is why the ecstasy of orgasm (Scholz, 89) is known as "la petite mort." But he will lose nothing more, for there is nothing more to lose than his being as a separate, individual self, constituted by time. And this he wants to lose, in exchange for endless, unindividual bliss. As Matussek puts it: "Faust geht die Wette ein, weil er sie just durch das Bemühen, sie zu gewinnen, zu verlieren hofft. Er will totalen Lebensgenuß (V, 1770–71) [. . .] einen Genuß, der nicht falsifiziert werden kann, weil er unbedingt ist" (366). Or, rather, Faust wants "Ekstase," "Verzückung," not merely "Genuß," however "unbedingt." Entry into bliss would be a resubmergence in the maternal womb and tomb — a *Liebestod*, which is how Gretchen imagines her love when she longs to expire in the rapture of Faust's kisses (3406–13) and when, in the prison scene of the *Urfaust*, she reproaches Faust: "Bist mein Heinrich und hast's Küssen verlernt! Wie sonst ein ganzer Himmel mit deiner Umarmung gewaltig über mich eindrang. Wie du küsstest als wolltest du mich in wollüstigem Todt ersticken" (41–44 [FA I.7.1, 537]; this is softened in the 1808 version).

Faust doubts that Mephistopheles will be able to bring about a moment so desirable that he will want it to last. His tempter and adversary has heard, however — from the Lord if he did not bring this knowledge with him to their interview — that permanence and "unbedingte Ruh" is what the human creature seeks. This is why he engineers the meeting with Margarete and the eventual moment of ecstasy that Faust will try to preserve. Faust and Mephisto both want the same thing: Faust's non-being in love and death. All of Faust's adventures from the signing of the wager on may be seen under the aspect of time and the longing for an ecstasy that, by definition, is attainable only in death. Like the Cabiri, Faust is a "sehnsuchtsvoller Hungerleider / Nach dem Unerreichlichen" (8204–05). In this respect, the song about the rat, which we have applied to Margarete, applies in an even more profound sense to Faust himself — to him who is "unbefriedigt jeden Augenblick."

"Wer immer strebend sich bemüht, / Den können wir erlösen." (11936–37). The soteriology of *Faust* continues to be misunderstood, in correlation with attempts to downplay the Eternal-Feminine as detracting from the honor due to Faust's individual merit. Niekerk argues that love is "only [. . .] of minor importance for Faust's final redemption" but that "Faust's willpower and eternal striving are *decisive*. The fact that Faust's soul is saved is a result of the fact that he 'immer strebend sich bemüht'" (18, his emphasis). The unreconstructed modernism of this view misses Goethe's point that individual merit is seldom crucial and that it is individual only as a point of intersection of multiple, complex forces. Goethe would have endorsed Sander L. Gilman's remark that "in the Shoah, individual action could not guarantee the salvation of any individual" (304). Brown reads God in the "Prologue in Heaven" as saying that "Mephistopheles' function is to keep man active so that God can reward him" (45) and as saying that Faust's striving is bound to be mistaken because this "is the condition of being human," therefore not a matter to be repented of or atoned for (46), but does the fact that humans are pathetic obviate the need for either repentance or atonement? And salvation is a blessing, not a reward, even for Faust whom the Lord promises to lead "in die Klarheit" (309) — in other words, Faust will not find his way into clarity without guidance. Albrecht Schöne cautions that "man [sollte] den 'weiblichen Schluß' der *Faust*-Dichtung [. . .] besser nicht anachronistischen Adaptionsversuchen unterwerfen und ihn für gynokratische Thesen und Programme in Anspruch nehmen" (816). But to recognize the emphasis attached to "das Ewig-Weibliche" as the subject of the last sentence in a twelve-thousand line poem presupposes no "gynokratische These," nor should a sexist prejudice in favor of the "active" principle oblige us to resist Goethe's unambiguous point that redemption is not to be earned through striving or any other exercise of autonomy. He often declared, as to Frédéric Soret, that we are not autonomous — "Mon oeuvre est celle d'un être collectif et elle porte le nom de Goethe" (cited in Schöne, 27) — and the conviction that we are dependent on one another informs his work, as may be seen in his concept of "Welt-literatur," his metaphors of symbiosis ("Amyntas") and parasitism (such as that of ants consuming the excrement of plant lice [letter to Knebel of 17 April 1782]) as well as in his mature understanding of "intertex-tuality" two centuries before the word became fashionable. The answer to Doctor Marianus's rhetorical question, "Wer zerreißt aus eigner Kraft / Der Gelüste Ketten?" (12026–27), is: no one, not "aus eigener Kraft." And a story of "the male's ceaseless striving and erring" (Schweitzer's formulation of a common view, 136) does not by the mere fact of its depiction assign *positive* value to this striving and erring, except insofar as human futility and perverseness — "Irrtümer auf Irr-tümer, Verirrungen auf Verirrungen" (thus Wilhelm Meister about his own life [HA 7, 446]) — may elicit a sad respect from any humane audience.

Böhm and, after him, Schöne convincingly read "Wer immer stre-bend sich bemüht" (11936–37) as meaning not "Whoever always strives" but as "*Wer* auch *immer* [. . .] " = "whoever it may be who is striving" (Schöne, 801). Goethe's modulates the ancient metaphor of the body as a prison of the soul (which escapes into freedom in death) into that of the *self* as a prison. "Whoever it may be who unceasingly strives, him (her) we can release, dissolve, set free" (cf. Trunz in HA 3, 738). The angels can *release* a soul from a life of frenzied activity, in-deed from selfhood itself.

"Unbedingte Thätigkeit, von welcher Art sie sey, macht zuletzt bankerotte" said Goethe (FA I.13, 40; Schöne, 787). Activity may be the story of our lives, but this is not so much a merit and a ground for "Erlösung" as an affliction from which we may one day be released. Faust's redemption involves not only release and absolution but also *dis*solution — the division of "geeinte Zwienatur" (11962–65) and the end of hypostasis in ecstasy. In the fifth of his *Hymnen an die Nacht*, Novalis wrote: "Noch einmal sah er freundlich nach der Mutter — da kam der ewigen Liebe *lösende* Hand, und er entschlief." Longing for dissolution informs the words to the moon of one of the most famous of Goethe's lyrical personae — "*Lösest* endlich auch einmal / Meine

Seele ganz" ("An den Mond"). This is why Faust's monologue in Gretchen's room "reëvokes the imagery of the speech to the moon" (Brown 1986, 101); it is also what motivates the willing seduction of the fisherman in "Der Fischer." Faust's longing is for release in the moonlight and then in union with Margarete, who means the same thing to him as moonlight (Brown 1992, 63) — like water, a solvent in which selfhood disappears. With the metaphor of dissolution by means of love — the ultimate *Menstruum universale* in *Faust* — Romanticism designates its "ideal of dissolving established limitations and determinations" (Schulte-Sasse, 30), including the limitation and determination of individuation. The angels' words: "Wer immer strebend sich bemüht, / Den können wir erlösen," are a commentary, not a vow.

Woman in *Faust* symbolizes mediation — indeed symbolism itself. It is the function of symbols to mediate. The mediatrixes in *Faust*, the rainbow of "Anmutige Gegend," and the Redeemer celebrated on Easter morning in the scene "Nacht" "share as symbols a property that distinguishes them from most other symbols, inasmuch as the idea they convey is identical with the principle by which they (and all other symbols) work [. . .]. They *do* that which they *mean*, and that which they mean is the principle that governs the life of man" (Dye, 972). Like the beautiful snake arched across the river in Goethe's "Märchen" or like the refracting spray of the waterfall in "Anmutige Gegend," woman bridges the chasm between the divine and the human, the high and the low, the sacred and the profane (like the Brahmana who becomes half adulteress in "Paria"). She is the way and the guide, out ahead of those she leads and on whom she works her magic — us. Even her mission as mediatrix is a given, for in *Faust* all being is a gift, a datum, and a donation, a *Gabe* and a *Begabung*. "Alles ist wie geschenkt" (FA I.2, 631). That this conception instrumentalizes the feminine does say something about the *Faust* drama's epistemological and soteriological framework. In Hart's witty formulation, Faust is "saved by the belle" (113). And it is as a promise of plenitude and a means of release from the particularity of selfhood that Faust sees Gretchen early on (2693–94). Hart believes "das Ewig-Weibliche" is "ultimately a feminized projection of [Faust] himself" (121). It is, rather, an imposition of male concepts on women. The view of woman as mediatrix projects a role upon woman from without and by her opposite, while making this projection visible and subject to criticism. Goethe's *Faust* tells us nothing about what it means to be female, only what femaleness means to men, and to women who have been taught to think like a man. If the word "uns" in the poem's last line does not refer to the world of men, it does encode the world according to men. In *Faust* the feminine is what brings us into being and transports us out of being again, and it is what gives us meaning while we are here. But the being in need of deliverance is made visible in this drama as well. Indeed, it would take no great leap of the imagination to think of Goethe's drama as the story of a needy male consciousness addressed to a *female* audience and showing that "der kleine Gott der Welt bleibt stets von gleichem Schlag" (281). It could have been written by a woman — given literary talent equivalent to Goethe's and the necessary independence of male patterns of thought.

Faust is a man propelled by love and longing. He owes his redemption not to his proud, lonely striving, but to Divine Love. Love, as Schöne notes (786), is the crucial word in this final scene, recurring fourteen times. But love is a gift and not to be earned, through striving or in any other way. In *Faust,* love is a *female* donation, embodied in the Mater gloriosa and the transfigured Margarete who intercedes on Faust's behalf. Schöne doubts that "das Ewig-Weibliche" refers exclusively to the feminine. And Hamlin would rescue "das Ewig-Weibliche" from the reductionist hermeneutics of erotic satisfaction and translate it into the aesthetic, in "a process of sublimation, whereby erotic desire is transformed into ritual celebration" (145). But although gender distinctions are complicated in *Faust* and in Goethe generally, and although the feminine is idealized, it would be illogical and inconsistent with the pervasive representation of females as intercessors in *Faust* to deny its vision of specifically *feminine* mediation. Reliance on this is central not only to *Faust* but to Western culture generally and its portrayal of passion and reception — "Schicksal" — as the defining fact of human being, true both of our coming into and going out of being and of all that befalls us and is given us to know.

Stripped of the old shell, Faust follows Gretchen upward. "Der früh Geliebte, / Nicht mehr Getrübte, / Er kommt zurück," (12073–75),[1] stripping off earth's bonds as he goes (12088–89; cf. 1114–15). But not under his own power. We can take Goethe at his word: "Das Ewig-Weibliche / zieht uns hinan."

---

[1] "Das Getrübte," from "Trübe" ("obfuscation"/"cloudiness" and derivative forms, e.g., "betrübt" ("obfuscated," "troubled") designates, in Goethe's *Die Farbenlehre*, a semi-opaque medium imparting color either to pure white light (from yellow to ruby red, as the opacity of the medium increases), or, if luminous, to pure dark (from violet to light blue). A familiar non-technical use may be found in Schubart's "Die Forelle" (musical setting by Schubert): "[Der Fischer] macht das Bächlein tückisch trübe [. . .]." Only after troubling the waters does the poem's fisherman catch the trout.

Acknowledgments

I want to thank Paul Bishop, Jane K. Brown, Carol Dye, Deirdre Vincent, and Bonnie Watkins for encouragement, criticism, and many helpful suggestions. My thanks also to David Pugh for reminding me of Schiller's extraordinary remark comparing Goethe to a prudish woman in need of being knocked up and humiliated. Neumann, whose dissertation I read only at the end of my work on this essay, has a chapter entitled "Figurationen des Weiblichen" (210). I gladly acknowledge his precedence.

Works Cited

Anchor, Robert. "Motherhood and Family in Goethe's *Faust*: Gretchen's Mother and the Gretchen Tragedy." *Historical Reflections/Réflexions Historiques* 23, 1 (Winter 1997). 29–48.

Arens, Hans. *Kommentar zu Goethes Faust I*. Heidelberg: Carl Winter, 1982.

———. *Kommentar zu Goethes Faust II*. Heidelberg: Carl Winter, 1989.

Atkins, Stuart. *Goethe's Faust: A Literary Analysis*. Cambridge, MA: Harvard UP, 1958.

Bennett, Benjamin. *Goethe's Theory of Poetry: Faust and the Regeneration of Language*. Ithaca: Cornell UP, 1986.

Bloch, R. Howard. *Medieval Misogyny and the Invention of Western Romantic Love*. Chicago: U of Chicago P, 1991.

Böhm, Wilhelm. *Goethes Faust in neuer Deutung*. Cologne: E. A. Seemann, 1949.

Breuer, Dieter. "Goethes christliche Mythologie. Zur Schlußszene des 'Faust.'" *Jahrbuch des Wiener Goethe-Vereins*. 84/85 (1980–81). 7–24.

Brown, Jane K. *Faust: Theater of the World*. New York: Twayne, 1992.

———. *Goethe's "Faust": The German Tragedy*. Ithaca: Cornell UP, 1986.

Burke, Kenneth. "Goethe's *Faust*, Part I." [1954] In *Language as Symbolic Action: Essays on Life, Literature, and Method*. Berkeley: U of California P, 1966. 145–62.

Busch, Ernst. "Die Transzendenz der Gottheit und der Naturmystische Gottesbegriff im Mütter-Symbol." [1949] In *Aufsätze zu Goethes "Faust II."* Ed. Werner Keller. Darmstadt: Wissenschaftliche Buchgesellschaft, 1992. 70–79.

Demetz, Peter. "The Elm and the Vine: Notes Toward the History of a Marriage Topos." *PMLA* 73 (1958). 521–32.

Dye, Robert Ellis. "The Easter Cantata and the Idea of Mediation in Goethe's *Faust*." *PMLA* 92, 5 (1977). 963–76.

Eissler, K. R. *Goethe: A Psychoanalytic Study 1775–1786*. 3 vols. Detroit: Wayne State UP, 1963.

Feise, Ernst. "Goethes Werther als nervöser Charakter." *The Germanic Review* 1 (1926). 185–253.

Gilman, Sander L. "Is Life Beautiful? Can the Shoah Be Funny? Some Thoughts on Recent and Older Films." *Critical Inquiry* 26, 2 (Winter 2000). 279–308.

Gray, Ronald D. *Goethe the Alchemist*. Cambridge: Cambridge UP, 1952.

Guenther, Margaret B. "*Faust*: The Tragedy Reexamined." *Beyond the Eternal Feminine: Critical Essays on Women and German Literature*. Ed. Susan L. Cocalis and Kay Goodman. Stuttgart: Akademischer Verlag Hans-Dieter Heinz, 1982. 75–98.

Hamlin, Cyrus. "Tracking the Eternal Feminine in Goethes Faust II." *Interpreting Goethe's Faust Today*. Ed. Jane Brown, Meredith Lee, and Thomas P. Saine. Columbia, SC: Camden House, 1994. 142–55.

Hart, Gail K. "Das Ewig-Weibliche nasführet dich: Feminine Leadership in Goethe's *Faust* and Sacher-Masoch's *Venus*." *Interpreting Goethe's Faust Today*. Ed. Jane K. Brown et al. Columbia, SC: Camden House, 1994. 112–22.

Heller, Peter. "Gretchen: Figur, Klischee, Symbol." *Die Frau als Heldin und Autorin*. Ed. Wolfgang Paulsen. Bern and Munich: Francke, 1979. 175–89.

Herwig, Henriette. *"Das ewig Männliche zieht uns hinab": Wilhelm Meisters Wanderjahre*. Tübingen: Francke, 1997.

Hölscher-Lohmeyer, Dorothea. "Natur und Gedächtnis: Reflexionen über die Klassische Walpurgisnacht." [1987]. In *Aufsätze zu Goethes "Faust II."* Ed. Werner Keller. Darmstadt: Wissenschaftliche Buchgesellschaft, 1992. 93–122.

Jantz, Harold. *The Mothers in Faust: The Myth of Time and Creativity*. Baltimore: Johns Hopkins UP, 1969.

Jantz, Rolf-Peter, "'Sie ist die Schande ihres Geschlechts'. Die femme fatale bei Lessing." *Jahrbuch der Deutschen Schillergesellschaft* 23 (1979). 207–21.

Kerényi, Karl. "Das Ägäische Fest. Die Meergötterszene in Goethes 'Faust II'" [1941] In *Aufsätze zu Goethes "Faust II."* Ed. Werner Keller. Darmstadt: Wissenschaftliche Buchgesellschaft, 1992. 160–89.

Kommerell, Max. *Geist und Buchstabe der Dichtung*. Frankfurt am Main: Vittorio Klostermann. 3rd ed. Tübingen, H. Laupp Jr., 1944.

Kuepper, Karl J. "Verführte Unschuld: Benennungen und Bezeichnungen für Gretchen in Goethes *Faust*." *Analogon Rationis: Festschrift für Gerwin Marahens zum 65. Geburtstag*. Ed. Marianne Henn and Christoph Lorey. Edmonton, Alberta: Marianne Henn and Christoph Lorey, 1994. 129–44.

Larrett, William. "Wilhelm Meister and the Amazons: The Quest for Wholeness." *Publications of the English Goethe Society*, N.S. 39 (1969). 31–56.

Mattenklott, Gert. "Faust II." In *Goethe-Handbuch*. Vol 2. *Dramen*. Stuttgart: Metzler, 1997. 391–477.

Matussek, Peter. "Faust I." In *Goethe-Handbuch*. Vol. 2. *Dramen*. Stuttgart: Metzler, 1997. 352–90.

Moog-Grünewald, Maria. "Die Frau als Bild des Schicksals: Zur Ikonologie der Femme Fatale." *Arcadia* 18.3 (1983). 239–57.

Neumann, Michael. *Das Ewig-Weibliche in Goethes "Faust."* Heidelberg: Carl Winter, 1985.

Niekerk, Carl H. "Sexual Imagery in Goethe's 'Faust II.'" *Seminar* 33: 1 (1997). 1–21.

Nietzsche, Friedrich. *The Birth of Tragedy*. Trans. Walter Kaufmann. New York: Vintage, 1967.

Petriconi, Hellmuth. *Die verführte Unschuld: Bemerkungen über ein literarisches Thema*. Hamburg: Cram, de Gruyter, 1953. 99–129.

Pruys, Hugo. *Die Liebkosungen des Tigers: Eine erotische Goethe Biographie*. Berlin: Edition q, 1997.

Requadt, Paul. *Goethes Faust I: Leitmotivik und Architektur*. Munich: W. Fink, 1972.

Rölleke, Heinz. "'Frau Marthe!' — 'Was soll's?': Der Name der Nachbarin in Goethes 'Faust' und anderwärts." *Jahrbuch des Freien Deutschen Hochstifts*. Tübingen, 1997. 64–68.

Saint-Armand, Pierre. "Terrorizing Marie Antoinette." Trans. Jennifer Curtiss Gage. *Critical Inquiry* 20, 3 (Spring 1994). 379–401.

Scholz, Rüdiger. "Der Müttermythos." In *Aufsätze zu Goethes "Faust II."* Ed. Werner Keller. Darmstadt: Wissenschaftliche Buchgesellschaft, 1992. 80–92.

Schöne, Albrecht, ed. *Faust. Kommentare*. Frankfurt am Main: Deutscher Klassiker Verlag, 1994. [FA 7.2.]

Schulte-Sasse, Jochen. "Romanticism's Paradoxical Articulation of Desire." *Theory as Practice: A Critical Anthology of Early German Romantic Writings*. Minneapolis: U of Minnesota P, 1997.

Schwerte, Hans. "Der weibliche Schluß von Goethes 'Faust.'" *Sprachkunst* 21 (1990). 129–43.

Schweitzer, Christoph E. "Gretchen and the Feminine in Goethe's *Faust*." *Interpreting Goethe's Faust Today*. Ed. Jane K. Brown et al. Columbia, SC: Camden House, 1994. 133–41.

Zabka, Thomas. *Faust II — Das Klassische und das Romantische: Goethes "Eingriff in die neueste Literatur."* Tübingen: Niemeyer, 1993.

The Problem of the Mothers

John R. Williams

IT IS A COMMONPLACE of *Faust II* criticism for commentators to claim that a particular episode or problem has received an inordinate amount of critical attention; and this is surely at least as true of the problem of the Mothers as of any other aspect of Goethe's encyclopedic and critically inexhaustible late work. In the interpretation of the Mothers, and of the three final scenes of Act 1 in which they feature — invisibly but centrally — the critical imagination has been allowed all the more free rein, on the one hand because of their very mysteriousness and inscrutability, the numinous awe with which they are surrounded, and on the other hand because of the unhelpful elusiveness of Goethe's own recorded comments on them.

Goethe's response to Eckermann's questionings on the subject was characteristically evasive; he merely repeated the bemused Faust's words ("Die Mütter! Mütter — 's klingt so wunderlich!"), and went on to reveal that he had found a reference in Plutarch to an ancient group of deities known as Mothers. That, Goethe asserted, was all he owed to traditional sources; the rest was of his own devising. To be sure, in the same report (10 January 1830) Eckermann goes on to give his own conclusions on the nature and function of the Mothers, which is as lucid a paraphrase of the textual evidence as most — but Goethe's reaction to his interpretation, if any, is not recorded:

> So, in ewiger Dämmerung und Einsamkeit beharrend, sind die Mütter schaffende Wesen, sie sind *das schaffende* und *erhaltende Prinzip,* von dem alles ausgeht, was auf der Oberfläche der Erde Gestalt und Leben hat. Was zu atmen aufhört, geht als geistige Natur zu ihnen zurück, und sie bewahren es, bis es wieder Gelegenheit findet, in ein neues Dasein zu treten. Alle Seelen und Formen von dem, was einst war und künftig sein wird, schweift in dem endlosen Raum ihres Aufenthaltes wolkenartig hin und her; es umgibt die Mütter, und der Magier muß also in ihr Reich gehen, wenn er durch die Macht seiner Kunst über die Form eines Wesens Gewalt haben und ein früheres Geschöpf zu einem Scheinleben hervorrufen will. Die ewige Metamorphose des irdischen Daseins, des Entstehens und Wachsens, des Zerstörens und Wiederbildens, ist also der Mütter nie aufhörende Beschäftigung. Und

wie nun bei allem, was auf der Erde durch Fortzeugung ein neues Leben erhält, das *Weibliche* hauptsächlich wirksam ist, so mögen jene
schaffenden Gottheiten mit Recht *weiblich* gedacht und es mag der
ehrwürdige Name *Mütter* ihnen nicht ohne Grund beigelegt werden.

The passage in Plutarch Goethe evidently had in mind is in chapter
20 of the *Life of Marcellus*, which refers to goddesses worshipped in
Engyium in Sicily who are called Mothers (Plutarch's *Lives*, 5, 489).
But source research has also identified a further passage in chapters 21
and 22 of Plutarch's *The Obsolescence of Oracles* that describes a soothsayer's account of a mysterious quasi-Platonic "Plain of Truth, in which
the accounts, the forms and the patterns [*tous logous kai ta eide kai ta
paradeigmata*] of all things that have come to pass and of all that shall
come to pass rest undisturbed; and round about them lies Eternity,
whence Time, like an ever-flowing stream, is conveyed to the worlds"
(Plutarch, *Moralia*, 5, 416–17).

This passage has been frequently and persuasively cited as a possible
additional source for Goethe's conception of the Mothers — though
few commentators have cared to point out that the soothsayer responsible for this striking vision is described in Plutarch as distinctly eccentric. And critics have gone a great deal further afield than Plutarch
in the search for antecedents and explanations of the Mothers episode,
discerning associations with Cybele, Gaia, Ops, Rhea and other *Magna
Mater* myths (which Goethe would have found in his mythological *va-
de mecum*, Benjamin Hederich's *Gründliches mythologisches Lexikon*
(1724, revised 1770); with Nordic deities of destiny (Norns); with various accounts of heroic descents into the underworld (Orpheus, Odysseus, Aeneas); with the Eleusinian Mysteries; with Hercules' theft of
the tripod from the Pythian Oracle; and (in the later *Rittersaal* scene)
with the stories of Pygmalion and Galatea, Endymion and Luna, and of
course the abduction of Helen by Paris. The Mothers have been seen in
terms of Plato's metaphysics, of the Goethean *Urphänomen*, of the
Kantian *Ding an sich*, of the Hegelian Absolute, of Leibnizian monadology, of Freudian and Jungian symbolism, and many other systems.

A survey of critical responses to the Mothers during the years 1900–
1938 can be found in Ada M. Klett (30–34), and more up-to-date surveys in Trunz (HA 3, 546–49), in the tendentious survey of Scholz
(242, footnote 40 and passim), and in Arens (225–57, 239–49, 273–
74 and passim). In a certain sense, the wheel of critical opinion has
come full circle since Friedrich Theodor Vischer summed up the typical
nineteenth-century bafflement, and indeed exasperation, with *Faust II*
in general and with this episode in particular, by describing the
Mothers, together with the mystical tripod, key, etc., with some

disapproval as belonging "zum Abstrusesten in Goethes Altersprodukt" (351). The overwhelming majority of twentieth-century critics has taken the episode of the Mothers and its attendant mysteries as a serious product of Goethe's imaginative myth creation; only relatively recently have some commentators subverted this approach by suggesting that the Mothers are an ironic product of Mephistopheles' (equally imaginative) myth creation.

As Rüdiger Scholz comments acerbically, the majority of modern interpreters "holt das Urbildliche der Mütter heraus" (242); and indeed, when commentators quote the passage from Plutarch's *Obsolescence of Oracles* in German translation, the terms *eide* or *paradeigmata* are actually rendered as "Urbilder" (thus for example Emrich, 215; Lohmeyer 1975, 392; Beutler, GA 5, 730). As early as 1842, Franz Thomas Bratranek had described the Mothers in terms of Platonic ideas as "die Urbilder alles Daseienden" (2, 44). For Ernst Beutler — who also sees Faust's experience of the Mothers as "das Erlebnis des Ewig-Weiblichen" — they are the source of *Urphänomene*, and the image of Helen conjured by Faust in the *Rittersaal* scene is "das Urphänomen, das Urbild der Schönheit" (GA 5, 730).

Conversely, others have argued that the Mothers cannot be the source of *Urphänomene*, since the Goethean *Urphänomen* exists in reality, it is both an abstract principle and an empirical experience — whereas the Mothers evidently inhabit a transcendent realm beyond known reality, and even the figure of Helen that Faust appears to conjure with the help of the Mothers is only a spectral shadow. Emrich in *Die Symbolik von Faust II* (1943) counters this with the observation:

> Während in der Frühklassik und Klassik Goethe noch daran glaubte, das "Urphänomen" in der Erscheinung selbst wahrnehmen und an ihr demonstrieren zu können, weisen seine späten Äußerungen immer mehr auf das "Unmögliche" des Urphänomens in den Erscheinungen und damit zusammenhängend auf den "Schauder" hin, den es bei unerwartet plötzlichem Hervorbrechen dann auslöse. (214)

For Emrich, the Mothers are the means of resurrecting archetypal beauty directly from the past, ready made, as it were, from a realm of ideality without any need for preparation, growth or development:

> Nicht eine wirkliche Antike erscheint in Helena einfach wieder, sondern das urphänomenal Schöne tritt auf als "Doppelreich" von Wahrheit und Fiktion, Traum und Wachheit, Idee und Erscheinung und enthüllt erst dadurch eine *wahre* Wirklichkeit [...]. Der glühende Schlüssel [...] ermöglicht den radikalen, entschlossenen Vorstoß ins Bereich des Transzendenten [...]. Die grenzlose Sphäre der Mütter

[. . .] bildet den abgründigen Urboden, auf dem allein wahre Schönheit sich behauptet. (219–22)

Gottfried Diener (1961) extends Emrich's portentous symbolism
into Jungian and alchemical systems. Faust's journey to the Mothers is
a descent into "jene gewöhnlich unbewußten und auch nie ganz be-
wußtseinsfähigen, überpersönlich-kollektiven Seelentiefen [. . .], in denen die archetypischen 'urtümlichen Bilder' wurzeln [. . .]. Der
schöpferische Seelengrund (des 'kollektiven Unbewußten') stellt sich
oft in Mutter-Symbolen dar" (66–67):

> Wenn also der Magier Faust die Geister der Helena und des Paris be-
> schwören will, in deren lebendigen Gestalten sich einst die Idee des
> Schönen musterhaft verwirklicht hat, wenn der *Seher* und *Dichter*
> Faust das Urbild der Schönheit als Urphänomen in der produktiven
> Phantasie sichtbar machen will, so muß er in die letzten Tiefen der
> Natur und der Seele hinabsteigen, wo die schaffenden Urkräfte und
> die ewigen Bilder zusammenwirken, muß dort den glühenden Dreifuß
> aufsuchen, der ihn einen Blick in die innersten Geheimnisse der nach
> Ideen verfahrenden Natur werfen läßt, und muß durch dessen Ver-
> mittlung den Abglanz der Ideen, also auch das Urphänomen der
> Schönheit […] aus unbewußten Lebensgründen nach oben in die gei-
> stige Helle des Bewußtseins zu ziehen suchen. (79–80)

Dorothea Lohmeyer (1975) also sees the realm of the Mothers as
"das Reich der Urformen der Natur" (128), but she rejects any association with Platonic concepts: "Die Welt der Goethischen Formen ist
nicht wie bei Plato als eine Welt des starren unbewegten Seins von der
Welt der Erscheinungen als der des Werdens getrennt; sondern das
Werden, die Metamorphose des Bildens und Umbildens der Formen,
ist bei Goethe in den Formen als dem Prinzip des Seins mitenthalten"
(129–30). Goethe's notion of *Urformen* is derived from Linné, not
Plato. The Mothers are not sources of Goethean *Urphänomene* —
"denn Urphänomene sind Erscheinungen, als solche immer ein Ge-
wordenes, und gehören, so sehr sie an der Urform teilhaben, dennoch
der sichtbaren Wirklichkeit an" — which the Mothers manifestly do
not. Nor can the "Bilder aller Kreatur" (line 6289) be explained as
Leibnizian monads or as Goethean entelechies, as Wilhelm Hertz had
suggested, for though these images are "regsam," they are "ohne Leben" — whereas energetic activity is precisely what characterizes the
monad (136).

Heinz Schlaffer (1981) purports to break with such heavily symbolic
interpretations of the Mothers: "Man wird allerdings von einem Rätsel
an andere gewiesen, wenn man sich mit dem bloßen Bild der Mütter
zufrieden gibt oder, dem Ratschlag der Kommentatoren folgend, in

und bei den Müttern die vagen Urbilder allen Lebens symbolisiert sieht" (104). But Schlaffer's allegorical interpretation of the episode does not break as radically with the doctrine of *Urbilder* as he appears to claim. Taking up Jantz's notion of the Mothers as "a repository of the ages" (Jantz, 29), Schlaffer characterizes them as "eine Allegorie der Geschichte," as "das Reservoir poetischer und historischer Erinnerung," as the guardians of "das Archiv der Zeiten"; they represent "die Summe des Gewesenen, worüber das moderne Wissen verfügen kann" (105–6). They rule over a museum of the past which the cultural imperialist Faust sets out to pillage in his search for Helen, rather as Lord Elgin and other Graecophiles pillaged the treasures of Greece: Faust's quest is "eine parasitäre Hoffnung, Historisches poetisch verlebendigen zu können" (108).

Werner Danckert (1951) rejects all philosophical interpretations of the Mothers in order to take the reader into the labyrinthine depths of primitive "tellurian" religious myth:

> Ein Stück tiefster Dichtung wie die Mütterszene kann nur dem ahnenden Symbolsinn, der Intuition entsprungen sein, keinesfalls als allegorische Einkleidung naturphilosophischer Lehrsätze [. . .]. Die Mütter sind wirklich die alten Erd- und Eimütter, die lebenwebenden Schicksalsmächte, der metaphysische Ort von Tod und Geburt [. . .]. Sie, die tellurischen Urmütter, entlassen die Entelechie zur Suche nach irdischer Verkörperung [. . .]. Goethes letzte, urgründliche Wirklichkeit ist eine Wirklichkeit der *Urbilder*. (552–55)

Alice Raphael's study, drawing on Jungian and alchemical symbolism, is more an embroidered fantasy on Goethe's text than any form of literary criticism. Faust's journey to the Mothers is a journey to the sublunary spheres; he "sinks into some form of trance, as he projects consciousness to the suprasensible realm"; in a state of "mystic introversion" he enters the "archetypal universe" to retrieve the *eidolon* of Helen (147). His intervention into the dumb-show of Paris and Helen is "a first alchemical effort to create a *coniunctio*. Since it fails, the experiment must be started anew. Faust's deepest need and desire is to unite with the feminine side of his nature, in order to recover the inner world of feeling, his lost values" (152).

On an altogether more sober, if more restricted, plane, Katharina Mommsen (1960) and Thomas Zabka (1993) consider Faust's journey to the Mothers in terms of identifiable literary references. Mommsen (233, 238, 247, 253, 257–61) traces precedents, motifs and patterns from the Arabian Nights, while Zabka interprets the episode as Goethe's satirical persiflage of early Romantic inwardness, subjectivity and irrationalism:

In Fausts Gang zu den Müttern zeigt sich Goethes Kritik an dem ro-
mantischen Weg nach innen. Wenn Faust die Phantome Helena und
Paris hervorbringt, werden das frühromantische Konzept der Einbildungskraft und der Magie-Begriff persifliert. Und wenn er schließlich
seine Kunstgebilde zu einem real-idealen "Doppelreich" (6555) er-
klärt, ist Schellings ästhetische Position um 1800 gemeint (140).

Critical opinion has also divided on the understanding of Faust's role in
his quest for the Mothers. Several critics have drawn inferences from
the manuscript variants of lines 6435–36 ("Die einen faßt des Lebens
holder Lauf, / Die andern sucht der kühne Magier auf"); Lieselotte
Blumenthal identified two earlier versions of line 6436, which read
"Die andern sucht getrost der Dichter auf," and "Die andern sucht der
kühne Dichter auf" (Blumenthal, 152). Just as Emrich saw behind
Faust's Plutus mask in the *Mummenschanz* a representation of the poet,
rather than of wealth as the patron of poetry (Knabe Wagenlenker), so
he sees Faust in the Mothers episode in the dual role of magus and poet: his retrieval of the figures of Paris and Helen from the transcendental sphere of the Mothers is a creative act of the poetic imagination. For
Blumenthal too, the manuscript variants indicate clearly enough that
Faust's role in the Mothers episode is not simply that of the "neophyte," or even of the fully-fledged "mystagogue." Goethe's conception of Faust's role and function had extended to include that of the
poet:

> Der Begriff des Magiers war umfassender geworden: er meinte nicht
> nur den Zauberer, sondern auf dem Wege über den Priester war Faust
> zum Dichter geworden [. . .]. Der neue Faust ist Zauberer, Priester
> und Dichter in eins, und je nach seiner Funktion innerhalb des
> Handlungsablaufs tritt das eine oder andere mehr hervor. (153)

Diener, Lohmeyer and Schlaffer — in their very different contexts — also discern in Faust the role of the creative poet; Arens seeks
to undermine such readings by pointing out that the Mothers, and the
dumb-show of Paris and Helen, are ultimately products of Mephistopheles' diabolical skills, not Faust's — are we therefore to assume
that art and poetry are in the gift of the Devil (277)?

A further point of critical contention concerns the relation of the
Mothers episode to the earlier scenes of Act 1 — the *Mummenschanz*
and the manufacture of paper money. For many critics, the difference
between the two sections of the act is radical. The opening scenes had
been played out in the worldly triviality of the courtly ambit; greed and
wealth had been the twin leitmotifs of that episode. Faust's journey to
the Mothers and the conjuration of Helen are concerned with infinitely
more profound themes and issues; it marks his abandoning of the frivo-

lity of the courtly milieu for the lofty cultural mission that will preoccupy him for the whole of the second and third Acts — his encounter
with, and conquest of, "die einzigste Gestalt," Helen of Troy. Mattenklott (1997) has defined this distinction:

> Helena erscheint nicht in der *Mummenschanz,* konnte in ihr nicht er-
> scheinen, denn in der Mythologie des *Faust II* gehört sie einer ande-
> ren Sphäre an als die Masken der Fastnacht. Diese waren in den
> allegorischen Kunstgestalten des höfischen Festes erschienen, das Ideal
> in den Verkleidungen, in denen die Hofgesellschaft es fassen konnte.
> Der Wunsch des Kaisers, Paris und Helena zu sehen, zielt auf mehr
> [. . .]. Nicht ein "Teufels-Liebchen" soll hier nun erscheinen, sondern
> eine antike Heroine [. . .]. Raum und Zeit entrückt ist die Müttergе-
> stalt nicht mehr bedingt, sondern als das Unbedingte aufgefaßt und
> selbst als die Bedingung der Schöpfung [. . .]. Zugang zu diesem
> Reich, Zugang zur antiken Kunstwelt als einem Seinsgrund, ist nicht
> durch irgendeine Kunstfertigung zu gewinnen, durch Zauber, durch
> Magie, sondern nur durch das Leben selbst. Das Gewesene ist nicht
> künstlich, ist nicht durch Bildung zu erschließen, sondern durch Er-
> zeugung. Darum weist der phallische Schlüssel Faust den Weg. [. . .]
> (412)

Other commentators choose to emphasise the similarities, indeed the
parallels, between the early and later episodes of Act 1: both are based
on the fundamental confusion of *Schein* and *Wesen.* Just as the crowd
(and the Emperor) fails to distinguish between appearance and substance, between paper money and true prosperity, so Faust fails to distinguish between illusion and reality in the dumb-show of Paris and
Helen. Both episodes end in catastrophe; to the *Flammengaukelspiel* of
the first corresponds the *Fratzengeisterspiel* of the second. When Mephistopheles protests to Faust: "Denkst Helenen so leicht hervor-
zurufen / Wie das Papiergespenst der Gulden" (lines 6197–98), he is
disingenuously misleading Faust — for both are phantom illusions.

Both Kruse (124–31) and Schlaffer (100) enumerate the textual and
thematic parallels between the paper money episode and the Mothers
episode. For Kruse, Faust's quest for Helen does not represent a higher
stage in Faust's progress: it is not a qualitative development; he does
not transcend the court milieu and the confusion of values it represents,
but only repeats the same confusion in a different register. Schlaffer
claims: "Im voraus ist die Erscheinung der Helena um den Kredit gebracht. Sie wird den Verdacht des 'Papiernen' nicht los [. . .]. Während
sie ins wirkliche Leben zu treten scheint, tritt sie in Wirklichkeit nur aus
dem literarischen Nachleben heraus" (101). Schlaffer also extends this
notion of Helen's unreality well beyond her phantom appearance in the

Rittersaal to her appearance in Act 3 — but in doing so, he indulges in some critical sleight-of-hand: when he quotes line 8783 in support of Helen's "allegorical" status analogous to the false substance of paper money ("Erobert', marktverkauft', vertauschte Ware du!"), he quotes it as if Mephistopheles' taunt related to Helen, whereas it is expressly directed not at her, but at her chorus of Trojan women as conquered spoils of war (Schlaffer, 102).

Some have reacted polemically against what Rüdiger Scholz imperiously dismisses as the "Vernebelungsinterpretation" of Emrich, Diener, Lohmeyer and those who seek ever deeper mystery or significance in the Mothers and their function in the episode — though Scholz only involves himself in an equally labyrinthine Freudian exegesis of Faust's quest:

> Die entscheidende Voraussetzung für Fausts Vereinigung mit Helena ist der Gang zu den Müttern. Obwohl die Bedeutung als Inzestphantasie so wenig kaschiert ist, daß sie eigentlich nur schwer zu übersehen ist, hat die "Faust"-Forschung trotz der überdeutlichen Hinweise auf die sexuelle Handlung infolge des bei den Forschern verinnerlichten Sexualtabus die Mütterszene mit allen möglichen Bedeutungen, aber nur selten mit der dargestellten, in Verbindung gebracht. Die sexuelle Berührungsangst der Interpreten hat besonders bei der Erklärung des Schlüssels zu grotesken Spekulationen geführt, um ihn nicht als Penis identifizieren zu müssen. (162)

To be sure, Scholz was by no means the first to see the talismanic key — "das kleine Ding" that behaves so perkily in Faust's hand, that will sniff out "die rechte Stelle" and guide him to the void where there are no locks or bolts — in phallic terms; but Scholz spells out the sexual connotations in scrupulous detail. He presents Faust's journey as Goethe's (*sic*) working out of sexual repressions and anxieties, of masturbation and incest fantasies. The journey is:

> als innerer Vorgang in Faust zu verstehen [. . .], psychisch als der Gang in sich selbst [. . .]. In der Form eines Mythos stellt Goethe die Wiedererinnerung verdrängter Wünsche, Erlebnisse und Phantasien der Kindheit dar [. . .]. Der Gang zu den Müttern ist psychisch die Aufhebung der Verdrängung, d.h. der Gang ins Unbewußte [. . .]. Die Handlung beschreibt wie in einer psychoanalytischen Kur Fausts Ängste, die Ursprünge der Konflikte anzugehen, seine Widerstände, die verdrängten Phantasien wiederzubeleben. (163–64)

One of the first modern critics to present a less portentously mystical, philosophical or symbolic analysis of the Mothers episode was Stuart Atkins (1958), who sees the whole construct of the Mothers, its attendant motifs, and the subsequent development of the action in the *Rit-*

tersaal scene, not as an example of Goethe's seriously imaginative poetic creativity, but as a "brilliant improvisation" on the part of Mephistopheles (133–34). That is, the Mothers, and Faust's journey to them,
are an ironic piece of inventive myth creation by the Devil. The "un-
prepossessing key" is a piece of theatrical magic which in the *Rittersaal*
scene becomes "simply a substitute for a magician's wand"; it and the
tripod are a kind of stage property supplied by Mephistopheles to bam-
boozle, first Faust, and subsequently the audience to which he presents
the spectacle of Paris and Helen (Atkins, 136–39). Atkins perceptively
points out the theatricality of Mephistopheles' pseudo-myth: he "coa-
ches" Faust in his role and rehearses with him the appropriate gestures
with the key (lines 6293–94); he instructs Faust to descend as if
through a stage trapdoor (line 6304); Faust re-emerges after line 6420
in the same theatrical manner; and the whole *Fratzengeisterspiel* is or-
chestrated and manipulated by Mephistopheles as director and stage
prompter.

Others have followed Atkins's lead. Albert Fuchs's interpretation
identifies Mephistopheles as "der Vater der Mütter. Er erfindet sie, um
nach dem Gesetz seines Wesens und Vorhabens Faust einmal mehr zu
hintergehen" (64–65). The episode represents a psychological struggle
between Faust and Mephistopheles, in which the Devil seeks to reassert
his authority over Faust by means of hypnotic illusion, by sending him
on a fool's errand to a mysterious realm that does not exist, giving him
as bogus talisman a key — "eine neue Ironie, da es ja nichts aufzu-
schließen gibt" (71). Faust initially — and correctly — suspects trickery
on Mephistopheles' part (lines 6249–54), but is soon caught up in his
compelling hypnotic spell. Nevertheless, Fuchs is still careful to emphasize the positive and productive result of Faust's quest — he finds his
"All" in Mephistopheles' "Nothing," and triumphs over trickery and
delusion:

> Das hypnotisch faszinierende Teufelsgespinst regte Fausts geistige Fä-
> higkeiten an [. . .]. Faust erblickt und begreift das Gesetz der Ent-
> wicklung, die das Prinzip aller Schöpfung ist, die Ordnung des
> Universums ausmacht und schließlich zur vollendeten, in der Frau
> verkörperten Harmonie führt. (73–74)

Hans Arens takes the demystification of the Mothers a step further:
the whole myth is a piece of trickery, "ein Schwindel Mephistos" (233).
Arens points out the contradictions, even the absurdities, of Mephistopheles' account: Faust must make a journey not only into "das Un-
betretene," but the "nicht zu Betretende"; he is given a key for a place
where there are no locks or bolts; he is told to descend — but he could

just as well ascend; the Mothers are enthroned beyond space and time, yet they sit, stand and walk around as if in a normal physical environment. Arens mocks the key, tripod and incense as the paraphernalia of magic hocus-pocus, and points out the absurdity of the tripod following Faust like a dog on a lead. The whole thing does indeed, as Faust remarks, recall the *Hexenküche* — it is not so much a profound mystery as a masterpiece of ironic mystification; Faust appears in the *Rittersaal* not as magus or poet, but as a wizard (*Wundermann*). Nevertheless, Arens, like Atkins and Fuchs, acknowledges that the experience takes on a quite different significance for Faust in the end: "in der 'Hexenküche' wie im 'Rittersaal', ist das Erlebnis und Ergebnis für Faust ein ganz anderes und höheres, als von Mephisto geplant war" (313); "das Wesentliche ist, nach Goethes Absicht, daß Mephisto etwas anzettelt, was für Faust eine ganz andere Bedeutung gewinnt, als jener auch nur denken konnte: die Schönheit" (277).

The striking gulf between interpretations of the Mothers episode as a serious poetic and creative myth on the one hand, and as an ironic masterpiece of Mephistophelian illusionism on the other, is nicely demonstrated in two recent critical editions of *Faust*. The commentary in the *Münchner Ausgabe* (1997), edited by Gisela Henckmann and Dorothea Hölscher-Lohmeyer, reiterates Lohmeyer's earlier findings:

> Die Mütter sind das Reich der Urformen der Natur, der ewigen, von der Vergänglichkeit ihrer stofflichen Substrate unabhängigen Formprinzipien [. . .]. Die Dreiheit ihrer Gebärden bezeichnet sie als das Prinzip des Seins, das in den drei Naturbereichen, dem mineralischen ("sitzen"), dem pflanzlichen ("stehn"), dem tierischen ("gehn") gleichermaßen gesetzlich bildend wirksam ist. (MA 18.1, 757)

To be sure, Lohmeyer concedes that Mephistopheles indulges in some trickery and charlatanism in the scene *Hell erleuchtete Säle*; but this does not vitiate either the solemn mystery of his vision of the Mothers or the significance of the *Rittersaal* scene. In the final scene of the act, his trickery gives way to theatrical illusion, as Faust creates a new dramatic art for the modern age:

> Aus der magischen Beschwörung als der Schöpfung Fausts ist das neue Theater geworden, das Theater einer naturwahren Kunst, wie sie die Antike schon einmal hervorgebracht hatte und wie sie in der Renaissance und dem deutschen Klassizismus um 1800 wiederum neu geschaffen wurde. (757)

Albrecht Schöne in the *Frankfurter Ausgabe* (1994) takes a quite different view:

Ins "Reich der Mütter" schauend, hat man freilich die zahlreichen sa-
tirischen Vorzeichen und Ironie-Signale übersehen [. . .]. Solche frei
schwebenden Interpreten-Konstrukte [as those of Emrich, Diener,
Lohmeyer, etc.] finden im Wortlaut des Textes keine Stütze. (FA 7.2,
477)

Schöne emphasizes the parallels between the *Flammengaukelspiel*
episode with its paper money sequel, and the *Fratzengeisterspiel* of Paris
and Helen, concluding that both are based on "das Grundmotiv des
Künstlichen, trügerisch Scheinhaften, Fiktiven, das diesen ganzen
1. Akt durchzieht" (465). Mephistopheles appears in *Hell erleuchtete
Säle* quite clearly as a charlatan, and Faust appears in the subsequent
Rittersaal scene as his assistant in illusion: "Diese kontrebalancierende
Zwischenszene entmythologisiert die orakelnde Rede des Mystagogen
in der *Finsteren Galerie* eben so wie die Offenbarungen, welche der ins
Priesterkleid gehüllte Faust im dämmerigen *Rittersaal* verkünden wird"
(473).

Schöne also goes on to characterize the dumb-show of Paris and
Helen as an illusionist spectacle devised by Mephistopheles with the
help of a magic lantern that projects images onto a screen of smoke (or
incense). Even so, Schöne cannot conclude that the episode is therefore
without serious significance for Faust, or for the drama as a whole:

Das alles besagt nun keineswegs, man habe das "Reich der Mütter" als
puren Schwindel, die Geistererscheinung als bloßen Trickbetrug, die
darauf bezogenen Verse nur als Schaumschlägerei zweier Showmaster
zu verstehen. So glatt geht im opalisierenden Zauberreich dieser Poesie die Rechnung zwischen Ernst und Scherz nicht auf. (478)

In the earlier narrative versions of the Faust legend, Faust's encounter
with Helen was by no means a central feature of the story (in Wid-
mann's 1599 version it had been consigned to a summary in his notes
to the text). Even in the 1587 *Historia*, it had been a relatively minor
sexual adventure: Helen was a succubus provided by Mephostopheles
(*sic*) as Faust's "Concubin und Beischläferin" in order to divert him
from any thought of the sacrament of marriage. In the theatrical versions, as far as we know of the details, Helen or Paris did not always
feature centrally: Faust conjured for his patron various mythical and historical figures such as Tantalus, Sisyphus, Pompey, Judith and
Holofernes, Samson and Delilah, David and Goliath, or Charlemagne.
Marlowe had certainly given Faustus's brief encounter with the classical
heroine a more resonant cultural significance as the "peerless dame of
Greece [. . .], the pride of Nature's works, / And only paragon of ex-
cellence"; but even here it is scarcely the central episode of Faustus's

career. It was Goethe who raised the figure of Helen to her symbolic status as the iconic emblem of mythical beauty, as the "einzigste Gestalt" who represented the perfection of the human form and the whole achievement of ancient classical culture; it was Goethe who elevated Faust's union with her to one of the two central encounters of Faust's career on earth and made it into the pivotal experience of the second part of the drama.

The third act of *Faust II* was conceived, and partly executed, as early as 1800 with the episode *Helena im Mittelalter* (FA 7.1, 671–79). The whole act was completed by June 1826, and published separately in volume 4 of the *Ausgabe letzter Hand* in 1827 as *Helena: Klassisch-romantische Phantasmagorie. Zwischenspiel zu Faust*. It was only then that Goethe set out to write what he called the "Antezedentien zu Helena"; in other words, almost the whole of *Faust II*, the material preceding and following the third act (except for some material from Act 5) was written around that central episode. Lines 4613–6036 of the first act were completed by January 1828, and were published that year in Volume 12 of the *Ausgabe letzter Hand*; the preparations or "antecedents" for the appearance of Helen in the third act, what is generally known as "Fausts Weg zu Helena" — that is, the remainder of Act 1 and the whole of Act 2 — was written during 1829 and 1830; the three scenes specifically relating to the Mothers (*Finstere Galerie, Hell erleuchtete Säle* and *Rittersaal*) were composed in December 1829 and January 1830.

So the central story of Faust's encounter with Helen was already long since completed when Goethe set out to devise Faust's first introduction to the heroine and chart his quest for her. His first meeting with her is not an encounter in which he appears on the soil of her homeland as her equal, indeed as her protector, an encounter (however symbolic, allegorical and "phantasmagoric") in which he is able to enter into a union with her and even to have a son by her — but a brief, spectral and shadowy encounter in which he is not even supposed to touch her, a vicarious encounter which, as a result of his confusion of illusion and reality, ends in a failure, an explosion. To be sure, it is a failure that inspires Faust to set out on his momentous quest, that fires in his (quite literally) unconscious mind the dream of Helen and the Greek ideal that will preoccupy, indeed obsess him over the following two acts; but this does not alter the fact that this first meeting ends in a spectacular failure, a catastrophe that is the equivalent, though in quite different allegorical terms, of the catastrophe that befell the Emperor in the *Flammengaukelspiel* earlier in the first act.

What strikes the reader or spectator is the sudden, unprepared, even arbitrary introduction of the figure of Helen into the action of *Faust II* — of the figure around whom, as we have seen from the very chronology of the composition, the whole symbolic and allegorical action appears to revolve: Faust and Mephistopheles have made the Emperor wealthy, now they are to entertain him (lines 6191–92). From such a casual request stems the whole Helen experience; Faust's first encounter with her begins as a trivial court entertainment for a frivolous and irresponsible patron.

Mephistopheles' initial reluctance to help Faust to conjure the spirits of Paris and Helen is puzzling. He not only protests that such a promise was foolish and rash, but warns Faust of the formidable difficulty, even the extreme peril, of such an enterprise — the Devil of the early *Faust* narratives and of the theatrical tradition had no such problems or doubts. And yet this show of reluctance is entirely characteristic of Goethe's Devil: had he not initially demurred when Faust demanded Gretchen, until he swiftly calculated that such a change in his plans would give him the opportunity to devastate two lives (or more), rather than one? Is his reluctance merely designed to whet Faust's appetite or to stimulate his curiosity — or is he genuinely embarrassed by the demand to conjure a classical heroine (lines 6209–10)? If so, his powers are severely limited: to someone who has overnight produced enough paper currency to create an illusion of inexhaustible wealth, and staged a spectacular and supernatural masquerade for the court, such a task should, as Faust suggests, be easily done "mit wenig Murmeln" (line 6207). Even Mephistopheles' protest that he has no access to or control over pagan demonology rings hollow. For all his exasperation with and feigned indifference towards classical antiquity, he displays sufficient knowledge of such things at various times: of Nereids, Thetis and Peleus (lines 6022–27), of Thessalian witches (lines 6979–83), of Ops, Rhea and the Parcae (lines 7988–91). And in Act 3 as Phorkyas (admittedly after having adopted a classical persona), he shows a remarkably detailed grasp of the myths of the heroic age and of Helen's biography (lines 8812–19, 8843–78), and is able to manipulate Helen and her Trojan women into Faust's protection.

Such pedantic references are in any case superfluous, for consistency of characterization and behaviour, or truthful reliability, are not things we can or should expect from Mephistopheles, who appears in *Faust* (and more especially in *Part Two*) in a bewildering series of masks and roles, each adapted to the prevailing situation. By definition, as it were, the Devil's word is not to be trusted (though this does not mean that he always speaks untruth). It soon becomes clear that Mephistopheles is able to fulfil Faust's (and the Emperor's) wishes — and indeed, he is contracted by the terms of his pact with Faust to fulfil those wishes (lines 1656–59). But if his mysterious and solemn invocation of the Mothers is a spurious myth of his own invention, the question remains: why should he go to such elaborate lengths to devise such a tale of such mysterious and inscrutable creatures, to be reached only across an unimaginable void after a journey attended by unheard-of dangers, for which Faust must be given careful instructions and be equipped with a magic talisman? It would have been a great deal simpler to cut out the mystification and let Faust in on the act. The answer to this might be that precisely in order to create the compelling illusion of his piece of theatre in the *Rittersaal* scene, Mephistopheles must make Faust believe in his myth — whether he does this by hypnotism, by stimulating Faust's own imagination, or by means of the power of language, or indeed by all three. He needs to exercise a hold over Faust so that Faust can conjure up the figures of Paris and Helen in a way that convinces the audience — and in a way that, as we shall see, leads ironically to Faust himself succumbing to the very illusion that he is helping to create. In other words, Goethe is signalling to his reader or audience Mephistopheles' role as the deviser and orchestrator of the whole sequence: as the creator of the Mothers myth in *Finstere Galerie*, as quack physician in *Hell erleuchtete Säle*, and as director of the dumb-show of Paris and Helen in *Rittersaal*.

Most commentators are led to accept the myth of the Mothers as *bare Münze*, as a serious and non-ironic creation of Goethe's imagination (in whatever symbolic or philosophical configuration they interpret it), because Mephistopheles' language, his eloquent and mysterious description of the way to the Mothers and their realm beyond the total desolation of the void, is so compelling. Lines 6239–48 in particular, a powerful evocation of utter emptiness that gains added force by being set against an equally eloquent evocation of a vivid seascape, the urgent insistence of "Du sähst doch etwas," the solemn description of the seat of the Mothers, their oracular attributes, their trance-like existence "umschwebt von Bildern aller Kreatur," are taken, reasonably enough, to be examples of Goethe's most compelling imaginative writing. This is all the more so because the lines "Gestaltung, Umgestaltung, / Des ewigen Sinnes ewige Unterhaltung" (6287–88) appear to adumbrate Goethe's own morphological credo of metamorphosis, and even to paraphrase aspects of his great poetic statement of the dynamic principle of transformation and re-creation in his late poem "Eins und Alles."

And yet there is no reason why the Devil should not be capable of devising and manipulating such language and such concepts in order to mystify Faust and to convince him that he is about to enter an utterly mysterious, timeless sphere to retrieve the spirit forms of Paris and Helen. Had he not already, in lines 6003–27, entranced the Emperor with an exotic vision of power and wealth, a submarine paradise worthy of Sheherezade? Had he not earlier, in Part One, invented a hilarious and imaginative account of Schwerdlein's life and death? Had not his spirits, even earlier, plunged Faust into a hypnotic "ocean of delusion", with their alluringly lyrical evocation of an Arcadian *Schlaraffenland* (lines 1447–1511)? There can be little doubt of the Devil's ability to create elaborate and compelling fiction; and Mephistopheles' hypnotic spell — as Faust himself realizes and points out (lines 6249–50) before he succumbs to it totally — could well be that of a master illusionist, a miracle worker, a *Wunderapostel* — in other words, of a Cagliostro.

Goethe's attitude to Giuseppe Balsamo, alias Cagliostro, as I have outlined elsewhere (Williams 1988), was one of fascination and repulsion. From as early as 1781 he had followed the master charlatan's career with an equal measure of interest and disapproval; he had even visited the magician's family in Palermo in 1787, and had followed the diamond necklace scandal of 1785 (in which he clearly believed, probably wrongly, that Cagliostro had been centrally involved) with horror, and in retrospect came to see the scandal as the beginning of the end for the Bourbon monarchy in France. Whatever the truth about Cagliostro's involvement in the affair, Goethe saw it as crucial, and the magician was demonized by Goethe as the very symptom and symbol of the corruption and decadence of the *ancien régime* in France. (In fact, Cagliostro had only limited success and influence in the court circles of Europe; he had enjoyed real power and prestige in Mitau, rather less in St. Petersburg, and still less in Paris, where he had duped only the vain and foolish Cardinal de Rohan. In spite of this, and in spite of being acquitted of involvement in the court scandal by the *Parlement*, he was still banished by Louis XVI for his suspected role in the affair.)

In 1791 Goethe had written a satirical comedy, *Der Groß-Cophta*, which lampooned, in a severely scaled-down provincial setting, the machinations of Cagliostro and the gullibility of his patrons. Although the scale and setting of the play do not remotely indicate the national, indeed international significance Goethe attributed to the necklace scandal at the French court, it is still an interesting illustration of Goethe's perception of the magician and of his infiltration of the higher echelons of society in the protagonist who is a clear lampoon of the self-styled Cagliostro: the "Graf Rostro di Rostro impudente."

Cagliostro and his many *confrères* in magical illusion (Saint-Germain, Schrepfer, Gaßner) would typically use a variety of tactics and devices for their ceremonies and spectacles — especially for the conjuration of spirits. They would insist on a period of strict initiation, often involving ordeals such as isolation or fasting, for their victims or "neophytes." They would be skilled in hypnotic suggestion, in theatrical effects and the use of stage properties: crystal balls or bowls of water, hidden voices, music, lighting, smoke, mirrors, and the projection of images by means of a magic lantern or similar apparatus. They would employ a medium who had been carefully coached in his or her role, and would issue dire warnings to their audience or victim not to approach or attempt to intervene in the spectacle they were witnessing — in case they should enquire too curiously into the mechanics of that spectacle; all depended on the willing suspension of disbelief on the part of an often-all-too-willing or credulous audience. And they would embellish their séances with arcane formulae, with alchemical or cabbalistic hocus-pocus; Cagliostro's speciality was his "Egyptian Rite," elaborated from Masonic and Rosicrucian ceremony and symbolism.

In the third act of *Der Groß-Cophta*, Graf Rostro provides for his patron the Domherr (a figure corresponding broadly to Cagliostro's historical victim the Cardinal de Rohan) an Egyptian ceremony with the help of his medium, the niece of the Marquise; his initiate or neophyte, the Ritter de Greville, is also being duped by the "Count." The scene is a temple, the ceremony is accompanied by music and singing, clouds of incense hang in the air, a tripod rises out of the floor, and the veiled figure of the medium, prompted by Graf Rostro, describes the actions of the "spirits" as she sees them in a glass ball. To be sure, there is no actual dumb-show here — the spectators experience the scene as it is described to them by the medium, and the spectral magic theatre of the *Rittersaal* is rather more elaborately staged; but otherwise, the parallels between the two episodes are striking.

Mephistopheles had already, in the earlier scenes of Act 1, played a role reminiscent of Cagliostro. He had infiltrated the court as a "Schalk" (line 4885), he had paraded his gifts of "Kalenderei" and "Chymisterei" (line 4974), he had prompted the Astrologer with a speech suggesting the fraudulent manufacture of gold and silver by alchemical processes, and used his persuasive gifts of suggestion in order to dangle a dream of unimaginable wealth before the Emperor and his entourage. In *Finstere Galerie*, the awesome ordeal of the journey he prescribes for Faust to the Mothers, the elaborate mystery and the sense of awe (*Schaudern*) he creates, the mysterious key he provides as talisman, all suggest the kind of total psychic dominance a master illusionist

like Cagliostro would exert over his victim, his "neophyte," or his medium. In the second scene of the Mothers episode, *Hell erleuchtete Säle*,
his role as magician or *Wunderapostel* is even more clearly signalled; he
prescribes an alchemical cure for freckles (lines 6323–28), and provides
a homeopathic remedy for a lame foot by kicking the patient with his
own *Pferdehuf* (6333–42). Some commentators relate the latter to one
of the spells of the *Merseburger Zaubersprüche*; more probably, it is a
satirical allusion to the methods of Samuel Hahnemann (1755–1843),
whose doctrine of *similia similibus curentur* (like is cured by like) was
the foundation of modern homeopathy — and whose work Goethe
considered little different from that of other contemporary quacks and
miracle-workers; in a letter to Johann Heinrich Meyer of 5 March 1820
he described Hahnemann caustically as "den neuen Theophrastus Paracelsus." The cure prescribed for a woman's unrequited love (lines
6347–54) may be based on traditional folk superstitions — or it may be
a persiflage of the techniques of Franz Anton Mesmer (1733–1815); at
all events, it is a further example of Mephistopheles' parade of quackery
and fraudulence (the emotional problems of the page are dealt with
more straightforwardly by means of diabolical advice).

The events of the *Rittersaal* scene are also consistent with the Cagliostro role of Mephistopheles; they bear all the hallmarks of a spirit
séance or conjuration. The astrologer is prompted by Mephistopheles,
who pops up comically from his *Soufflierloch*; he describes the scene,
encourages the audience's suspension of disbelief — "Durch magisch
Wort sei die Vernunft gebunden" (line 6416) — and emphasizes
Faust's appearance, not as a magus or poet, but as a magician ("ein
Wundermann"). At this point, Faust assumes his role as medium with a
solemn invocation of the Mothers (lines 6427–38). Now, this might be
the speech of someone who has indeed witnessed the awesome presence of ineffable deities enthroned "hehr in Einsamkeit" — or it might
be the trance-like vision of someone who has wholly succumbed to
Mephistopheles' hypnotic spell (a third alternative, that Faust is know-
ingly conniving in a piece of Mephistophelian — or Cagliostrian — deception, is unlikely, given Faust's subsequent behavior). It has been
persuasively argued (for example, by Arens, 270 and 309–10) that
Faust's grandiose invocation contains nothing that Faust (or the reader) did not already know about the Mothers from Mephistopheles'
description of them in the scene *Finstere Galerie*; it is simply a more
rhetorical and theatrical reformulation of what he has been told about
them.

The spectacle proceeds as a "Geister-Meisterstück" (line 6443); the
court audience, much less involved than Faust, treats the whole episode

simply as a show put on for its amusement, commenting and gossiping accordingly. And indeed, in this they may well be showing a healthier skepticism than Faust, for as the scene moves towards its climax, Faust three times becomes wholly carried away by the illusion. What is interesting is not so much Faust's reaction, but Mephistopheles' ripostes: three times he urgently warns Faust not to interfere. The first time (line 6501) he orders him to control himself and not to step out of his role as medium or collaborator: "So faßt Euch doch und fallt nicht aus der Rolle!"; the second time (lines 6514–15) he warns him urgently to keep clear of the spectral action: "Ruhig! Still! / Laß das Gespenst doch machen, was es will"; the third time (line 6546) he frantically tries to convey to Faust that this is a spectacle of his, Faust's, own making: "Machst du's doch selbst, das Fratzengeisterspiel!" This revealing remark can only indicate that, at least as far as Mephistopheles is concerned, Faust is helping to create the illusion to which he then succumbs, with catastrophic results.

There are two earlier enigmatic remarks by Mephistopheles that must also be considered here; for on the face of it, they appear to contradict the notion that the Mothers are an improvised Mephistophelian invention — indeed, they appear to indicate that Mephistopheles believes in the objective reality of the Mothers and of the extreme perils of the journey that he himself has so hair-raisingly evoked. In lines 6305–6, in a typically conspiratorial aside to the audience, he comments:

> Wenn ihn der Schlüssel nur zum besten frommt!
> Neugierig bin ich, ob er wiederkommt.

And in line 6366 he appears to appeal directly to the Mothers to release Faust: "O Mütter, Mütter! Laßt nur Fausten los!" Of those commentators who insist that the myth of the Mothers is of Mephistopheles' devising, none has given a fully satisfactory explanation of these remarks. And yet the reader's understanding (or the actor's "reading") of these lines is crucial to the interpretation of the whole Mothers episode. The first remark can certainly be read ironically, as Mephistopheles' provocative comment on his own powers of mystification — with a nod and a wink, or even a knowing leer, to the audience. His appeal to the Mothers to release Faust can also be read as part of the theatricality of the whole show — even as a signal to his witting or unwitting accomplice, Faust, that the scene is set, and he can now appear in his role as *Wundermann* or medium; alternatively, it might be read as a signal to the *stage* audience that the spectacle is about to start, or as a device to rid himself of the importunate crowd of "patients" pestering him. His final sardonic comment to the audience (lines 6564–65) is an altogether less ambiguous statement of his perception of the whole episode.

No final or unequivocal conclusion can be drawn on the interpretation of the Mothers episode, on whether they are the creations of a serious Goethean myth of transcendental archetypes of creation and metamorphosis, guardians of a repository of mythical or historical images — or whether they are the ironic creations of Mephistophelian mystification. Those commentators who interpret the episode as a piece of theatrical illusionism invented and manipulated by the Devil — and the parallels to *Der Groß-Cophta* or to the fraudulent spirit séances of contemporary *Wunderapostel* are surely too close to ignore — still find themselves unable to demystify the Mothers completely, and concede that since the episode culminates in the appearance of no less a figure than Helen of Troy, and since the appearance of the heroine fires Faust with the heroic ambition to seek and possess the Greek ideal, there must be more to the whole thing than simply a Mephistophelian trick. In other words, Faust does indeed find his "All" in the Devil's "Nothing."

It is undeniable that the myth of the Mothers, and even the spirit séance of the *Rittersaal,* are compelling constructs; this is no ordinary piece of charlatan illusionism of the kind lampooned by Goethe in *Der Groß-Cophta*, or by Schiller, for example, in his unfinished novel *Der Geisterseher* (1787–89). After all, it is no mere Cagliostro, no ordinary *Wunderapostel* who is orchestrating events here, but the Devil himself; the figures of Paris and Helen appear to be charged with some kind of occult energy, and the result of Faust's unprogrammed intervention is not simply the unmasking of an elaborate fraud, as it is in Goethe's comedy or in Schiller's novel, but an explosion that paralyses Faust until he sets foot on the soil of Helen's homeland. Just as Faust's first encounter with Gretchen was to develop in a quite different direction from the casual lechery envisaged by Mephistopheles (and indeed initially by Faust himself), so the consequences of Faust's first encounter with Helen are far more momentous than either of them had imagined when they set out simply to fulfill the Emperor's whim.

Nevertheless, the Helen of Act 1 is not remotely the Helen of Act 3. She is the product of a collaboration between Faust and Mephistopheles, in which Faust is indeed acting as the Devil's catspaw, though no doubt unwittingly; she is the product of a theatrical piece of higher, even supernatural, illusionism; she is the spectral image of the Greek heroine, inaccessible to Faust except as a phantom form: "ein Schauspiel nur." In order to find and possess Helen, Faust cannot simply grab impatiently at this specter in a frenzy of besotted jealousy; he must first submit to a long process of personal and cultural maturity, he must make a far lengthier, far more complex and substantial journey than his trance-like, if intrepid, journey to the Mothers. He must travel, not through a trackless void, but back through historical time, and to Greece. In the teeming mythical throng of the *Klassische Walpurgisnacht* he must experience, vicariously and at first hand, the whole primitive pre-classical spectrum of archaic Greek religious myth, the pre-history of Helen herself, as it were; he must descend to Hades, and transform himself into a Frankish knight who has colonized the Peloponnese, in order to reach the stage where the "barbarian" is fit to claim possession of the classical heroine — in however "phantasmagoric" or symbolic a form. In short, he must embark on his own classical education.

For all the thematic parallels and textual correspondences drawn by Schlaffer and Kruse between the earlier scenes of Act 1 and the three closing scenes, for all the common confusion of appearance and reality, illusion and substance that underlies both the *Mummenschanz* sequence and the *Fratzengeisterspiel* of the *Rittersaal*, the introduction of the motif of Helen of Troy into the development of Act 1 in lines 6183–86 does mark a distinct and significant hiatus in the symbolic and dramatic action of *Faust II*. It is the point at which the dramatic allegory begins to leave the political and historical context that informs the "imperial" scenes of lines 4728–6172 (and which will return to occupy the whole action of Act 4), and embarks on the cultural allegories with which the second and third Acts are concerned. In the imperial scenes of Act 1 we witnessed a realm on the brink of catastrophic social, economic and political disaster; the parallels to the *ancien régime* in France prior to 1789 are there to be drawn (see Williams 1987, 125–34; 1993, 91–95). At almost exactly the same point in historical time, Goethe set out on his own classical education, on his Italian journey, which was to culminate in the period of Weimar Classicism.

Of course Acts 2 and 3 of *Faust II* are not simply a biographical allegory of Goethe's personal commitment to classical ideals, or of Weimar Classicism; they also adumbrate the successive responses of Western civilization to the cultural heritage of Greece over a vast historical period. Act 3 begins as Euripidean tragedy, moves through the era of the Germanic migrations, the Crusades, and the Renaissance, modulating into the neo-classicism of the seventeenth and eighteenth centuries, up to and including Weimar Classicism, in the final operatic episode of the death of Euphorion and the return of Helen to Hades. It may well be that in Faust's early spectral encounter with Helen, Goethe is adumbrating both his own immature response to classicism and that of western culture as a whole. M. G. Druian has made the interesting suggestion that Faust's fourteen-line encomium to the phantom Helen in lines 6487–500 reads like a clumsily executed Petrarchan sonnet — that is, Faust is here "a man of the Renaissance" who expresses his furious emotional turmoil in this flawed poetic form.

However skeptically or ironically we may judge the strangely compelling Mephistophelian myth of the Mothers, or its theatrical and satirical aftermath in the *Fratzengeisterspiel* of the *Rittersaal* scene, and in spite of the fact that the whole sequence ends in such apparent disaster for Faust, the episode is clearly of profound consequence to Faust's career and to the development of the action of *Faust II*. Faust will indeed find his All in Mephistopheles' Nothing; he will find that All, however, not in the vague and obscure realm of insubstantial forms inhabited by the Mothers, nor in the spectral dumb-show that he himself helps to stage for the court, but only after a lengthy educative mission, after a long quest at the end of which he will be fit to possess "die einzigste Gestalt."

Works Cited

Arens, Hans. *Kommentar zu Goethes Faust II*. Heidelberg: Winter, 1989.

Atkins, Stuart. *Goethe's Faust: A Literary Analysis*. Cambridge, MA.: Harvard UP, 1958.

Blumenthal, Lieselotte. "Goethes letztes Gedicht." *Goethe. Neue Folge des Jahrbuchs der Goethe-Gesellschaft*. 16 (1954). 143–60.

Bratranek, Franz Thomas. *Erläuterungen zu Goethes Faust* (1842). 2 vols. New ed. Salzburg: Klosterneuburg, 1957.

Danckert, Werner. *Goethe: Der mythische Urgrund seiner Weltschau*. Berlin: de Gruyter, 1951.

Diener, Gottfried. *Fausts Weg zu Helena: Urphänomen und Archetypus*. Stuttgart: Klett, 1961.

Druian, M. Gregory. "A Note on *Faust II*, lines 6487–6500." *German Quarterly*. 47 (1974). 432–35.

Emrich, Wilhelm. *Die Symbolik von Faust II*. 3rd ed. Frankfurt am Main: Athenäum, 1957.

Fuchs, Albert. "Die Mütter. Eine Mephistopheles-Phantasmagorie." In: Albert Fuchs, *Goethe-Studien*. Berlin : de Gruyter, 1968. 64–81.

Jantz, Harold. *The Mothers in "Faust": The Myth of Time and Creativity*. Baltimore: Johns Hopkins UP, 1969.

Klett, Ada M. *Der Streit um Faust II seit 1900*. Jena: Frommann, 1939.

Kruse, Jens. *Der Tanz der Zeichen: Poetische Struktur und Geschichte in Goethes Faust II*. Königstein (Taunus): Hain, 1985.

Lohmeyer, Dorothea. *Faust und die Welt: Der zweite Teil der Dichtung. Eine Anleitung zum Lesen des Textes*. Munich: C. H. Beck, 1975.

Mattenklott, Gert. "Faust II." *Goethe-Handbuch*. Vol. 2. *Dramen*. Ed. Theo Buck. Stuttgart & Weimar: Metzler, 1997. 391–477.

Mommsen, Katharina. *Goethe und 1001 Nacht*. Berlin: Akademie-Verlag, 1960. New ed. Frankfurt am Main: Suhrkamp, 1981.

Plutarch. "The Life of Marcellus." *Plutarch's Lives*. Trans. Bernadotte Perrin. Loeb Classical Library. Cambridge, MA: Harvard UP, 1917. Vol. 5. 435–523.

———. "The Obsolescence of Oracles." *Plutarch's Moralia*. Trans. Frank Cole Babbitt. Loeb Classical Library. Cambridge, MA: Harvard UP, 1936. Vol. 5. 350–501.

Raphael, Alice. *Goethe and the Philosophers' Stone: Symbolical Patterns in "The Parable" and the Second Part of Faust*. London: Routledge & Kegan Paul, 1965.

Schlaffer, Heinz. *Faust Zweiter Teil: Die Allegorie des 19. Jahrhunderts*. Stuttgart: Metzler, 1981.

Scholz, Rüdiger. *Die beschädigte Seele des großen Mannes. Goethes "Faust" und die bürgerliche Gesellschaft*. Rheinfelden: Schäuble, 1982.

Vischer, Friedrich Theodor. "Zum zweiten Teile von Goethes Faust" (1861). In: Fr. Th. Vischer. *Kritische Gänge*. Ed. Robert Vischer. 2nd ed. Munich: Meyer & Jessen, 1920–22. Vol. 2. 320–64.

Williams, John R. "Mephisto's Magical Mystery Tour. Goethe, Cagliostro and the Mothers in *Faust, Part Two*." *Publications of the English Goethe Society*. 58 (1988). 84–102.

———. *Goethe's Faust*. London: Allen & Unwin, 1987.

———. "Die Deutung geschichtlicher Epochen im zweiten Teil des *Faust*." *Goethe-Jahrbuch*. 110 (1993). 89–103.

Zabka, Thomas. *Faust II — Das Klassische und das Romantische: Goethes "Eingriff in die neueste Literatur."* Tübingen: Niemeyer, 1993.

The Classical and the Medieval in *Faust II*

Anthony Phelan

IN *FAUST*, THE LATE MEDIEVAL OR EARLY MODERN WORLD enfolds classical antiquity and is in turn enfolded by it. This is centrally true in Act 3 of Part Two, the Helena Act. Here a Greek tragedy takes the stage in which a medieval castle becomes the scene of Faust and Helena's love and, in its turn, encloses the Arcadian idyll that briefly realizes their union in the life of Euphorion. This pattern of concentric actions in the Helena Act will concern us later in this essay; but the classical realm confronts most readers of Goethe's drama in another way, as a matter of cultural reference or allusion. In some cases these allusions are incidental, but more often than not they send us scurrying to the commentaries provided by generations of *Faust* scholars. Ironically enough, modern readers may be doing no more than Goethe himself in this respect, for he constantly had recourse to the encyclopedic knowledge garnered by Benjamin Hederich in his *Gründliches mythologisches Lexikon* (revised in 1770), and he took some material from early nineteenth-century studies of classical mythology by Georg Friedrich Creuzer and the philosopher Friedrich W. J. von Schelling. When the Theatre Director of the "Vorspiel auf dem Theater" says that his learned audience outstrips his skills in providing popular entertainment, Goethe is half defining the audience he *hopes* for — and half acknowledging the huge resources he and his readers will need for the play that is to follow:

> Ich weiß, wie man den Geist des Volks versöhnt;
> Doch so verlegen bin ich nie gewesen;
> Zwar sind sie an das Beste nicht gewöhnt,
> Allein sie haben schrecklich viel gelesen.
>
> (43–46)

Faust will indeed be a learned play, evolving from the tragedy of a scholar ("Gelehrtentragödie"); and we need to rely on commentators who can match this wide knowledge of classical literature and mythology, but not every reference carries the same weight. Early in the drama Faust's assistant, Wagner, imagines he has overheard him reciting a passage from a Greek tragedy, and wanders in, in his nightcap and night-gown, in order to improve his own rhetorical skills. It would be point-less to speculate which of the Greek tragedians might provide a suitable text for this false assumption. If anything, it will be the purpose of the whole drama to emancipate itself from the imitation of Greek models and from the narrow scholasticism which sees the literature and my-thology of antiquity only in this light. On the other hand, the classical references of Goethe's play are not merely decorative; are more than the "Dekor des gebildeten Diskurses" (Jamme, 208). When Faust, in the Walpurgisnacht scene, euphemistically tells the attractive young witch he is dancing with that he has dreamt of an apple-tree on which two beautiful apples were hanging, and his partner clarifies the eroti-cism by reference to Paradise (where Eve plucked an apple), Mephi-stopheles unmasks their lack of candor in his own coarse ("wüst") and downright version (4128–43). Indeed, editions before the Frankfurter Ausgabe suppress the devil's obscenity by retaining Goethe's "An-standsstriche." The biblical allusion is not allowed to decorate or con-ceal the "real" meaning.

Wagner's only interest is in improving his rhetoric. His utilitarian attitude to the art of antiquity is smug and self-satisfied, as is his esti-mation of the relationship of past and present in general: for him schol-arly learning is "Zu schauen, wie vor uns ein weiser Mann gedacht, / Und wie wir's dann zuletzt so herrlich weit gebracht" (572–73). This belief in human progress is a symptom, for Faust, of Wagner's limited intellectual aspirations: his response "O ja, bis an die Sterne weit!" (574) is heavy with irony. There is a gulf between the narrow mind of the Famulus and his own attempt to reach for the stars. This contrast between spiritual and intellectual limitation and a fearless yearning for the vastness of the universe itself is focussed in one of the dominant im-ages for Faust's world as a prison ("Kerker"). Although the Theater Di-rector of the "Vorspiel" promises that the play will move at breath-taking speed "Vom Himmel durch die Welt zur Hölle," in Part One the stations of Faust's life seem seriously limited. He moves, via the ba-nalities of "Auerbachs Keller" and the "Hexenküche," from one con-fined space to another — from his "hochgewölbtes enges gotisches Zimmer" to the more domestic constraints of Gretchen's "kleines rein-liches Zimmer" (before 2678), until the play ends with Faust's flight from outside a prison cell which he had already anticipated in Gretchen's room: "In diesem Kerker welche Seligkeit!" (2694).

On the way, the expansiveness of Faust's soliloquy in "Wald und Höhle" is soon deflated and, like Gretchen's domestic beginnings, he too is "Umfangen in der kleinen Welt" (3355). Here Faust's own intellectual range is compromised, as John Williams points out, by the fact that his lyrical statement of faith in response to Gretchen's naïve question appears in the context of the play "as specious and evasive, as the rhetorical smokescreen of a subtle and complex mind" (Williams, 106). Even the promised extremities of the "Walpurgisnacht" are deflected by Mephistopheles' preference (for whatever reasons) for "kleine Welten" (4045) (see Schöne 1982, 351–52). The world of Part One is straitened and confined — a far cry from the vision of the macrocosm which first excites Faust's desire for a fuller experience than that afforded by his scholarly surroundings in a sixteenth-century university.

It is this dark and superstitious world which places Faust at the dawn of the modern age, and at the historical limit of the late Middle Ages. Yet his initial state of mind is essentially one of boredom: the higher faculties of the medieval university provide no further stimulus for him, and in what follows there is something essentially random about his attempts at cabbalism and conjuration, speculative suicide or Bible translation. His efforts with the beginning of St. John's Gospel associate him historically with the philological advances of the Renaissance and Reformation. It is the rediscovery of the languages and cultures of antiquity that nourished both the humanist revival with new access to classical and biblical Greek (and Hebrew) and their respective literatures, and thus also opens the way for the knowledge of the classical world in the late medieval context. Faust's willingness to abandon the sacred text for a version better suited to his own proclivities, however, suggests an unfocussed intellectual restlessness, and a desire to mould the original to his own taste. Here the Logos is progressively transformed from "Wort" via "Sinn" and "Kraft" to read the opening of St. John's prologue as "Im Anfang war die Tat." Translation is only possible in Faust's own image. His questing mind, his Hamlet-like pursuit of self-transcendence, skull in hand and contemplating "not to be," beats against the limits of his own prison — "Weh! steck' ich in dem Kerker noch?" (398) — but he achieves only glimpses of a greater order of experience. Even in the spectacle of the sign of the macrocosm, the vision fades in the very moment that it is acknowledged — "Welch Schauspiel! Aber ach! ein Schauspiel nur!" (454) (see Bennett, 22–23).

The historical parts of Part Two of Goethe's play allude to a similar period. In the sketch for a conclusion which Goethe drafted for his autobiographical work, *Dichtung und Wahrheit*, in 1816, the scenes following "Anmutige Gegend" are placed in the imperial court at Augsburg, and the Kaiser is Emperor Maximilian I (HA 3, 435–37.). The council of state assembled in this second scene of *Faust II* provides a much broader frame of reference, however; the empire described by

the reports of Chancellor, Treasurer, Steward and General reveals a
state on the verge of fiscal collapse and anomie. Its early modern context points towards the political strand of the play. What begins in this
act with the devilish invention of paper money is taken up again in the
apparent conflict between Emperor and Anti-Emperor staged by
Mephistopheles in Act 4 and concludes in Faust's attempt in Act 5 to
establish an independent colony on land reclaimed from the sea and
granted to him as sovereign territory in return for his "military" support. The early modern world of the empire generally points beyond its
own limits, then, to the collapse of feudal order, the emergence of early
capitalism from mercantilism, and towards the revolutionary movements
of the eighteenth and nineteenth centuries. It is this wider field of contemporary reference to which Goethe alludes in his comment on Part
Two of 17 February 1831 to Eckermann: "Es erscheint hier eine höhere,
breitere, hellere, leidenschaftslosere Welt, und wer sich nicht etwas um-
getan und Einiges erlebt hat, wird nichts damit anzufangen wissen."

Readers need to have their wits about them. Goethe's own sense is
evidently that Part One presents a world of narrowness, darkness and
passion which will be contrasted with the lighter and more open texture
of Part Two. Yet it is clear that the less elevated material of Part One is
entirely appropriate to the Faust tradition. Goethe draws on the popular
transmission of the legend through its puppet-play version based on
Marlowe's *Dr. Faustus,* and Nikolaus Pfitzer's 1674 redaction and ab-
breviation of the original *Historia von D. Johann Fausten* of 1587.
Goethe had probably read the shortened version as a child (Matussek,
352; Müller, 204). This material combines low comedy, recalling Til
Eulenspiegel's pranks, with an enduring Lutheran anxiety about theological authority, as well as an interest in uncertain states of mind caught
between dream, hallucination, and illusion. For example, chapter 24 of
the *Historia von D. Johann Fausten*, entitled "Wie Doct. Faustus in die
Hell gefahren," turns out to be "eine lauter Phantasey oder traum" (*Historia*, 53). But it is also the Faust book material which associates Faust
with the evocation or conjuration of figures from classical antiquity.

In the *Historia* Faust is, among other things, a kind of travelling
magician and miracle worker. His tricks are performed for the entertainment and edification of the aristocracy or at the expense of self-
confident peasants. The third part of the Faust book concentrates on
his necromancy as performed "an Potentaten Höfen." Chapter 33
opens this section with an account of Faust's performance for Emperor
Charles V, who wishes to see Alexander the Great and his spouse. (The
desired historical figure clearly corresponds to the position of Faust's
patron.) Helen of Troy is another of these conjurations. She appears in

Christopher Marlowe's play almost as an afterthought, invoked for the
satisfaction of some of Faustus's fellow scholars; after he has once again
come close to repentance, he asks "to have unto my paramour / That
heavenly Helen which I saw of late" and greets her with the lines forever associated with her in English:

> Was this the face that launched a thousand ships
> And burnt the topless towers of Ilium?
> Sweet Helen, make me immortal with a kiss.
>
> (Marlowe, lines 1377–79)

Like his German successor, Goethe's Faust seems to fall under the spell
of a figure whose appearance he has himself stage-managed. However,
it is the scholarly context of Helen's appearance here and in its precur-
sor, the Faust book, that identifies her as a figure of classical learning
and as an object of desire. In the Faust book, Faustus conjures "die
schöne gestalt der Königin Helenae / Menelai Haußfraw" (*Historia*,
97) as an after-dinner entertainment for his students; when they ask for
a repeat performance, however, Faustus insists that they make do with a
portrait ("Conterfey") of Helen — a substitution which perhaps provides the basis for the equivocations associated with Helena's "presence" in Part Two of *Faust*.

Helena, the most important representative of antiquity, first appears
in *Faust* within the context of the courtly entertainments of the Palati-
nate, but the form which these take and the carnival masks which cross
the stage en revue prepare for Helen's appearance as a figure from classical antiquity in the final scene of the act. The second scene of Act 1
insistently presents the financial difficulties of the Reich, and Mephistopheles, in the guise of the emperor's new fool, offers to solve the
problem with the promise of hidden treasure. This is to provide a secure financial basis for the state. The inaccessibility of such buried
hoards subsequently leads to the introduction of paper money, at
Mephistopheles' suggestion. He and Faust wryly justify their inflation-
ary policy in the "Lustgarten" scene (6097–130). In the characterization of a courtly culture on the cusp of modern capitalist relations,
however, the paper money scene is important because it raises questions
about how values, ideas and other abstractions are represented.

In the scenes at the imperial court the ruse of introducing paper
money to solve the financial crisis is only one of a variety of illusions
that define different categories of representation. In the course of the
play this question of how values are staged is consistently associated
with the recovery of the classical world in the medieval or modern
context. First, the courtly masquerade of the "Mummenschanz" intro-

duces a form of allegorical carnival from Rome: as gardeners, fisher-
men, bird-catchers and woodmen cross the stage, the court reviews the
hierarchical social order of the empire. Goethe's restoration of the archaic form of allegory and the concomitant introduction of a new level
of generalization and abstraction were identified by Heinz Schlaffer, in
a now unfashionable argument, as fixing the dominant form of the
whole subsequent drama as allegorical (Schlaffer, 76–77; and see Schöne 1994, 55–56 and 430–32). Strictly speaking, this term applies only
to the masque of Plutus staged by Faust and Mephistopheles, which
finally involves the Emperor himself in the role of Pan leading the Wild
Hunt. However, the classical persona of the god of Wealth which Faust
adopts is anticipated, as the series of figures becomes increasingly abstract, by "die griechische Mythologie" which the Herald summons
earlier in the masquerade. He needs mythological characters here to fill
in for absent "Nacht- und Grabdichter" (before 5299). These writers'
preoccupation "mit einem frisch erstandenen Vampyr" decodes them as
Goethe's Gothic and Romantic contemporaries (which also enables us
to recognize a parallel between this carnival action and the contemporary allusions of the "Walpurgisnacht" and "Walpurgisnachtstraum" in
Part One: the cultural allusions of *Faust* are not merely antiquarian).
The arrival of the Graces, the Fates and the Furies gives a first glimpse
of classical order, measure, and proportion: in this account, the scissors
with which the Fate Klotho cuts the thread of life stay safely inside their
sheath, and the Furies themselves will only wreak their vengeance on
the promiscuities of court life. This mythological sequence in the
masque assimilates the figures of mythology to the decorum of the
court — and Goethe himself relies on their contemporary assimilation
in his own time through the encyclopedism of Hederich's *Lexikon* (see
Schöne 1994, 438–40). Hederich's account of Chiron, for instance,
explains the "eigentliche Historie" and "anderweitige Deutung" of the
mythical figure (Schöne 1994, 710–11).

The mythical masquerade has little antiquarian substance, then. It
extends the pastoral view of social stratification which began in the
masks of the "Gärtnerinnen" and "Gärtner" with an indulgent reflection on the amatory mores of the court, in a style which perhaps recalls
playful rococo versions of mythical material such as Wieland's *Comische
Erzählungen* or *Die Grazien*. The courtly entertainment thus illustrates
Faust's complaint to Wagner:

> Was ihr den Geist der Zeiten heißt,
> Das ist im Grund der Herren eigner Geist,
> In dem die Zeiten sich bespiegeln.
>
> (577–79)

Such assimilation is disrupted by the masque of Plutus. Up to this point the emblems of the masque have been controlled by the Herald. The arrival of an elephant in what seems to be an emblem of good government looks like the *pièce de résistance* of the entertainment, but the intervention of the obscure Zoilo-Thersites (often read as another mask of Mephistopheles), who mocks the stability of the triumphal procession, makes it clear that other and magical forces are now in play which overwhelm the herald's hermeneutic control. As the Boy Charioteer instructs the baffled Herald:

> Herold auf! nach deiner Weise,
> Ehe wir von euch entfliehen,
> Uns zu schildern, uns zu nennen;
> Denn wir sind Allegorien,
> Und so solltest du uns kennen.
>
> (5528–32)

His difficulty is resolved here by description, a relatively static "reading-off" of attributes; but the Herald's uncertainty is also the first in a series of mistakes about representation. The speaking flowers in the gardeners' masque are answered here by a staging of wealth. Value or valuables are twice brought to the stage and lead to a confusion in the understanding of the courtly audience and its imperial patron. The Boy Charioteer, who identifies himself as poetry and extravagance ("Bin die Verschwendung, bin die Poesie" [5573]) scatters jewelry among the courtiers which turns into beetles and butterflies the moment they try to seize it. This should be sufficient indication that what poetry represents is never simply a tangible good — and not even a practicable ornament! But the distinction between illusion, representation and reality is now unclear. The women of the courtly audience next mistake the "real" dragons drawing Faust-Plutus's chariot for part of the stage-set of the court masque. The assimilation and control of the allegorical structure earlier in the courtly entertainment has now been completely disrupted by the magical intervention of Faust and Mephistopheles.

Next Faust unleashes in the masque of Plutus the magical simulacra of gold, in the forms of jewelry and money. This time the Herald, as master of ceremonies, immediately recognizes the mistake — "Sind doch für euch in diesem Spiel / Selbst Rechenpfennige zuviel" (5731–32). It is a good point — for such tokens or counters would have no value in themselves, even though they are able to represent it. And Mephistopheles, as Avarice, provides another form in which the truth of these events can be measured in his own tongue-in-cheek description of the action, before providing a crass exposure of the eroticism implied in the earlier masques by making a huge golden phallus. Plutus and Avarice do not allow for the pretty assimilation and moralization of mythical figures that occurs in the "Mummenschanz" and Hederich. Instead Plutus reveals an aspect of the court which does not so happily coincide with the courtiers' amour-propre.

In their greed they seek to appropriate directly and immediately what is merely *represented* within the theatrical framework of the masque of Plutus. This play with the illusory representations of value anticipates the second appearance of the theme, in Goethe's larger argument, when the circulation of assignats or paper money is proposed by Mephistopheles and Faust to deal with the insolvency of the Reich. In his recent commentary on the play, Gert Mattenklott suggests that Mephistopheles' lines "Nimm Hack' und Spaten, grabe selber, / Die Bauernarbeit macht dich groß" (5039–40), towards the end of the court discussion of hidden treasure, in fact invite the Emperor to recognize and participate in *labor* as the true source of social wealth in a proper relationship to Nature. Hederich's *Lexikon* might confirm this when he notes of Plutus, god of wealth, "Er bemerket aber an sich nichts, als den Reichthum selbst, der von der Ceres [Plutus's mother], das ist vom Feldbaue, am besten ernähret wird" (column 2032); but, by the same token, Mattenklott is inclined to dismiss the significance of the paper money episode as not essential to Goethe's conception of the imperial scenes (412–14). However, the doubling of the pattern which takes the illusion or the representation of gold for the real thing insists on the role of representation in the illusions of the masque. Money provides a good case of the instability of representation, because it combines the transmission of an actual equivalence, a price, with the general possibility of equivalence which can be defined as exchange-value; and these two functions underline the appropriateness of the masque of Plutus and the fiscal policy of Mephistopheles in an action which now moves from allegory to another kind of entertainment.

The early modern court has thus far exploited the figures of classical mythology to flatter its sense of its own sophistication, and to excuse its morals. Faust's appearance has suggested that other forces might be invoked in myth — but his own magical contribution also emphasizes the illusions of representation. The only unaccountably primal force in the masque of Plutus is the charioteer, Knabe Lenker, who is not a figure of myth at all, but the extravagance of poetry itself.

The classical world is invoked directly in the next entertainment requested by the emperor. As Faust explains to an apparently alarmed Mephistopheles,

> Der Kaiser will, es muß sogleich geschehn,
> Will Helena und Paris vor sich sehn;
> Das Musterbild der Männer so der Frauen
> In deutlichen Gestalten will er schauen.

(6183–86)

The formulation carefully marks continuity with the masques that have preceded, but also a change in the form. The notion that Helen of Troy and her lover Paris should appear as "Musterbild der Männer und der Frauen" suggests that an element of abstraction survives in the Emperor's desire: the figures can be moralized as instances of human perfection — of heroism or beauty. On the other hand, however, "Helena und Paris vor sich" and "in deutlichen Gestalten" indicate a desire for historical authenticity: the Emperor wants to see the real thing. The satisfaction of the Emperor's request involves Faust's descent to the Mothers, and Mephistopheles provides instruction for this journey as well as a strangely phallic "key" which will enable Faust to return with the magical tripod. This apparatus will permit him to command the return of Helen and Paris. The Mothers sound as though they are another borrowing from antiquity, but in fact they are Goethe's own invention. For some readers these "Mütter" (see John Williams's essay in this volume) touch the most profound conceptions of Goethe's creative imagination as goddesses of the primordial forms which are only knowable through metamorphosis (Mattenklott, 412–14); for others, such as Stuart Atkins, who speaks of the "ultimate absurdity of beings ignorant of their own identity," and includes the Phorcyads and Cabiri as well as the Mothers, they are another of Goethe's "serious jokes" (Atkins, 183), and the piece of stage business in which Faust practises the attitudinizing of a professional magician (at 6293) suggests that the *entertainment* of the Emperor and his court by a charlatan is still not far from Goethe's mind.

The stage direction, "Dämmernde Beleuchtung," of "Rittersaal" (before 6377) indicates a darkened auditorium as the representational space, the "venue" for the next appearance of the classical world at the emperor's behest — "Kaiser und Hof sind eingezogen," as audience; and this anticipation of theatrical activity is confirmed by the Herald's uncertainty about his task:

> Mein alt Geschäft, das Schauspiel anzukünden,
> Verkümmert mir der Geister heimlich Walten.

(6377–78)

Instead of the carnival review of the earlier scenes, figures of classical antiquity are to be staged. A theatrical performance is due but one with unusual characteristics. While the physical disposition of the theatre can be described, neither actors nor script will easily answer to the familiarities of the craft. The court Astrologer is next to speak and he announces the beginning of the drama, but first the "Rittersaal" is occupied by *another* theater:

> Die Mauer spaltet sich, sie kehrt sich um,
> Ein tief Theater scheint sich aufzustellen,
> Geheimnisvoll ein Schein uns zu erhellen,
> Und ich besteige das Proszenium.
>
> (6395–98)

Once again Goethe draws our attention to the fact that "der Raub der Helena," as the Astrologer will call the show later (6548), is being put on in the late medieval or early modern context of the court. What is seen on the stage, the Astrologer says, is

> Massiv genug, ein alter Tempelbau.
> Dem Atlas gleich, der einst den Himmel trug,
> Stehn reihenweis der Säulen hier genug [. . .]
>
> (6404–06)

The scene, that is to say, is set outside a Greek temple, and the passing allusion to a figure of Greek mythology serves to underline the milieu. This set is sufficient to provoke the court Architect:

> Das wär' antik! Ich wüßt' es nicht zu preisen,
> Es sollte plump und überlästig heißen.
> Roh nennt man edel, unbehülflich groß.
> Schmalpfeiler lieb' ich, strebend, grenzenlos;
> Spitzbögiger Zenit erhebt den Geist;
> Solch ein Gebäu erbaut uns allermeist.
>
> (6409–14)

This polemical response contrasts the classical columns of antiquity with medieval Gothic architecture characterized by its slimmer pillars and pointed arches. The framework of the classical representation continues to be the aesthetics of a broadly conceived middle ages.

Albrecht Schöne has argued that, at this stage in the play, Faust and Mephistopheles should be understood, at least in part, as a couple of hucksters, exploiting the technology of the magic lantern to produce their stage effects (1994, 476–78; and on the "Laterna magica," 479–84). And Neil M. Flax (1979), in an interesting article on the origins of the term "Phantasmagorie" in the subtitle of Act 3, pointed out that technical means were known to Goethe's theater which could realize such an effect by means of projection. Mephistopheles' intervention from the prompter's box partly confirms that he is manipulating events in some way, and that the Astrologer is once more ventriloquizing lines devised as part of Faust's entertainment — and not for the first time: Mephistopheles had provided a script for the same figure near the beginning of the "Kaiserliche Pfalz" scenes (see Osman Durrani's essay in this volume). The recovery of spirits from the world of antiquity is possible only as a put-up job and a trick of the light. It remains striking, however, that the clarification occurs *after* the Astrologer has begun to speak. We cannot be certain whether the "tief Theater" appears at his behest or whether he is already a figure in Faust's and Mephistopheles' play. For it is not until he enters upon the stage, at the end of his speech, that his role as quasi-Shakespearean chorus properly begins. Against the Gothic preferences of the architect, the astrologer insists on a willing suspension of disbelief.

Faust's return as a stage entry underlines the theme of showmanship: Mephistopheles had promised that once he has touched the "Dreifuß" with the key which takes him to the Mothers, "Gelassen steigst du, dich erhebt das Glück, / Und eh' sie's merken, bist mit ihm zurück" (6295–96). Goethe's stage direction after line 6420 reads almost as a parody of Mephisto's words: "Faust steigt auf der andern Seite des Proszeniums herauf." And he does so already in costume: "Im Priesterkleid" announces the astrologer, "bekränzt, ein Wundermann." It would be convenient to see this as the final complement to the theatrical details deployed so far: the theatrical space, the set, the rule of heteronymous discourse in "speaking lines," costume, and the entrance of an actor. But Goethe immediately complicates the matter. The Astrologer continues by speaking of "ein Wundermann, / Der nun vollbringt, was er getrost begann." Furthermore, his line "Er rüstet sich, das hohe Werk zu segnen" (6425) echoes Faust's enthusiasm before his descent to the Mothers: "Die Brust erweitert, hin zum großen Werke" (6282). We, as audience, can recognize the allusion; it is only Mephistopheles who is in a position to make it. *He* speaks in the Astrologer, and his burlesque irony will (as usual) undo any attempt to take this dramatic entry too seriously. So, not for the last time in the play, we are bound to ask what Faust thinks he is doing as he prepares to conjure the spirit of Helen of Troy for the court's entertainment. His stage direction "großartig" suggests a dramatic performance. Certainly the speech does not do what Mephistopheles had suggested — "Und hast du ihn [den Dreifuß] einmal hierher gebracht, / So rufst du Held und Heldin aus der Nacht" (6297–98). Instead he invokes the Mothers, *performing* the stage role of magus, and calling to this stage "Des Lebens Bilder, regsam, ohne Leben" (6430), lifeless representations of life. The presentation of antiquity as myth is never quite stable here; its uncertain status as performance, along with the obscurity of the dominant theatrical authority unsteadies the truth of what is seen.

It is significant that this is the first magical operation independently undertaken by Faust since the opening of the drama. "[. . .] der Magie ergeben" notoriously amounts to very little until this point, when Faust enacts a necromantic operation (whatever else it may be) at the request of the Emperor. In a magical theater — "Nichts hindert mehr," says the Astrologer as the "tief Theater" appears, "hier ist Magie zur Hand" (6393) — Faust performs (in both senses) magic: the complicity of magic and theater is plain enough, and is reflected in the references to *The Tempest* which enclose Part Two from the appearance of Ariel in "anmutige Gegend" to Faust's Prospero-like abjuration of magic in "Mitternacht" of Act 5. Such a framework of illusion and sleight of hand on the part of the two showmen compromises the glimpse of ideal classical beauty which the return of Helen might promise. Like magic, theater produces effects through the utterance of verbal formulae. In a more than antiquarian sense it is a ritual act. And because it produces the same effects, it testifies to the emptiness of the magic it mimes, and which it is always ready to occupy with its empty verbalizations.

The ironies of this pattern are myriad. In a mirror-image of "die griechische Mythologie" in the "Mummenschanz," Goethe focuses on the erotic fantasies of the ladies of the court, in order to throw Faust's growing passion for Helen into greater relief. Now it is his turn to fall under the spell of representation, and so to misunderstand it.

> Du bists's, der ich die Regung aller Kraft,
> Den Inbegriff der Leidenschaft,
> Dir Neigung, Lieb', Anbetung, Wahnsinn zolle.
> (6498–500)

This provokes Mephistopheles to intervene from the prompter's box: "So faßt Euch doch und fallt nicht aus der Rolle" (6501). So we were right to see Faust playing out a role when he climbs onto the proscenium, thus *theatricalizing* the return of the classical on his return to the upper world. His role is in some mysterious way separate from the representation of Paris and Helen, which can only *appear* on the stage but must remain disembodied. They are characters on the stage, and yet not quite actors in the play. Our attention flickers between a number of distinct theatrical frames: the "tief Theater," the theatrical space of the

"Rittersaal," and ultimately the theater, be it physical or mental, in which we watch the play (see Barry, 269).

This movement between the mutually ironic levels of the representation is the theme of the debate in the stage-audience which opens the presentation of "The Rape of Helen." As Paris begins to doze, one of the chamberlains complains that such behavior is inappropriate. This recalls the hypocrisy of the courtiers, in their excusal earlier of their own erotic propensities. The response of the court-ladies and of the "Kämmerer" himself turns on the mimetic and actorly qualities of the performance:

> KÄMMERER. Die Flegelei! Das find' ich unerlaubt!
>
> DAME.   Ihr Herren wißt an allem was zu mäkeln.
>
> DERSELBE. In Kaisers Gegenwart sich hinzuräkeln!
>
> DAME.   Er stellt's nur vor! Er glaubt sich ganz allein.
>
> DERSELBE. Das Schauspiel selbst, hier sollt' es höflich sein.
>
> DAME.   Sanft hat der Schlaf den Holden übernommen.
>
> DERSELBE. Er schnarcht nun gleich; natürlich ist's, vollkommen!
>   (6466–71)

The Kämmerer is making a point about the form in which the Judgment of Paris, the myth which explains the origins of the Trojan War, fought because of Helen, is transmitted. Paris is traditionally presented as a shepherd lad challenged to choose between the beauty of three goddesses. By recognizing the naturalism of the acting, the Kämmerer can also identify the anti-pastoral force of the attractive "Schäfer-knecht" who snores when he falls asleep. The comic detail recalls once again the light-hearted use of classical myths in rococo painting and literature ("DAME: Endymion und Luna! wie gemalt!" [6509]). In the theatrical framework, however, the lady has the profounder insight in saying "Er stellt's nur vor": he is only acting, and so *represents* his belief that he is alone. She responds as if she were watching an actor playing the role of Paris; and in at least one important sense, as an actress herself, that is exactly what she sees. As "Hofdame," however, she too has been tricked by the magic of this performance. Somehow the character she watches *is* Paris, his simulacrum or shade, but if his identity is to appear, to be presented, it must split from his substance to become a role, a mere part. Paris enacts himself, and the chamberlain's complaint about this "Schauspiel" is not without its justification. There is perhaps something unsettling about the presentation of Paris and Helena, who become something like their own Doppelgänger. As Faust's invocation makes clear, they are "des Lebens Bilder, regsam, ohne Leben," shadowy, liminal presences. His play is uncanny.

What shuttles back and forth across the irony of Mephistopheles the prompter, and between the different frames within which the classical myth is presented, is a sense of equivocation. The attempt to recover the classical must remain ambiguous, whether it is the recovery of Greece, of which the "Gothic" architect complains, or the classical wellspring of beauty itself which Faust senses at the sight of Helen. Faust loses sight of just this ambiguity in the representation in attempting to embrace Helen and turning his "key" on Paris. As a result the illusory reality evaporates and Faust is left unconscious.

The pattern which, as we have seen, frames the classical world in the medieval is repeated again in the first part of Act 2. Faust has been returned by Mephistopheles to the narrow Gothic room in which his journey had begun in Part One. Here Homunculus, the artificial manikin "created" by Wagner's alchemy, is able to read Faust's dreaming, unconscious thoughts. He is still under Helen's spell; as Mephistopheles says: she has paralyzed him (6568). He dreams therefore of Leda and the swan, and hence of the conception of Helen who is the product of their union. In transposing the vision of antiquity to a dream, the scene introduces a further form in which the classical can be perceived. The myth of Helen's conception is described as if it were a tableau vivant, much as the encounter between Paris and Helen at the end of Act 1 had been described by members of the court. After the allegorical masques and magic lantern show of Act 1, the scene of Helen's conception has become an erotic aspiration for Faust, and a longing for Greece itself. Looking round at the Gothic setting in which he has read Faust's dream, Homunculus uses the same word as the imperial architect in Act 1 to describe its style: "Spitzbögig" (6929). The contrast of styles is now enriched in another way when Homunculus points out that this is the northern style of Mephistopheles' home territory, whereas Faust's recovery must take them all to Greece.

It will be the classical thread, in the form of Faust's pursuit of Helena, that guides the continuing development of the drama. Its central significance has not always been recognized. In his *Study of Goethe*, Barker Fairley made no attempt to conceal his irritation at the "formal inappropriateness" of "this intrusion" (Fairley, 192). But Homunculus' recognition of philhellenism as the source of Faust's collapse immediately heralds the prospect of a "klassische Walpurgisnacht," understood in contrast to the northern witches' Sabbath of Part One:

HOMUNKULUS.   [. . .]
Jetzt eben, wie ich schnell bedacht,
Ist klassische Walpurgisnacht;
Das Beste, was begegnen könnte.
Bring ihn zu seinem Elemente!

MEPHISTOPHELES.   Dergleichen hab' ich nie vernommen.

HOMUNKULUS.   Wie wollt' es auch zu euren Ohren kommen?
Romantische Gespenster kennt ihr nur allein;
Ein echt Gespenst, auch klassisch hat's zu sein.
(6940–47)

In these lines the relationship of a medieval world to antiquity is complicated once again by a more contemporary contrast between Classical and Romantic as literary and aesthetic movements in Goethe's own time.

Before this issue can be addressed, the form in which the world of antiquity is presented must be considered. Homunculus, Mephistopheles, and Faust fly in on their magical coat and disturb the gloomy ruminations of Erichtho the Thessalian witch, who opens Act 2 by recalling the decisive battle on the Pharsalian Fields between Caesar and Pompey. Erichtho begins in the iambic trimeter of Greek tragedy, imagining "hellenischer Sagen Legion" (7028) gathering about the critical moment of political confrontation (on the temporality of this speech, see Schöne 1994, 534; and on the trimeter, see Ritchie Robertson's essay in this volume). But the presentation of antiquity, and of a pre-classical and archaic world in a German drama is neatly ironized by a mistake made by Mephistopheles in one of his early encounters, with the griffons:

Glückzu den schönen Fraun, den klugen Greisen!

GREIF *schnarrend.*   Nicht Greisen! Greifen! — Niemand hört es gern,
Daß man ihn Greis nennt [. . .]
(7092–94)

Of the many jokes and gags in Act 2 this is one of the most lighthearted: Mephistopheles' mistake depends on the look of German black-letter print, *Fraktur,* in which an f and an s, with its long descender, are distinguishable only by the fine line which crosses the f. The implications of the error are charming: Mephistopheles inadvertently calls the mythical creatures "old women" by failing to make the distinction: it is as if he were unable to decipher his German script and so mispronounces the unfamiliar name. Similarly the archaic realm of antiquity presents its utter difference as alien and unreadable in the transcription of the "Klassische Walpurgisnacht." For the moment, Erichto's quantitative metre is supplanted by northern, Germanic accented lines — in great variety.

In the narrative of Act 2 taking the audience through a Greek landscape and introducing its denizens, two important features are apparent. The three northern visitors — Faust, Mephistopheles, and Homunculus — follow essentially separate paths. Plot in the usual sense of the word has been reduced to the merest motivation: Faust appears in Mephistopheles' colloquy only to ask the sphinxes whether they have seen Helen — their Egyptian background makes this likely, given that in one myth, dramatized in Euripides's *Helen*, Helen survives the Trojan War in Egypt. However, the sphinxes belong to an earlier period ("Wir reichen nicht hinauf zu ihren Tagen" [7197]) and direct him to seek Chiron, the centaur. In staring into the waters of the river Peneus, Faust recalls his earlier vision of Helen's conception — "Sind's Träume? Sind's Erinnerungen?" (7275) — before Chiron duly arrives to carry him to Manto the sibyl who will offer to smuggle Faust down into Hades for an audience with Persephone from whom, like Orpheus, he may be able to secure Helen's release. Homunculus seeks a path to development in the material world, instructed by the Greek philosophers of fire and water, Anaxagoras and Thales; and Mephistopheles to sexual gratification amid the grotesqueries of Greek myth.

The last scene of the act will celebrate the splendors of the sea in the extravagant Aegean festival which provides the context for Homunculus's impassioned journey. Guided and enflamed (Thales says "verführt" [8469]) by Proteus, he sets out to encounter Galatea. In the course of the act very few named characters (Chiron, Manto; Seismos, Anaxagoras, Thales, Nereus, and briefly Galatea herself) speak at any length; and the majority of the act is taken up with generic encounters — with nymphs, sirens, lamias, empedusas and the rest. The "klassische Walpurgisnacht" presents an *array* of mythical creatures from Greek myth but, unlike the various allegories of the *Mummenschanz* with its thematic development, they are no longer governed by the principle of readability. There are certainly striking parallels between Acts 1 and 2, especially their conclusions: for just as Faust's attempt to embrace the image of Helen causes her evaporation and his swoon, Homunculus's "herrisches Sehnen" (8470) ejaculates his being into the sea at the feet of Galatea. Similarly, the series of mythical encounters experienced by Faust, Homunculus, and Mephistopheles echoes the review pattern of the *Mummenschanz*; but the classical "Walpurgisnacht" becomes a broad spectrum of equal forces which Goethe, in his conversation with Eckermann of 21 February 1831, saw in republican terms, compared to the monarchical presentation of the *Mummenschanz* organized under a controlling principle: "Die klassische [Walpurgisnacht] aber ist durchaus republikanisch, indem alles in der Breite nebeneinandersteht, so daß der eine so viel gilt wie der andere." Such equalization testifies to the enormous freedom of structure in the second part of Act 2. The "Klassische Walpurgisnacht" provides a catalogue of the arcane and archaic Greece of philology: culled from the pages of Hederich's *Lexikon*, this antiquity repeats the archival form of the source. That is why only Homunculus achieves the completion of an *action* in Act 2: he comes to represent the dematerialized dreams and memories of antiquity struggling towards realization in a new and material way, which Goethe imagines as the developmental potential of the sea.

The mythical creatures of the "Klassische Walpurgisnacht" are dual species — from the sphinxes and griffons through to the sirens, lamias, and empedusas encountered by Mephistopheles, to Chiron the centaur who carries Faust and the sea creatures of the Aegean festival. This hybrid nature makes them thematically appropriate to the act in which the characters become ontologically unstable. Homunculus, for instance, is ambiguous in a contrasting way, as a presence without a body or a potential for spontaneous self-realization for which Proteus is the foil. The Cabiri (Kabiren) of whom the Nereids and Tritons sing that they are "alle noch nicht fertig" (8201), exhibit the same mysterious ambiguity, and demonstrate the fertility and purpose of Goethe's mythopoeia. They are not even properly Greek divinities at all, and it remains unclear how many of them there are. Borrowing details of their genealogy and attributes from Hederich, but also from Romantic studies of mythology, Creuzer's *Symbolik und Mythologie der alten Völker* and Schelling's essay on the Cabeiri, *Über die Gottheiten von Samothrace*, Goethe playfully releases these ancient tutelary gods of shipwrecked sailors from such syncretistic scholarship to be the guardians of Homunculus, wrecked against Galatea's shell, and in their own way to recall the whole Faustian project of desire for the unattainable (8204–05) (see Zabka, 123 and 137).

At the beginning of Act 3 this unattainable object finally appears when Helena steps on to the stage to say "Bewundert viel" (see Phelan 1989; 1990). After the emblematic (and assimilated) framework in which figures from classical mythology appear in the imperial masquerade, and after the ontological instabilities which are developed from it in the "Klassische Walpurgisnacht," here Goethe seems to dispense with the cavils and qualifications of theatricality. Helen of Troy steps on to the stage of *Faust* and, without further ado, begins to speak. Yet this opening also accomplishes a dislocation: from the extravaganza by the Aegean, the action moves to a setting outside the palace of Menelaus in Sparta. This shift of location is necessary because it establishes the conventions for Goethe's impersonation of the Greek tragedians. The emergence of the forms of Greek drama at this point is a powerful disruption, and Helena herself is dislocated. Although she claims that she has come by sea, with Menelaus, after the fall of Troy, we have to assume that she is not speaking the truth. Faust, we know, has made two descents from the plane of human life — once to the Mothers in Act 1 and once to the Underworld in Act 2 — in his efforts to bring Helena to the stage; if, on the other hand, she is not lying, then something very odd has happened to chronology.

The appearance of Helena outside the palace and upon this stage is determined by other forces, however. Earlier, in Part One, Faust had been "attracted [. . .] to an ideal, unapproachable vision of female beauty" (Boyle, 57) which has been identified with Helena, and is partly so identified by Faust himself when he speaks of "ein Schaumbild solcher Schöne" (6497). Faust's quest is for Helena's full presence, and it reaches a preliminary climax when Manto offers to smuggle him down into Hades. In that case, however, we are bound to ask what he thinks *he* is doing in his encounter with Helena. Are we to think that Faust "acts out" a meeting with her or is he deceived by Mephistopheles? Does Helena know her lines and, therefore, what to expect? Or is she no more than a puppet manipulated by Mephistopheles and hence no more materially present than in her ghostly and explosive appearance for the imperial court?

A recent commentator explains this paradox in Helena's stage appearance in terms of her existential insecurity, claiming that she is "a figure revivified from Hades, uncertain as to whether she is a phantom, an eidolon, or a living individual" (Williams, 164). But this possibility emerges only some 400 lines into the act in Helena's exchange with Phorcyas (8834–81). Helena's identity is not only dispersed across a wide range of literary and mythical "texts," to which Mephisto alludes in these lines: even as absolute beauty she seems to be constituted in and by her differential relationship with Mephistopheles in the guise (taken up at the end of the classical Walpurgis night) of the ultimately ugly Phorcyas. Yet, however alarming the power which Mephistopheles' existential opposition gives him, such an interpretation merely stabilizes in allegorical form the dislocation of theatrical representation which takes place in relation to personality, identity, chronology, and motivation when Helena steps on to the stage.

The ambiguous position of Helena, together with Faust's role in staging the classical revival of Act 3, offers a reflexive summary of the whole project of Goethe's classicism: the return of some element of antiquity from the past and its reinstatement in the present. Hence, the whole action of the Helena act gives new meaning to the term representation, which is now a restoration to presence. Consequently, Goethe's retrospective and ironic account of "Classicism," as appropriating and so authorizing (and authoring) antiquity, destabilizes the personal identity of its central figure by insisting on her allusive character. As one much praised and much blamed (8488), Helena seems to know this in the announcement of her arrival. But here too, her words exceed her knowledge, for the praise and blame to which she might historically refer, as it were, would be those of the Greeks or the Trojans, while *we* know that her words imply the whole tissue of myth transmitted not only by Greek literature, but also by Shakespeare, for example, in *Troilus and Cressida* — of which she can know nothing.

Helena appears on stage from the beach, having just landed on her native shore, and announced the fact at the opening of the earliest version of the act. The self-contextualisation of 8488 is a later addition. "Vom Strande komm' ich, wo wir erst gelandet sind" (8489), the words with which Helena arrives in the text of 1800, is accessible to a range of readings. Primarily, we take "we" ("wir") to refer to Helena, Panthalis and the chorus of Trojan women. But it soon becomes clear that the audience is also involved in this arrival: either because we, too, have "just landed," arriving from the coast of the Aegean and the end of Act 2 so that now we are all properly in "classical" Greece; or because the audience has long been in Greece and Helena and her entourage have only just landed. But at another level, the line must also mean "I, Helena, re-emerge from those German shores where we have only recently arrived" in the sense that "I am a product of the interest shown in Greece by the *German* literary revival of the late eighteenth century."

The ambiguities of Helena's arrival derive from the "shifters," "wo" and "erst." Neither in narrative, nor in dramatic discourse, nor in literary allusion, nor in self-naming can her presence be assured. Nevertheless, in this littoral existence, Goethe has found an appropriate form of speech for her, not always easily, but in a passing impersonation of the iambic trimeter of Greek tragedy. After the relative ease of the first two lines of Act 3, the sheer weight of classical vocabulary, of place names and mythology, makes it clear that a new kind of writing is beginning, marked perhaps by the point (8490) where the substitution of a tribrach announces the instability of the iambic pulse still dominating lines 8488–89. The meter of Helena's speech in the scene of classical tragedy is answered by the forms of the Trojan chorus in strophe, antistrophe and epode.

Wherever Helena is, Greek is not spoken there, but German regulated by classical prosody. Helena has returned to her own from those realms where she is the object of praise and blame. It is because she is admired that she has this "place" in antiquity, but her imaginary biography consists of necessary supplements; there is no essential or fundamental "Helen of Troy" about whom a succession of stories are told: rather, Helena *is* the stories, in all their contradictory variety, and no one of them presents a single truth to which the others are accretions. Mephistopheles-Phorkyas spells this out until Helena loses consciousness: "Ich schwinde hin" (8881). Recovered, Helena receives the news that a sacrificial axe awaits her and that Menelaus will hang her chorus "erstaunt und erschreckt" but in a carefully rehearsed stage tableau, "in bedeutender, wohlvorbereiteter Gruppe" (before 8930). Helena is restored in *Faust* but she continues to be framed by the theatricality of the presentation.

Phorkyas is able to frighten Helena and her Trojan women into accepting refuge in Faust's *Burg,* which is carefully described as medieval in architecture. By a neat irony the classical Phorkyas matches the medievalism of the imperial architect in Act 1 by comparing the two building styles to the detriment of the classical: "[. . .] dort / Ist alles senk- und waagerecht und regelhaft. / Von außen schaut sie! himmelan sie strebt empor" (9021–23). In the course of the chorus following Helena's acceptance of advice from this "Widerdämon" (9072), and with the help of some stage mists, Mephistopheles keeps his word — "Sogleich umgeb' ich dich mit jener Burg" (9049); but the encounter with Faust is itself a highly staged affair. The Trojan Women notice how well drilled Faust's "Knaben und Knappen" are as they re-set the stage, and Helena's welcome to this German territory takes the form of another masque, as Leonard Forster showed. Faust's watchman, Lynkeus, is supposed to have failed in his duty by not reporting Helena's arrival. His "excuse, however, is neither classical not medieval; its mode is that of the Renaissance, and it is fitting that it should be so, as Lynkeus is presented as being the first in the castle to see the brilliance of the ancient world concentrated in the person of Helena" (Forster, 152; compare with Neumann, 231–32). Thus, the Renaissance provides the bridge between the classical and the medieval-romantic, as the first great European recovery of antiquity which has now been restored again through the project of Weimar classicism; but it can also provide a point of contact with the Romantic generations through the implied

celebration of Petrarch, who along with Dante and Boccaccio constantly figures in the Romantic canon of modern poets (in Friedrich
Schlegel, for instance, in "Epochen der Dichtkunst" in *Gespräch über
die Poesie* [1800], and in the "Prolog" to the novel *Lucinde* [1799]).

Faust secures Helena in language, in the forms of Germanic verse.
In this respect, the prosodic and dramatic forms are not incidental but
fundamental to the classical *renovatio*, for the balance or equivocation
between two metrical schemes in "classical verse" is supposedly resolved in two *voices* harmonized and united by rhyme. First, Helena
had to be brought *within* the castle walls, and then her approach to the
moment of consummation is marked by a drift from the metrical regu-
latives of Greek towards blank verse, until she finally asks in relation to
the masque of Lynkeus:

> HELENA.   Doch wünscht' ich Unterricht, warum die Rede
>   Des Manns mir seltsam klang, seltsam und freundlich.
>   Ein Ton scheint sich dem andern zu bequemen,
>   Und hat ein Wort zum Ohre sich gesellt,
>   Ein andres kommt, dem ersten liebzukosen.
>
> FAUST.   Gefällt dir schon die Sprechart unsrer Völker,
>   O so gewiß entzückt auch der Gesang,
>   Befriedigt Ohr und Sinn im tiefsten Grunde.
>   Doch ist am sichersten, wir üben's gleich;
>   Die Wechselrede lockt es, ruft's hervor.
>
> HELENA.   So sage denn, wie sprech' ich auch so schön?
>
> FAUST.   Das ist gar leicht, es muß von Herzen gehn.
>   Und wenn die Brust von Sehnsucht überfließt,
>   Man sieht sich um und fragt —
>
> HELENA.   wer mitgenießt.
>
>   (9367–80)

As the exercise in "Wechselrede" proceeds, Faust and Helena are con-
joined in the present ("Die Gegenwart allein — ist unser Glück"
[9382]). In their second dialogue they rhyme with themselves, and
Helena intensifies the formal constraints by adding "internal rhymes"
(May, 163) in an ecstasy of "being present": "Ich fühle mich so *fern*
und doch so nah, / Und sage nur zu *gern*: Da bin ich! da!" (9411–12)
where the final "internal rhyme" is self-identical ("Da [. . .] da"). Helena, the figure of classical antiquity, seems thus to have transcended
the dimensions of time ("die Gegenwart allein") and space ("so fern

und doch so nah") to arrive without detour or deferral in undivided presence. Indeed, Faust prohibits critical reflection on this unique destiny since such presence is ethically imperative, however momentary: "Dasein ist Pflicht, und wär's ein Augenblick" (9418); momentary it may be, but it is also a *dream* of union between Greece and Germany, classical and medieval (9414). In being thus contracted to Helena, Faust appears embarrassingly close to satisfying the conditions of his initial contract with Mephistopheles. Indeed, the key word "Augenblick" brings Mephistopheles-Phorkyas back to the stage on cue. But far from demanding his rights, he simply pours scorn on Helena's and Faust's loving rhymes in a parody of their speech which demonstrates his own skill as a rhymester and, far from incidentally, drives Faust back to the iambic trimeter for his next lines. Menelaus now threatens to return — or seems to — and Faust takes up his role as a medieval commander.

Phorkyas's intervention also heralds a renewal of the threat posed by Menelaus, this time in military terms. It is this external pressure which triggers the final meeting of Faust and Helena, the Germanic, medieval, Romantic culture and the classical. It appears to take place on classic ground in a fantasy of Arcadia. The classical features here — the *locus amoenus,* the cave of love making — are unsettled by the energy of the child Euphorion who is born to Helena and Faust, but what drives the act to conclude the encounter between the two great literary traditions is the threat of war. It is well known that Goethe identified Euphorion's Icarean flight toward the sun with Byron's death at Missolonghi (see his conversation with Eckermann, 5 July 1827). This otherwise arcane parallel is foregrounded by the stage action so that, almost uniquely, a contemporary moment provides a perspective for the remainder of the act, with its recurrent effects of *trompe l'oeil,* its feints and theatrical frames.

The classical modalities of Euripides have enclosed Faust's medieval castle, and in turn this scene has provided the context of yet another classical allusion in Arcadia. Euphorion, however, insists on wider horizons. His flight takes him out of the confines and constraints of the "Schattiger Hain" — "Keine Wälle, Keine Mauern, / Jeder nur sich selbst bewußt" (9855–56) — surrounded by its "rings umgebende Felsenteile" (before 9574), itself defended from military invasion by Faust's armed men. Euphorion's symbolic identification, not only with the extravagance of poetry in Knabe Lenker, but more particularly with Byron, takes the action beyond itself. The Greek war of liberation situates both the philhellenism of the Helena action and the Romantic medievalism of "Innerer Burghof" in relation to the most pressing demands of modernity. Helena is floating in an ahistorical space not merely as an anachronism, but because the Weimar classicism of which she is the final expression is itself a form of relation to the modern age which requires the *renovatio* of classical revival, and which is itself measured against its Renaissance predecessors in the masque of Lynkeus; similarly, the medieval world is an instance of the Romantic stock-taking of modern experience in relation to a different and Germanic past. Goethe positions himself in relation to current literary debates by configuring the medieval world of the Romantic imagination and the classicism that he had himself espoused in a single act.

> Goethe, der gerade das klassische Altertum unhistorisch und gleichsam im luftleeren Raum sich vor Augen zu stellen lebenslang sich bemüht hatte, entwirft nun in der klassisch-romantischen Phantasmagorie "Helena," das erste große, durch die Vergangenheit des Deutschtums selbst geschaute Bild der Antike. (Benjamin, 736)

Walter Benjamin's Goethe article (written for but not included in the *Great Soviet Encyclopaedia* [1929]) reflects that a traditional German social formation together with its life-values ("Deutschtum") reaches its limit in the imaginative reconstruction of a medieval/early modern world. Because it is past, it provides the unavoidable framework through which the classical itself must be reassessed. The resolution of the contemporary split between classicists and the romantics, figured throughout the parts of *Faust* considered here as the worlds of the classical and the medieval, was the main sense of the Helena-Act, Goethe wrote on 27 September 1827 to his friend Karl Jakob Ludwig Iken. What the flight of Euphorion achieves in the play goes far beyond that local diplomatic difficulty. By relating the classical and the archaic to the medieval world, and then through Missolonghi to the most contemporary concerns of his day, Goethe opens up these reconstructions of myth and antiquity to our contemporaneity also, as Max Kommerell realized:

> Die antike Form kämpft mit der vordringenden modernen, und doch bedeutet dies luftigfreie Spiel einen ins Herz schneidenden Verzicht, da es auf die Frage, welche Zeit ist, eine unausweichliche Antwort gibt. (193)

Works Cited

Atkins, Stuart. *Goethe's Faust: A Literary Analysis.* London: Oxford UP, 1958.

Barry, David. "Turning the Screw in Goethe's 'Helena.'" *German Life and Letters.* 39 (1986). 268–78.

Benjamin, Walter. "Goethe." *Gesammelte Schriften.* Ed. Rolf Tiedemann et al. Vol. 2.2. Frankfurt am Main: Suhrkamp, 1991. 705–39.

Bennett, Benjamin. *Goethe's Theory of Poetry.* Ithaca and London: Cornell UP, 1986.

Boyle, Nicholas. *Goethe: Faust, Part One.* Cambridge: Cambridge UP, 1987.

Fairley, Barker. *A Study of Goethe.* Oxford: Oxford UP, 1947.

Flax, Neil M. "Goethe's 'Faust II' and the Experimental Theatre of his Time." *Comparative Literature.* 31 (1979). 154–66.

Forster, Leonard. "Lynkeus' Masque in Goethe's *Faust II.*" In *The Icy Fire: Five Studies in European Petrarchism.* Cambridge: Cambridge UP, 1969. 148–68.

Hederich, Benjamin. *Gründliches mythologisches Lexikon.* [Reprint] Darmstadt: Wissenschaftliche Buchgesellschaft, 1996.

Historia von D. Johann Fausten. Ed. Stephan Füssel and Hans Joachim Kreutzer. Stuttgart: Reclam, 1988.

Jamme, Christoph. "Goethes Mythen-Bastelei im *Faust II.*" In *Interpreting Goethe's Faust Today.* Ed. Jane K. Brown et al. Columbia, SC: Camden House, 1994. 207–18.

Kommerell, Max. "Vielheit der Formen im Helena-Akt." In *Aufsätze zu Goethes Faust II.* Ed. Werner Keller. Darmstadt: Wissenschaftliche Buchgesellschaft, 1991. 190–94.

Marlowe, Christopher. *Dr Faustus.* Ed. David Ormerod and Christopher Wortham. Nedlands WA: U of Western Australia P, 1989.

Mattenklott. Peter. "Faust II." *Goethe Handbuch.* Ed. Bernd Witte et al. Vol. 2. *Dramen.* Stuttgart: Metzler, 1996. 391–477.

Matussek, Peter. "Faust I." In *Goethe Handbuch.* Ed. Bernd Witte et al. Vol. 2. *Dramen.* Stuttgart: Metzler, 1996. 352–90.

May, Kurt. *Faust II. Teil: In der Sprachform gedeutet.* [1936] Frankfurt am Main: Ullstein, 1972.

Müller, Joachim. "Faust und Helena: Der arkadische Traum: Genese und dramatisches Medium." *Jahrbuch des Wiener Goethe-Vereins.* 86–88 (1982–84). 199–227.

Neumann, Michael. "Faust und Helena." In *Aufsätze zu Goethes Faust II*. Ed. Werner Keller. Darmstadt: Wissenschaftliche Buchgesellschaft, 1991. 227–42.

Phelan, Anthony. "Goethe's 'Euphrosyne' and the Theatres of *Faust Part Two*." *Publications of the English Goethe Society*. 59 (1989). 59–78.

———. "Deconstructing Classicism: Goethe's *Helena* and the Need to Rhyme." In *New Ways in Germanistik*. Ed. Richard Sheppard. Oxford: Berg, 1990. 192–210.

Schlaffer, Heinz. *Faust Zweiter Teil: Die Allegorie des 19. Jahrhunderts*. Stuttgart: Metzler, 1981.

Schöne, Albrecht. *Götterzeichen, Liebeszauber, Satanskult: Neue Einblicke in alte Goethetexte*. Munich: C. H. Beck, 1982.

———, ed. *Faust. Kommentare*. Frankfurt am Main: Deutscher Klassiker Verlag, 1994. [FA 7.2]

Williams, John R. *Goethe's Faust*. London: Allen and Unwin, 1987.

Zabka, Thomas. *Faust II — Das Klassische und das Romantische*. Tübingen: Niemeyer, 1993.

Progress and Restorative Utopia in *Faust II* and *Wilhelm Meisters Wanderjahre*

Franziska Schößler

B Y COMMON CONSENT, Goethe's late works are concerned, at least in part, with the radical innovations and the progressive consciousness of the revolutionary change in the early years of the nineteenth century (Kaiser, 18; Böhme, 1988, 208–33; Degering, 522). In one of the maxims in the "Betrachtungen im Sinne der Wanderer," part of the novel *Wilhelm Meisters Wanderjahre,* Goethe speaks of the inexorable growth in the number of steam engines (Schmidt 1999, 215); he mentions "die Lebhaftigkeit des Handels, das Durchrauschen des Papiergelds, das Anschwellen der Schulden, um Schulden zu bezahlen" — it is an age which is truly "veloziferisch" (HA 8, 289). Yet, equally, Goethe's later writings recall what was lost or abandoned as obsolete with the advent of these economic, aesthetic, ethical, and medical innovations, whose significance is investigated in *Wilhelm Meisters Wanderjahre* and *Faust II* (Jeßing, 135). Goethe inscribes in his late works the signature of past epochs and ways of thinking, and he outlines, often in the subtextual space, restorative utopias that are sometimes taken to be his actual, esoteric message (Böhme 1986, 249–72; Schlaffer 1978, 212–26), and which throw into relief the deficits that accrue to progress. If, in Goethe's late texts, historical conditions overlap, and if mythological stories, pre-Socratic, neo-Platonic, or palimpsest-like references to pre-bourgeois conditions are contained within modernizing tendencies (Schmidt 1999, 216), then this complex layering of periods of time serves to criticize inexorable progress (Birk, 243–66). More important, this progress is described with extreme precision and apparent neutrality. It is not new to see parallels in the figures of Faust and Wilhelm Meister (Jockers, 148–59) but, rather than placing these two protagonists at the center of my discussion, I have regarded them as an opportunity to link various themes and diverse modern developments.

Taking the time of Goethe as the beginning of the modern age, I wish to investigate in more detail the two poles of this vast historical panorama. To begin with, I will offer from an economic viewpoint (also adopted in the texts themselves) a profile of the contours of bourgeois modernity. For Goethe presents us with the replacement of an economy based on subsistence by one based on commerce, which involves making business out of artificial needs, imaginary demands, imaginary desires, and their illusory satisfaction. Thus, at least at first glance, the object of enquiry that forms the topic of this paper turns out to be, suprisingly enough, fantasy — both what it can do, and how it can be corrupted, for all artificially aroused needs are rooted in the imagination, as becomes clear in the Carnival Masquerade in *Faust II*, and within the realm of the Oheim in the *Wanderjahre*. The economic development that is driven by the modernization of society can, at the same time, be considered from a textual, poetological perspective.

That Goethe thought of himself as something of an expert in economic matters should not surprise us, for he had already, during his *Sturm und Drang* phase, immersed himself in the experiments of the physiocrats (Mahl, 173) and read up on the advanced economic concepts of his brother-in-law, Johann Georg Schlosser, whose work of 1784, entitled *Xenocrates oder über die Abgaben* and dedicated to Goethe, had gone beyond physiocratic notions and stressed the importance of imaginary needs (Binswanger, 152). Goethe also became acquainted with the Scottish economist Adam Smith, thanks to his friend Georg Sartorius and the critical commentary on his work by Johann Georg Büsch (*Abhandlung von dem Geldumlauf in anhaltender Rücksicht auf die Staatswirtschaft und Handlung*, 1780).

Over and against this mimetic diagnosis of a new kind of structure of need, which Goethe carries out and which is based on the notions of ceaseless striving and an eternal postponement — in other words, a reformulation of the typical Faustian movement from an economic perspective — I shall oppose, in the second part of this essay, the restorative dimension of Goethe's late works, which on closer inspection are revealed to be inextricably bound up with these innovations. Beyond the aspects of modernity he depicts, Goethe repeatedly outlines a vision, inspired by neo-Platonism, of a micro-macrocosmic order, which represents humanity as ethical beings within a well-structured cosmos. Within this sphere, the fundamental movement dominating economic processes is repeated, albeit on a higher level; and so eternal striving, which characterizes economic activity, is presented (following the monadology of Leibniz) as the entelechy of an active soul. This conception leaves its mark not only on Faust's elevation in Act 5, but also on one of the most mysterious figures of the *Wanderjahre*, the venerable and mystically gifted woman Makarie. Goethe's restorative utopias are, however, not re-evoked in a straightforward manner, but the fact of their anachronistic nature is displayed both in the form of ironic relativizations and in an esoteric narrative style. As a result, the main question to be answered in this essay is what interpretation we should place on the obvious parallels between, on the one hand, the processes of everyday economic activity as depicted in the Carnival Masquerade and in the Oheim's garden in the *Wanderjahre*, and, on the other, the redemptive visions staged above the figure Makarie and during the elevation of Faust to the Mater gloriosa.

The Carnival Masquerade: The Phantasmagoric Play with Artificial Needs

The masked ball at the imperial palace, played out in the first Act of *Faust II* as well as the preceding episode in the throne-room, is, in historical terms, constructed out of many layers. As Goethe once remarked (in a letter to J. K. Lavater of 19 February 1781): "Man übertäubt mit Maskeraden und glänzenden Erfindungen oft eigne und fremde Not," and thus the ball takes place in the context of financial corruption and ruin (Schöne, 426). The action itself contains several allusions to various potentates and their financial wheelings and dealings. When, for example, the Emperor in Goethe's drama is hoping for credit from a rich Jew — the Steward complains that "der Jude wird mich nicht verschonen" (4870) — we can detect a reference to the dependence of the emperor Rudolf II on the court banker Moderechaj Meisel. By the same token, the arrival of the elephants and Pluto's quadriga goes back to Andrea Mantegna's sequence of nine pictures, *The Triumphal Procession of Julius Caesar* (1490), but there are also similarities with Albrecht Dürer's *Triumphal Procession of Kaiser Maximilian* (1512), and Charles Le Brun's *Triumphal Procession of Alexander the Great in Babylon* (c.1673); indeed, the iconography of imperial self-display finds many echoes in Goethe's treatment of the decline of sovereign power. Moreover, other details of the triumphal procession refer back to the cultural practice known as the trionfi (triumph), much loved in the Renaissance and Baroque, although this age is, on closer examination, presented in terms of its retrospective definition. For even though that age was one "newly born," it was nevertheless not until between 1825 and 1830 that the concept of the "Renaissance" entered literary French discourse, and became the fashionable term used to designate an epoch (Skalweit, 11; Schmidt 1999, 219). Accordingly the action acquires a specifically modern signature; there are allusions to revolutionary stirrings, be they those of the French Revolution, or of the disturbances of July 1830 which were flaring up at the time of the composition of *Faust II* (Metscher, 285). The Chancellor complains:

Doch ach! Was hilft dem Menschengeist Verstand,
Dem Herzen Güte, Willigkeit der Hand,
Wenn's fieberhaft durchaus im Staate wütet
Und Übel sich in Übeln überbrütet? [. . .]
Indessen wogt in grimmigem Schwalle
Des Aufruhrs wachsendes Gewühl.

                                    (4778–81, 4793–94)

Moreover, we are made aware of the egotism central to bourgeois economic thought when the Treasurer remarks:

Gleichgültig wurden Lieb' und Haß.
Die Ghibellinen wie die Guelfen
Verbergen sich, um auszuruhn;
Wer jetzt will seinem Nachbar helfen?
Ein jeder hat für sich zu tun.
Die Goldespforten sind verrammelt,
Ein jeder kratzt und scharrt und sammelt,
Und unsre Kassen bleiben leer.

                                    (4844–51)

Goethe is thinking here not just of the threshold of the modern era, but also of the emerging epoch of bourgeois modernity around 1800.

To begin with, the action revolves around the empty state coffers of the ailing empire, as well as the phantasmagoric consolidation of the budget, which Mephistopheles decides to initiate. He allows bills of exchange to be issued on subterranean treasure, which belongs (according to the so-called "Golden Bull" of Karl IV) to the Emperor; Mephisto says: "Das alles liegt im Boden still begraben, / Der Boden ist des Kaisers, der soll's haben" (4937–38). Nevertheless, the economic strategies and procedures we see here are essentially modern ones; what is being created is paper money, which appears under the guise of an adventurous search and alchemical passion for gold, but which, on closer inspection, turns out to be based on modern commercial principles, that is, on a close association of economics and fantasy. The Emperor, whose belief in astrology reminds us of Wallenstein, becomes involved with a highly speculative project, which must be seen against the background of numerous failed attempts to bring paper money into circulation (Binswanger, 50) and in which, in order to be successful, the imagination has to play a major role. For the creation of this money proceeds, seen in the cold light of day, from sheer nothingness. The mineral treasure is not immediately available, and the labor costs required to attain it have not been included in the calculations; the paper is literally banking on nothing. But the belief that the paper is based on something of actual value enables the transactions with the imperial bills of exchange to take place, at least until such time as the valueless notes are refused and no longer accepted. So it is imagination, the power of fantasy, that lies behind the success of the creation of this money, even if it is the authority of the Emperor that guarantees the value of the bills of exchange, replacing the link between currency value and the intrinsic value of gold. The money thus created in *Faust II* can be described as state money, for it is the money that the state, in a sovereign gesture, declares to be the means of payment — as Werner Sombart put it, "im Anfang ist ein Staatsakt" (1.1, 402) — and which, unlike other currencies, is not based on material goods. The creation of money is based on a belief in imperial authority, which also turns out to be a purely imaginary greatness, since the empire is, right from the start, ailing (Metscher, 283); and, incidentally, Goethe had always argued in his reports on the mint in Weimar for coinage to be secured against gold.

The Emperor makes value out of nothing, and it is precisely the imagination of the masses that enables transactions with unsecured bills of exchange to take place. Thus, it comes as no surprise when the creation of value is treated as equivalent to alchemy and the hunt for treasure (see Binswanger), for the process of creating money is equal, right down to the smallest details, to the search for the philosophers' stone. The magic rituals of Paracelsus to raise treasure offered Goethe a model, and the crowd murmurs suspiciously about "Kalenderei — Chymisterei" (4974). As Sombart has pointed out, paper money was, in fact, initially "von den Fürsten als eine Art des Goldmachens angesehen," and it took some time before "die innere Gesetzmäßigkeit dieser Geldform" was grasped, only for it still to be regarded "als 'Teufelswerk,' als Zauberwerk" (1.1, 427). According to Sombart, the first experiments with paper money failed because of the "Unvermögen der Staatsorgane, mit diesem gefährlichen Werkzeug umzugehen" and because of the "tiefe[n] Mißtrauen [. . .] gegen diese Geldform, das sich namentlich im 18. Jahrhundert erst recht einstellte (als Folge der Schwindelmanöver in der ersten 'Gründerzeit')" (1.1, 427). Nevertheless, the creation of paper money is not set up simply in a relationship of analogy to alchemy, for the latter also functions as a statement of the fact that everything is for sale, that all objects are commodities. The Astrologer speaks, while Mephistopheles prompts him ("bläst ein") — this literally two-faced origin of his speech corresponds to the transformative adoption of an obsolete discourse: "Das übrige ist alles zu erlangen: / Paläste, Gärten, Brüstlein, rote Wangen" (4967–68) (Schmidt 1999, 222). The alchemical doctrine of correspondences, which relates planets and metals to each other, is quoted merely to advertize and celebrate the fact that all goods are purchasable. In the ailing imperium a truly buccaneering spirit, a modern kind of adventurism, is gaining a foothold; sudden wealth derives from the phantasms of imperial authority as well as from easily uncovered mineral treasure.

Equally, the imagination plays a crucial role in the ensuing Carnival Masque, for it makes clear a certain structure of desire which promotes the circulation of commodities. The economic analysis of commercial principles continues from the perspective of suppliers and consumers, as we are made aware of the process by which artificial needs are created by fantasy and fashion. In the course of the masque, various figures and characters, both mythological and typological, appear, beginning with the Flower Girls. They arrange a decorative display of fruit, creating the appearance of life in Arcadia, but its purpose is obviously to advertise. The Gardeners sing: "Unter lustigen Gewinden, / In geschmückter Lauben Bucht, / Alles ist zugleich zu finden: / Knospe, Blätter, Blume, Frucht" (5174–77). Here we see the return of the cipher of paradise, of the simultaneity of blossom and fruit, part of the topos of the eternal spring (which Goethe also uses in the description of Alkinoos's paradise-like garden in his drama fragment, *Nausikaa*). But what follows next in *Faust II* makes it unmistakably clear that this paradisiacal plenitude owes its origins to an extensive choice of goods and hence, in a quite profane manner, to import trade; in the stage instructions, we read that "unter Wechselgesang, begleitet von Gitarren und Theorben, fahren beide Chöre fort, ihre *Waren stufenweis* in die Höhe zu schmükken und auszubreiten" (my emphasis). While establishing a link with the concept of a naturally organized hierarchy, the "chain of being," this detail at the same time ironically subverts it. In place of the harmonious, graduated arrangement of natural phenomena and their paradisiacal plenitude, an extensive choice of goods emerges, which is arranged purely out of commercial considerations in a decorative way, "in Stufen." Moreover, both fruit and flowers are only available for purchase at the same time because of the independence from the natural seasons created by importing goods. By the same token, however, nature itself is appropriated to commercial ends, and becomes merely decorative, as the Flower Girls sing: "Tragen wir in braunen Locken / Mancher heitern Blume Zier; / Seidenfäden, Seidenflocken / Spielen ihre Rolle hier" (5092–95). Here too nature plays its part, for it serves the function of making the range of goods appear disguised as the fullness of paradise, even though the real purpose is to create artificial appetites and hence fragment the relation between what is offered by

nature as available and what is consumed, so that the natural relationship between need and what nature provides is destroyed. (Not the
least of the reasons why Italy had impressed Goethe was the way in
which the relationship between the gifts of nature and what was required for nourishment was present there, as opposed to the situation
where "nordische Industrie" obtained.) Thus, it is quite logical when
fantasy and fashion make an entrance at this point in *Faust II*, and we
see what it is that extends need into the infinite and makes us imagine
the immeasurable — the fundamental basis of the commercial system
(Binswanger, 134). This unending yearning, this striving, is sustained,
in *Faust II*, by fashion (which, according to Sombart, generates both
"Wechselhaftigkeit" and "Vereinheitlichung der Bedarfsgestaltung"
[1.2, 744]), as well as by fantasy, which creates things that are unusual,
unknown, and above all, new. A fantasy garland comments thus on itself: "Bunte Blumen, Malven ähnlich, / Aus dem Moos ein Wunder-
flor! / Der Natur ist's nicht gewöhnlich, / Doch die Mode bringt's
hervor" (5132–35); and the challenge of rosebuds contribute the following lines: "Mögen bunte Phantasien / Für des Tages Mode blühen,
/ Wunderseltsam sein gestaltet, / Wie Natur sich nie entfaltet" (5144–
47). Fashion constitutes the essential motor of the production of luxu-
ries, constantly tempting the consumer with new products; for as Sombart tells us, what the consumers of luxury goods "vor allem
verlangten, war: daß die Ware 'frisch und neu' sei" (2.2, 896). In the
first act of *Faust II*, Goethe offers an account of this commercial
framework, the business of imaginary needs and fashion accessories,
and uncovers, down to its very detail, the relationship between commercial industry and the production of luxury goods, not to mention
the mass production of goods. In his short essay entitled *Kunst und
Handwerk* (1797), Goethe warned of the dangerous consequences of
such production of luxury goods, which arises with the mechanical
production of goods and, as far he was concerned, ushers in the decline
of "wahre Kunst":

> Dagegen hat alles was der bloß mechanische Künstler hervorbringt,
> weder für ihn noch für einen andern jemals ein solches Interesse.
> Denn sein tausendstes Werk ist wie das erste und es existieret am Ende
> auch tausendmal. Nun kommt noch dazu daß man in den neueren
> Zeiten das Maschinen- und Fabrikwesen zu dem höchsten Grad hin-
> aufgetrieben hat und mit schönen, zierlichen, gefälligen vergänglichen
> Dingen durch den Handel die ganze Welt überschwemmt. Man sieht
> aus diesem, daß das einzige Gegenmittel gegen den Luxus, wenn er
> balanciert werden könnte und sollte, die wahre Kunst und das wahr
> erregte Kunstgefühl sei, daß dagegen der hochgetriebene Mechanis-

mus, das verfeinerte Handwerk und Fabrikenwesen der Kunst ihren völligen Untergang bereite. (WA 1.47, 58)

In *Faust II* this very process, which Goethe saw proceeding "mit unaufhaltsamer Gewalt," has taken shape in the form of all the allegorical figures of the Masque.

As a result, it would be right to say that there is a direct connection between allegorical form and economic innovation (see Schlaffer 1981, 34). The principle of artificial arousal of needs is reflected in the form of presentation — in allegory. If the value of products is proportionate to an artificially generated desire, by means of which commodities acquire "chimerical significance," and if being and appearance become separated — as is, for example, the case with the gold, of which Sombart says it became the "mächtige Triebkraft" behind historical processes (1.2, 536) — then the form of allegory can itself be described in an analogous manner. Its significance is not exhausted in appearances, and it is something heteronymous; frequently, as a result of this devaluation of its sensuous shape, allegory has been described as ghostly, as being like a chimera. Friedrich Theodor Vischer, for instance, wrote in 1841 of "das Gespenst der Kunst, die Allegorie [. . .] das einem bestimmten sinnlichen Gebilde die ihm lebendig zugehörende warme Seele ausweidet und dafür einen ihm fremden, der Vielseitigkeit individueller Beseelung durch seine Abstraktheit widersprechenden Begriff hineinstopft" (in Schlaffer 1981, 34). Commodities whose value has been enhanced precisely through the creation of artificial needs and advertising correspond just as little to their intrinsic value as the sensuous embodiment of allegory does to its abstract meaning; in the play, the Herald becomes increasingly unable to explain the allegories (Schmidt 1999, 223). In this respect, the allegorical figures of the Carnival Masque are very well suited to making manifest to the spectator the principle of artificially awakening needs; what, and who, is hiding behind the masks remains undetectable.

Yet not only fashion and fantasy arouse artificial desires: eroticism plays a crucial role in this process too. If desire is structured around imaginary values, then at the same time an intimate link is created between Eros and economics; according to traditional topoi, the woman appears as the very incarnation of seduction (Schlaffer 1991, 55–69). The Gardeners, for example, sing the praises of the goods on display, but at the same time they invoke the erotic power of seduction exercised by the shop assistants, the Flower Girls: "Bieten bräunliche Gesichter / Kirschen, Pfirschen, Königspflaumen, / Kauft! denn gegen Zung' und Gaumen / Hält sich Auge schlecht als Richter" (5162–65).

Eroticism, then, is nothing less than an instrument of marketing strategy. The opposite also becomes true: love and marriage are up for sale. The Gardeners' encomium is followed immediately by the monologue of the Mother speaking to her Daughter, which is about the economic provision for the Daughter by means of, as it were, the business of marriage (just as a similar topic constitutes the theme of the opening conversation between Barbara and Mariane in *Wilhelm Meisters Lehrjahre*). The Mother looks back nostalgically at her earlier hopes: "Dachte dich sogleich als Braut, / Gleich dem Reichsten angetraut, / Dachte dich als Weibchen" (5182–84). Over and beyond this little monologue, however, love and economics find analogous forms of expression, which is possible because, in both areas, there is an endless desire that cannot be satisfied with whatever it possesses, and so is pushed by insatiable yearning ever onward to "true fulfillment." That is why one of the Furies says what she does: Megaera, while being a mythological figure, is appropriate for modern times (the Herald says about the Furies' mythological status: "Die jetzo kommen, werdet ihr nicht kennen, / Wärt ihr noch so gelehrt in alten Schriften; / Sie anzusehn, die so viel Übel stiften, / Ihr würdet sie willkommne Gäste nennen. // Die *Furien* sind es, niemand wird uns glauben, / Hübsch, wohlgestaltet, freundlich, jung von Jahren" [5345–50]), and she says of the eternal goad of unsatisfied yearning: "Und niemand hat Erwünschtes fest in Armen, / Der sich nicht nach Erwünschterem törig sehnte" (5373–74). This is true of both love — and commerce. In both realms, there is endless desire, which is perpetuated by longing, more precisely by phantasmagoric images, in other words by the imagination. Here Faustian striving takes on specifically modern contours, shaped as it is beyond the concrete form of Faust by the ceaseless striving for the satisfaction of artificial desires so structured that their gratification is impossible.

That this desire for money, possessions, satisfaction is, fundamentally, phantasmagorically determined and is based on a perpetual deferral, is shown by the Boy Charioteer, who also represents a certain kind of poetry in an age of transition (Metscher, 281). He conjures up riches out of nothingness, just as Mephistopheles does the paper money; it is all, to use the German expression, *aus der Luft gegriffen*. For what he offers the public is utterly insubstantial: "Hier seht mich nur ein Schnippchen schlagen, / Schon glänzt's und glitzert's um den Wagen. / Da springt eine Perlenschnur hervor." Snapping his fingers in all directions, he goes on: "Nehmt goldne Spange für Hals und Ohr, / Auch Kamm und Krönchen ohne Fehl, / In Ringen köstlichstes Juwel" (5582–87). The crowd grabs greedily at these unexpected gifts, thus exhibiting how easy it is to tempt them by all that glisters or by, to use an expression applied to art itself, mere "beautiful appearance" (*schöner Schein*), and at the same time revealing the desire for gold and possessions to be a delusion. For what is actually gained is by no means what is wanted; held in the hand, a string of pearls turns into horrible beetles ("Käfer"). This entire performance is a means of showing us that any range of goods for sale — however promising — lures us with false appearances, and that what we finally possess is never what we really wanted: "Wie doch der Schelm so viel verheißt / Und nur verleiht, was golden gleißt" (5604–05). At the same time, the concept of appearance (*Schein*) leads us to the realm of aesthetics. Even in "beautiful form" (*schöner Schein*), which constitutes the essence of art, the masses are deceived, and they want to be deceived: *mundus vult decipi*, as Thomas Mann would say. The crowd, like the Emperor, does not just want to own things, it wants entertainment; it is because of this demand that the ruler orders the necromantic ceremony that will call up Helena. Faust realizes that there is in fact a link between the wish to be rich and the wish to be entertained, and that the latter follows the former, when he declares: "Erst haben wir ihn reich gemacht, / Nun sollen wir ihn amüsieren" (6191–92). In this way, Horace's dictum about *docere* and *delectare* is recalled, but also inverted. The new slogan is "profit," instead of "utility" or edification, and amusement instead of entertainment. And that is why Helena is, above all, merely an insubstantial spectre, created out of nothingness, just like the gifts of the Boy Charioteer.

The Garden of the Oheim — *Chrematistik* Displacing *Öconomia*

The commercial principle of creating infinite demand by means of luxury and fashion, as presented in the Carnival Masque, proves to be of equal significance in understanding *Wilhelm Meisters Wanderjahre*, and in particular the section dealing with the realm of the Oheim, which Wilhelm enters after his stay with the "second Joseph." The economic behavior of the Oheim has long been regarded as characteristic of the eighteenth century, with the result that its explicit orientation towards making profit has been overlooked or relativized; for example, Erich Trunz speaks of the Oheim leading a life of "aufklärerischer Eudämonismus" (in HA 8, 570; see Fink, 127; John, 142). On the other hand, Thomas Degering has noted that "der Standard-Satz der Nationalökonomie, daß jeder in der Verfolgung seines Privatwohls zugleich und ungewollt das Wohl aller (anderen) mitrealisiere, ist bei diesem alten Herrn keine graue Theorie" (126), pointing out the Oheim's self-interested behaviour, and the military quality of his world (the estate is surrounded by spring-guns and high walls) (133). What in *Faust II* was staged as theatrical-allegorical action is, by contrast, treated here discursively, in the form of conversations allowing the utilitarian character of the Oheim's agricultural, capitalist enterprise to emerge unmistakably.

When he visits the Oheim in the *Wanderjahre*, Wilhelm comes across a similar vegetable garden to the one Lothario planted in the *Lehrjahre*. Fruit trees can be seen on all sides, vegetable plots, storage plants; not a trace, then, of the aristocratic pleasure-garden, or even aristocratic farming as traditionally practised. On the Oheim's estate, the transition from feudal society to capitalist economics has taken place; instead of a lord of the manor, entrusted with the duty to protect, and whose rule is, according to the ideal, bound by ethical guidelines, we have a big landowner who is concerned only with economic interests, even managing to integrate the needy into his business enterprise, rather than dispensing charity. In the terminology of Otto Brunner, *Ökonomik* (or how to run a household), which involves both ethical and political considerations, is replaced by *Chrematistik*, the core of modern economics (260). In other words, *Chrematistik* signifies economic transactions for the sake of profit, not for subsistence — a principle that received one of its first condemnations from Aristotle. For Aristotle, business and trade were permissible only within strict limits or "soweit sie die vollständige Autarkie des Hauses ergänzen. Verwerflich sind die 'unsichtbaren Vermögen,' die aus Geldhandel und Geldleihe entstehen" (Brunner, 251); and thus, for ethical reasons, pure profit is rejected. On the territory of the Oheim, a new kind of economics has emerged — the kind that established itself in the course of the eighteenth century and consisted, above all, in a radical rationalization of economic activity (Brunner, 242), being less concerned with the home than with the market (300). With the appearance in 1809–1812 of Albrecht Thaer's *Grundsätze der rationellen Landwirtschaft*, the essence of economics becomes concerned with capitalist agriculture and, above all, profit (321). The primary concern of the Oheim's activities is likewise profit making, or *Chrematistik*; and so his garden can be read as a deliberate *Kontrafaktur* (or "imitation," from the Latin *contrafactura*) of the Garden of Paradise, and of the Golden Age (as, for example, depicted by Ovid in terms of an abundance of nature fulfilling every imaginable need), since it is exclusively designed to satisfy artificially created needs. Nevertheless, everyone talks about the Oheim's apparently altruistic motivation, and his niece, Juliette, tells us: "Alles dies geschah dem großen, nahen Gebirg zuliebe. Der treffliche Mann, Kraft und Vermögen zusammenhaltend, sagte zu sich selbst: 'Keinem Kinde da droben soll es an einer Kirsche, an einem Apfel fehlen, wonach sie mit Recht so lüstern sind; der Hausfrau soll es nicht an Kohl noch an Rüben oder sonst einem Gemüse im Topf ermangeln, damit dem unseligen Kartoffelgenuß nur einigermaßen das Gleichgewicht gehalten werde'" (HA 8, 67). The products of the Oheim's fields enhance the monotonous food that the barren landscape can provide; in fact, during his stay with the "second Joseph" in the opening chapter of the *Wanderjahre*, Wilhelm enjoys eating delicious cherries and, in the second version of the *Wanderjahre*, a passage is inserted about the children being "im Begriff, Kirschen zu handeln; eigentlich aber feilschte Felix, der immer etwas Geld bei sich führte. Nun machte er sogleich als Gast den Wirt, spendete reichliche Früchte an seine Gespielen, selbst dem Vater war die Erquickung angenehm, *mitten in diesen unfruchtbaren Mooswäldern*, wo die farbigen, glänzenden Früchte noch einmal so schön erschienen" (my emphasis; HA 8, 14). The cherries are foreign to the inhospitable environment of the mountains, and have to be transported in, increasing the price, a point which is in turn thematized: "Sie trage solche weit herauf aus einem großen Garten, bemerkte die Verkäuferin, um den Preis annehmlich zu machen, der den Käufern etwas zu hoch geschienen hatte" (HA 8, 14). Such transport makes "hohen Wert" out of "Stoffen aus dem Bereich minderen Werts" or, to put it another way, the transport produces the difference between the purchase and sale price, this creating added value (Binswanger, 44). Goethe's description of economic processes is extremely precise, and accordingly the Oheim, despite his apparently altruistic intent, covers his costs. Or as Gustav Radbruch puts it: "Der Oheim nützt also andern, indem er zunächst sich selber nützt; [. . .] seine soziale Auffassung des Privateigentums beruht auf dem liberalistischen Gedanken von der prästabilisierten Harmonie des Eigennutzes mit dem Gemeinnutz" (91).

    If the Oheim's agricultural production is aimed at export, and at the satisfaction of the needs of those who live in the mountains, his transactions anticipate the nineteenth century. For the principles of self-sufficiency persisted in Germany well into the nineteenth century. According to Sombart, two-thirds of total production were consumed on the farmers' estates themselves (2.2, 629), and precisely the agricultural economy remained for a long time "im Banne des Bedarfsdeckungsprinzipes und des Traditionalismus befangen" (2.2, 631). Not so the Oheim, with his capitalist, agricultural enterprise and his "luxury products," as we should have to call them. Even the cherries, which Wilhelm enjoys while staying with the "second Joseph," are really luxury articles; and Sombart points to the link between the luxury industry (among other things) and capitalist development: "So bleiben denn in

Wahrheit als die beiden Stammwurzeln, aus denen die kapitalistische Industrie erwachsen ist: Luxusbedarf und Heeresbedarf" (2.2, 862). The Oheim provides the mountain dwellers with goods that cannot be grown in their own region; moreover, alpine areas are seldom self-sufficient or autarkical, as among other things Lenardo's diary shows. So it is extremely important that, in Goethe's novel, commercial economic principles are shown at work in the vicinity of mountainous areas. Thanks to the Oheim, the principle of maintenance by means of subsistence can be overcome.

That pleasure and luxury are in fact of significance in this functionally organized sphere is, by the same token, illustrated by the meals Wilhelm consumes in this part of the novel. The Oheim, whose table-manners are, to say the least, innovative (his table moves about and is, like him, mobile), sets up the following rule for the meals over which he presides: "Will man die Menschen ergötzen [. . .] so muß man ihnen das zu verleihen suchen, was sie *selten oder nie* zu erlangen im Falle sind" (HA 8, 71) — or at least that is what the women remember him saying. The Oheim's table is stacked with various tasty delights, with rare culinary treats; what arrives on his table are luxury goods, just as, later on in the *Wanderjahre*, crayfish are served. That said, this form of pleasure derived from rare commodities and delicacies is presented in the course of the novel as disastrous and is commented upon as such. In his last letter to Natalie, Wilhelm gives a report of the death of his first close friend. The beautiful young son of a fisherman, Adolf, is given the task of fishing for crabs, which the Pfarrerin "den Gästen als *eine Seltenheit* nach der Stadt mitgeben wolle" (my emphasis; HA 8, 272). The lad goes in search of them, but as he tries to get hold of these delicacies, he finds an early death by drowning, and thus the hunt for culinary rarities comes to a fatal conclusion.

The process of awakening and satisfying artificial desires is thus presented in the *Wanderjahre* as a major principle of economic innovation, but it is subjected to covert criticism, for example, by the death of Adolf. The close link between Eros and economics dominating in *Faust II* is, however, absent from the *Wanderjahre*.

Following these observations on the innovative economic aspects of the two works of the late period of Goethe's life, I should like to turn to a quite different dimension of these texts and examine the premodern concepts — particularly the idea of restorative utopia — they also incorporate, beginning with *Faust II*.

Mater Gloriosa — Neo-Platonic Utopia or Calvinistic Work Ethic?

Ceaseless striving — the quintessence of what it means to be Faustian — reaches its culmination in Act 5 of the play, when Faust has become an old man, and dominates the project of land reclamation as well as, once he has died, the apotheosis of Faust. The aging and the deceased Faust are united by this governing motif of *Streben*. Faust's elevation is presented as the continuation of his earthly striving: he strives, in a hierarchically organized cosmos, "hinan zu höherm Kreise," from one heavenly sphere to another, following the tradition of Dante's *Divine Comedy*. There are, in fact, important parallels between Dante's vision, led from Beatrice to the Divine, and the concluding scene of *Faust II*. Faust rises through the spheres of Heaven, just as Dante ascends through the various angelic hierarchies (which are based on a schema derived from Dionysius the Pseudo-Areopagite) (Schmidt 1991, 389). Faust approaches the Mater gloriosa, who is surrounded by penitent women: "Dort ziehen Fraun vorbei, / Schwebend nach oben. / Die Herrliche mitteninn / Im Sternenkranze, / Die Himmelskönigin, / Ich seh's am Glanze" (11991–96). This image corresponds to that of the Virgin Mary surrounded by penitent women, which goes back to medieval conceptions and traditional Marian iconography, yet there are also parallels with Dante (Schmidt 1999, 300). For just as Beatrice leads Dante upwards (gazing into her eyes, he sees reflected in them the light of God, and he then contemplates the angelic circles directly), Gretchen becomes, in her elevated and impersonal form, the woman who guides Faust. Significantly, the Plotinian notion of mutual guidance acquires importance in the writings of Dionysius (Schmidt 1991, 402). The Mater gloriosa commands her: "Komm! hebe dich zu höhern Sphären; / Wenn er dich ahnet, folgt er nach" (12094–95). And in the act of redemption itself, Faust is placed under the sign of love, as is the case in Dante's vision. In *Faust II*, we read: "Denn das ist der Geister Nahrung, / Die im freien Äther waltet: / Ewigen Liebens Offenbarung, / Die zur Seligkeit entfaltet" (11922–25). And the Pater Ecstaticus tells us: "Daß ja das Nichtigste / Alles verflüchtige, / Glänze der Dauerstern, / Ewiger Liebe Kern" (11862–65). In the cosmogony of the *Divine Comedy*, Love is equally central, for "all loving beings" arise from Love itself and create the earth, indeed the universe: "In sua eternità di tempo fuore, / Fuor d'ogni altro comprender, come i piacque, / S'aperse in nuovi l'eterno amore."

But for all the seemingly Christian pathos of this redemption, which stands in radical disjuncture with the crude earthly machinations of Faust's craze for progress, Act 5 of *Faust II* is by no means an affirmative adoption of Catholic thought. Rather, this tradition is, as Jochen Schmidt (1991) has shown, subjected to a mystical demythologization by covering Catholic teaching with a layer of neo-Platonism and, in particular, the notion of a developing entelechy and a mystical vision. As Faust is admitted into Heaven, he is, in accordance with neo-Platonic ideas, cleansed of earthly stains, and his *Steigerung* is brought about by a process of instruction which renders his entelechy pure spirit. And it appears it is precisely Faust's activity, his never-ending striving, that makes possible this transformation of his entelechy in the hereafter. In the last years of his life, Goethe laid great emphasis on the view that activity creates permanence, or eternity, telling Eckermann: "Die Überzeugung unserer Fortdauer entspringt mir aus dem Begriff der Tätigkeit; denn wenn ich bis an mein Ende rastlos wirke, so ist die Natur verpflichtet, mir eine andere Form des Daseins anzuweisen, wenn die jetzige meinem Geist nicht ferner auszuhalten vermag" (4 February 1829). Activity guarantees that the individual soul develops in a way that transcends earthly life — a notion that Goethe took up from Humboldt, who spoke of the human character as being in perpetual motion that never comes to an end: "Da der Charakter in einer fort-währenden Thätigkeit ist, so verändert sich mit jedem Augenblick das Verhältniss seiner Fähigkeiten.[. . .] Diese Thätigkeit ist es [. . .], in der wir, nebst dem Verhältniss derselben [i.e. der Kräfte], den Sitz des ei-gentlichen Charakters zu finden glaubten" (Humboldt, 61; cited in Dippel, 139). Against this background Faust's redemption appears as a neo-Platonically inspired vision, which incorporates Goethe's notions of immortality. At the same time, the elevation of the soul to the abso-lute in *Faust II* seems a self-conscious anachronism; or as Jochen Schmidt has argued, by setting up the vision of a cosmos beyond all history in opposition to the historical end of the earthly cosmos, Goethe emphasizes the out-dated nature of traditional cosmological thought. Becoming aware of this out-datedness is achieved by reflect-ing on the *historical* tradition, in which Goethe himself was rooted and which persists in his outlook on the world in the form of an ideal, but it is an ideal that, in the light of the experience of modernization in the nineteenth century, recedes into the imaginary and is projected into poetic-mythological representation and hence the next world (1999, 302).

There remains, however, the question of whether Faust's elevation can simply be regarded as a *Kontrafaktur* opposed to the modern world, or whether it also functions as an integral part of that modernity and is thus intimately bound up with modernization. Hannelore Schlaffer has emphasized the ironic undertone of the *Schlußszene*, an ironic quality shared with other concluding scenes in Goethe's works (1994, 102–11). As has been already mentioned, Faust's elevation follows the same trajectory as his economic activities: his tireless striving just keeps going (Schmidt 1991, 384). The famous lines of his final redemption, concentrated in epigrammatic form, tell us that *"wer immer strebend sich bemüht, / Den können wir erlösen"* (11936–37), and we further learn: "Und hat an ihm die Liebe gar / Von oben teilgenommen, / Begegnet ihm die selige Schar / Mit herzlichem Willkommen" (11938–41). This principle could be described, as Adorno has done, as "[eine] Maxime innerweltlicher Askese" (134), not far removed from Calvinist convictions. Thus seen, Goethe anticipates Max Weber's thesis that the capitalist work ethic developed from Protestant and, above all, Calvinist thought (Borchmeyer; Kaiser, 41). The words are conspicuously presented as a quotation, which seems to come from another world, not the heavenly one, and is, as such, out of place here. Moreover, the contribution of the hereafter is even further reduced by the use of "gar," which, as Adorno pointed out, "lehrhaft [. . .] den Zeigefinger in die Höhe [streckt]" (134) — "Und hat an ihm die Liebe gar / Von oben teilgenommen." To strive in this world is, according to the maxim, sufficient *movens* to reach *this* Heaven; the Love from the next world is no more than an accident of redemption. In other words, it is the immanent conduct of one's life, or what one does in this world, that decides one's fate in the next. Thus it seems to be irrelevant whether God favours the "good" (because active) soul and bestows his love upon him. This world decides what happens in the next; transcendence does not determine redemption. From which one might draw the conclusion, which our analysis of the *Wanderjahre* supports: at the end of *Faust II*, the bourgeois doctrine of work and activity appears in transfigured, transcendent form; and those very principles — untiring activity and insatiable desire — that, on the threshold of a new era, initiate the economic processes of modernity, acquire a kind of divine aura. Not only is the Heaven that awaits Faust a projection of earthly life, it is also designed to receive the man of technological and economic progress, transfiguring the immanent principles of ceaseless striving he embodies and giving him the appearance of transcendence.

Seen from this perspective, the idiosyncratic love ethic of Faust's apotheosis (which I would hesitate to call spiritualized) cannot be traced entirely to the influence of the Platonic conception of Eros (Schmidt 1991, 394). I would argue that the final apotheosis of *Faust II*, in contrast to Plato, evokes sensuous love, the seductions of this world, not a transcendent *eidos* of another world. As a result, that love ethic acquires a specific meaning. We cannot fail to notice the sensuous nature of Eros in the final apotheosis, and its dialectic structure: the gracious forgiveness of sins brings to the fore Faust's offenses and his sensuous (and sensual) desire. Doctor Marianus talks of "those who are easily seduced," and evokes in vivid terms the dangers of love:

> Dir, der Unberührbaren,
> Ist es nicht benommen,
> Daß die leicht Verführbaren
> Traulich zu dir kommen.
>
> In die Schwachheit hingerafft,
> Sind sie schwer zu retten;
> Wer zerreißt aus eigner Kraft
> Der Gelüste Ketten?
> Wie entgleitet schnell der Fuß
> Schiefem, glattem Boden?
> Wen betört nicht Blick und Gruß,
> Schmeichelhafter Odem?
>
> (12020–31)

If we assume that in the *Schlußszene* the immanent principles of desire, striving, and activity return in transfigured form, then it becomes clear why the Feminine appears here once again as a seduction, as a principle of desire that causes (man's) desire to become unending: we see the triumph of the entire feminine art of seduction which was played out in the domain of the Carnival Masque. As a love ethic, it looks very different from the one in Dante's vision. The final apotheosis becomes analogous, in a very precise way, to modern economic processes: not only does the performance principle return, but also desire, which the woman, the feminine principle, symbolizes. It is to this same movement — perpetual postponement, eternal yearning — that the genesis of artificial needs and their merely apparent satisfaction are subjected, and it equally dominates Faust's assumption, which thereby acquires the appearance of the earthly raised to a higher level. Faust's heaven is a reflection of the earth, the earth projected and transfigured — a thought Goethe had already formulated in a quite different context in his "Prometheus" poem. The conclusion of *Faust II* can thus be read in two ways, which is not unusual for Goethe's late works: first, as a nostalgic retrospective on a neo-Platonically inspired cosmology; and second, as the transfiguration of immanent principles, of the worldly ethos of activity, of ceaseless striving, which characterizes Faust's project of land-reclamation and colonization. Seen in this light, both the neo-Platonic and Catholic references have the function of evoking the appearance of transcendence; more precisely, traditional elements are employed, in the modern world of pure immanence, to preserve the appearance of transcendence, and at the same time to legitimize those immanent values that drive modernization forward, that is, its tireless hustle and bustle. Mystical striving for the Eternal Feminine — a notion completely alien to, for example, Plotinus — can, from this perspective, be seen as the apparent legitimation of that very desire presented in the Carnival Masque scene under the sign of economics.

So in contrast to some other works by Goethe, in Hannelore Schlaffer's view, in the case of *Faust II* the spectators are confronted with this play with transcendence in a particularly direct way. In the drama Goethe wrote toward the end of his life, the ironic objections are much less easy to notice than in, for example, *Die Wahlverwandtschaften*; above all, there is no narrator who might relativize the apotheosis (1994, 68). That said, we might detect in the fact that an analogy is conspicuously set up between economic activities in this world and spiritual events in the next nothing less than a device for creating irony.

Makarie — Priestess or Artificial Center

The figure of Makarie in *Wilhelm Meisters Wanderjahre*, supported by our reading of Faust's assumption, is equally susceptible to a similarly dual interpretation, and in similar terms to the Marian vision in *Faust II*. Through Makarie, the notion — no longer valid in the collectively based communities — that there is an analogy between microcosm and macrocosm (the neo-Platonic concept of "the chain of being") celebrates its return. For Makarie, the ethical analogy between humanity and the world is still in place and, according to the Astrologer: "Sie erinnert sich von klein auf ihr inneres Selbst als von leuchtendem Wesen durchdrungen, von einem Licht erhellt, welchem sogar das hellste Sonnenlicht nichts anhaben konnte. Oft sah sie zwei Sonnen, eine innere nämlich und eine außen am Himmel" (HA 8, 449). This integration into the cosmos carries ethical significance, and since Makarie's spirit is "von überirdischen Gesichten erfüllt," that is why "ihr Tun und Handeln [blieb] immerfort dem edelsten Sittlichen gemäß" (HA 8, 450). Moreover, as far as she is concerned, the ancient ethical concept of *kalokagathia* (the Greek educational ideal of Goodness and Beauty) retains its validity. This ideal is represented in the conclusion of the novella *Der Mann von funfzig Jahren*, by the beautiful widow; as it is also later by Susanne, explicitly referred in Lenardo's diary as "die Gute-Schöne." In *Der Mann von funfzig Jahren*, Makarie functions as an "ethical mirror," for we are told that she, "im Vorhalten eines sitt-

lich-magischen Spiegels, durch die äußere verworrene Gestalt irgendei-
nem Unglücklichen sein rein schönes Innere gewiesen und ihn auf
einmal erst mit sich selbst befriedigt und zu einem neuen Leben auf-
gefordert hat" (HA 8, 223). Makarie is the ennobling, ethical mirror
that allows her own beauty and goodness to appear in the other person.
By looking in the "mirror of Makarie" the beautiful widow reforms
herself and becomes a truly compassionate being.

Makarie, too, is a Marian figure; she too is a saint, surrounded by
penitent women. She dispenses absolution, is free of the burden of
earthly cares, and, being full of grace, brings about reconciliation and
teaches love. Right at the end of the *Wanderjahre*, when the Emigrants
meet up again before their huge undertaking, Philine and Lydie fall at
the feet of Makarie: "Es war merkwürdig genug, die beiden Sünderin-
nen zu den Füßen der Heiligen zu sehen. Zu beiden Seiten lagen sie
ihr an den Knieen, Philine zwischen ihren zwei Kindern, die sie lebhaft
anmutig niederdrückte" (HA 8, 441). Makarie releases the tearful Lydie from her earthly hardships by the sacred gesture of the laying-on of
hands, and there is the suggestion of the rising soul, a spiritual elevation: "Lydie richtete sich auf, erst auf ihre Kniee, dann auf die Füße,
und schaute zu ihrer Wohltäterin mit reiner Heiterkeit. 'Wie geschieht
mir!' sagte sie, 'wie ist mir! Der schwere, lästige Druck, der mir, wo
nicht alle Besinnung, doch alles Überlegen raubte, er ist auf einmal von
meinem Haupte aufgehoben, ich kann nun frei in die Höhe sehen,
meine Gedanken in die Höhe richten'" (HA 8, 441). Thanks to Makarie, the mediatrix, the "sittlicher Spiegel," the soul can concentrate on
higher things as well as on a purer form of love. When Jarno meets Lydie, he exclaims: "'Es ist das erstemal, daß du mir offen und liebevoll
entgegenkommst, das erstemal, daß du mich ans Herz drückst, ob ich
es gleich längst verdiente'" (HA 8, 441). Makarie promises that the
human soul may yet become divine. Lydie tells Makarie that "[Mon-
tan] soll erfahren, was er dieser Göttlichen schuldig ist, und sich mit
mir dankend niederwerfen" (HA 8, 441). And she also embodies the
thought that the human soul develops like an entelechy, and persists on
the other side of death. In the interpolated essay by the Astronomer,
we read (with reference to Makarie): "Wir hoffen, daß eine solche En-
telechie sich nicht ganz aus unserm Sonnensystem entferne, sondern,
wenn sie an die Grenze desselben gelangt ist, sich wieder zurücksehnen
werde, um zugunsten unsrer Urenkel in das irdische Leben und
Wohltun wieder einzuwirken" (HA 8, 452). (According to Hannelore
Schlaffer, the trajectory described by Makarie through the universe is
based on the astronomical theories of Johann Elert Bode [1747–1826],
and the star they observe is the planet Uranus, discovered in 1781

[1980, 185].) The motion of her soul is imagined as cyclical, eternally recurring (Schlaffer 1980, 185).

Yet the figure of Makarie, in which Catholic and neo-Platonic elements are once again combined, is in various ways relativized, problematized, even ironized, as such critics as Jochen Schmidt (304), Hannelore Schlaffer (1980, 186), and Jane K. Brown (69–70) have maintained. On one hand, the anachronistic quality of her character is made manifest when she is described as "ätherische Dichtung" (HA 8, 452). On the other, Makarie's gifts appear in the external form of a disease: in the Astronomer's essay (whose authenticity is nevertheless questionable [cf. HA 8, 448]), we read: "Solange sie die Anschauungen geheimhielt, gehörte viel dazu, sie zu ertragen; was sie davon offenbarte, wurde nicht anerkannt oder mißdeutet, sie ließ es daher in ihrem langen Leben nach außen als Krankheit gelten, und so spricht man in der Familie noch immer davon" (HA 8, 450). We might at this juncture recall that Goethe, talking about "jenseitige Fragen," spoke approvingly of the esoteric form, which is used in the *Wanderjahre* to preserve Makarie's secret: "Solch unbegreifliche Dinge liegen zu fern, um ein Gegenstand täglicher Betrachtung und gedankenzerstörender Spekulation zu sein. Und ferner: wer eine Fortdauer glaubt, der sei glücklich im stillen" (conversation with Eckermann, 25 February 1824). But the Astronomer's statement stresses the complete loss of transcendent horizons within the community in which Makarie has her place, since only under such conditions is it possible for her visions to be explained as speculative musings. Moreover, Makarie is marked in a physical way, just as are other figures in Goethe's works who distinguish themselves by their particular sensitivity (Schiff, 145); and she belongs to that line of similarly disadvantaged figures that includes Mignon and Ottilie. The cosmic harmony that can still be detected in Makarie causes her physical disintegration. Furthermore, the esoteric nature of Makarie's declarations underscores the exclusivity and, in a certain sense, the loss of validity within the modern collective social form of the harmony between humanity and the world. Such esotericism can also be seen from a different perspective, as Degering has shown in his study *Das Elend der Entsagung*.

Degering's assessment of Makarie's ideas is that they are delusional, and he argues that the company around Lenardo actually constructs this delusion for reasons that are, in fact, quite rational (249). He wants to show that Makarie becomes an instrument for concealing the lack of any consolatory metaphysical systems in a society well underway to becoming modern. For him, the "empty middle" is hidden by turning traditional conceptions to modern purposes. Religion and myth are retained for the purpose of offering consolation, not least because, for example, they make it possible for the emigrants to bow to their fate with patience and tenacity, and the eclectic system of belief is maintained in the Pedagogic Province precisely in order to make bearable the sufferings of emigration. According to Degering, the functional role played by Makarie is signalled by the high degree of theatricality that bestows dignity on her. Particularly significant in this respect is her first entrance, when Wilhelm visits her in her castle. Makarie appears from behind a green curtain, just as the secret society, the Turm-Gesellschaft, uses theatrical devices during Wilhelm's initiation in the *Lehrjahre*. In the *Wanderjahre*, the following happens: "Angela, so nannte man die durch Gestalt und Betragen einnehmende Schöne, verkündigte sodann die Ankunft Makariens; ein grüner Vorhang zog sich auf, und eine ältliche, wunderwürdige Dame ward auf einem Lehnsessel von zwei jungen, hübschen Mädchen hereingeschoben" (HA 8, 115).

Such a critical reading of the text is confirmed in the way Makarie promotes the end of art, which is often regarded in the novel as a sign of the times. Flavio, "der immer leidenschaftliche Dichter," writes a poem and "die gute Dame, obgleich ungern, verstand sich hiezu [ihm zuzuhören], und es ließ sich allenfalls anhören, ob man gleich dadurch weiter nichts erfuhr, als was man schon wußte, nichts fühlte, als was man schon gefühlt hatte" (HA 8, 438). And the poem should have been shorter — a rejection of art for reasons of utility, which is expressly represented at this point by Makarie. Moreover, ironic touches are added to the Marian iconography at the end of the *Wanderjahre*. Philine sinks to her knees in front of Makarie, but we must remember that this gesture is performed by the happy-go-lucky Venus figure of the *Lehrjahre* (modelled on Prévost's *Manon Lescaut*), in front of a figure symbolizing the Virgin Mary — a decidedly odd image. The strangeness of this scene has been noted by Adolf Muschg: "Philine vor Makarie: welche Zusammenstellung von Leicht- und Tiefsinn, und wieviel ironisches Licht — und wie wenig kultivierte Moral — fällt von der einen Figur auf die andere!" (122). Such irony makes Makarie appear questionable, and the model of microcosm and macrocosm seems to have become merely something acted out, around which society, in the throes of modernization, can orient itself, in order to conceal the cosmic homelessness of humanity and to compensate for the loss of ethical guidelines.

A central figure of the *Wanderjahre* can thus be read in terms of two different points of view. From the perspective of society entering the era of modernity, Makarie is a memento of a past world, which is theatrically re-evoked in order to camouflage the vacuum arising from the loss of ethical guidelines and metaphysical convictions. Modern society retains traditions in order to continue to enjoy their effects of consolation and solidarity, and so metaphysical notions become quotations used to cover up the functionalism, the pure immanence of modern society. From another perspective, the figure of Makarie offers a means of recalling an obsolete conception of microcosm and macrocosm as a nostalgic horizon of desire, or as a restorative utopia, which is placed in opposition to the innovating tendencies of this new society. The development of the soul as an entelechy, the overcoming of death, the notion of cyclical return, suggested by Makarie, all counteract and balance the apocalyptic mood that prevails in the final chapter of the *Wanderjahre.*

Such a dual interpretation proves to be fruitful in the case of these two late works, particularly in the context of their respective visions of redemption. In *Faust II*, we are presented with an apotheosis that derives from Catholic as well as neo-Platonic patterns of thought. At the same time, however, if we pay attention to its ironic signals, this conclusion can be described as a theatrical re-enactment of traditional visions of redemption which are inscribed in the structures of the modern world — if the eternal deferral of fulfillment, seduction, the desire for ever more novelty and for chimerical values dominate this world, an endless striving for "das Ewig-Weibliche" also dominates the next. Love and profit — both realms are ruled by an unending desire, which is kept alive by (traditional) phantasmagoric images, as the Carnival Masque and the final apotheosis both show. Just as in the *Wanderjahre* we find, as Degering points out, that Makarie's tendency towards the infinite corresponds to the wanderer's desire to traverse the earth (258), so too we find an analogy with, on the one hand, the elevation of Faust and, on the other, the profane passions of the crowd. In the case of both *Faust II* and *Wilhelm Meisters Wanderjahre*, if we take into account the way in which transcendent concepts are functionalized in the world of progress, and if we see how Heaven represents a compensatory projection of the earthly — only then can we become aware of this crucial analogy between secular and celestial activity and its explosive potency.

Translated by Paul Bishop

Works Cited

Adorno, Theodor W. "Zur Schlußszene des Faust." In *Noten zur Literatur*. Ed. Rolf Tiedemann. Frankfurt: Suhrkamp, 1981. 129–38.

Binswanger, Hans Christoph. *Geld und Magie: Deutung und Kritik der modernen Wirtschaft anhand von Goethes Faust*. Stuttgart: Weitbrecht, 1985.

Birk, Manfred. "Goethes Typologie der Epochenschwelle im vierten Akt des *Faust II*." In *Aufsätze zu Goethes* Faust II. Ed. Werner Keller. Darmstadt: Wissenschaftliche Buchgesellschaft, 1991. 243–66.

Böhme, Hartmut. "Lebendige Natur: Wissenschaftskritik, Naturforschung und allegorische Hermetik bei Goethe." *Deutsche Vierteljahrsschrift für Literaturwissenschaft und Geistesgeschichte*. 60 (1986). 249–72.

———. "Eros und Tod im Wasser: 'Bändigen und Entlassen der Elemente': Das Wasser bei Goethe." In *Kulturgeschichte des Wassers*. Frankfurt am Main: Suhrkamp, 1988. 208–33.

Borchmeyer, Dieter. *Höfische Gesellschaft und französische Revolution bei Goethe: Adliges und bürgerliches Wertsystem im Urteil der Weimarer Klassik*. Kronberg/Ts: Athenäum-Verlag, 1977.

Brown, Jane K. *Goethe's Cyclical Narratives:* Die Unterhaltungen deutscher Ausgewanderten *and* Wilhelm Meisters Wanderjahre. Chapel Hill: U of North Carolina P, 1975.

Brunner, Otto. *Adeliges Landleben und europäischer Geist: Leben und Werk Helmhards von Hohberg 1612–1688*. Salzburg: Mueller, 1949.

Degering, Thomas. *Das Elend der Entsagung: Goethes* Wilhelm Meisters Wanderjahre. Bonn: Bouvier, 1982.

Dippel, Lydia. *Wilhelm von Humboldt: Ästhetik und Anthropologie*. Würzburg: Königshausen und Neumann, 1990.

Fink, Gonthier-Louis. "Die Auseinandersetzung mit der Tradition in *Wilhelm Meisters Wanderjahren*." *Recherches Germaniques*. 5 (1975). 89–142.

Hering, Robert. *Wilhelm Meister und Faust und ihre Gestaltung im Zeichen der Gottesidee*. Frankfurt am Main: G. Schulte-Bumke, 1952.

Humboldt, Wilhelm von. "Das achtzehnte Jahrhundert." *Werke*. Ed. Albert Leitzmann. Vol. 2 (1796–1799). Berlin: Walter de Gruyter, 1904.

Jeßing, Benedikt. *Konstruktion und Eingedenken: Zur Vermittlung von gesellschaftlicher Praxis und literarischer Form in Goethes* Wilhelm Meisters Wanderjahre *und Johnsons* Mutmaßungen über Jakob. Wiesbaden: Deutscher Universitäts-Verlag, 1991.

Jockers, Ernst. *Mit Goethe: Gesammelte Aufsätze.* Heidelberg: Winter, 1957.

John, Johannes. *Die Aphorismen in Goethes Romanen.* 2nd ed. Rheinfeld, Berlin: Schäuble, 1993.

Kaiser, Gerhard. *Ist der Mensch zu retten? Vision und Kritik der Moderne in Goethes* Faust. Freiburg: Rombach, 1994.

Mahl, Bernd. *Goethes ökonomisches Wissen: Grundlagen zum Verständnis der ökonomischen Passagen im dichterischen Gesamtwerk und in den "Amtlichen Schriften."* Frankfurt am Main: Peter Lang, 1982.

Metscher, Thomas. "Faust und die Ökonomie." In *Aufsätze zu Goethes* Faust II. Ed. Werner Keller. Darmstadt: Wissenschaftliche Buchgesellschaft, 1991. 278–89.

Muschg, Adolf. *Goethe als Emigrant: Auf der Suche nach dem Grünen bei einem alten Dichter.* Frankfurt am Main: Suhrkamp, 1986.

Radbruch, Gustav. "Goethe: Wilhelm Meisters sozialistische Sendung." In *Gestalten und Gedanken: Zehn Studien.* 2nd ed. Stuttgart: Köhler, 1954. 84–111.

Schiff, Julius. "Mignon, Ottilie, Makarie im Lichte der Goetheschen Naturphilosophie." *Goethe Jahrbuch.* 9 (1922). 133–47.

Schlaffer, Hannelore. *Wilhelm Meister: Das Ende der Kunst und die Wiederkehr des Mythos.* Stuttgart: J. B. Metzler, 1980.

———. "Paradies und Parodie: Die letzten Szenen in Goethes letzten Werken." In *Interpreting Goethe's* Faust *Today.* Ed. Jane K. Brown, Meredith Lee, Thomas P. Saine. Columbia, SC: Camden House, 1994. 102–11.

Schlaffer, Heinz. "Exoterik und Esoterik in Goethes Romanen." *Goethe Jahrbuch.* 95 (1978). 212–26.

———. *Faust: Zweiter Teil: Die Allegorie des 19. Jahrhunderts.* Stuttgart: J. B. Metzler, 1981.

———. "Der Aufzug der Allegorien: Zur Mummenschanz." In *Aufsätze zu Goethes* Faust II. Ed. Werner Keller. Darmstadt: Wissenschaftliche Buchgesellschaft, 1991. 55–69.

Schmidt, Jochen. "Die 'katholische Mythologie' und ihre mystische Entmythologisierung in der Schluß-Szene des *Faust II.*" In *Aufsätze zu Goethes* Faust II. Ed. Werner Keller. Darmstadt: Wissenschaftliche Buchgesellschaft, 1991. 384–417.

———. *Goethes Faust, Erster und Zweiter Teil: Grundlagen — Werk — Wirkung.* Munich: C. H. Beck, 1999.

Schöne, Albrecht, ed. *Faust. Kommentare.* Frankfurt am Main: Deutscher Klassiker Verlag, 1994. [FA 7.2]

Skalweit, Stephan. *Der Beginn der Neuzeit: Epochengrenze und Epochenbegriff.* Darmstadt: Wissenschaftliche Buchgesellschaft, 1982.

Sombart, Werner. *Der moderne Kapitalismus* [1927]. 3 vols. Berlin: Deutscher Taschenbuch Verlag, 1969.

"Was die Welt im Innersten zusammenhält": Scientific Themes in Goethe's *Faust*

Peter D. Smith

IN HIS SCIENTIFIC STUDIES Goethe contributed to the fields of botany, comparative anatomy, meteorology, and geology, as well as developing original theories of morphology and color. However, in the positivist nineteenth century Goethe was unfairly categorized as a literary genius who completely misunderstood the scientific endeavor. Goethe's *Farbenlehre* (1810), the culmination of his critique of Isaac Newton's *Opticks* (1704), was the work that contributed most to this impression. In the nineteenth century the evident success of science in explaining the mechanisms of biological, chemical, and physical systems gave no cause to question the intellectual inheritance of Newton. The advance of science seemed incontestable and hence the temptation to reject Goethe's scientific writings as the work of a misguided dilettante was very great. As Maren Partenheimer has shown, however, not all scientists were so dismissive: Hermann von Helmholtz (1821–94), Ernst Haeckel (1834–1919), and Rudolf Virchow (1821–1902) were important exceptions. The interest shown by such prominent scientists demonstrates that one should not reject Goethe's scientific work because it does not conform to the textbook view of the "progress" of science. Indeed, the twentieth century has witnessed a revaluation of Goethe's scientific ideas. The newly perceived complexity of the physical world and an awareness of the limitations of nineteenth-century empiricism (for which Newton's *hypotheses non fingo* became the credo), has resulted in scientists in the vanguard of new ideas turning to Goethe: the physicists Werner Heisenberg (1901–1976), Carl Friedrich von Weizsäcker (born 1912), and Ilya Prigogine (born 1917), the biologists Adolf Portmann (1897–1982) and Wolfgang Schad, and chaos theorist Mitchell Feigenbaum (born 1945) (Gleick, 163–66), as well as scientists working on quantum theory (Bastin, 321–34). Many contemporary commentators on Goethe's approach to science, such as Henri Bortoft and Frederick Amrine, are discovering close parallels with our modern understanding of the scientific process. For, as John Neubauer (1997; 1998) rightly argues, in Goethe's mature scientific writings is expressed a sophisticated understanding of the experimental process, one that takes account of the observing subject as well as the institutional context in which scientific work takes place.

In *Wilhelm Meisters Wanderjahre* (1829) this concept of science is memorably described as "zarte Empirie": "Es gibt eine zarte Empirie, die sich mit dem Gegenstand innigst identisch macht und dadurch zur eigentlichen Theorie wird" (Book 2, "Betrachtungen im Sinne der Wanderer" [HA 8, 302]). This notion embraces a scientific methodology that is empirical while including the observer-scientist in the experimental equation, that accepts the role of theory in framing acts of cognition, and that views scientific ideas as competing *Vorstellungsarten*, or ways of thinking about the world (Kleinschnieder, 91–136). The *Vorstellungsarten* of science can be seen as part of a conceptual tradition that includes Platonic nature philosophy and Renaissance alchemical ideas. Goethe's science was resolutely anti-mechanistic and opposed contemporary Cartesian dualism with a philosophy that viewed the "universe as a dynamic, organic and divine whole" (Nisbet, 6). Indeed, as Jeremy Adler (1998) has shown, it is an approach that owes much to the idealist philosophy of Schelling, but which never surrenders its fundamental empiricism. Far from being the empty rhetoric of a dilettante, Goethe's scientific worldview was a carefully thought out and systematic engagement with contemporary science and with the complexity of the natural world.

According to the physiologist Emil du Bois-Reymond (1818–1896), Goethe's scientific work was the "totgeborene Spielerei eines autodidaktischen Dilettanten" (Bois-Reymond). In contrast, Goethe considered his contributions to science and particularly the theory of color to be of profound importance, as a conversation with Eckermann of 19 February 1829 reveals:

> Auf Alles, was ich als Poet geleistet habe, [. . .] bilde ich mir gar nichts ein. Es haben treffliche Dichter mit mir gelebt, es lebten noch Trefflichere vor mir, und es werden ihrer nach mir sein. Daß ich aber in meinem Jahrhundert in der schwierigen Wissenschaft der Farbenlehre der Einzige bin, der das Rechte weiß, darauf tue ich mir etwas zu gute, und ich habe daher ein Bewußtsein der Superiorität über Viele.

For Michael Böhler the "tragische Ironie" of this passage is reminiscent of the blind Faust's misinterpretation of the sound of the spades: Goethe's *Farbenlehre* did not provide the inspiration for a new science of color and light but was largely ignored by mainstream scientists (Böhler, 315). Nevertheless, the fact that Goethe was so convinced of the significance of his *Farbenlehre* indicates the central role his scientific research must play in any exegesis of Goethe's thought or literary work. Of no work is this more true than of his *Faust*.

The *Faust* project developed in parallel with his most important scientific ideas. According to Ruprecht Matthaei, Goethe worked simultaneously on *Faust* and the *Farbenlehre* for at least forty years (62). In Goethe's diaries, comments relating to both works appear in close relation to each other (see his entries for March-July 1806). Nevertheless, as Horst Albert Glaser has pointed out (12), we should be wary of interpreting Goethe's literary works as mere explications of his scientific ideas. Texts such as *Die Wahlverwandtschaften* (1809) allude to many *Vorstellungsarten* — the chain of being, Renaissance *sympathia*, as well as contemporary chemical theories of elective affinity (Adler 1987). He invoked many competing paradigms to describe the natural world, and wove them all together into a complex and richly textured fabric. Yet the work itself, although clearly a product of the Goethean scientific worldview, never propagandizes but instead reflects the intricate mystery of nature and the complexity of the human relation with the material realm. Similarly the chronologically disparate series of works that constitute *Faust* focuses explicitly on the problematic relationship between humankind and nature. However, as we will see, there are moments when parallels can be established between Goethe's science and *Faust*, parallels which cast light both on the hermeneutic possibilities of the text and on contemporary scientific debates.

For Goethe, scientific and literary work was unified by the attempt to give form to the heterogeneous realm of nature: "Wie sehr mich die Formung des Formlosen, ein gesetzlicher Gestaltenwechsel des Unbegrenzten erwünscht sein mußte, folgt aus meinem ganzen Bestreben in Wissenschaft und Kunst" ("Luke Howard to Goethe" [HA 13, 304]). As we will see, in both his science and literature Goethe developed an alternative approach to nature, one that was not reductive but which sought to represent the complex interconnectedness of nature. He supplements the empirical and quantifiable aspirations of science with a phenomenological emphasis that valorizes individual experience. This view is powerfully present in Faust's description of the waterfall, a literary moment that contains clear resonances with the *Farbenlehre*.

Faust's desire, in the opening scene of Part One, to understand "was die Welt / Im Innersten zusammenhält" (382–83) results from his dissatisfaction with conventional scholarship, with knowledge derived from books. Standing in his Gothic study, "Beschränkt von diesem Bücherhauf" (402), Faust turns initially to magic for enlightenment. Ironically it is a book, "dies geheimnisvolle Buch, / Von Nostradamus' eigner Hand" (419–20), that opens the world of magical experience to him, despite the fact that Michel de Notredame (1503–1566) left no single text. However, it is in this book that Faust sees the symbols of the macrocosm and the "Erdgeist." What Goethe depicts here is the hermetic tradition, the natural philosophy of Agrippa von Nettesheim (1487–1535), of Paracelsus (1493–1541), and of Emanuel Swedenborg (1688–1772), amongst others. Goethe's interest in alchemy is well documented, dating back to his friendship with Susanna Katharina von Klettenberg in Frankfurt during 1768–1769 (see, e.g., Mesh-hadi, 11). For the mature Goethe, however, such ideas did not in themselves offer the way to an understanding of nature (Matussek 1992, 119–21). Indeed, in his "Versuch einer Witterungslehre" (written 1825, pub. 1833), Goethe rejected "die astrologischen Grillen": "wir wagten den Mond, die Mitplaneten und ihre Monde, zuletzt die gegeneinander unbeweglichen Gestirne als mitwirkend zu betrachten, und der Mensch, der alles notwendig auf sich bezieht, unterläßt nicht, sich mit dem Wahne zu schmeicheln, daß wirklich das All, dessen Teil er freilich ausmacht, auch einen besondern merklichen Einfluß auf ihn ausübe" (HA 13, 307). Nevertheless, the *a priori* assumption of the unity of humankind and nature expressed in such works provided a model for Goethe's future scientific writings: "Die Magia naturalis entsprach in ihrer Einheit, die sich bis ins Theologische erstreckte, einer Einheit suchenden Grundveranlagung Goethes, und so sind in seine Naturanschauung unauslöschlich Elemente dieses merkwürdigen Kosmos eingegangen" (Kuhn, 108). Thus it is the holistic vision of the chain of being encapsulated in the sign of the macrocosm that inspires Faust:

> Wie alles sich zum Ganzen webt,
> Eins in dem andern wirkt und lebt!
> Wie Himmelskräfte auf und nieder steigen
> Und sich die goldnen Eimer reichen!
> Mit segenduftenden Schwingen
> Vom Himmel durch die Erde dringen,
> Harmonisch all das All durchklingen!
>
> (447–53)

It is this same vision of the unity of nature dating from the mid 1770s which, as we will see, characterizes the description of the waterfall in Part Two, written some fifty years after this scene in Faust's study. Although the concept of unity inspires Faust, he dismisses the theoretical lore of alchemy. He clearly has no illusions about his father's alchemistic preoccupation with nature and his attempts in the "schwarze[n] Küche" (1039) to cure the plague: "So haben wir mit höllischen Latwergen / In diesen Tälern, diesen Bergen / Weit schlimmer als die Pest getobt" (1050–53). Despite his fascination with magical symbols, Faust is decidedly not an alchemist.

But Faust's famulus, Wagner, is an adept. The stage directions prefacing the scene in Wagner's laboratory (Part Two, Act 2) indicate that an alchemical procedure is underway: "im Sinne des Mittelalters, weitläufige unbehülfliche Apparate zu phantastischen Zwecken." Wagner, who according to his own famulus "sieht aus wie ein Kohlenbrenner, / Geschwärzt vom Ohre bis zur Nasen" (6678–79), is standing by the furnace staring intently into the alembic. Like Faust, Wagner is on a quest to discover "was die Welt / Im Innersten zusammenhält," and it is a secret which he believes will be revealed by the Promethean lore of the alchemists. Hans Mayer has pointed out that Wagner's experiment is not the result of original research but a dutiful recreation of an alchemical recipe: "Wagner verhält sich durchaus nicht fragend und in wissenschaftlicher Neugier experimentierend. Er besitzt Gewißheiten. Die verdankt er den überlieferten Rezepten.[...] Da er alles gelesen hat, weiß er jetzt, auf welche Mischung es bei der Menschenschöpfung ankommen muß" (Mayer, 192). Unlike Faust, Wagner never progresses beyond the idea that the ultimate secret of life and nature can be discovered through scholastic work. The Homunculus is the "Produkt eines Viellesers und Vielwissers" (Mayer, 193).

Clearly, as many commentators have observed, Paracelsus is the source for Wagner's alchemistic recipe for creating "ein homunculum" (Paracelsus, 312, 317). Yet as Schöne (1994) has convincingly claimed, this scene does not have its origins in Renaissance natural philosophy alone, as there are also fascinating parallels with contemporary chemistry, in particular the discovery by Friedrich Wöhler (1800–82) that the ammonium salt of cyanic acid could be easily isomerized into urea. This isomerization of ammonium cyanate into crystals of urea was first carried out by Wöhler in 1828. By synthesizing an organic substance from chemicals derived from inanimate matter, Wöhler presented a profound challenge to the vitalistic theories of his day. Wöhler reported his discovery to his former teacher, the great chemist Jöns Jacob Berzelius, who replied on 7 March 1828:

> Nachdem man seine Unsterblichkeit beim Urin angefangen hat, ist wohl aller Grund vorhanden, die Himmelfahrt in demselben Gegenstand zu vollenden [...]. Sollte es nun gelingen, noch etwas weiter im Produktionsvermögen zu kommen (vesiculae seminales [seminal vesicles] liegen ja weiter nach vorn als die Urinblase), welche herrliche Kunst, im Laboratorium der Gewerbeschule ein noch so kleines Kind

zu machen. — Wer weiß? Es dürfte leicht genug gehen. (quoted in
Schöne 1994, 144)

The reference to the creation of a "small child" in Wöhler's laboratory
is meant ironically but it is also strikingly similar to what actually occurs
in Wagner's "schwarze[n] Küche." Goethe was kept informed about
Wöhler's experiments by his friend Johann Wolfgang Döbereiner
(1780–1849), professor of chemistry at Jena since 1810. Indeed it is
possible, as Schöne contends, that Goethe had Wöhler's experiment in
mind when he wrote the scene in Wagner's laboratory in late 1829:

> Was man an der Natur Geheimnisvolles pries,
> Das wagen wir verständig zu probieren,
> Und was sie sonst organisieren ließ,
> Das lassen wir kristallisieren.
>
> (6857–59)

Wagner's use of the word "kristallisieren," which is echoed by Mephistopheles (6864), may well be a direct reference to Wöhler's creation of
crystals of urea in his groundbreaking experiment. As in *Die Wahlverwandtschaften*, Goethe skillfully intermingles alchemical and contemporary chemical allusions in his depiction of Wagner's experiment. Both the
Paracelsian recipes from the hermetic tradition and the scientific attempt
to synthesize living matter by a non-organic, artificial process are depicted
here. Both approaches to nature are also implicitly called into question.

Wagner's experiment is one he has repeated many times without
success: "O daß ich's diesmal nicht verliere!" (6829). The reason for
his current success is not due to his alchemical or scientific skills but to
the presence of Mephistopheles, as Homunculus acknowledges: "bist
du hier / Im rechten Augenblick? ich danke dir" (6885–86). Wagner's
creation is deeply flawed in its conception: his objective is to create a
being of pure intellect, "ein Hirn, das trefflich denken soll" (6869).
Mephistopheles facilitates the creation of this being. The researcher,
who rejects living, breathing nature and dwells instead among dusty
tomes, gives birth to a creature which is indeed pure intellect. It is not
surprising, therefore, that the Homunculus cannot exist in the real
world and must remain protected *in vitro*. Ironically Wagner's creation
is not satisfied with being *Geist* alone and desires "zu entstehen!"
(7858), as the Greek philosopher Thales says:

> Er ist, wie ich von ihm vernommen,
> Gar wundersam nur halb zur Welt gekommen.
> Ihm fehlt es nicht an geistigen Eigenschaften,
> Doch gar zu sehr am greiflich Tüchtighaften.
>
> (8247–50)

As Homunculus learns from Proteus, to be truly born he needs to be first dissolved in the Aegean Sea: "Vermähle dich dem Ozean" (8320). Here the Aegean represents nature's alembic; its waters the alcahest in which true "Mischung" can occur and life develop. This is not the artificial, mechanical "Mischung" that Wagner initiates in his furnace but the gradual organic process of becoming. True being, it is suggested, is not created in a test-tube but occurs gradually through time and as a result of the processes of nature:

> Da regst du dich nach ewigen Normen,
> Durch tausend, abertausend Formen,
> Und bis zum Menschen hast du Zeit.
>
> (8324–26)

This immersion in the sea also symbolizes the elemental meeting of opposites: "Hochgefeiert seid allhier, / Element' ihr alle vier!" (8484–87). The fire of Homunculus's birth and the vital presence of Mephistopheles who (as is made clear in the "Hochgebirg" scene in Part Two) also represents the element of fire, is combined with its opposite, the element of water. Polarity was a fundamental concept in Goethe's idea of nature and one which was linked to the similarly important notion of *Steigerung* or intensification. These two concepts he termed (in an unusually mechanistic metaphor) the "zwei großen Triebräder aller Natur":

> Der Begriff von Polarität und von Steigerung, jene der Materie, insofern wir sie materiell, diese ihr dagegen, insofern wir sie geistig denken, angehörig; jene ist in immerwährendem Anziehen und Abstoßen, diese in immerstrebendem Aufsteigen. Weil aber die Materie nie ohne Geist, der Geist nie ohne Materie existiert und wirksam sein kann, so vermag auch die Materie sich zu steigern, so wie sichs der Geist nicht nehmen läßt, anzuziehen und abzustoßen. ("Erläuterung zum aphoristischen Aufsatz 'Die Natur'" [HA 13, 48])

Homunculus — symbolizing *Geist* — cannot develop further without the qualities of *Materie*. As we will see in the discussion of the waterfall, polarity and intensification are key concepts for Goethe's science and also play a central role in Faust's progress towards understanding. The artificial synthesis of life that Wagner attempts through alchemy results in an unviable life form: Homunculus must be reborn through the element of water. As we have seen, Wagner's experiment also engages with contemporary advances in chemistry. The vitalistic implication of this scene is that animate matter cannot be synthesized or crystallized in a laboratory test-tube. Life is not merely a mechanical process but something elemental, mysterious, and intimately bound up with the fundamental laws of nature, which for Goethe included *Polarität*.

Faust does not witness the experiment of his former famulus: he is unconscious throughout, dreaming of Helena. It is clear, however, that he would have scorned Wagner's experiments, which without Mephistopheles' help would have resulted only in yet another issue of soot and hot air. In Part One Faust derided the alchemical experiments of his father and rejected his technical instruments still adorning his study:

> Ihr Instrumente freilich spottet mein
> Mit Rad und Kämmen, Walz' und Bügel:
> Ich stand am Tor, ihr solltet Schlüssel sein;
> Zwar euer Bart ist kraus, doch hebt ihr nicht die Riegel.
> (668–71)

Scientific instruments alone are not sufficient to raise the "Schleier" of Nature: "Das zwingst du ihr nicht ab mit Hebeln und mit Schrauben" (675). Indeed, although he valued meteorological instruments (HA 13, 306), Goethe rejected scientific theories that relied too heavily on instrumental evidence, a shortcoming of Newton's work, as he argued in a letter to Zelter of 22 June 1808:

> Der Mensch an sich selbst, insofern er sich seiner gesunden Sinne bedient, ist der größte und genaueste physikalische Apparat, den es geben kann. Und das ist eben das größte Unheil der neuen Physik, daß man die Experimente gleichsam vom Menschen abgesondert hat und blos in dem was künstliche Instrumente zeigen die Natur erkennen, ja was sie leisten kann dadurch beschränken und beweisen will.

Before instruments can be of help, "Geist" (674) working through direct experience must first grasp the subtle interrelatedness and lawfulness of the natural world: "daß alle natürlichen Dinge in einem genauen Zusammenhange stehen" ("Über den Granit," written 1784, pub. 1877 [HA 13, 255]). Neither books nor elaborate scientific instruments will afford the Faustian individual this knowledge. It is not the "Wort" that leads to understanding but the deed: "Im Anfang war die Tat!" (1225, 1237). It is the Faustian striving for personal knowledge — and "streben" is a crucial verb in this dynamic text — that characterizes what Goethe understood as the essential approach of the scientist to nature: the active observation and reflexive *Erkennen* of phenomena as part of an interrelated whole. For the route to self-knowledge and knowledge of nature was a parallel process, as Goethe suggested: "Der Mensch kennt nur sich selbst, insofern er die Welt kennt, die er nur in sich und sich nur in ihr gewahr wird. Jeder neue Gegenstand, wohl beschaut, schließt ein neues Organ in uns auf"

("Bedeutende Fördernis durch ein einziges geistreiches Wort," 1823 [HA 13, 38]). In his important essay on the methodology of science written in 1792, "Der Versuch als Vermittler von Objekt und Subjekt," Goethe goes beyond Newton's *experimentum crucis* and places the act of repeated experimentation at the center of the relationship between subject and object: "Die Vermannigfaltigung eines jeden einzelnen Versuches ist also die eigentliche Pflicht eines Naturforschers" (HA 13, 18). The experiment — which for Goethe has more in common with *Erleben* than the contrived laboratory experiments of Galileo and Newton (Krohn, 404) — becomes for the scientist-observer a physical and intellectual act ("Tat"). It is quite different from Wagner's arid scholasticism ("Wort"), which is driven by the Cartesian dualism that dominates Western science. Instead it is the expression of Faust's dynamic and very human complexity: "Zwei Seelen wohnen, ach! in meiner Brust" (1112). This evocative phrase, far from echoing Wagner's attempt to dislocate mind from body, denotes Faust's symbolic embodiment of nature's polarity: humankind belongs to the unity of nature and must therefore share its essential polarity. Faust's dynamic striving represents an innate desire for *Steigerung,* a desire for heightened understanding that will illuminate his own condition and that of nature. This understanding can only be achieved through an intellectual and physical experience (*Erleben*) of nature which Goethe saw as central to the scientific experiment (*Versuch*).

Faust's desire to know "was die Welt / Im Innersten zusammenhält" is a phrase which could have been uttered by any scientist from Galileo to Einstein. Initially the sign of the macrocosm offers Faust intimations of nature's holistic complexity and the Erdgeist a blinding vision of nature's splendor. And yet Faust is unable to attain the level of understanding and insight into nature for which he longs: "Der große Geist hat mich verschmäht, / Vor mir verschließt sich die Natur" (1746–47). Mephistopheles promises Faust the means to achieve this breakthrough. However, Mephistopheles has no desire to satisfy Faust's deep need for understanding — he is, after all, from Hell and not Heaven. Instead, by feeding Faust's innate tendency toward "übereiltes Streben" (1858), Mephistopheles hopes to bring Faust to a point where he will despise "Vernunft und Wissenschaft" (1851). It is this cynical attitude towards scientific knowledge and experience that is the measure of evil in Goethe's nineteenth-century *Faust,* as Martin Swales argues in this volume. For Goethe and for his contemporaries the systematic study and investigation of nature was a sacred task, "denn sie wird für Welt und Nachwelt unternommen" (HA 13, 20). Ultimately, Mephistopheles fails in his attempt to dampen Faust's passionate desire for knowledge. But I believe that Mephistopheles does succeed in leading Faust astray in his quest to understand nature and self. He achieves this by fuelling Faust's impatience, his "übereiltes Streben," a characteristic which, as I have argued elsewhere, he shares with Eduard in *Die Wahlverwandtschaften* (Smith 2000, 29–92).

The tragic Gretchen episode is a direct result of Faust's impetuous desire (aided by the witch's philter): "Wenn nicht das süße junge Blut / Heut nacht in meinen Armen ruht, / So sind wir um Mitternacht geschieden" (2636–38). In his wish to possess Gretchen we see the profoundly negative dimension to Faust's valorization of "Tat": it is an *übereiltes* attempt to *erkennen* (know) and thus to *verstehen* (understand) the world which anticipates Faust's exploitative stance of Part Two, Act 4. In the Gretchen scenes *Erkennen* is to be understood in its Biblical sense. However, it was commonplace at this time to personify "die Natur" as a woman whose secrets were to be uncovered by the male scientist, as is illustrated in Goethe's praise of the meteorologist Luke Howard: "Es gibt vielleicht kein schöneres Beispiel, welchen Geistern die Natur sich gern offenbart, mit welchen Gemütern sie innige Gemeinschaft fortdauernd zu unterhalten geneigt ist" (HA 13, 305; cf. the essay "Die Natur," written 1782–1783 [HA 13, 45–47]). Faust's obsessive desire to possess Gretchen results in her death at the end of Part One; in the penultimate act of Part Two this same "übereiltes Streben" leads to the deaths of the harmless old couple, Baucis and Philemon. In "Der Versuch," Goethe warns "den handelnden, so auch den stillen, von allen Leidenschaften gesichert scheinenden Beobachter" against "Übereilung" and against other qualities detrimental to the practice of science, including: "Einbildungskraft, die ihn schon da mit ihren Fittichen in die Höhe hebt, wenn er noch immer den Erdboden zu berühren glaubt, Ungeduld, Vorschnelligkeit, Selbstzufriedenheit, Steifheit, Gedankenform, vorgefaßte Meinung, Bequemlichkeit, Leichtsinn, Veränderlichkeit" (HA 13, 11 and 14–15). In a thinly veiled criticism of Newton's method, Goethe argues for repeated and careful empirical investigation of natural phenomena. Such work he writes "kann nicht sorgfältig, emsig, streng, ja pedantisch genug vorgenommen werden" (HA 13, 20). Goethe viewed nature as a complex, interrelated whole and accordingly individual experiments were inadequate, leading to hasty generalizations:

> In der lebendigen Natur geschieht nichts, was nicht in einer Verbindung mit dem Ganzen stehe, und wenn uns die Erfahrungen nur isoliert erscheinen, wenn wir die Versuche nur als isolierte Fakta anzusehen haben, so wird dadurch nicht gesagt, daß sie isoliert seien,

es ist nur die Frage: wie finden wir die Verbindung dieser Phänomene, dieser Begebenheit. (HA 13, 17)

The complexity of nature required scientist-observers to adopt an attitude of selfless receptivity and become "gleichgültige und gleichsam göttliche Wesen" (HA 13, 10). Indeed, it is an attitude which Faust, in his involvement with Gretchen and in the last scenes of Part Two, fails utterly to live up to. In contrast, Faust's experience at the beginning of Part Two represents the point at which he comes closest to this ideal. Significantly it is a scene in which Mephistopheles is absent.

Part Two begins with Faust's "Heilschlaf," his psychological and physical recovery from the loss of Gretchen. He awakes "auf blumigen Rasen" and feels the earth inspiring him to continue with his quest: "Du regst und rührst ein kräftiges Beschließen, / Zum höchsten Dasein immerfort zu streben" (4684–85). Faust stands as if reborn in the light of the rising sun. There is an echo here of the lines cited by Faust (and probably invented by Goethe) as he is inspired by the sign of the macrocosm: "'Auf, bade, Schüler, unverdrossen / Die ird'sche Brust im Morgenrot!'" (445–46). Indeed, it is as if the "Vorahnung" of the mystical symbol were made manifest and Faust is able to experience an ideal natural world, an Eden (4694). For the first time since the Easter walk in Part One, Faust pauses in his "übereiltes Streben" and examines the living world of nature around him. Without Mephistopheles' cynical presence Faust raises his eyes skywards (4695), a motif of inspiration familiar from narrative painting. Yet the sun rising above the mountains is too bright for human eyes: "schon geblendet, / Kehr' ich mich weg, vom Augenschmerz durchdrungen" (4702–703). This act of averting his eyes from the sun becomes for Faust a symbol of his "sehnend Hoffen" (4704), the unquenchable dissatisfaction that drives him onwards and which following Gretchen's death he interprets as potentially tragic: "Des Lebens Fackel wollten wir entzünden, / Ein Feuermeer umschlingt uns, welch ein Feuer!" (4709–710). Clearly this moment has its parallel in Faust's inability to look upon the flaming Erdgeist, a moment of Promethean hubris whose origins lie in Faust's impetuous and impatient desire for knowledge. Bertolt Brecht, in his final version of *Leben des Galilei* (1955), forms this theme of fire into a deeply suggestive intertext:

> Hütet nun ihr der Wissenschaften Licht
> Nutzt es und mißbraucht es nicht
> Daß es nicht, ein Feuerfall
> Einst verzehre noch uns all
> Ja, uns all.
>
> (Brecht, 286)

This warning to the audience at the beginning of Brecht's final scene describes how the enlightening "Fackel" of Galilean science has been perverted to create the technology of atomic destruction: Faust's "Feuermeer" has become an all too real threat of atomic "Feuerfall." Like Faust, Brecht's Galileo is also impatient for knowledge of "was die Welt / Im Innersten zusammenhält," and like Goethe's protagonist he pays for this knowledge with his sight, the faculty that defines both characters' relation to the world.

As in his encounter with the Erdgeist, Faust must avert his eyes from the radiance of the sun. Yet in Part Two Faust no longer despairs at his inability to confront the light. Instead he turns away: "So bleibe denn die Sonne mir im Rücken!" (4715). Faust turns his back on the fiery light of the sun and looks instead at a mountain waterfall, a movement which is itself symbolic of the fundamental *polarity* ("Polarität") in nature which Faust is seeking to comprehend. This movement from fire to water also echoes the brief lifespan of the Homunculus, the product of fire, which needed to know (*erkennen*) its opposite element in order to be born. The radiant Homunculus consisted of pure *spirit* ("Geist"), and represents an abnegation of nature's essential polarity. Faust's desire to gaze into the radiance of the Erdgeist and the sun symbolizes his "übereiltes Streben," a hubristic, Promethean act to gain access to pure knowledge of nature which is not the result of personal experience, of experimental *Erleben*. The Homunculus is the product of a similarly hubristic act: Wagner despises the natural realm and, rather than studying nature, he searches the books of the alchemists for a shortcut that can only lead to a dead-end. At the beginning of Part Two following the Gretchen tragedy, Faust literally turns his back on his earlier approach and stands as if reborn, contemplating the forms of nature.

Faust's experience of the waterfall represents a moment of insight and self-knowledge that forms a still center at the heart of Goethe's dynamic masterpiece. It also provides a wonderfully nuanced demonstration of the ontological significance of natural phenomena within Goethe's science. As we have seen, the direct observation of nature — "die Gegenstände der Natur an sich selbst und in ihren Verhältnissen untereinander zu beobachten" — was the touchstone of Goethe's science (HA 13, 10). The sight of this cascading waterfall and rainbow, which was based on Goethe's own experience of the Rhine waterfall at Schaffhausen on 18 September 1797, provides a concrete symbol of the relation between humankind and nature:

> Allein wie herrlich, diesem Sturm erprießend,
> Wölbt sich des bunten Bogens Wechseldauer,
> Bald rein gezeichnet, bald in Luft zerfließend,
> Umher verbreitend duftig kühle Schauer.
> *Der* spiegelt ab das menschliche Bestreben.
> Ihm sinne nach, und du begreifst genauer:
> Am farbigen Abglanz haben wir das Leben.
>
> (4721–27)

In the description of the waterfall and the rainbow we have a model of Goethe's mature approach to science and epistemology. There is a clear movement here from observation, to description and then, in the final three lines, to metaphor and theory, a movement from "Analyse" to "Synthese." At this moment Faust is for the first time sufficiently self-aware, even self-critical, to accept that the sun (and the Erdgeist) cannot be confronted directly. Instead Faust turns to nature itself. Through his active observation of the waterfall and the associated phenomenon of the rainbow, Faust realizes that true understanding of nature is not to be attained by magical shortcuts. It is now apparent — although not to Faust himself — that it is Faust's *Übereilung* that prevents him from grasping "was die Welt / Im Innersten zusammenhält." True knowledge can only be reached through the direct observation of natural phenomena: the dual experience of physical nature through the senses and the intellect. The insufficiency of knowledge derived solely from books is apparent, as is the inadequacy of alchemy and the reductive formulae of chemistry and physics: "es sind symbolische Hülfsmittel, hieroglyphische Überlieferungsweisen, welche sich nach und nach an die Stelle des Phänomens, an die Stelle der Natur setzen und die wahre Erkenntnis hindern, anstatt sie zu befördern" (*Zur Farbenlehre* [HA 13, 321–2]).

In the *Farbenlehre*, Goethe developed a sophisticated account of the phenomenon of color which rejected Newton's mathematical "Dekomposition" of light (HA 13, 50) and proposed a phenomenological and physiological alternative. Goethe attempted to expand the contemporary language of nature, "Natursprache" (HA 13, 316), to develop a descriptive vocabulary based on detailed and repeated observations of color as manifested within nature. Color for Goethe was not just a quantifiable constituent of light but the key to understanding the complex and interrelated whole of nature. Goethe rejects naïve Baconian empiricism: "das bloße Anblicken einer Sache kann uns nicht fördern" (HA 13, 317). In an important passage that expresses Goethe's mature view of the scientific process he continues: "Jedes Ansehen geht über in

ein Betrachten, jedes Betrachten in ein Sinnen, jedes Sinnen in ein Ver-
knüpfen, und so kann man sagen, daß wir schon bei jedem aufmerksa-
men Blick in die Welt theoretisieren" (HA 13, 317). For this reason
the observer (that is, the scientist) must guard against "Abstraktion"
and proceed "mit Bewußtsein, mit Selbstkenntnis, mit Freiheit [. . .],
mit Ironie" (HA 13, 317). Although the inductive approach is rejected,
abstraction and the over-dependence on hypotheses (an accusation lev-
eled at Newton and his deployment of the *experimentum crucis*) indicate the scientist-observer's failure to be guided by the phenomenon
and result in a science that is "lifeless": "Am widerwärtigsten sind die
kricklichen Beobachter und grilligen Theoristen; ihre Versuche sind
kleinlich und kompliziert, ihre Hypothesen abstrus und wunderlich"
(*Wilhelm Meisters Wanderjahre*, Book 2, "Betrachtungen im Sinne der
Wanderer" [HA 8, 302]). (For further discussion of this point, and this
passage, see Franziska Schößler's essay in this volume.) Such a science
can only offer mechanistic and reductive accounts of nature, which like
Wagner's experiments are destined to produce only partial explanations. In contrast, Goethe envisages a science that is "recht lebendig
und nützlich" (HA 13, 317), a principle he applied to his own works
on science in which he aimed at recreating the living complexity of nature: "so muß dem Leser die Natur entweder wirklich oder in lebhafter
Phantasie gegenwärtig sein" (HA 13, 321). In science, as in literature,
Goethe strove for the "lebendige Wirkung" (HA 13, 321).

Goethe's *Farbenlehre* contains an extraordinary catalogue of visual
phenomena, ranging from observations of color as a physiological
event, to its physical manifestation in nature. Goethe's enumeration of
diverse instances of color in nature is intended to enable the reader to
experience the complexity of the phenomenon. Yet it is envisaged that
the reader will move beyond this complexity and grasp the fundamental
principles suffusing the observations and thus achieve an individual understanding of the underlying order, or "Zusammenhang," in nature.
In this way Goethe's science, like his literary works, sought to give form
to both nature's bewildering diversity of phenomena and to our otherwise disordered experience of this heterogeneity — "die Formung des
Formlosen" (HA 13, 304). Goethe's term for these archetypal forms
which manifested the underlying order and lawfulness of nature was the
"Urphänomen." Color was one such "Urphänomen." According to
Goethe, color is a sign of nature's inherent lawfulness, a concept which
cannot otherwise be visualized. The polarity of light and darkness produces color in nature when a turbid medium is present:

> Wir sehen auf der einen Seite das Licht, das Helle, auf der andern die
> Finsternis, das Dunkle; wir bringen die Trübe zwischen beide, und aus

diesen Gegensätzen, mit Hülfe gedachter Vermittlung, entwickeln
sich, gleichfalls in einem Gegensatz, die Farben, deuten aber alsbald,
durch einen Wechselbezug, unmittelbar auf ein Gemeinsames wieder
zurück. (HA 13, 368)

Goethe cites the example of the color of the sky and the sun: the density of the atmosphere provides the turbid medium through which we
observe both the darkness of space and the blinding light of the sun.
This enables Goethe to explain the different colors of the sun at morning and midday: "Die Sonne wird durch eine Röte verkündigt, indem
sie durch eine größere Masse von Dünsten zu uns strahlt. Je weiter sie
heraufkommt, desto heller und gelber wird der Schein" (HA 13, 363).
Similarly, the blue of the sky is dependent on the density of the atmosphere relative to the observer:

> Wird die Finsternis des unendlichen Raums durch atmosphärische,
> vom Tageslicht erleuchtete Dünste hindurch angesehen, so erscheint
> die blaue Farbe. Auf hohen Gebirgen sieht man am Tage den Himmel
> königsblau, weil nur wenig feine Dünste vor dem unendlichen finstern
> Raum schweben; sobald man in die Täler herabsteigt, wird das Blaue
> heller, bis es endlich in gewissen Regionen und bei zunehmenden
> Dünsten ganz in ein Weißblau übergeht. (HA 13, 363)

According to Goethe, the observation of this *Urphänomen* in nature
leads ideally to an understanding in the percipient of the underlying
unity present in the diversity and complexity of nature.

Goethe's scientific methodology involves a hierarchy of knowledge:
beginning on the most basic level with experiences which can be classi-
fied and explained empirically, this process leads up the scale of understanding, "wobei uns gewisse unerläßliche Bedingungen des Er-
scheinenden näher bekannt werden" (HA 13, 367). This knowledge of
the interconnectedness of phenomena leads in turn to an understanding of underlying principles, "höhere Regeln und Gesetze, die sich aber
nicht durch Worte und Hypothesen dem Verstande, sondern gleichfalls
durch Phänomene dem Anschauen offenbaren" (HA 13, 368). This
fundamental lawfulness is grasped, not through hypotheses or formulae, but through observation: "Das Höchste wäre, zu begreifen, daß
alles Faktische schon Theorie ist. Die Bläue des Himmels offenbart uns
das Grundgesetz der Chromatik. Man suche nur nichts hinter den Phä-
nomenen; sie selbst sind die Lehre" (*Wilhelm Meisters Wanderjahre*,
Book 2, "Betrachtungen im Sinne der Wanderer" [HA 8, 304]). The
identification of the *Urphänomen* is the pinnacle on Goethe's hierarchical scale of scientific understanding. Once the observer has reached this
point Goethe describes how there follows a rapid descent from this
epistemological peak which enables the observer to grasp the funda-

mental interrelatedness of nature down to the smallest detail: "[die Urphänomene sind] völlig geeignet [. . .], daß man stufenweise, [. . .],
von ihnen herab bis zu dem gemeinsten Falle der täglichen Erfahrung
niedersteigen kann" (HA 13, 368). For Faust, the waterfall and rainbow represent just such a moment of profound insight into the lawfulness and wonder of nature. The water vapor created by the waterfall
forms the perfect turbid medium through which the *Urphänomen* of
color can be manifested: the light of the sun and the darkness of the
surrounding rocks reproduce in microcosm the polarity of nature.
Faust's observation of the "bunten Bogens Wechseldauer" (4722), the
Urphänomen, affords him insight into the paradoxical polarity and yet
unity of nature. It is a paradox reflected in the simultaneous ascent and
descent necessary to grasp the significance of the *Urphänomen*, movements repeated in the soaring rainbow and the plunging waterfall. True
understanding lies not in confronting the blinding light of the sun but
in the *Urphänomen*, in the act of identifying and giving form to the
otherwise invisible lawfulness of nature: "Am farbigen Abglanz haben
wir das Leben" (4727).

Faust also translates the image of the rainbow into a metaphor of
human cognition: truth is ultimately only manifested in reflections of
reality. The rainbow is not the result of a Newtonian "Dekomposition"
of light, a product of refraction, but is literally for Faust the "Abglanz,"
or reflection, of the sun's radiance in the myriad droplets of water.
Only in this way can humankind gaze upon the sun *qua* truth which, as
Goethe wrote in the introduction to his *Witterungslehre*, was never
amenable to unmediated perception:

> Das Wahre, mit dem Göttlichen identisch, läßt sich niemals von
> uns direkt erkennen, wir schauen es nur im Abglanz, im Beispiel,
> Symbol, in einzelnen und verwandten Erscheinungen; wir werden es
> gewahr als unbegreifliches Leben und können dem Wunsch nicht ent-
> sagen, es dennoch zu begreifen.
> Dieses gilt von allen Phänomenen der faßlichen Welt [. . .]. (HA
> 13, 305)

The rainbow, a representation of the polarity of light and darkness, allows Faust to glimpse the *Urphänomen* behind the diversity of appearances: it is the realization of the permanent and the eternal in the flux
of *natura naturans*. It is — to cite Faust's wonderful oxymoron — a
sign of nature's "Wechseldauer." In the rainbow Goethe provides the
supreme metaphor of the metaphysical reality of law in nature: something which is not visible but which must be comprehended through
observation of phenomena, through *Versuche*. The *Urphänomen* was
Goethe's attempt to give form to this elusive absent-presence (to use

another oxymoron). The rainbow reveals the *Urphänomen* of color and according to Goethe: "Die Farben sind Taten des Lichts, Taten und Leiden" (HA 13, 315). For this reason it is highly appropriate that Faust, who valorizes deeds above words, should be granted insight into nature through the deeds of light. Faust, as he stands on the mountain in the light of the rising sun, like Caspar David Friedrich's *Wanderer above the Sea of Mist* (1810), is able without the aid of his dusty tomes or Mephistopheles to gain a moment of profound insight into "was die Welt / Im Innersten zusammenhält." Unlike Wagner's experiment, it is a moment of true understanding, and it demonstrates the dynamic and positive aspect of Faust's ceaseless *Streben*.

In a fragmentary statement of 1799, Goethe describes how the act of knowing and understanding is itself an expression of the polarity of nature: "Wenn wir einen Gegenstand in allen seinen Theilen über-sehen, recht fassen und ihn im Geiste wieder hervorbringen können; so dürfen wir sagen, daß wir ihn im eigentlichen und im höhern Sinne an-schauen, daß er uns angehöre, daß wir darüber eine gewisse Herrschaft erlangen. Und so führt uns das Besondere immer zum Allgemeinen, das Allgemeine zum Besondern" (WA 2.11, 164). He then proceeds to sketch the fundamental polarity of existence:

> Wir und die Gegenstände,
> Licht und Finsterniß,
> Leib und Seele,
> Zwei Seelen,
> Geist und Materie,
> [. . .]
> Zwei Körperhälften,
> Rechts und Links,
> Atemholen.
>
> (WA 2.11, 164–65)

This extraordinarily economical yet highly suggestive enumeration clearly evokes Faust's existential problem — "Zwei Seelen wohnen, ach! in meiner Brust!" Yet it also encompasses the moment of insight in front of the waterfall, the act of knowing which is simultaneously a pro-cess of giving form to nature. It is this moment of understanding which is also a meta-cognitive act, an understanding of the essential interrelat-edness of self and nature (Schweitzer, 391), that leads Faust to gain "Herrschaft" over nature, and specifically over the element of water. For as the writer of the *Farbenlehre* is keen to point out, an under-standing of the laws of nature leads (as Francis Bacon realized) to practical knowledge: "Dem Techniker, dem Färber hingegen muß unsre Arbeit durchaus willkommen sein" (HA 13, 328).

Faust's final confrontation with nature — one of the great treatments of this theme in any national literature — concerns the attempt to control the power of the sea. Critics have generally taken one of two conflicting approaches to Acts 4 and 5, seeing them as either endorsing technological utopianism or as challenging the universal validity of Enlightenment science. In support of the former, one can cite Goethe's active involvement in silver and copper mining at Ilmenau from 1776–1777 and his role in the practical application of science in the course of his official duties in the duchy of Sachsen-Weimar-Eisenach (Hahn, 247). However, Goethe's criticisms of Newtonian science have also been seen as an indication that Goethe represented a reactionary tendency in science, one that posed a threat to the "progress" of science and technology. As we will see, this polarization is not helpful in understanding the significance of Faust's attempt to control nature. Moreover, attempts to view Part Two as a general critique of industrialization are anachronistic, as Harro Segeberg has argued (13–46). Rather, I believe that the significant issue here is Faust's attitude to the natural world. The application of science and the agenda of technological progress that played such a formative role in the nineteenth century (although belatedly in Germany), is of course important but only in so far as it relates to Faust's approach to nature and in particular his "übereiltes Streben."

It is clear that Faust's fascination with the sea and more generally with the element of water (as is evidenced by the waterfall monologue), stands in opposition to the fiery catastrophism of Mephistopheles as expounded in the "Hochgebirg" scene (Part Two, Act 4). The disagreement between Mephistopheles and Faust (and that between Anaxagoras and Thales in the "Klassische Walpurgisnacht") parallels the contemporary geological debate concerning the formation of the earth's surface. Two paradigms were contending for authority: the Vulcanist (or Plutonist) account, which saw volcanic and seismic activity as the main tectonic principle, and the Neptunist paradigm which foregrounded the sedimentary and erosional effects of a primal ocean. The latter view is expressed by Thales: "Im Feuchten ist Lebendiges erstanden" (7856). It was a debate in which Goethe took an active interest, favoring the Neptunist paradigm for its gradualist approach which supported his own morphological theory of the development of life forms, illustrated by the following conversation with Riemer on 19 March 1807:

> Die Natur kann zu allem, was sie machen will, nur in einer *Folge* ge-
> langen. Sie macht keine Sprünge. Sie könnte zum Exempel kein Pferd
> machen, wenn nicht alle übrigen Tiere voraufgingen, auf denen sie
> wie auf einer *Leiter* bis zur Struktur des Pferdes heransteigt.

Another reason for Goethe's opposition to Vulcanism was its apparent justification of revolutionary activity in society, as Mephistopheles' catastrophist rhetoric makes clear:

> Nun haben wir's an einem andern Zipfel,
> Was ehmals Grund war, ist nun Gipfel.
> Sie gründen auch hierauf die rechten Lehren,
> Das Unterste ins Oberste zu kehren.
>
> (10087–90)

Indeed, this fallacious linking of natural and social history is echoed by the French revolutionary leader St. Just in the play *Dantons Tod* (1835) (Act 2, Scene 7) by another scientist and writer, Georg Büchner. As I have argued elsewhere, St. Just in Büchner's play uses the language of science to equate natural catastrophes with the Revolution: both follow natural laws and lead inevitably to human victims (Smith 2000, 93–150). Significantly, Goethe began writing Act 4 just months after the bloody excesses of the July 1830 Revolution in France, which he described on 12 September 1830 in a letter to Knebel as "die Reprise der Tragödie von 1790" (see Schöne 1994, 149).

Throughout *Faust* the element of water represents gradualism and metamorphosis, as Proteus says to Homunculus:

> Im weiten Meere mußt du anbeginnen!
> Da fängt man erst im kleinen an
> Und freut sich, Kleinste zu verschlingen,
> Man wächst so nach und nach heran
> Und bildet sich zu höherem Vollbringen.
>
> (8260–64)

Having disputed Mephistopheles' version of the formation of the earth's surface, Faust also rejects his attempts to distract him from his "unbefriedigt" striving (11452) with offers of sensual gratification (10155–76). Faust's mind is on other matters: "Mein Auge war aufs hohe Meer gezogen" (10198). It is as if the oxymoronic "Wechsel-dauer" of the rainbow created by the interaction of water and sun has been translated into a fascination with the constant motion of waves crashing against the shore:

> Da herrschet Well' auf Welle kraftbegeistet,
> Zieht sich zurück, und es ist nichts geleistet,

> Was zur Verzweiflung mich beängstigen könnte!
> Zwecklose Kraft unbändiger Elemente!
> Da wagt mein Geist, sich selbst zu überfliegen;
> Hier möcht' ich kämpfen, dies möcht' ich besiegen.
>
> (10216–21)

Faust feels that the purposeless force of the unharnessed elements brings into question his own ceaseless striving, as if the ocean's waste of energy is an indictment of his own behavior. From this arises Faust's vision of nature's forces tamed and exploited:

> Das herrische Meer vom Ufer auszuschließen,
> Der feuchten Breite Grenzen zu verengen
> Und, weit hinein, sie in sich selbst zu drängen.
>
> (10229–31)

As Schöne suggests, Faust's plan for creating "ein neptunistisches Reich" (1994, 149) out of the land reclaimed from the sea contrasts both with Mephistopheles' Vulcanism and with the Empire which in the following scene ("Auf dem Vorgebirg") descends into civil war: it is indeed the result of "wie Teufel die Natur betrachten" (10123). More important, Faust's constant striving for knowledge and experience is given concrete form in this struggle against the primal element of the sea. Whereas Wagner ignores the phenomena of nature but seeks to control life through alchemistic texts, Faust in Part Two engages directly with the natural world: he observes, understands and ultimately seeks power over nature. The element which the Homunculus needs in order to become a human being is now the element with which Faust must struggle in order to realize his own potential.

In his *Witterungslehre*, Goethe describes how the elements are always ready "seinen eigenen wilden wüsten Gang zu nehmen" (HA 13, 309). Despite humankind's hard-won dominion over nature, Goethe argues that we must be ever vigilant: "Insofern sich nun der Mensch den Besitz der Erde ergriffen und ihn zu erhalten Pflicht hat, muß er sich zum Widerstand bereiten und wachsam erhalten" (HA 13, 309). As we have seen, Faust's experience of the waterfall has given him an insight into the lawfulness of nature, an insight which includes an understanding of the vital role of empirical observation as the way to grasp the *Urphänomen*. In the *Witterungslehre* Goethe states that it is knowledge of nature's lawfulness that is essential if we are to control the wild elements: "Das Höchste jedoch, was in solchen Fällen dem Gedanken gelingt, ist, gewahr zu werden, was die Natur in sich selbst als Gesetz und Regel trägt, jenem ungezügelten, gesetzlosen Wesen zu imponieren" (HA 13, 309). Even with this knowledge the battle for control is never-ending, and the sea in particular is cited as a formidable opponent: "Die Elemente daher sind als kolossale Gegner zu betrachten, mit denen wir ewig zu kämpfen haben, und sie nur durch die höchste Kraft des Geistes, durch Mut und List im einzelnen Fall bewältigen. [. . .] Ebenso unruhig möchte das Wasser die Erde, die es ungern verließ, wieder in seinen Abgrund reißen" (HA 13, 309).

Contemporary events such as the construction of a new harbor at Bremen in 1826–1829 may have influenced Goethe in his decision to make the sea into the focus of Faust's final engagement with nature (see Eckermann's comment of 10 February 1829 and Goethe's diary for 2 July 1829). However, the technology employed by Faust's laborers is primarily pre-industrial ("Hack' und Schaufel" [11124]), a fact that undermines interpretations that view these final scenes as either a parable of "Fortschrittsoptimismus" or indeed as a critique of industrialization (Matussek 1992, 312–15). Baucis's description of the drainage work has been cited in defense of this latter argument. Her reference to the "Flämmchen" and "Feuergluten," which appear in the night where in the morning there is a dam or canal, could describe steam-driven machinery (often referred to at this time as "Feuermaschinen"). Equally, given the association of Mephistopheles with fire, they could merely indicate his employment of will-o'-the-wisps to light the nighttime excavations. Whatever the technology employed, the human cost is clear: "Menschenopfer mußten bluten, / Nachts erscholl des Jammers Qual" (11127–28). Suffering of this kind was a very real part of such works, as Schöne has noted in his commentary on *Faust*: at the end of the eighteenth century in Prussia a thirty-six kilometer stretch of canal cost 1,500 lives in the sixteen months it took to construct (FA 7.2, 716–17). The old couple is rightly afraid of their "Gottlos" neighbor (11131): it is clear that this is inhuman, not to say demonic, work. Whatever demonic methods Mephistopheles uses to complete the labor, there is, however, no suggestion that magic is used to overcome the laws of nature. Faust's understanding of the laws of nature gives rise to his desire to control the sea and enables him to devise a practical and effective system of drainage. It is Faust's skill and knowledge that achieves success here in contrast to the failure of both his father's attempts at medicine and Wagner's alchemical creation of life. By the end of his life — and many years have passed since the experience of the waterfall — Faust has attained a deep and practical knowledge of nature. And yet it is clear that Faust's achievements have been won at a price. The suffering of the workers and the death of the harmless old couple are obvious signs of this, but the relationship of the scientist-observer Faust with nature has also suffered.

Faust's role in the deaths of Baucis and Philemon results from his "übereiltes Streben," his fatal flaw that Mephistopheles is keen to nurture. If Mephistopheles fails to distract Faust with the promise of debauchery, he succeeds in fueling his impatient desire for power over nature. This, together with his increasing reliance on Mephistopheles, results in Faust losing contact with the empirical reality of nature, symbolized by his experience beside the waterfall, when it will be remembered Mephistopheles was absent. By enabling him quickly to attain every goal, Mephistopheles alienates Faust from the world of experience. The understanding of nature derived from individual experience has, however, given Faust the power to control the sea without recourse to magic or Mephistopheles. Following the death of Baucis and Philemon and before his encounter with the spirit Sorge, Faust realizes that Mephistopheles, by feeding his impatient desire, is isolating him from that existential encounter with nature which is the source of true knowledge:

> Könnt' ich Magie von meinem Pfad entfernen,
> Die Zaubersprüche ganz und gar verlernen,
> Stünd' ich, Natur, vor dir ein Mann allein,
> Da wär's der Mühe wert, ein Mensch zu sein.
> Das war ich sonst, eh' ich's im Düstern suchte,
> Mit Frevelwort mich und die Welt verfluchte.
> Nun ist die Luft von solchem Spuk so voll,
> Daß niemand weiß, wie er ihn meiden soll.
> Wenn auch ein Tag uns klar vernünftig lacht,
> In Traumgespinst verwickelt uns die Nacht [. . .].
>
> (11404–413)

Faust is no longer able to see the world for what it is: he has lost touch with the reality of nature. He can no longer stand before nature "ein Mann allein," as he did at sunrise in the beginning of Part Two. As if to underline Faust's current failing, Sorge removes the power of sight from the aged man. His cryptic comment, "Allein im Innern leuchtet helles Licht" (11500), seems to underline the asymmetry that exists in Faust's relation to the world: reality exists now in his imagination and not in the world of phenomena. Indeed the loss of his sight does not seem to concern him unduly: his true vision lies in his mind, in his *Geist*, and not in his eyes. In the *Farbenlehre* Goethe describes the eye as having been called into being by light: "und so bildet sich das Auge am Lichte fürs Licht, damit das innere Licht dem äußeren entgegentrete" (HA 13, 323). This mystical statement, which echoes the philosophy of Plotinus (AD 204–70), was perhaps more revealing in its earlier, unrevised, form: "Das Auge als ein Geschöpf des Lichtes leistet alles, was das Licht selbst leisten kann. Das Licht überliefert das Sichtbare dem Auge; das Auge überliefert's dem ganzen Menschen. Das Ohr ist stumm, der Mund ist taub; aber das Auge vernimmt und spricht. In ihm spiegelt sich von außen die Welt, von innen der Mensch. Die Totalität des Innern und Äußern wird durchs Auge voll- endet" (HA 13, 642). Here the function of the eye as mediator be- tween self and world is apparent. The eye performs a role analogous to the turbid medium in manifesting the phenomenon of color from the polarity of light and dark. Self and world meet on the liminal mem- brane of the eye. Here polarity is comprehended and surmounted and the individual attains an insight into the lawful interrelation of self and nature. This is accomplished through the mediation of the eye. As Pe- ter Michelsen has said, Faust's emphasis on his inner light indicates his "Verlust der Beziehung zur Welt" (30). The unity of inner and outer realms that Goethe posited as an ideal condition is not present in Faust. He sees only his vision of what might be and not what is: "die Augen, die das Unendliche sehen wollen, sehen nichts" (Michelsen, 34). Just as mere empiricism is inadequate to probe nature's secrets but requires the active spirit ("Geist") to give form to what is invisible, so Faust's vi- sion of the future needs to be balanced by the facticity of phenomenal experience. His "übereiltes Streben" leads him away from nature and into the future. Blinded, Faust continues to see before him "ein para- diesisch Land" (11569), believing he can hear the sound of workers busy furthering this goal. However, this Eden is a hollow echo of the one experienced at the beginning of Part Two: in reality the lemures are digging his grave. It is a moment of crushing irony and reveals Faust's utopian vision to be a dangerous dream. As Peter Matussek has pointed out, the classical topos of the blind seer is here inverted into one of "die visionäre Verblendung" (1998, 231). Just as Newton (at least in Goethe's account) failed to gather sufficient or appropriate ex- perimental evidence to justify his theoretical abstractions concerning the phenomenon of color, so Faust's "übereiltes Streben" and his reliance on Mephistopheles results in hubristic visions as unviable as Wagner's Homunculus. Even Faust's utterance of the words which Mephistophe- les has waited so long to hear are in the subjunctive mood: a mere pre- monition of what might be (11585). And yet, of course, this "Vor- gefühl," this deceptive vision of what could be, is also deeply expressive of Faust's constant *Streben*, his quest for understanding. This moment reveals both the tragedy and the hope that the figure of Faust embodies. The overweening ambition of humankind and its creative energy are, like the "zwei Seelen," inseparably part of the human condition.

In the final analysis Mephistopheles fails in his goal of distracting Faust from science and knowledge. Indeed, at the beginning of Part Two, Faust does attain a deep understanding of nature and of "was die Welt / Im Innersten zusammenhält," intimations of which he had experienced through the sign of the macrocosm and the appearance of the Erdgeist. However, Mephistopheles does succeed in corrupting Faust's relationship to nature by encouraging Faust's innate "übereiltes Streben," an activity that results in his blindness to the world around him. Faust's ceaseless striving has a human cost: Gretchen, Baucis and Philemon, not to mention the countless laborers sacrificed to the accelerated toil on his land-reclamation project. In this respect the play is undeniably a critique of contemporary trends (Schlaffer, 124–36) and Goethe does not obscure this negative dimension to the quest for knowledge and power that is the scientific theme of this text. But equally there is a positive side to this equation: namely Faust's profound experience of the waterfall and the rainbow. It is this experience that ultimately is at the core of the play and of Goethe's scientific studies: the individual encounter with the phenomena of nature which enables the essential lawfulness of *Materie* and *Geist* to be grasped and the task of the "Formung des Formlosen" to begin (HA 13, 304).

Works Cited

Adler, Jeremy. *"Eine fast magische Anziehungskraft": Goethes "Wahlverwandtschaften" und die Chemie seiner Zeit.* Munich: Beck, 1987.

———. "The Aesthetics of Magnetism: Science, Philosophy and Poetry in the Dialogue Between Goethe and Schelling." *The Third Culture: Literature and Science.* Ed. Elinor S. Shaffer. Berlin: de Gruyter, 1998. 66–102.

Bastin, Ted, ed. *Quantum Theory and Beyond: Essays and Discussions Arising from a Colloquium.* Cambridge: Cambridge UP, 1971.

Böhler, Michael. "Naturwissenschaft und Dichtung bei Goethe." *Goethe im Kontext: Kunst und Humanität, Naturwissenschaft und Politik von der Aufklärung bis zur Restauration. Ein Symposium.* Ed. Wolfgang Wittkowski. Tübingen: Niemeyer, 1984. 313–40.

Bois-Reymond, Emil du. *Goethe und kein Ende.* Leipzig: Veit & Comp., 1883.

Bortoft, Henri. *The Wholeness of Nature: Goethe's Way of Science.* New York: Lindisfarne P / Edinburgh: Floris Books, 1996.

Brecht, Bertolt. *Werke.* Vol. 5. Eds. Werner Hecht *et al.* Berlin: Aufbau; Frankfurt am Main: Suhrkamp, 1988.

Büchner, Georg. *Sämtliche Werke und Briefe: Historisch-kritische Ausgabe mit Kommentar.* Vol. 1. Ed. Werner R. Lehmann. Hamburg: Wegner, 1967.

Glaser, Horst Albert, ed. *Goethe und die Natur: Referate des Triestiner Kongresses.* Akten Internationaler Kongresse auf den Gebieten der Ästhetik und der Literaturwissenschaft, 1. 2nd ed. Frankfurt am Main: Lang, 1988.

Gleick, James. *Chaos: Making a New Science.* London: Heinemann, 1988.

Hahn, Karl-Heinz. "'Die Wissenschaft erhält ihren Werth, indem sie nützt': Über Goethe und die Anfänge der technisch-wissenschaftlichen Welt." *Goethe-Jahrbuch* 96 (1979). 243–57.

Heisenberg, Werner. "Das Naturbild Goethes und die technisch-naturwissenschaftliche Welt." *Goethe-Jahrbuch* 29 (1967). 27–42.

Kleinschnieder, Manfred. *Goethes Naturstudien: Wissenschaftstheoretische und -geschichtliche Untersuchungen.* Abhandlungen zur Philosophie, Psychologie und Pädagogik, 75. Bonn: Bouvier/Grundmann, 1971.

Krohn, Wolfgang. "Goethes Versuch über den Versuch." *Goethe und die Verzeitlichung der Natur.* Ed. Peter Matussek. Munich: Beck, 1998. 399–413.

Kuhn, Dorothea. "Goethe und die Chemie." D. Kuhn. *Typus und Metamorphose: Goethe-Studien.* Ed. Renate Grumach. Marbach am Neckar: Deutsche Schillergesellschaft, 1988. 106–19.

Matthaei, Rupprecht. "Die Farbenlehre im Faust." *Goethe* 10 (1947). 59–148.

Matussek, Peter. *Naturbild und Diskursgeschichte: "Faust"-Studie zur Rekonstruktion ästhetischer Theorie.* Germanistische Abhandlungen, 75. Stuttgart: Metzler, 1992.

———. "Formen der Verzeitlichung: Der Wandel des Faustschen Naturbildes und seine historischen Hintergründe." *Goethe und die Verzeitlichung der Natur.* Ed. Peter Matussek. Munich: Beck, 1998. 202–32.

Mayer, Hans. "Der Famulus Wagner und die moderne Wissenschaft." *Gestaltungsgeschichte und Gesellschaftsgeschichte: Literatur-, Kunst- und Musikwissenschaftliche Studien.* Eds. Käte Hamburger and Helmut Kreuzer. Stuttgart: Metzler/Poeschel, 1969. 176–200.

Mesh-hadi, Nabil. *Die Einschätzung der Alchemie in Faust-Deutungen.* Europäische Hochschulschriften Reihe 1, Deutsche Literatur und Germanistik, 299. Frankfurt am Main: Lang, 1979.

Michelsen, Peter. "Fausts Erblindung." *Deutsche Vierteljahresschrift für Literaturwissenschaft und Geistesgeschichte* 36 (1962). 26–35.

Neubauer, John. "'Ich lehre nicht, ich erzähle': Geschichte und Geschichten in Goethes naturwissenschaftlichen Schriften." *Goethe-Jahrbuch* 114 (1997). 164–73.

————. "Goethe and the Language of Science." *The Third Culture: Literature and Science*. Ed. Elinor S. Shaffer. Berlin: de Gruyter, 1998. 51–65

Nisbet, H. B. *Goethe and the Scientific Tradition*. Publications of the Institute of Germanic Studies, 14. London: Institute of Germanic Studies, 1972.

Paracelsus (Theophrast von Hohenheim). *Sämtliche Werke*. I. Abteilung: Medizinische, naturwissenschaftliche und philosophische Schriften. Vol. 11. Ed. Karl Sudhoff. Munich: Oldenbourg, 1928.

Partenheimer, Maren. *Goethes Tragweite in der Naturwissenschaft: Hermann von Helmholtz, Ernst Haeckel, Werner Heisenberg, Carl Friedrich von Weizsäcker*. Berlin: Duncker & Humblot, 1989.

Portmann, Adolf. "Goethe and the Concept of Metamorphosis." *Goethe and the Sciences: A Reappraisal*. Boston Studies in the Philosophy of Science, 97. Ed. Frederick Amrine, Francis J. Zucker, and Harvey Wheeler. Dordrecht: Reidel, 1987. 133–45.

Prigogine, Ilya. *From Being to Becoming: Time and Complexity in the Physical Sciences*. New York: W. H. Freeman, 1980.

Schad, Wolfgang. *Man and Mammals: Toward a Biology of Form*. Trans. Carroll Scherer. Garden City, New York: Waldorf P, 1977.

————, ed. *Goetheanistische Naturwissenschaft*. 4 vols. Stuttgart: Verlag Freies Geistesleben, 1982–85.

Schöne, Albrecht. "'...wie Teufel die Natur betrachten' (*Faust*, V. 10,123)." *Goethe-Jahrbuch* 111 (1994). 141–50.

————, ed. *Faust. Kommentare*. Frankfurt am Main: Deutscher Klassiker Verlag, 1994. [FA 7.2]

Schweitzer, Frank. "Naturwissenschaft und Selbsterkenntnis." *Goethe und die Verzeitlichung der Natur*. Ed. Peter Matussek. Munich: Beck, 1998. 383–98.

Segeberg, Harro. *Literarische Technik-Bilder: Studien zum Verhältnis von Technik- und Literaturgeschichte im 19. und frühen 20. Jahrhundert*. Studien und Texte zur Sozialgeschichte der Literatur, 17. Tübingen: Niemeyer, 1987.

Smith, Peter D. *Metaphor and Materiality: German Literature and the World-View of Science, 1780–1955*. Oxford: European Humanities Research Centre, 2000.

Weizsäcker, Carl Friedrich von. "Goethe and Modern Science." *Goethe and the Sciences: A Reappraisal*. Boston Studies in the Philosophy of Science, 97. Ed. Frederick Amrine, Francis J. Zucker, and Harvey Wheeler. Dordrecht: Reidel, 1987. 115–32.

Further Reading

Böhme, Hartmut. "Lebendige Natur-Wissenschaftskritik, Naturforschung und allegorische Hermetik bei Goethe." *Deutsche Vierteljahrsschrift für Literaturwissenschaft und Geistesgeschichte* 60 (1986). 249–72.

Burwick, Frederick. *The Damnation of Newton: Goethe's Color Theory and Romantic Perception*. Quellen und Forschungen zur Sprach- und Kulturgeschichte der germanischen Völker, n.s. 86 (210). Berlin: de Gruyter, 1986.

Cassirer, Ernst. "Goethe und die mathematische Physik: Eine erkenntnistheoretische Betrachtung." *Idee und Gestalt: Goethe, Schiller, Hölderlin, Kleist.* E. Cassirer. 2nd ed. Berlin, 1924; repr. Darmstadt: Wissenschaftliche Buchgesellschaft, 1981. 33–80.

Erpenbeck, John. "' . . . die Gegenstände der Natur an sich selbst . . . ': Subjekt und Objekt in Goethes naturwissenschaftlichem Denken seit der italienischen Reise." *Goethe-Jahrbuch* 105 (1988). 212–33.

Fink, Karl J. *Goethe's History of Science.* Cambridge: Cambridge UP, 1991.

Fischer, Hans. *Goethes Naturwissenschaften.* Zurich: Artemis, 1950.

Laine, Barry. "By Water and by Fire: The Thales-Anaxagoras Debate in Goethe's *Faust.*" *Germanic Review* 50 (1975). 99–109.

Richter, Karl. "Das 'Regellose' und das 'Gesetz': Die Auseinandersetzung des Naturwissenschaftlers Goethe mit der Französischen Revolution." *Goethe-Jahrbuch* 107 (1990). 127–43.

Rueger, Alexander. "The Cultural Use of Natural Knowledge: Goethe's Theory of Color in Weimar Classicism." *Eighteenth-Century Studies* 26 (1992–1993). 211–32.

Salm, Peter. *The Poem as Plant: A Biological View of Goethe's Faust.* Cleveland, Ohio: P of Case Western Reserve U, 1971.

Schmidt, Alfred. *Goethes herrlich leuchtende Natur: Philosophische Studie zur deutschen Spätaufklärung.* Munich: Hanser, 1984.

Sepper, Dennis L. "Goethe, Colour and the Science of Seeing" *Romanticism and the Sciences.* Ed. Andrew Cunningham and Nicholas Jardine. Cambridge: Cambridge UP, 1990. 189–98.

Smith, Peter D. "German Literature and the Scientific World-View in the Nineteenth and Twentieth Centuries." *Journal of European Studies* 27 (1997). 389–415.

Stephenson, R. H. *Goethe's Conception of Knowledge and Science.* Edinburgh: Edinburgh UP, 1995.

Goethe's *Faust* and the Philosophers

Cyrus Hamlin

SINCE THE FIRST APPEARANCE of Goethe's fragment of *Faust* in his *Schriften* (1790), the drama has been closely associated with philosophy. The initial readers of the drama included many of the most important philosophical followers of Immanuel Kant during the 1790s — all of them belonging to a younger generation than the poet, just coming of age at that time — and their enthusiasm for the fragment was boundless, primarily because they identified the central problem of *Faust* with the central issue of post-Kantian Idealism. Such had certainly not been the intention of the poet, who first composed his drama at a time (early 1770s), when Kant's critical philosophy had not even been conceived. Yet the publication of the Faust-Fragment in the same year that Kant published his *Kritik der Urteilskraft* seems in retrospect to have been more than an accident of cultural history. A few of these initial responses deserve mention.

The earliest public response is found in a short review by August Wilhelm Schlegel (1767–1845) in the Göttingen *Gelehrter Anzeige* for 1790, where the bewildering diversity of tone and style in *Faust* is emphasized together with the sustained focus on the central character in his striving to experience all aspects of human existence: "Nur das *eine* Gesetz scheint sich der Dichter gemacht zu haben, dem freiesten Gange seines Geistes zu folgen. Daher die plötzlichen Übergänge von populärer Einfalt zu philosophischem Tiefsinn, von geheimnisvollen magischen Orakeln zu Sprüchen des gemeinen Menschenverstandes, vom Erhabenen zum Burlesken" (112). Even more remarkable was the response of Schlegel's younger brother Friedrich (1772–1829) in his essay "Über das Studium der griechischen Poesie" (written 1795, pub. 1797), one of the founding documents of German Romanticism, which first established the polarity between Classical and Romantic poetry, including the opposition between what he calls "aesthetic tragedy" (*ästhetische Tragödie*) and "philosophical tragedy" (*philosophische Tragödie*). The former is exemplified by the ancient Greeks, notably Sophocles; the latter by Shakespeare, above all in *Hamlet*. The character of Hamlet is defined as the quintessential philosophical tragic hero:

"Es gibt vielleicht keine vollkommnere Darstellung der unauflöslichen Disharmonie, welche der eigentliche Gegenstand der philosophischen Tragödie ist, als ein so gränzenloses Mißverhältnis der denkenden und der tätigen Kraft, wie in Hamlets Charakter" (248). Yet Goethe's *Faust*, adds Schlegel, were the drama completed, would surpass even the masterpiece of Shakespeare, since "was dort [in *Hamlet*] nur Schicksal, Begebenheit — Schwäche ist, das ist hier [in *Faust*] Gemüt, Handlung — Kraft. Hamlets Stimmung und Richtung nämlich ist ein Resultat seiner äußeren Lage; Fausts ähnliche Richtung ist ursprünglicher Charakter" (260). To this view may be added the well-known comment by the poet Friedrich Schiller (1759–1805), to whom Goethe turned for advice on how to complete the drama when he first began work again on the fragment in June 1797. Schiller wrote in his letter of 23 June 1797 that:

> der "Faust," das Stück nämlich, bei aller seiner dichterischen Individualität, die Foderung an eine symbolische Bedeutsamkeit nicht ganz von sich weisen kann, wie auch wahrscheinlich Ihre eigene Idee ist. Die Duplizität der menschlichen Natur und das verunglückte Bestreben, das Göttliche und das Physische im Menschen zu vereinigen, verliert man nicht aus den Augen; und weil die Fabel ins Grelle und Formlose geht und gehen muß, so will man nicht bei dem Gegenstand stille stehen, sondern von ihm zu Ideen geleitet werden. Kurz, die Anfoderungen an den "Faust" sind zugleich philosophisch und poetisch, und Sie mögen sich wenden, wie Sie wollen, so wird Ihnen die Natur des Gegenstandes eine philosophische Behandlung auflegen, und die Einbildungskraft wird sich zum Dienst einer Vernunftidee bequemen müssen.

By the time Goethe came to complete Part One of his drama around the turn of the eighteenth to the nineteenth century, a reading of the Faust-Fragment as fundamentally philosophical had already been established, above all from the perspective of early Romantic literary theory, and Goethe was fully aware of this response, centered as it was in nearby Jena.

The two most powerful philosophical readings of the Fragment also originated in Jena and were also presumably known to Goethe, at least indirectly, at the time he returned to work on the drama. These readings may be documented, if only partially, from writings published by Schelling (1775–1854) and Hegel (1770–1831). It should be noted that Schiller wrote to Goethe from Jena on 16 March 1801, offering his best wishes for further progress in the composition of *Faust*, "auf den die hiesigen Philosophen ganz unaussprechlich gespannt sind." Goethe responded on 20 March 1801 with a cautionary word: "Keinen eigentlichen Stillstand an 'Faust' habe ich noch nicht gemacht, aber mitunter nur schwache Fortschritte. Da die Philosophen auf diese Arbeit neugierig sind, habe ich mich freilich zusammenzunehmen." Which philosophers could these have been other than Schelling and Hegel — the latter only recently arrived in Jena — who were living together and had recently decided to found a *Kritisches Journal der Philosophie* that they would co-edit? A philosophical reading of the Faust-Fragment had indeed developed in Jena, even if Schelling and Hegel were more likely the recipients than the instigators, above all through contact with Schiller and the Schlegels.

Schelling first mentions *Faust* in a short essay "Über Dante in philosophischer Beziehung," published in the *Journal* in 1803, where the *Divine Comedy* is presented as the only valid model for modern poetry in its attempt to equal the mythical totality of world represented in the Homeric epics. Within this Romantic re-reading of Dante, clearly indebted to the work done on the *Commedia* during the preceding decade by A. W. Schlegel, Schelling refers to Goethe's *Faust* — known at that time only from the published Fragment — as "das einzige deutsche Gedicht von universeller Anlage," and describes it as bringing together "die äußersten Enden in dem Streben der Zeit durch die ganz eigenthümliche Erfindung einer partiellen Mythologie" (576). He adds that *Faust* is both more Aristophanic as comedy than Dante but in a more poetic sense also more divine. Schelling offers a more fully articulated view of the Faust-Fragment in his lectures on the *Philosophie der Kunst* (delivered at Jena in 1802–03, published posthumously in 1859), which he discusses as a mixture of tragedy and comedy within modern literature. The central problem of the drama, so argues Schelling, arises from the confrontation of the individual subject and the "In-itself" (*An-sich*) of the universe. Faust seeks to "enjoy the infinite as infinite," which is impossible for the finite subject, and this results in an "eternal contradiction": "Des Unendlichen als Unendlichen kann nicht das Subjekt als Subjekt genießen, welches doch ein nothwendiger Hang desselben ist. Hier also ein ewiger Widerspruch" (382). Quoting in its entirety the monologue of Mephistopheles in what later became the second Study scene (1851–67), Schelling argues that the drama offers a twofold direction to Faustian striving: on the one hand, "der unbefriedigte Durst, das Innere der Dinge zu schauen und als Subjekt zu genießen, [. . .] die unersättliche Begier außer dem Ziel und Maß der Vernunft durch Schwärmerei zu stillen"; and, on the other, "sich in die Welt zu stürzen, der Erde Weh, der Erde Glück zu tragen," as Mephisto promises to do with an allusion to the legend of the punishment of Tantalus, surrounded by food and drink but unable ever to satisfy his hunger and thirst (382–3). "Auch hier nämlich ist es ewig unmöglich," so concludes Schelling, "als Endliches des Unendlichen theilhaftig zu werden" (383). Once again, Schelling compares *Faust* with Dante's *Divine Comedy*, at least in the apparent tendency of the Fragment. Even more significant is his claim that Goethe's drama has assumed "seine wissenschaftliche Seite [. . .], so daß, wenn irgend ein Poem philosophisch heißen kann, dieses Prädikat Goethes Faust allein zugelegt werden muß" (384). Because of their immense suggestiveness and wide-ranging significance, Schelling's concluding remarks on *Faust* deserve to be quoted in full:

> Der herrliche Geist, der mit der Kraft des außerordentlichen Dichters den Tiefsinn des Philosophen vereint, hat in diesem Gedicht einen ewig frischen Quell der Wissenschaft geöffnet, der allein hinreichend war, die Wissenschaft in dieser Zeit zu verjüngen, die Frischheit eines neuen Lebens über sie zu verbreiten. Wer in das wahre Heiligthum der Natur dringen will, nähere sich diesen Tönen aus einer höheren Welt und sauge in früher Jugend die Kraft in sich, die wie in dichten Lichtstrahlen von diesem Gedicht ausgeht und das Innerste der Welt bewegt. (384)

For his part, Hegel never addressed Goethe's *Faust* directly in a sustained reading in any work, although his pronouncement much later in his lectures at the university in Berlin on *Aesthetics* (published posthumously as edited by his student Hotho, 1835–9) has often been cited, namely that *Faust* is "die absolute philosophische Tragödie" (557). In his initial systematic philosophical work, however, *Phänomenologie des Geistes* (1807), written during his years at Jena, Hegel includes at least a sustained allusion to the Faust-Fragment as central instance for what he terms Desire and Necessity ("Die Lust und die Notwendigkeit") as a sub-heading of his chapter on Reason ("Vernunft") entitled "The Realization of Rational Self-Consciousness through Itself" ("Die Verwirklichung der vernünftigen Selbstbewußtseins durch sich selbst"). Of interest with reference to Schelling's reading is the fact that Hegel also quotes the monologue by Mephistopheles, though only the first two and the last two lines, slightly emended (on purpose?) and without indication that they are not continuous:

> Es verachtet Verstand und Wissenschaft
> des Menschen allerhöchste Gaben —
> es hat dem Teufel sich ergeben
> und muß zugrunde gehn.
>
>   (271)

What Mephistopheles says in fact, initially addressing the absent Faust directly and then describing him in the third person, is as follows:

> Verachte nur Vernunft und Wissenschaft,
> Des Menschen allerhöchste Kraft, [. . .]
> Und hätt' er sich auch nicht dem Teufel übergeben,
> Er müßte doch zugrunde gehn!
>
> (1851–2; 1866–7)

Hegel translates the action of the drama, involving the devil's judgment against Faust, ironic as that may be from the perspective of the reader, into a description of self-consciousness in this particular phase of its development (referred to in Hegel's citation as "Es"). His description is characteristically abstract and without the passage from *Faust* it would probably not be recognized as a philosophical paraphrase of Goethe's drama at all.

> Insofern [das Selbstbewußtsein] aus der sittlichen Substanz und dem ruhigen Sein des Denkens zu seinem *Fürsichsein* sich erhoben, so hat es das Gesetz der Sitte und des Daseins, die Kenntnisse der Beobachtung und die Theorie als einen grauen, eben verschwindenden Schatten hinter sich; denn dies ist vielmehr ein Wissen von einem solchen, dessen Fürsichsein und Wirklichkeit eine andere als die des Selbstbewußtseins ist. Es ist in es statt des himmlisch scheinenden Geistes der Allgemeinheit des Wissens und Tuns, worin die Empfindung und der Genuß der Einzelheit schweigt, der Erdgeist gefahren, dem das Sein nur, welches die Wirklichkeit des einzelnen Bewußtseins ist, als die wahre Wirklichkeit gilt. (270–71)

Of interest for an assessment of Goethe's *Faust* in relation to post-Kantian Idealist philosophy is the substitution by Hegel of *Verstand* for *Vernunft* in the first line he quotes, though he retains the term for science which Fichte's philosophy had featured, *Wissenschaft,* a term which remained central to Hegel's notion of philosophy as system of thought. From Mephistopheles' point of view Faust has abandoned precisely those faculties or capacities of mind which became central to German philosophy in the wake of Kant: reason and science; and by entering into a contract with the devil, he has abandoned himself to forces and directions of experience which would be the very opposite of philosophical. Hegel also clearly views this in conjunction with Faust's attempt to conjure the Earth Spirit, where — quite erroneously, if we follow the outcome of Faust's confrontation with the Spirit — true reality (*Wirklichkeit*) is taken to be identical with the reality of individual consciousness, as Hegel asserts in the passage just quoted. The outcome, according to the traditional legend of Dr. Faustus, would be eternal damnation at the hands of the devil. Goethe has Mephisto say, however, that Faust would be damned — *zugrunde gehen* — even if he had not entered into a pact with the devil. Hegel seems to feel, by contrast, that such damnation is precisely what the devil imposes as a direct result of abandoning the mind's "all highest gifts" of philosophical reason. He goes on to describe the immediate consequences for human action in terms that also still allude to *Faust*:

> [Das Selbstbewußtsein] stürzt also ins Leben und bringt die reine Individualität, in welcher es auftritt, zur Ausführung. Es macht sich weniger sein Glück, als daß es dasselbige unmittelbar nimmt und genießt. Die Schatten von Wissenschaft, Gesetzen und Grundsätzen, die allein zwischen ihm und seiner eigenen Wirklichkeit stehen, verschwinden als ein lebloser Nebel, der es nicht mit der Gewißheit seiner Realität aufnehmen kann; es nimmt sich das Leben, wie eine reife Frucht gepflückt wird, welche ebensosehr selbst entgegenkommt, als sie genommen wird. (271)

Hegel's image of plucking the ripe fruit could well be an allusion to the seduction of Gretchen. It would be an error, however, to interpret Hegel's comments here as if he were offering his own reading of Goethe's Fragment. Instead, he adapts the situation and even some of the terms from the drama to fit his abstract philosophical argument concerning the developmental process of self-consciousness. Nonetheless, Hegel's brief paraphrase subsequently produced at the hands of his students several abstruse monographs on Goethe's *Faust*, Part One, notably by H. F. W. Hinrichs (*Aesthetische Vorlesungen über Goethe's Faust*, 1825) and C. F. Göschel (*Über Goethe's Faust und dessen Fortsetzung*, 1824), which translate the entire drama into such abstruse and often incomprehensible philosophical terms. This so-called Hegelian phase of Faust criticism led to a vehement polemic by the leading critic of Goethe's *Faust* in the nineteenth century, Friedrich Theodor Vischer, in a book-length survey of such philosophical readings ("Die Literatur über Goethe's Faust. Eine Uebersicht," published in the *Hallische Jahrbücher für deutsche Wissenschaft und Kunst*, 1839).

Why did Goethe's *Faust* have such an impact on the philosophers? More specifically, why did the published Fragment of 1790 impress the entire generation of post-Kantian Idealists at Jena, including the early Romantics, as a philosophical tragedy? These questions are important for any assessment of the drama in relation to philosophical issues, particularly to the degree that an implicit affinity exists between the central issue of the drama as Goethe conceived it from the outset of his work on *Faust* and the central issues for philosophy as defined by the Idealists at Jena, including Schelling and Hegel. An answer may be provided by considering those aspects of the drama fragment, few as they are, which are cited as the basis for a philosophical reading: the monologue of Mephistopheles about his relationship with Faust, and the initial encounter of Faust with the Earth Spirit. In the first instance, though the passage was presumably composed for publication in the Fragment, the devil emphasizes that Faust has abandoned precisely those faculties of mind — *Vernunft und Wissenschaft* — that would constitute the primary resources of all philosophical thinking. The outcome of this stratagem, implying essentially that Faust has entered into league with the devil, as the traditional legend would require, is expected to be, by Mephisto's surmise, that Faust is doomed, indeed will suffer shipwreck and sink: *zugrunde gehn*. The second instance, which is so crucial for Hegel's reading: "the Earth Spirit has entered into Self-consciousness," constitutes the primal scene of the drama, presumably the first conceived by the young poet, where instead of conjuring the devil, as the traditional legend would require, Faust invokes the magical sign that calls the *Erdgeist* to appear. The result, as every reader of Goethe's drama knows, is a categorical rejection of Faust by the Spirit, a complete failure by the human mind to comprehend (*begreifen*) this unmediated, transcendent force, which appears as a horrific vision within a crimson flame and threatens to overwhelm and annihilate Faust. To Faust's assertion: "Der du die weite Welt umschweifst, / Geschäftiger Geist, wie nah fühl' ich mich dir!" (511–2), the Earth Spirit replies as it disappears: "Du gleichst dem Geist, den du begreifst, / Nicht mir!" (513–4). The central issue for a philosophical reading of Goethe's *Faust* as tragedy is contained in these two moments from the drama. Faust in his guise as scholar and learned teacher, which in effect should qualify him as professor of philosophy — no less than Kant, Schelling, or Hegel — rejects all academic learning as inadequate to providing what he most desires: "Daß ich erkenne, was die Welt / Im Innersten zusammenhält, / Schau' alle Wirkenskraft und Samen, / Und tu' nicht mehr in Worten kramen" (382–5).

Two later formulations by Faust of his fundamental existential desire, both presumably composed for the publication of the Fragment in 1790, provide further clarification of Faust's tragic dilemma and its significance for the project of philosophy as understood by post-Kantian Idealism. The first occurs at the outset of the fragmentary scene of dialogue between Faust and Mephistopheles, the first appearance of the devil in the Fragment, located in the middle of what subsequently became the second Study scene, immediately following Faust's pact and wager with the devil. In a six-line utterance that begins essentially in mid-sentence, Faust reiterates both the nature of his desire and his essential resignation about achieving what he wants:

> Und was der ganzen Menschheit zugeteilt ist,
> Will ich in meinem innern Selbst genießen,
> Mit meinem Geist das Höchst' und Tiefste greifen,
> Ihr Wohl und Weh auf meinen Busen häufen,
> Und so mein eigen Selbst zu ihrem Selbst erweitern,
> Und, wie sie selbst, am End' auch ich zerscheitern.
>
> (1770–5)

To a degree which seems uncanny in retrospect, Faust here anticipates the central project of Idealist philosophy in its attempt to achieve a comprehensive system of knowledge or a science of experience, a *Wissenschaftslehre*, to use Fichte's term, or a *Phänomenologie des Geistes*, to cite Hegel's title for the book originally intended to be called *Wissenschaft der Erfahrung des Bewußtseins*. Unlike the philosophers, however, Faust has embraced the demonic powers of Mephistopheles as the means to his end, nor does he have any illusions about the realistic possibility that he will achieve what he wants, even with the devil's help.

The second passage occurs at the end of the blank verse monologue by Faust that opens the scene "Wald und Höhle," which was also composed, perhaps while Goethe was still in Italy, for publication in the Fragment. Faust in his invocation of the Earth Spirit, motivated by gratitude for everything he has received — "Erhabner Geist, du gabst mir, gabst mir alles, / Warum ich bat" (3217–8) — turns to acknowledge his dependence on Mephistopheles (*den Gefährten*) for his quest to attain the beautiful image (*jenem schönen Bild*) which transfixed his gaze in the "Hexenküche" scene.

> O daß dem Menschen nichts Vollkommnes wird,
> Empfind' ich nun. Du gabst zu dieser Wonne,
> Die mich den Göttern nah und näher bringt,
> Mir den Gefährten, den ich schon nicht mehr
> Entbehren kann, wenn er gleich, kalt und frech,
> Mich vor mir selbst erniedrigt, und zu Nichts,
> Mit einem Worthauch, deine Gaben wandelt.
> Er facht in meiner Brust ein wildes Feuer
> Nach jenem schönen Bild geschäftig an.
> So tauml' ich von Begierde zu Genuß,
> Und im Genuß verschmacht' ich nach Begierde.
>
> (3240–50)

We may surmise that Faust's resignation with regard to the unending process of desire and the failure of satisfaction (*Genuß*) to end this quest for fulfillment (*Vollkommnes*) is intended to define a universal truth about human existence, which thus identifies the hero of Goethe's drama, even within the initial published Fragment, to be a symbol for mankind in general. To this extent the philosophical tragedy of *Faust* signifies also for philosophy as such the essential tragic condition of human nature.

Based on the evidence presented from the Faust-Fragment and the response of philosophical readers, it may be argued with some conviction that the reputation of Goethe's *Faust* as a philosophical tragedy emerged from specific statements and situations in the drama that were not in themselves explicitly or intentionally philosophical. At the time when the Fragment was published, soon after Goethe's return from his sojourn in Italy, nothing of the new philosophy in Germany could have been known to him. There is no doubt, however, that the poet encountered the work of Kant soon afterward, beginning apparently with the *Kritik der Urteilskraft* (1790) and then moving to the *Kritik der reinen Vernunft* (3rd edition, 1790). Goethe's annotated copies of both these works are preserved in his library in Weimar. It is also certain that the development of Idealism at the University of Jena, above all through the work of Fichte and Schelling during the decade that followed, were well known to Goethe, whether he felt any sympathy with their teaching or not. It appears that he was more interested in Schelling's *Naturphilosophie* than in Fichte's *Wissenschaftslehre*. By the time he returned to work on *Faust* in the last years of the decade, essentially completing Part One of the drama by 1801, even though the work was only published in 1808, Goethe was fully aware of the response to his published Fragment by the philosophical readers at Jena and presumably understood precisely why the figure of Faust as portrayed in the Fragment could be regarded as the prototype for the protagonist of a philosophical tragedy. That the basis for such a reading had been established for the drama from the outset, at least in Faust's encounter with the Earth Spirit, could not be denied. To what extent Goethe may have concurred with such a philosophical reading is difficult to say. Beyond question, however, the manner in which Part One of the drama was subsequently completed indicates at least an implicit response to this reading, indeed even a conscious, programmatic concern to develop these philosophical implications to a higher, more fully articulated level. It is not by accident that *Faust*, Part One, was published with the generic subtitle, *Eine Tragödie*, the only work in Goethe's entire career that is so designated. The question still to consider, however, is the extent to which the material added in Part One could itself be considered "philosophical."

Not everything in the drama lends itself to a philosophical reading. Just as the Gretchen sequence from the earliest stage of composition achieves an immediacy of human interest and pathos that resists abstraction and reflection, so also does the Walpurgis Night, composed for Part One in 1798/99 (with some subsequent changes and additions), lead the reader or audience into a scene of indiscriminate debauch, which defies all philosophy. In this portion of the drama, following tendencies of human excess established initially in the drinking scene of "Auerbachs Keller in Leipzig" and subsequently intensified in the rejuvenation of Faust in "Hexenküche," Goethe elaborates a satirical view of the human condition in its social contexts, where excess, debauch, bestiality and the banal hold sway. Even the tableau of representative and largely anonymous human stereotypes of social life in the scene "Vor dem Tor" serves primarily to expose human folly to a degree of ridicule. This aspect of *Faust*, which is even further developed in Part Two — notably in the Carnival scene of Act 1 — provides a sense of theatrical show and display that heightens the sense of play and satire that qualifies Goethe's drama ultimately to be compared with the work of Petronius, Rabelais, Cervantes or Swift and other satirists as a universal spectacle of human folly. Nothing in all this could be confused with philosophy, nor does the satirical view of society in any way affect the existential dilemma of Faust in his quest for the satisfaction of his longing. The further elaboration of the philosophical dimension of the drama is found in the focus on Faust himself in the scenes that fill the gap — "die große Lücke," as Goethe called it — between the conjuring of the Earth Spirit in "Nacht" and the appearance of the Student at the end of the second "Studierzimmer" scene. Here, more than anywhere in *Faust*, Goethe's mature skill as a dramatist develops a sense of the moral and existential dilemma of the central protagonist. It would be an error to claim that Faust's varied statements of self-concern in themselves have philosophical implications; yet much that transpires here may well be understood as the intentional dramatic and poetic representation of philosophical issues as Goethe applied them to his philosophical tragedy.

A central figure of thought and experience for Faust is the circular movement of the mind out of itself into the realm of nature or the external world and, subsequently, the reflective return to self-consciousness, a process which corresponds exactly to what Friedrich Schlegel called the structure of Idealism and Hegel more famously labeled the dialectical process of thought. The earliest instance of this

pattern for Faust occurs in the opening monologue, composed as part
of the *Urfaust*, where he responds to the moonlight shining through
the stained-glass window of his study by imagining himself to be outside enjoying the pleasures of communing with nature:

> Ach! könnt' ich doch auf Bergeshöhn
> In deinem lieben Lichte gehn,
> Um Bergeshöhle mit Geistern schweben,
> Auf Wiesen in deinem Dämmer weben,
> Von allem Wissensqualm entladen,
> In deinem Tau gesund mich baden!
>
> (392–7)

Abruptly, Faust comes to himself with the realization that he has only
been imagining such bliss and that in reality he is still enclosed in his
study like a prison cell, surrounded by all the artificial apparatus of his
academic learning:

> Weh! steck' ich in dem Kerker noch?
> Verfluchtes dumpfes Mauerloch,
> Wo selbst das liebe Himmelslicht
> Trüb durch gemalte Scheiben bricht!
>
> (398–401)

This same pattern of imagined experience recurs in a more paradigmatic form in Faust's response to the sunset in "Vor dem Tor," where
he stands on the summit of a hill and projects himself upon a visionary
journey, accompanying the sun as departing divinity on its journey beyond the horizon:

> Betrachte, wie in Abendsonneglut
> Die grünumgebnen Hütten schimmern.
> Sie rückt und weicht, der Tag ist überlebt,
> Dort eilt sie hin und fördert neues Leben.
> O daß kein Flügel mich vom Boden hebt,
> Ihr nach und immer nach zu streben!
> Ich säh' im ewigen Abendstrahl
> Die stille Welt zu meinen Füßen,
> Entzündet alle Höhn, beruhigt jedes Tal,
> Den Silberbach in goldne Ströme fließen.
>
> (1070–9)

Faust's reverie leads him to imagine the infinite vista of his immortal
flight: "Vor mir den Tag und hinter mir die Nacht, / Den Himmel
über mir und unter mir die Wellen" (1087–8); but again abruptly, as

signaled by his cry of distress ("Ach!"), he returns to self-consciousness and realizes that this is all but a dream or projection of his fancy, though nonetheless an experience inborn to every human being ("Doch ist es jedem eingeboren" [1092]). This pattern or structure of mental experience also defines the famous assertion Faust subsequently makes to Wagner about the two souls that dwell within his breast:

> Zwei Seelen wohnen, ach! in meiner Brust,
> Die eine will sich von der andern trennen;
> Die eine hält, in derber Liebeslust,
> Sich an die Welt mit klammernden Organen;
> Die andre hebt gewaltsam sich vom Dust
> Zu den Gefilden hoher Ahnen.
>
> (1112–7)

These two souls function primarily as signals of desire, impulses or urges (*Triebe*), as both Fichte and Schiller defined the dynamics of human consciousness in terms of opposite yet equally essential forces or agencies of the mind, the one directed outward into the world (Schiller's *Stofftrieb*), the other inward toward the realm of thought and reason (Schiller's *Formtrieb*). Only through the dynamic, indeed dialectical interaction of both is experience constituted (as both Fichte and Hegel argue). Of course, this is not to suggest that Goethe consciously adapted a philosophical doctrine in Faust's formulation — though he was certainly familiar at least with Schiller's argument in *Über die ästhetische Erziehung des Menschen in einer Reihe von Briefen* (1795) — but rather that the formulation resulted directly from the dramatic realization of precisely that process of experience described by the philosophers as the foundation of cognition.

Similar patterns of experience and thought occur throughout Faust's statements in the course of these scenes, where implicit philosophical structures may be defined. This holds true, for instance, in the elaborate monologue that fills the latter half of the opening scene "Nacht," composed for Part One, where Faust's reaction to the failure of his encounter with the Earth Spirit leads to a suicidal despair in the face of his recognition that he cannot fulfill his desire for communion with the Spirit. Nowhere in Goethe's drama does Faust speak in a manner so closely resembling the existential soliloquies of Shakespeare's *Hamlet*, above all in the famous "To be or not to be" speech, which would affirm — perhaps by design! — the claim made by Friedrich Schlegel that Goethe's drama as philosophical tragedy would surpass the masterpiece of the genre. Also significant is the imagery that Goethe employs to describe the imagined outcome for Faust of drinking the poison and annihilating himself. Once again a journey outward is envisioned, leading beyond the limits of selfhood into new and unknown realms of transcendent experience.

> Ich fühle mich bereit,
> Auf neuer Bahn den Äther zu durchdringen,
> Zu neuen Sphären reiner Tätigkeit.
> Dies hohe Leben, diese Götterwonne,
> Du, erst noch Wurm, und die verdienest du?
> Ja, kehre nur der holden Erdensonne
> Entschlossen deinen Rücken zu!
> Vermesse dich, die Pforten aufzureißen,
> Vor denen jeder gern vorüberschleicht.
> Hier ist es Zeit, durch Taten zu beweisen,
> Daß Manneswürde nicht der Götterhöhe weicht,
> Vor jener dunkeln Höhle nicht zu beben,
> In der sich Phantasie zu eigner Qual verdammt,
> Nach jenem Durchgang hinzustreben,
> Um dessen engen Mund die ganze Hölle flammt;
> Zu diesem Schritt sich heiter zu entschließen,
> Und wär' es mit Gefahr, ins Nichts dahinzufließen.
>
> (703–19)

Again and again, the pattern of poetic imagery and the structure of the experiential process defined by Faust for himself sustains the legitimacy of comparison to central philosophical doctrines from Idealism. I shall name only selected instances, without analyzing Faust's formulation in detail. His response to the choruses of the Easter liturgy overheard in a church outside his study at the end of "Nacht" introduces the central importance of memory, specifically the remembrance of personal experience from childhood, as an alternative to religious faith, and it is the power of such remembrance — a characteristic feature of European Romantic poetry! — that turns Faust away from his resolve to commit suicide and wins him back, however reluctantly, to the slings and arrows of existence in the world.

> Dies Lied verkündete der Jugend muntre Spiele,
> Der Frühlingsfeier freies Glück;
> Erinnrung hält mich nun mit kindlichem Gefühle
> Vom letzten, ernsten Schritt zurück.
> O tönet fort, ihr süßen Himmelslieder!
> Die Träne quillt, die Erde hat mich wieder!
>
> (779–84)

Faust's initial speech when he appears with Wagner in "Vor dem Tor,"
celebrating the new life that springtime brings to both nature and society, reaffirms the intimate correlation between natural process in the
world and the temper of the human mind, including Faust's own as he
hears the festive sounds of song and dance among the villagers:

> Ich höre schon des Dorfs Getümmel,
> Hier ist des Volkes wahrer Himmel,
> Zufrieden jauchzet groß und klein.
> Hier bin ich Mensch, hier darf ich's sein!

> (937–40)

In the first Study scene, when Faust has returned from his walk at evening, accompanied by Mephistopheles disguised as a poodle, his mood
turns pensive and reflective, as expressed in a series of statements about
the pleasures of repose and mental relaxation, the temporary cessation
of the will and desire as a symbol of fulfillment. The devil understand-
ably cannot tolerate such tones of contentment and constantly inter-
rupts with his agitated barking. The irony of this comic interlude
anticipates, of course, the role that Mephisto is shortly to play in
Faust's career as his companion throughout the remainder of the
drama. Readers will recall the assertion of the Lord in the "Prolog im
Himmel," a scene which also deserves to be interpreted with reference
to the philosophical condition of the Faustian mind, where he states:

> Des Menschen Tätigkeit kann allzuleicht erschlaffen,
> Er liebt sich bald die unbedingte Ruh;
> Drum geb' ich gern ihm den Gesellen zu,
> Der reizt und wirkt und muß als Teufel schaffen.

> (340–3)

Equally important for the philosophical implications of Faust's situation
in Goethe's drama is his attempt to translate the opening line of the
Gospel of St. John into German, where the Greek term *Logos* is first
rendered as "Wort," then "Sinn," next "Kraft," and finally "Tat"
(1224–37). This famous sequence invites commentary, which it has
often received, with reference to the theological implications of Faust's
reading, where the originary Deed would signify the primal act of divine creation through God's utterance, as stated in the opening chapter
of Genesis: "Let there be light!" Equally, this sequence of alternatives
evokes the central issues for a semiotic theory of language within the
context of Romanticism, where the basic relation of sign to signified
("word" to "sense") is shifted to consider that every utterance in language consists essentially of the expression of mental energy (that is,

"force"), which is immediately acknowledged to be the primal constitutive procedure for all action (that is, "deed"). The assertion that action is the essential criterion for all creation, whether verbal or
existential or theological, corresponds to Fichte's central claim in his
Wissenschaftslehre that the primal constitutive event of all consciousness
and thought is the positing of the self in action: "die Tathandlung oder
Sichselbstsetzen des Ichs." We need not refer Faust's choice of Deed as
preferable to Word for the originary Logos to Fichte's philosophical
theory of knowledge, yet clearly there is a profound similarity between
them, which suggests that the philosophical implications of Faust's position in the drama are fully compatible with the philosophical theories
of German Idealism.

Other moments in the sequence of scenes that fill this gap in the
drama, which would deserve comment with regard to their philosophical implications but will not be further considered here, may be mentioned in passing. The self-presentation of Mephistopheles in the first
Study scene demonstrates categorically how this devil is unsympathetic
to all philosophizing, indeed to all speculative thought. As he asserts
later in the second Study scene: "Ein Kerl, der spekuliert, / Ist wie ein
Tier, auf dürrer Heide / Von einem bösen Geist im Kreis herumge-
führt, / Und rings umher liegt schöne grüne Weide" (1830–3). His
animosity towards the light, as an antithetical power that sprung from a
primeval darkness, to which he belongs, also indicates the influence —
here as elsewhere in *Faust* — of Goethe's research into the nature of
color:

> Das stolze Licht, das nun der Mutter Nacht
> Den alten Rang, den Raum ihr streitig macht,
> Und doch gelingt's ihm nicht, da es, so viel es strebt,
> Verhaftet an den Körpern klebt.
> Von Körpern strömt's, die Körper macht es schön,
> Ein Körper hemmt's auf seinem Gange,
> So, hoff' ich, dauert es nicht lange,
> Und mit den Körpern wird's zugrunde gehn.
>
> (1351–8)

A direct, intentional analogy may be perceived between this striving of
the light, its dependence on the materiality of bodies and the prospect
that it, along with the bodies, will be destroyed (*zugrunde gehn*) and
Faust's own existential condition as one who strives, is never satisfied
and will also be destroyed. The song of the invisible spirits that puts
Faust to sleep through hypnosis at the end of the scene (1447–
1505) — a tour de force of Goethe's lyric genius — exactly resembles

the pattern of imaginative projection by Faust's mind into a communion with nature, as discussed with reference to the moonlight in "Nacht" and the sunset in "Vor dem Tor." In this case, however, no reflective turn of the mind occurs and no return to self-consciousness, so that Faust in response to this sweet music is left sound asleep. At a further extreme of existential gesturing is the curse that Faust utters against everything that pertains to his life and his relation to the world at the outset of the second Study scene (1583–606). Even more extreme than the inclination to suicide in the scene "Nacht," this stance of absolute despair establishes in the character of Faust the stance of an incipient nihilism, which appears to be destructive of everything that constitutes human experience and human values and functions in this scene as preparation for the contract which Mephistopheles subsequently offers in accord with the traditional legend of Dr. Faustus.

There remains one more crucial event in this sequence of scenes that is perhaps the most significant in the entire drama for an assessment of its philosophical implications. This is the pact scene between Faust and Mephistopheles, which takes place in the second Study scene, the moment of contractual agreement between the devil and the learned doctor, derived from the traditional legend of Dr. Faustus and unavoidably programmatic for the relationship between them as it develops through the remainder of the drama. As every reader knows and critics always enjoy pointing out, what begins as a version of the traditional pact — Mephisto asserts: "du sollst, in diesen Tagen, / Mit Freuden meine Künste sehn, / Ich gebe dir, was noch kein Mensch gesehn" (1672–4); to which Faust responds with the question: "Was willst du armer Teufel geben?" (1675) — is quickly transformed into a personal wager posed by Faust to the devil. The terms for this wager are set by Faust quite explicitly:

> Werd' ich beruhigt je mich auf ein Faulbett legen,
> So sei es gleich um mich getan!
> Kannst du mich schmeichelnd je belügen,
> Daß ich mir selbst gefallen mag,
> Kannst du mich mit Genuß betrügen,
> Das sei für mich der letzte Tag!

> (1692–7)

Mephisto accepts these terms, which seem to recapitulate the basic configuration of Faustian desire — a striving toward satisfaction (*Genuß*), which if ever achieved would be characterized by contentment and repose (*beruhigt . . . auf ein Faulbett*) — and which also recall the terms of agreement between the Lord and the devil from "Prolog im Himmel," that the function of the devil would be to goad Faust without cease ever onward in the activity of his quest (324–35). But Faust goes on to specify with more precision the terms that would define the successful conclusion of the wager, terms that have become as well known as any statement in the entire drama:

> Werd' ich zum Augenblicke sagen:
> Verweile doch! du bist so schön!
> Dann magst du mich in Fesseln schlagen,
> Dann will ich gern zugrunde gehn!

$$(1699–702)$$

The images used to describe the hypothetical triumph of the devil, which would also constitute the destruction (*zugrunde gehen*) of Faust, remain remarkably consistent throughout the drama. The condition that would determine such a triumph, however, here introduced for the first time, deserves careful scrutiny within the context of philosophical theories of beauty current at the time Goethe composed this scene and fully familiar to him.

What Faust envisions is the possibility that his longing might in some situation find complete resolution and satisfaction. Yet he describes this both in temporal terms as a moment that he would want to endure (*Verweile doch*) and in aesthetic terms as a condition that he calls beautiful (*schön*). The source for such a formulation is found in Schiller's *Über die ästhetische Erziehung des Menschen*, a work that Goethe knew well and the argument of which to a large extent he may be assumed to have supported. Schiller wrote under the immediate influence of Fichte's *Wissenschaftslehre* (1794) and was attempting to unite ideas derived from Kant's ethical philosophy and his aesthetic theory. In the central section of the letters (11 to 15) Schiller traces the development in the individual mind of the dialectical interaction of the two basic opposing forces or impulses — *Stofftrieb* and *Formtrieb*, mentioned above in conjunction with Faust's claim to have two opposing "souls" within his breast. This dynamic opposition constitutes experience for the individual, and the challenge for culture and education is to achieve a balance or harmony between the two. If they were ever to be fully reconciled, argues Schiller (Letter 14), which would only be possible in the perfection (*Vollendung*) of human existence, it would constitute "the Idea of Humanity" (*die Idee seiner Menschheit*). In actual experience such a complete reconciliation is impossible, he acknowledges, but if it were achieved it would in fact constitute a symbol of the completed destiny (*ausgeführten Bestimmung*) of human existence. As is well known, Schiller proceeds to assert (Letter 15) that such a symbolic manifestation of the ideal of humanity is only possible as Beauty (*Schönheit*). It is, furthermore, through the encounter with the beautiful as manifested in works of art that the mind may be educated to an understanding of this ideal, a condition where reason and nature would become one, where freedom and necessity would be fully reconciled.

The influence of Schiller's theory of beauty in art on the emergence of a Romantic aestheticism during the decade or so following its publication would be impossible to overstate, even where its legitimacy was called into question by such critics as Friedrich Schlegel, who in one of his best known aphorisms, *Athenaeum-Fragment* 116, speaks of Romantic poetry as "progressive and universal" (*eine progressive Universalpoesie*). A much more immediate influence may be perceived in the poetry of Friedrich Hölderlin (1770–1843), close friend and former roommate of both Schelling and Hegel in the Tübingen Seminary, who in an unpublished preface drafted for his novel *Hyperion, oder der Eremit in Griechenland* (1797/9) argued as follows:

> Jenen ewigen Widerstreit zwischen unserem Selbst und der Welt zu endigen, den Frieden alles Friedens, der höher ist, denn alle Vernunft, den wiederzubringen, uns mit der Natur zu vereinigen, zu *einem* unendlichen Ganzen, das ist das Ziel all unseres Strebens, wir mögen uns darüber verstehen oder nicht. Aber weder unser Wissen noch unser Handeln gelangt in irgend einer Periode des Daseins dahin, wo aller Widerstreit aufhört, wo Alles Eins ist [. . .] Wir hätten auch keine Ahndung von jenem unendlichen Frieden, von jenem Sein, im einzigen Sinne des Worts, wir strebten gar nicht, die Natur mit uns zu vereinigen, wir dächten und wir handelten nicht, es wäre überhaupt gar nichts, wir dächten selbst nichts, wenn nicht durch jene unendliche Vereinigung, jenes Sein im einzigen Sinne des Worts vorhanden wäre. Es ist vorhanden — als Schönheit; es wartet, um mit Hyperion zu reden, ein neues Reich auf uns, wo die Schönheit Königin ist. — (236–7)

Similar ideas were also put forward about the ideal of beauty in art by Schelling in the concluding section of his *System des transzendentalen Idealismus* (1800), published in the same year that Goethe composed the sequence of scenes for the gap in *Faust*. Schelling argues that the ultimate goal of all philosophy, as with human culture itself, is to become poetry in its highest sense as the medium of beauty as ideal. Within the work of art, he argues in essential agreement with Schiller, all human conflict is resolved and the duality of reason and nature, as Kant had understood it, is overcome. The beautiful manifests as symbol the highest ideal of humanity and provides the model or goal for all thought and action, for all human striving. Such ideas had become familiar by this time and received intensive debate within the circles of Romanticism at Jena precisely at the turn of the eighteenth to the nineteenth century, when Goethe completed Part One of his drama, about which, as Schiller wrote to him (cited above), the philosophers in Jena were so keenly interested.

Once again the relation of philosophical ideas to Goethe's formulation in *Faust* cannot be defined as direct and uniform. The terms that Faust sets for his wager with Mephistopheles, upon which their entire career together through the remainder of the drama is grounded, do not in themselves define a program for aesthetic education in the manner of Schiller, nor does the wager specify precisely what the "beautiful moment" might be. Yet in the context of the drama, above all in the context of Faust's several descriptions in his monologues of the central dilemma of his existence, it becomes clear that the goal defined for his career with the devil would coincide precisely with the kind of ideal experience that was projected by Schiller and the Romantics for beauty. But Faust, it should be noted, makes it clear in offering this wager with the devil that he does not believe it possible that his terms could ever be met. Nor does Mephistopheles appear to realize that in accepting the wager he is in effect going against himself. He emphasizes, both in his conversation with the Lord in the "Prolog im Himmel" and in his monologue just following the pact scene, that he intends to lead Faust astray, to drag him through the nitty-gritty of life, to provoke and challenge him in his desire and will, so that indeed his striving will never be resolved, no beautiful moment will ever be realized, and ultimately Faust, as is several times predicted, will be destroyed (*zugrunde gehn*). The philosophical implications of Faust's wager must thus be viewed with a double sense of irony, since Faust is a radical skeptic about the possibility that the wager could be won and the role of Mephistopheles, whether he recognizes this or not, works directly against the terms of the wager. Ultimately, the wager must be understood within the parameters of Faust's tragic situation, which relegates the concept of the beautiful moment to a kind of negative norm, placing all aspects of the dramatic action in opposition to itself.

The outcome of an inquiry into the role of philosophy in *Faust* is thus paradoxical. The central concerns of post-Kantian Idealism are clearly reflected in all aspects of the existential dilemma defined by Faust for himself, specifically in the material composed for the drama around 1800. Yet the philosophical programs developed within the context of Romanticism are all challenged and called into question by the drama. Goethe as poet, of course, never intended his play to provide answers to philosophical questions, nor did he seek to apply philosophical ideas *as such* to *Faust* and to prove the validity of such ideas through the action of the drama. Yet the importance of philosophy for interpreting the full implications of Goethe's drama remains beyond dispute, even if most readers and scholars have missed or ignored the relationships resulting from the reciprocal influence between philosophy and poetry as traced in the present argument, an influence, on one hand, which the drama exerted on philosophical ideas, notably concerning the genre of philosophical tragedy, and subsequently, on the other, an influence of the philosophical readings elicited by the published Fragment upon the poet himself, especially when he returned to work on *Faust* around 1800, in order to complete Part One of the drama.

It would be possible, of course, to trace the further development of these central thematic concerns of Goethe's drama through Part Two, though the question of philosophy becomes far more diffuse and complex within the poetic medium of the poet's last and most supreme literary achievement. Of particular importance would be the continuing legitimacy of Faust's wager with Mephistopheles and the question of the beautiful moment. It may be argued, for instance, that the union between Faust and Helena in Act 3, where a kind of mythical or symbolic marriage is achieved through the act of exchanging rhymes (9411–18), fulfills implicitly the terms of the wager by achieving such a beautiful moment. Faust's final statement in this sequence even acknowledges the primacy of the moment for their union: "Dasein ist Pflicht und wär's ein Augenblick" (9418). But no reference is given here to the wager, and Mephistopheles, who enters blustering in rhyme immediately afterwards, does not press the point. Faust's final speech in Act 5, furthermore, where as an old man blinded by Care he imagines the achievement of his future utopian vision for the city he has built upon the tidal lands, recapitulates the terms of his wager, as if it were now fulfilled by anticipation: "Im Vorgefühl von solchem hohen Glück / Genieß' ich jetzt den höchsten Augenblick" (11585–6). These are moments of central importance for Goethe's drama, but it would be difficult to claim that philosophical issues still provide legitimate criteria for understanding what happens.

Goethe's poetic imagination privileges symbolic and mythical forms of action and experience in ways that are elaborated and expanded in Part Two beyond anything that could have been anticipated from the issues presented in Part One. By the time the poet came to compose these later scenes, furthermore, the question of philosophy in European culture had greatly shifted away from the concerns of Romantic Idealism. The larger reaches of Part Two, especially where Faust and Mephistopheles enter the court of the Emperor in Act 1, pursue the mythological mysteries of the Classical Walpurgis Night in Act 2, engage in the warfare resulting from the devil's economic reform in Act 4, and finally attempt the construction of Faust's brave new world on the tidal lands in Act 5, all leave far behind the explicit issues which philosophy had raised in response to the initial published Fragment. Yet the conjunction of poetic concerns and philosophical responses with regard to the Fragment, both in the drafting of a theory of philosophical tragedy and the ideal of aesthetic education and also in Goethe's implicit response to these ideas in the completion of Part One, may be regarded as a uniquely fortuitous event in the emergence of modern Western thought. No other poetic work of such importance as Goethe's *Faust* ever challenged the central ideas of philosophy in so productive a way, resulting in significant innovative theories in philosophy to which the poetic work also responded in its own terms. We may not choose to identify these philosophical issues through our reading of *Faust*, since the drama far transcends philosophy as such, yet such philosophical issues remain central, if never adequately clarified and interpreted, for a critical assessment of Goethe's drama within the cultural, intellectual and literary contexts of its time.

Works Cited

Hegel, Georg Wilhelm Friedrich. *Phänomenologie des Geistes*. In *Werke*. Ed. Eva Moldenhauer and Karl Markus Michel. Vol. 3. Frankfurt am Main: Suhrkamp, 1986.

————. *Vorlesungen über die Ästhetik III*. In *Werke*. Ed. Eva Moldenhauer and Karl Markus Michel. Vol. 15. Frankfurt am Main: Suhrkamp, 1986.

Hölderlin, Friedrich. "Die vorletzte Fassung. Vorrede." In *Sämtliche Werke* [Stuttgarter Hölderlin-Ausgabe]. Ed. Friedrich Beissner. Vol. 3. *Hyperion*. Stuttgart: W. Kohlhammer, 1957. 235–7.

Schelling, Friedrich Wilhelm Joseph von. "Über Dante in philosophischer Beziehung." In *Werke*. Ed. Manfred Schröter. Vol. 3. *Schriften zur Identitätsphilosophie 1801–1806*. Munich: C. H. Beck'sche Verlagsbuchhandlung, 1958. 572–83.

————. *Philosophie der Kunst, Besonderer Teil (aus dem handschriftlichen Nachlaß)*. In *Werke*. Ed. Manfred Schröter. Ergänzungsband 3. *Zur Philosophie der Kunst, 1803–1817*. Munich: C. H. Beck/R. Oldenbourg, 1959. 134–387.

Schlegel, August Wilhelm. "Aus einer Rezension des 7. Bandes von Goethes 'Schriften.'" [1790] In *Goethe im Urteil seiner Kritiker. Dokumente zur Wirkungsgeschichte Goethes in Deutschland*. Ed. Karl Robert Mandelkow. Vol. 1. 1773–1832. Munich: C. H. Beck, 1975. 111–12.

Schlegel, Friedrich. *Über das Studium der griechischen Poesie*. In *Kritische Friedrich-Schlegel-Ausgabe*. Ed. Ernst Behler. Vol. 1. *Studium des klassischen Altertums*. Paderborn, Munich, Vienna: Ferdinand Schöningh/ Zurich: Thomas-Verlag, 1979. 217–367.

The Diachronic Solidity of Goethe's *Faust*

R. H. Stephenson

> Wer kann was Dummes, wer was Kluges denken,
> Das nicht die Vorwelt schon gedacht?
>
> (6809–10)

IT MAY BE AN EXAGGERATION to claim that Goethe's inner solidarity "was a direct result of his early studies in alchemy" (Gray, 182). But it is nonetheless clear that the magic and Kabbalistic material that he built into his *Faust* from its inception appealed as strongly as did other aspects of Gottfried Arnold's *Unparteiische Kirchen- und Ketzergeschichte* (1698–1700) to his life-long interest in modes of thought and feeling that are co-terminous with the Western cultural tradition. It is, after all, in his writings in Rome — celebrated in Elegies VII and XV especially of his *Römische Elegien* as the "eternal" city of tradition, as the definitive meeting-point of those two tap-roots of our tradition, classical antiquity and Christianity — that Goethe first articulates the peculiar sense of experiential depth that awareness of a long, historical perspective (evoked specifically by the pyramid of Cestius and the ruins of the imperial palaces) inspires in him:

> Kehr' ich nun in mich selbst zurück, wie man doch so gern tut bei jeder Gelegenheit, so entdecke ich ein Gefühl, das mich unendlich freut, ja, das ich sogar auszusprechen wage. Wer sich mit Ernst hier umsieht und Augen hat zu sehen, muß solid werden, er muß einen Begriff von Solidität fassen, der ihm nie so lebendig ward.
>
> Der Geist wird zur Tüchtigkeit gestempelt, gelangt zu einem Ernst ohne Trockenheit, zu einem gesetzten Wesen mit Freude. (HA 11, 135)

A sound understanding of the present (as he remarked to von Müller in 1827, noted in the latter's diary on 23 August) requires a knowledge of "crucial turning-points" (*Hauptmomente*, as he calls them in the "Historical Part" of his *Farbenlehre* [HA 14, 56]) in our shared cultural history: key cultural forms which, at ever higher levels of refinement, recur over and over again in the cyclical — or, rather, helical — pattern that he discerned in the Western tradition (HA 12, 383). One result of

this diachronic mode of perception is the simultaneous experience of
the Past-in-the-Present ("im Gegenwärtigen das Vergangene") that
Goethe extolled in the paintings of Ruysdael (HA 12, 138), and which
is perhaps most blatantly represented in the double titles of each
stanza — one Greek, one Christian — of his "Urworte. Orphisch"
(Schantz, 44). Another result of such a perspective "through time" is
breadth, since "es geht mit der Kunst wie mit dem Leben: je weiter
man hineinkommt, je breiter wird sie" (*Italienische Reise* [HA 11,
105]). What Fritz Strich identified as the unique "symbolische Tiefe
und Weite" of Goethe's *Faust* (Strich, 17) — what Barker Fairley called
"a panoramic exceeding that of any other poem" — is intimately linked
to the text's peculiar way of "gathering up the past [. . .] and incorporating it into the present" (Fairley, 35). The vast richness of cultural
material that Goethe built into his play (and mirrored in its rich diversity of dramatic and poetic forms) has recently been codified (by Ulrich
Gaier) using the following eight categories of possible "readings": religious, scientific, magical, historicist, sociological, economic, anthropological, and poetic. My aim in this essay is not to contest the
usefulness of such re-presentation of Goethe's *Stoff* (provided, too, by
the Munich and Frankfurt editions) but to seek to corroborate a
growing consensus among commentators in the second half of the
twentieth century and incipient twenty-first century about what Goethe
is doing with this wealth of cultural material. After all, in letter, conversation, and diary-entry, as in his published work, from at least as early as
his reading of Arnold's *Kirchen- und Ketzergeschichte*, there is,
throughout his life, continuous and explicit reference to the Present's
polar relationship to the Past and the therefore intrinsically time-bound
nature of human experience. The famous *Spruch* to that effect in the
West-östlicher Divan could be glossed by many other instances of his insistence on the necessity of entertaining a diachronic perspective:

> Wer nicht von drei tausend Jahren
> Sich weiß Rechenschaft zu geben,
> Bleib im Dunkeln unerfahren,
> Mag von Tag zu Tage leben.
>
> (HA 2, 49)

The fact that Goethe transcends the two-thousand-year starting-point
of Dionysius Exiguus's sixth-century invention of a calendar which
took its date from the birth of Christ is not without significance (as
Goethe pointed out in a letter to Wilhelm von Humboldt of 22 October 1826) for an understanding of his *Faust*. Three thousand years
takes us back roughly to the putative Fall of Troy, to the establishment

of Greek (and Jewish) culture over and against such "eastern" influences as Egypt and Persia. In other words, such a time frame takes us back to the supposed birth of a recognizably *Western* culture, one that has been characterized above all by an ever-widening diffusion of a learned tradition (Whitehead, 105) that, in terms of print, reached an unprecedented height in Goethe's own day and, in terms of electronic media, yet higher levels in our own. It is precisely such a Westernized, i.e., generally informed, audience that, the Direktor tells us in the "Vorspiel auf dem Theater," *Faust* is to address:

> Zwar sind sie an das Beste nicht gewöhnt,
> Allein sie haben schrecklich viel gelesen.
>
> (45–46)

Such diachronic hints abound in the play. For example, in the "Schattiger Hain" scene in Act 2 of Part Two, the age-old debate on the nature of genius (precocious, overflowing energy, all-consuming and many-faceted; yet, without self-discipline, tending to degeneration and dissolution) is hinted at in the dialogue between Phorkyas and the Chorus over and over again, in order to ensure that the reader/spectator grasps the through-time perspective (9574–78). The Chorus' allusion to Icarus (9901) in respect of Euphorion, like the blasé lines with which they greet Phorkyas's enthusiastic description of Euphorion's seemingly miraculous powers — "Nennst du ein Wunder dies, / Kretas Erzeugte?" (9629–30) — anticipate the full world-weary weight of their declaration that there is nothing new under the sun:

> Alles, was je geschieht
> Heutigen Tages,
> Trauriger Nachklang ist's
> Herrlicher Ahnherrntage.
>
> (9637–40)

Indeed, the whole of Act 3, like the play of which it may in this sense be taken to be paradigmatic, is quite explicitly embedded in the three-thousand-year-old framework of Western culture, as Helena's wistful words to Faust after the death of Euphorion make unambiguously clear:

> Ein altes Wort bewährt sich leider auch an mir:
> Daß Glück und Schönheit dauerhaft sich nicht vereint.
>
> (9939–40)

Part of Helena's function, like that of many other characters in Part Two — the Sphinxes, for example (7241–48), or Manto, about whom

"Time revolves" (7481) — is to reflect on the whole length of the
Western tradition of which they are witnesses. But it is Mephistopheles
(who, by his own testimony, has been on earth for at least one hundred
thousand years [10211]), who consistently plays this role throughout
the whole play — and, in doing so, evokes a traditional function of the
Devil in Western literature; as Byron has it in *The Deformed Transformed* (in lines quoted to Goethe by Eckermann on 29 November
1826):

> The Devil speaks truth much oftener than he's deemed,
> He hath an ignorant audience.

For Mephisto (often quoting Scripture, in the time-honored fashion of
the Devil [see Osman Durrani's essay in this volume]), never tires of
reminding his much-read, but presumably ahistorically-minded, audience of the repetitive nature of his human experience:

> Wer lange lebt, hat viel erfahren,
> Nichts Neues kann für ihn auf dieser Welt geschehen.
>
> (6861–62)

Human history evinces, to his cynical mind, no progress, by dint of the
fact that human beings are congenitally incapable of real development:

> [Der Mensch] scheint mir, mit Verlaub von Euer Gnaden,
> Wie eine der langbeinigen Zikaden,
> Die immer fliegt und fliegend springt
> Und gleich im Gras ihr altes Liedchen singt.
>
> (287–90)

In his view, as he insistently reminds us, the Modern is only a "version"
of the Classical, and vice versa ("es ist ein altes Buch zu blättern"
[7742]); and his citing of 1 Kings 21 to point out the long history of
the kind of injustice that Philemon and Baucis suffer at the hands of the
powerful (11287) is only one instance of Mephisto's clear-sighted (indeed, as in "Trüber Tag," ruthless) diachronic "take" on "present" experience: "Auch hier geschieht, was längst geschah" (11286).
      The abundance of diachronic hints, throughout the whole length of
this vast text, establishes a frame of reference in which the general tendency of any work of art to transcend the historical period in which it is
set and the everyday conception of "unity of time" — "den Poeten
bindet keine Zeit" (7433) — is specifically *shaped* to direct the specta-
tor/reader to attend to more than the illusory "present" of the action
(and to more than the *Zeitkritik* it contains). Goethe's *Faust* is designed, on every level of its organization, to remind us of the recurrent

nature of those forms of life which we may blithely mistake for givens but which are, in fact, cultural artefacts, inherited from the deep past. This is, at least, the nub of the critical consensus (brought to theoretical distinctness in Wilkinson [1972]) that has grown in the last fifty years or so among some of those commentators who have grappled with the "high degree of extra-textual allusiveness" (Lamport, 119) in the work. Fairley's "sophisticated retrospection," like Jantz's "symbolic extension" share with Wilkinson's "tragedy in the diachronic mode" a concern to account for a salient fact of the text: namely, that whether it is dealing with theology (Pelikan [1995]), or economics (Destro [1997]), with the dramaturgy of the theatre (Schanze [1989]), or poetological semiotics (Kruse [1985]), its astonishing wealth of material is the result of Goethe's attempt to trace the ramifications of those recurrent modes of thought, feeling, and being that have come to constitute, along the whole length of its history, what we know as Western culture. In corroborating this growing consensus in the secondary literature, the aim of this essay is, then, to reinforce the relevance of Goethe's *Faust* to a generation that sees itself as inhabiting a postmodern age that seeks in such texts as Josten Gaarder's *Sophie's World* (1991) and Richard Tarmas's *The Passion of the Western Mind* (1991) an orientation in the otherwise bewildering welter of cultural forms that we have inherited from our tradition.

We do not need to regress to the psychologizing character-studies so popular in *Faust* criticism in the early twentieth century in order to accept Stuart Atkins's contention that the exposition of Faust's character is virtually completed in "Vor dem Tor" (Atkins, 38), and that the character we are first introduced to in Mephistopheles' satirical caricature (300–07) turns out to be "a man of deep feeling, rich intellect, inexhaustible vitality [. . .] [with] faith in the innate worth of Man" (Atkins, 26). Moreover, he is a character who both develops and achieves: the Faust we encounter in Act 3 of Part Two ("Innerer Burghof") has, for example, achieved the embodiment he sought in Act 2; he has, according to the leader of the Chorus (9182–87), attained to a mature and distinguished demeanor (so different from the unworldly scholar of "Nacht"). Similarly, in Act 5, we witness Faust in the role of the wise and creative elder, achieving, if only in imagination, a vision of the fate of posterity that gives him (at least an anticipatory moment of) peace (11559–86). And, as Philemon testifies to the returning Wanderer in "Offene Gegend," the opening scene of the final act, there can be no doubt about Faust's great achievement:

> Das Euch grimmig mißgehandelt,
> Wog' auf Woge, schäumend wild,
> Seht als Garten Ihr behandelt,
> Seht ein paradiesisch Bild.
>
> (11083–86)

On the other hand, Faust also evinces, beyond the specificity of his being and doing, a general pattern that is familiar enough for Jantz to see
in him a manic-depressive type, alternating hyperbolically from hubristic euphoria to the depths of melancholy, from self-glorification as an
Übermensch (490, 500) to self-denigration as a *Wurm* (653) (Jantz
1978, xx). Moreover, a tendency is discernible within these fluctuations: Faust, as Barker Fairley has it, "embodies an impulse" — to strive
after ideals beyond his attaining, but of which his awareness is ever-
renewed (118). There is, however, no indication in the text that such
idealistic activism is unique to Faust; indeed, other characters, notably
the Student (1896–1900) and Euphorion (9779–84), share them. Far
from "being a challenging newcomer among the great themes of literature," the idea "that activity is man's defining characteristic, and that
its timeless continuation has an intrinsic value even before we consider
its particular goals" (Reed, 79) is, in fact, the fundamental Western
(that is, Platonic) doctrine that the very meaning of existence consists
in being a factor in activity. It is, therefore, misleading, here and elsewhere, to restrict the perspectives opened up by Goethe's *Faust* to "the
traditions of thought already definitely associated with the figure of
Faust" (Atkins, vi). Goethe freely deviates from the Faust legend in
many ways (Holsovsky-Weill); and it would be a peculiarly perverse
twist of the genetic fallacy to insist that, because the Faust material has
its source in historical fact and in the Renaissance turmoil of a universe
centered on God giving way to one centered on Man, Goethe's Faustian character is to be associated only with Renaissance themes. After all,
the whole body of legendary tradition that had gathered round Johannes, or Georg, Faustus's name by the time of his death in c. 1540 was
itself age-old. As E. M. Butler (1948 and 1952) demonstrated, "the
myth of the Magus" stretches back far beyond the Renaissance, to precisely the dawn of Western civilization that Goethe evoked with his
three-thousand-year perspective. The magus who does wonders without God's aid (Strich, 26) takes us back to the Hellenistic Age when
"the complex of general ideas forming the imperishable origin of Western thought [. . .] was handed over to University professors" of the
Faustian type (Whitehead, 132–33). In other words, the restless tension, embodied, in varying degrees and varying modes, by Goethe's

Faust, between speculation and erudition, between "knowledge-by-description" and "knowledge-by-acquaintance," between the Mind and the Body, which runs right through the play, is no mere idiosyncrasy of his character, nor just a symptom of his psychological type, nor even a trace of his origins in Renaissance myth-making. It is rather the reflection of a duality in Western anthropological thought, stretching from Plotinus to Pascal, that places humanity in-between the divine and the animal. Nor was Goethe being in the least bit original in broadening the significance of Faust in this way. Christopher Marlowe had already given Faust (in 1592) something of that paradigmatic status qua Western Man that Goethe's character embodies, by elevating him into a Promethean figure who yearns and strives for superhuman knowledge and lusts insatiably for power and life:

> O what a world of profit and delight,
> Of power, of honour, of omnipotence.
> (Marlowe, 9; cf. 374–75)

Goethe's Faust is not, then, "a poetic figure, in which specific Goethean life-rhythms find expression" (Requadt, 388); nor is he "modern man" (even if "modern" be taken to mean post-Renaissance) (Binswanger et al.). Faust, as Goethe represents him, is Western Man in essence, whose restlessness (as Socrates, Aquinas, Augustus, Pascal — and Lacan — attest) results from an unending desire for that of which he is in want (7459–60).

In view of Mephisto's own insistence on his having been witness to every significant event in the history of the world (including its geological history) — "'s Ehrenpunkt, der Teufel war dabei!" (10125) — it hardly seems necessary to labor the point of the diachronic dimension of his character. However obscure may be the Devil's origins in the monotheistic religions of the West, and however controversial the role of Satan in the Book of Job, chapters 1 and 2 (to which Goethe's "Prolog im Himmel" makes emphatic reference), the fact remains that, in this play, the Devil is portrayed (as is itself traditional [Mason, 173–74]) as a (severely limited) opponent to God in a pairing that is co-extensive with the Western tradition. His Judaeo-Christian origins certainly make Mephisto feel, to some extent at least, uncomfortable in Greece (compare 7044–47, say, with 7676–78). But even here he finds close parallels to his own deeply ambivalent, hermaphroditic, nature. Indeed, in the hideous, ancient hag, Phorkyas, he is delighted to find the perfect persona for his protracted sojourn in Greece (7993). As an unreconciled, yet inextricably interrelated, opponent of God, he torments the Creatures because he, too, is tormented by his own perplexity at his own ambivalent nature; as the Sphinx notes: "Sprich nur dich selbst aus, wird schon Rätsel sein" (7132). In one of those deft exploitations of syntactical ambiguity that abound in his writing, Goethe expresses the baffling complexity of "the Problem of Evil" — of the Devil's relation to the light:

> Ich bin ein Teil des Teils, der anfangs alles war,
> Ein Teil der Finsternis, die sich das Licht gebar.
>
> (1349–50)

For in this self-definition, the feminine relative pronoun may, with equal justice, be taken as either subject of the verb, *gebären*, or as its object. In the first case, "darkness gives birth to light" (Mephisto's conscious preference); in the second, "light gives birth to darkness" (something Mephisto strenuously denies). Thus, within the metaphoric economy of the play, even Mephisto is a child of light! There is, then, even in him, a spark of all that light symbolizes in Goethe's *Faust*: goodness, love, reason, the divine impulse of the Universe. The problematic complicity of Good and Evil that so exercised the Church Fathers and gave rise to the tradition of theodicy-writing could hardly be more tellingly embodied than in this highly intelligent, witty, urbane, and yet deeply sadistic and perverse devil, of whom Byron is reported to have said that he was "one of the finest and most sublime specimens of human conception" (in Kennedy, 154). Like Faust, Goethe's devil is certainly a vivid character. And like Faust, he is at the same time a psychological type — that of the *esprit de contradiction*, at odds with himself and the world (4030; 9072–73). But, more significantly still, Mephisto, like Faust, represents a long Western tradition of thought.

Where Faust represents romantic idealism, Mephisto (as Fairley rightly points out [19]) represents the impulse to cynicism and nihilism that accompanies intelligence unrelated to, and untempered by (repressed) feeling and imagination: a would-be value-free realistic outlook. He has no brief for intellect or for aesthetic sensibility; his attitude is rather that of the highest practical intelligence — of *Verstand* rather than *Vernunft* — of judging only by optimal results, never by ideals. As Homunculus acknowledges, Mephisto's destructive aggression can come in useful: "Du bist gewandt, die Wege mir zu kürzen" (6890). He has the fox-like gifts of Odysseus (indeed he much resembles Goethe's Reineke), which — as *techné* — are as much a part of the make-up of Western civilization as the more rarefied attitudes of Faust. Even Mephisto's apparently pointless, because unwinnable, bet with God over Faust's soul (312) has its own kind of logic, given his situation. In the same spirit as the *Sponti-Spruch*, "Du hast keine Chance —

nutze sie!", Mephisto — hoping against hope — adopts the gambler's "you-never-know" attitude: "Wer weiß, wie noch die Würfel fallen?" (10295). And it is his indomitable will-to-win, against all odds, that makes him so effective. In Part Two it is he, not the prating Imperial Cabinet, who solves (albeit temporarily) the financial crisis in Act 1; it is he, not the plodding Wagner, who produces Homunculus (6885–86); and it is he, not Faust, who wins the war in Act 4. He is, indeed, "ein Teil von jener Kraft, / Die stets das Böse will und stets das Gute schafft" (1335–36); for he reflects the fact that Good has so often been secured in our history by intelligent management, in contrast to the Evil that has too often been caused by clumsy idealism (10689). It is, therefore, wholly characteristic of his penetrating intelligence that Mephisto should be the most pointed of diachronic commentators. While his conscious denial of idealism blinds him to much (in particular, to the progressive values of the attainment of greater beauty, truth, and goodness), it does have the compensatory virtue of allowing him to see, with great perspicuity, the massive inheritance from the past that goes into making the present. It also enables him to alert the reader to the fundamental stupidity of forgetting the relevance of the past, of ever thinking that it is over and done with:

> Vorbei! ein dummes Wort.
> Warum vorbei?
> Vorbei und reines Nicht, vollkommnes Einerlei!
> Was soll uns denn das ew'ge Schaffen!
> Geschaffenes zu nichts hinwegzuraffen!
> "Da ist's vorbei!" Was ist daran zu lesen?
> Es ist so gut, als wär' es nicht gewesen,
> Und treibt sich doch im Kreis, als wenn es wäre.
> Ich liebte mir dafür das Ewig-Leere.
>
> (11595–603)

It is in large part owing to the Devil's diachronic truth-telling that the audience is in a position to read the play in the way it is designed to be read.

The doubling of the characters of Faust and Mephisto, by means of which they both evince a recognizable type and represent, through time, a traditional outlook, is also a distinguishing characteristic of the other figures in the drama. For this kind of stereoscopic co-ordination of two different modes of perception and thought — embracing simultaneity and succession respectively — Goethe used the term "Archetype" (*Urform*) in his scientific work, to cover both the basic form and its metamorphosis in time (Stephenson 1995, 12, 55–59, 68). The resultant model embraces both the static type-concept *and* a mental picture (an *Idee*) of the phenomenon's growth-pattern, its genetic profile. Analogously, in *Faust* Goethe produces characters who represent, allegorically, ideas that are constituent of the Western tradition. (Indeed, it is this archetypal quality that (mis)led C. G. Jung, and some of his followers, to undertake psychoanalytical studies of many of the figures in the play [see Jantz, 1962].) In Part Two, where a wealth of mythological material amplifies the unique and personal to the point where it becomes blatantly typical in nature, we find ourselves in a world of sophisticated awareness, on the characters' part, of the forms and symbols that shape experience. It is a world of self-conscious retrospection, in which Faust falls in love with Helena, eminent example of a figure-as-traditional-symbol: of consciously cultivated and alluring beauty. Beauty/Helena is shown forth in "Vor dem Palaste" as both positive and negative: playful (8500), of the highest value and efficacy (8516–23), and joy-giving (8601–03); but, on the other hand (in Phorkyas's bitter tirade), Beauty is said to be arrogant in its irrelevance to practical life (8765–70), ready always to prostitute itself (8775–78), vampyric in its essential parasitism (8821), and tending to arouse fanatical, egotistic possessiveness (9061–62).

What Helena embodies, then, and promotes by her very being, is a (debatable) value that has been discussed (together with the two others of an age-old triad, Truth and Goodness) throughout the tradition of Western thought, as Phorkyas-Mephistopheles makes unambiguously clear in evoking the antiquity of the question of Beauty's moral deficit: "Alt ist das Wort, doch bleibet hoch und wahr der Sinn" (8754). Similarly representative of a recurrent idea is the witch, Erichtho, who, at the opening of the "Klassische Walpurgisnacht," delivers a prologue which clearly functions as an indication of the diachronic intent of what follows:

> Überbleicht erscheint mir schon
> Von grauer Zelten Woge weit das Tal dahin,
> Als Nachgesicht der sorg- und grauenvollsten Nacht.
> (7009–11)

Here on the Pharsalian Plain was fought a battle — between Pompey and Julius Caesar — which is, for her, paradigmatic ("ein großes Beispiel") of the recurrent structure of power politics (7018), as it is for Mephistopheles, who, at the mention of Pharsalus by Homunculus (6955), expatiates on the unendingly repetitive nature of such power-struggles in general:

> O weh! hinweg! und laßt mir jene Streite
> Von Tyrannei und Sklaverei beiseite.
> Mich langeweilt's; denn kaum ist's abgetan,
> So fangen sie von vorne wieder an.
>
> (6956–59)

And, significantly enough for a diachronic reading of the text, he adds that such repetitive forms of behavior occur unconsciously and are clear only to those who pay them self-conscious attention:

> Und keiner merkt: er ist doch nur geneckt
> Vom Asmodeus, der dahinter steckt.
> Sie streiten sich, so heißt's, um Freiheitsrechte;
> Genau besehen, sind's Knechte gegen Knechte.
>
> (6960–63)

Erichtho herself represents a view of history, itself traditional, as an unending cyclical repetition of power-struggles between haves and have-nots, in which Might always prevails:

> Keiner gönnt das Reich
> Dem andern; dem gönnt's keiner, der's mit Kraft erwarb
> Und kräftig herrscht.
>
> (7013–15)

Her resigned acceptance of the recurrence of such phenomena — "Wie oft schon wiederholt' sich's! wird sich immerfort / Ins Ewige wiederholen . . ." (7012–13) — is itself repeated throughout the play, constantly underlining its diachronic temper. Nowhere is this more amusingly in evidence, perhaps, than in Mephisto's resigned acceptance of the Baccalaureus's brash solipsism:

> Dies ist der Jugend edelster Beruf!
> Die Welt, sie war nicht, eh' ich sie erschuf;
> Die Sonne führt' ich aus dem Meer herauf;
> Mit mir begann der Mond des Wechsels Lauf.
>
> (6793–96)

In rejecting both experience and inherited wisdom (6758–61), the Baccalaureus opposes the Devil's urgent sense of the relevance of the long past (6815–18) and, simultaneously, gives voice to that high evaluation of novelty-for-novelty's sake that is no less traditional than conservatism in the West's development.

The diachronic temper of Part One is — "genau besehen" — no less clear in some of the minor characters who appear there. The Baccalaureus is, after all, that same fresh-faced student who appeared in the so-called "Schülerszene," in which we hear not only an echo of Faust's ambitious strivings voiced in the opening scene of "Nacht," but also recurrent issues in the history of Western-style education. Mephisto's satire, in reponse to the Student's naïve enthusiasm, on logic-chopping and its inhibition of spontaneous thought (1918–21) has resonated down the centuries since at least the Sophists, as has the recurrent unease about both analysis, to which Mephisto gives trenchant (and, for the Student, encouraging) expression (1936–39), and that pre-eminent tool of Western thought, theory (2038–39), which, as the hypothetical method, underpins scientific work from Hippocrates and Euclid to Newton and Darwin. Although in "Auerbachs Keller" Goethe turns from the life of the mind emphasized in the preceding scenes (the so-called "Gelehrtentragödie") to the life of feeling, at its coarsest, in the foolish and clumsy ribaldry of drunks, this should not blind us to its diachronic import. Certainly what the "lustige Gesellen" embody is indeed life at its most insipid (Strich, 83): forced gaiety barely masking vicious *ressentiment* (Atkins, 58–61). But the scene is not to be dismissed as Mason suggests: it is, as Coleridge remarked, a most significant representation (Mason, 185). This "microcosmic self-justification through alcohol" (Jantz 1978, 168) presents not so much "the Tavern of Life" (Atkins, 57) as "the Tavern of *Western* Life." For what these temporarily uninhibited buffoons represent here is the long tradition of a Western drug-culture, tolerated in the spirit of "ergo bibamus": drink as release from repressive — political (2092) — forces, a cultivated (if insipid) safety-valve concurrent with our cultural history. Similarly in the witches and other phantasmagoric creatures of the "Walpurgisnacht," Goethe presents an orgy — an "erotischer Rausch" (Strich, 74) — of feeling at its most primitive. But sexual gratification here, both in its direct (3974–85) and indirect (4165–71) forms, is a representative of the variety of modes, from brazen crudity to sadistic, verbal aggression, that the history of *Western* sexuality evinces. Equally the various familiar types — the "Spaziergänger aller Art" — who populate the "vaudeville tableau" (Atkins, 34) of the scene "Vor dem Tor" express the common concerns of everyday life (to which Faust has been drawn back by the childhood nostalgia evoked by the Easter bells): food, drink, sex, financial pressure, class-snobbery, and simply idle curiosity. But what is portrayed here has, too, its diachronic quality, evident for example in the characteristically Western isolation (even alienation) of the *savant* from the crowd, in which Wagner delights (944) and against which Faust chafes (940). Indeed, the tension between Wagner and Faust, which is sublimated into intellectual discussion, is itself a striking instance of the diachronic temper of Part One.

Each character voices opinions that are consonant with his own personality and outlook; but their opposing views are by no means idiosyncratic positions. When, for example in "Nacht," Wagner puts great stress on the power of persuasion — "Wie soll man sie durch Überredung leiten?" (533) — he is not simply representing either a cardinal tenet of Renaissance humanism; nor is he merely echoing the kind of slogan commonplace enough in the Enlightenment for a Gottsched to champion. Rather, what Wagner is insisting upon is of the essence of the progressive, liberal, outlook as it has recurred, again at least since the Sophists, down to more recent philosophers of the likes of Bertrand Russell, Max Horkheimer, or Jürgen Habermas. Similarly, Faust's rejoinder — "Wenn ihr's nicht fühlt, ihr werdet's nicht erjagen" (534) — is not merely a repetition of a cardinal doctrine of the *Sturm und Drang*, nor just another version of Shaftesbury's theory of "inner form." Rather Faust is articulating a view, held at least since Gorgias and more and more prevalent in the advertising industry of our own day, that people are best managed by an appeal to their feelings. In fact, it is Wagner's belief in the progressive accumulation of knowledge that most clearly signals his representative, diachronic function. He spells out in "Vor dem Tor" to Faust his vision of the passing-on of learned tradition:

> Wenn du, als Jüngling, deinen Vater ehrst,
> So wirst du gern von ihm empfangen;
> Wenn du, als Mann, die Wissenschaft *vermehrst*,
> So kann dein Sohn zu höhrem Ziel gelangen.
>
> (1060–63; my emphasis)

And it is precisely this stolidly one-sided quantitative approach of his that, as Mephistopheles, in Act 2 of Part Two, slyly insinuates to the Baccalaureus (in his ambiguous use of *Beschlagner*), is Wagner's intellectual weak spot:

> Doch Euer Meister, das ist ein Beschlagner:
> Wer kennt ihn nicht, den edlen Doktor Wagner,
> Den Ersten jetzt in der gelehrten Welt!
> Er ist's allein, der sie zusammenhält,
> Der Weisheit täglicher *Vermehrer*.
>
> (6642–46; my emphasis)

In this (for *Faust*, wholly characteristic) way, two of the fundamental categories in Western thought from Aristotle to Kant (Quality and Quantity) are re-presented in vivid, dramatic terms.

There is, as has been noted, a widespread misconception of Gretchen's character: she is too often seen as the totally innocent victim

(Jantz 1978, 31). But no less misleading is the related, and equally widespread, misconception (in which Jantz himself participates) that she is, in some sense, "natural" and culture-free: "she is," claims Jantz, "as much confined to [her natural environment] as a plant is to its soil" (33). Gretchen's little world is actually as far from being "natural" as it is from being innocent. It is clear, for example, from Faust's first exchange with her (2605–08) that we are in a world of rigid sociocultural role-playing, in which the title "Fräulein" is reserved for those of a higher class than Gretchen's. And Faust has entered this world via "Auerbachs Keller" and "Hexenküche," in both of which scenes coarse, violent feeling has been barely held in check by recourse to the culturally-determined forms of, respectively, drunkenness and the infantile pursuit of speciously rejuvenating thrills. Gretchen is, in fact, presented as steeped in traditional, conventional, cultural forms which, like her church-going, form the narrow limits of her — initially, very proper — behavior. It is entirely characteristic of her, for instance, that she should, in "Der Nachbarin Haus," repudiate Mephisto's lewd suggestions with the prim rejoinder, "Das ist des Landes nicht der Brauch" (2949); that she should take such pride in her economically solid, respectable background (3116–18); and that the anxious question about Faust's religious position should be formed in conventional terms of taking communion (3425–26). And the strong cultural overtones of Gretchen's character, especially in her relationship with Faust, transcend the socio-economic context which Georg Lukács adduced in describing her fate as "die Tragödie des verführten Bürgermädchens [. . .] unter den vielen Übergriffen des verkommenen Feudalismus" (226). Whether or not the Gretchen episode is a *Kontrafaktur* of the patriarchal idyll of the *Song of Songs* (as recently suggested [Simpson, 16]), it is clear that she is, like the other characters of this drama, in part a symbolic figure (Atkins, 73). In, for instance, the short scene, "Dom" (3776–84), we are witness to terrible remorse on Gretchen's part: a mixture of guilt, and grief, and fear; in other words, that characteristically Western (Christian) mode of feeling — of acknowledging present responsibility for past behavior — that Nietzsche was out, with his doctrine of *Vergessen*, to undermine and destroy, as a psychological correlate of Western (Platonic) idealism which makes us ashamed of our own "imperfections" in action. Likewise, in the harrowing final scene, "Kerker," when Faust returns to save Gretchen and finds her delirious, though determined to accept the death-penalty imposed on her for killing her illegitimate child by Faust as penance for the guilt she feels at her many transgressions of her moral code — we are witness (as in the case of Ottilie in *Die Wahlverwandtschaften*) to the wholly Western conviction that loss (at its extreme, of life) has redemptive power. For Schopenhauer, this was "a clear and vivid presentation" of "Verneinung des Willens" (*Die Welt als Wille und Vorstellung*, Book 1, section 68). Surely its more obvious meaning for a Western audience would be that of a peculiarly Christian conception of ethical responsibility, of "blame," in the words of a contemporary philosopher, as "the charac-teristic reaction of the [Christian] morality system":

> The remorse or self-reproach of guilt [. . .] is the characteristic first-personal reaction within the system, and if an agent never felt such sentiments, he would not belong to the morality system or be a full moral agent in its terms. (Williams, 177, 198)

Gretchen, then, is as much a (diachronic) cultural construct as any other of the characters in the play.

If, on the one hand, the diachronic stamp of the characters, and the frequent hints strewn across the text, encourage the reader/spectator to recall from the Western cultural tradition parallels to the play's dra-matic action and thematic import, the closely-woven texture of the work's highly-wrought rhetorical and aesthetic structure ensures, on the other, that the reader is restrained from making any arbitrary asso-ciations. For, clearly, what is adduced must not violate the form of the play, because in that case the reader/spectator's attention would be taken outside, rather than retained within, the work of art, and aes-thetic interest would yield to an historico-intellectual concern. The "playful cross-references" that Fairley discerned (drawing on Wil-loughby's conception of the play's "morphology") are, as Jantz puts it, "woven into the texture of the play" (Fairley, 81–82; Jantz 1978, 102).

Moreover, while the action of Part One is held together by the headlong rush of its episodic structure, Part Two follows an *ordo natu-ralis* that lends it a sense of fundamental cohesion. We move from an allegorical presentation of Society in Act 1, through the search for em-bodiment, undertaken by the Mind released by the social fostering of reflexion (Humphrey, 51–52), in Act 2, to the joys and dangers of achieved embodiment in beautiful form in Act 3; in Act 4, empowered by aesthetic experience and imbued with a profound sense of form, Faust seeks, through violent struggle, the power to impose order, which he achieves, with the usual mixed results, in Act 5. And each act is held in the controlled arc of a series of near-climaxes until the final climactic crisis of the last act. This overarching structure is underpinned by a variety of rhetorical devices: by the "interlude" connecting groups of scenes, in the way "Wald und Höhle" marks a transition in Faust from flirtation with Gretchen to guilt-ridden seduction (Jantz 1978,

93, 97); by the diverse use of internal parallels (Jantz 1978, xxi):
Faust's debate with Wagner, for instance, is mirrored in both Mephisto's with the Student and Faust's own dialogue with the Devil —
just as the same or similar statements are put into the mouths of different, often contrasting, characters (compare Wagner in lines 558–9 and
601 with Mephisto in lines 1787 and 1582), creating a sense of overlap
and basic coherence. And these parallels extend across not only Part
One but the play as a whole: in Act 2, for instance, we return in "Rittersaal" to the concerns of "Vorspiel auf dem Theater," just as in the
opening scene of the final act, we return, like the Wanderer, to the little
world of Part One. So densely organized are these interconnections
that at whatever significant point we strike the verbal surface of *Faust*,
we are able to follow up a pattern of meaning running through the
whole play (Willoughby 1970, 102). Myriads of leitmotifs create an
intensely thick surface, across which the most distant parts are drawn
tightly together (Requadt, 25–26). In the very second line of the play
(in the dedicatory prologue, "Zueignung") appears the word *trüb*, for
example, with synonyms *Dunst und Nebel* just five lines later. The poet
is creating out of vague, opaque depths and bringing his creation to
light. This process of creation — from the murky depths from which all
life issues (and to which it may fall and return) — almost always underlies the pervasive light/dark imagery of the play. *Trüb* denotes the
middle stage, as it were — vague, half-lit, dreary — the human condition, caught between the light of heaven and the gloom of hell. So,
when Faust complains of the twilight in his "narrow, Gothic room"
(400–1), the reader/spectator hears an extra resonance by virtue of this
network of interconnections — just as, at the very end of the play,
Gretchen's description of the dead Faust as "[der] nicht mehr
Getrübte" (12074) harks back to the Angels' celebration of the risen
Christ, who is said to have endured "die betrübende [. . .] Prüfung" of
life and death on earth (759–61). In much the same way, the motifs of
"knowing-by-description" (*erkennen*) and "knowing-by-acquaintance"
(*begreifen, fassen*) — those "two souls" in Faust's breast (1112) — are
brought together very late in the play, indicating the slow process of
integration that Faust undergoes. Whereas in "Nacht" Faust alternates
on the one hand between longing for intellectual insight —

> Daß ich erkenne, was die Welt
> Im Innersten zusammenhält,
> Schau' alle Wirkenskraft und Samen
>
> (382–4)

and, on the other, sensuous prehension — "Wo fass' ich dich, unendliche Natur?" (455) — in the heroic monologue in which he defies "Sorge" shortly before his death in Act 5, he articulates his hard-won belief in the human capacity to understand the world by virtue of a co-ordination of *both* modes of apprehension:

> Er stehe fest und sehe hier sich um;
> Dem Tüchtigen ist diese Welt nicht stumm.
> Was braucht er in die Ewigkeit zu schweifen!
> Was er erkennt, läßt sich ergreifen.
>
> (11445–8)

Such word and phrase echoes, heightened throughout by the magical power of Goethe's poetry (Stephenson 1993), hold together, in a finely-spun web, a vast rhetorical structure. But it does not follow, simply because "we ultimately come to see [the parts] as all co-existing synchronically in the greater whole," that they "are more readily perceived synchronically than diachronically" (Lamport, 127–30). The two tendencies are manifestly at work simultaneously.

Since my aim in this essay is the limited one of corroborating an already available theory about the play, and since "the fallacy of misplaced completeness" (Willoughby 1973, 110) is to be avoided here as elsewhere, I shall attempt to give final reinforcement to the validity of the approach by offering a synoptic survey of some aspects of the play which seem, to me at least, to be as paradigmatic of Goethe's diachronic intent as those already analyzed by Wilkinson (in 1957, 1971, and 1972). The scene "Saal des Thrones," from Act 1 of Part Two, for instance, introduces us to the "great world" of top-level politics: a "cabinet-meeting" presents us with a paradigm of political debate. The Kanzler, who emphasizes the stress and strains the law is subject to, outlines a catalogue of the perennial problems of society: the impotence of the individual in a society lacking in respect for the law (4778–81), where crime often goes unpunished (4787–90), a sense of morality is missing (4792–802), and the legal system itself is corrupt (4805–6). The Heermeister stresses the breakdown of social order (4814–30), and the Schatzmeister, the consequent dissolution of the economic system (4831–50). There then follows the (to us very familiar, but by no means merely "modern") cut-and-thrust of argument and counter-argument about how to deal with these social ills. Mephisto puts the progressive point of view, urging a rational solution; the Kanzler urges the conservative case for caution, and reliance on trust and authority (rather than Nature and Reason). Mephisto, in insinuating money as both the core problem (4890) and the key solution (4927), reduces the complexity of the socio-political problems to economic, indeed simply financial, terms. Adroitly, and in perfect consonance with that contempt for humankind he voices in "Prolog im Himmel," he appeals, like any demagogue, to delusory confidence building (4877–84). And to the implicit question, "Where is the money to come from?", he answers by appealing to faith in hidden (that is, unknown) resources and human resourcefulness (4893–96), before deploying his *tour de force* by handing over to an *expert* (represented here by that age-old wise counsel, the Astrologer) (4947–48), whose pretentious (and meaningless) jargon (4955–70) eventually helps close the deal. Here, then, as in the trade in fashion and fantasy in "Weitläufiger Saal" or the discussion of money as, at bottom, a mere social convention in "Lustgarten," recurrent economic debates are re-presented that are co-extensive with the history of Western civilization. Just as there is nothing necessarily "modern" about love being for sale or the use of eroticism as a marketing tactic ("Weitläufiger Saal"), and just as the artificial arousal of economic needs was as much a part of everyday life in the Roman Empire as in our own day — so, too, money as a steering-mechanism in the service of socio-political ends invites a diachronic response: after all, it is common enough for the decidedly non-expert Gretchen to comment on the phenomenon in "Abend" (2802–4).

Similarly, just as the exchange between the Baccalaureus and Mephisto, in "Hochgewölbtes enges gotisches Zimmer," rehearses a debate stretching back over millennia, between brilliant innovation on the one hand and sound continuity on the other, so, too, in the historico-mythical "Klassische Walpurgisnacht," we hear resonances of all the cults, myths, and theories of growth and evolution that have made up the long Western preoccupation with the "Eros, der alles begonnen!" (8479). For the "Klassische Walpurgisnacht" represents that groping of mind after embodiment (7114–5) that Ernst Cassirer dubbed "symbolic form," in which the decisive synthesis of Mind and World is undertaken. Nowhere is this clearer than in the debate between the pre-Socratic philosophers, Thales and Anaxagoras, with its obvious diachronic relevance, in the scene "Am obern Peneios, wie zuvor." The aspect of natural formation expounded by Anaxagoras is the violent, revolutionary, eruption from below, as in Seismos's breakthrough (7570, 7865–68). Thales' theory, by contrast, is emphatically evolutionary (7861–64). Far from being an apology for Goethe's own commitment to a (tempered) version of geological Neptunism; and equally far from being merely a sideways look at contemporary politics in the 1830s, this exchange (along with its far-reaching political implications) reflects a "great geological controversy," one that is not only as old as speculation on the origin of the earth: it remains today, though in more refined terms, a live issue in geology (Hallam, 180). It is also alive in the on-going challenge to classical evolutionary Darwinism, posed by the Gouldian theory that proposes sustained stasis giving way, in unpredictable ways, to the sudden appearance of new phenomena. It is entirely typical of the diachronic modality of Goethe's *Faust* in general, and of the diachronic response invited by the "Klassische Walpurgisnacht" in particular, that Mephisto's advice to Homunculus, to the effect that embodiment presupposes error, should reflect so exactly the evolutionist doctrine that development progresses "by the curious procedure of making random copying errors" (Gardner, 123):

> Damit man seiner Kunst und Gunst sich freue,
> Erschafft er gleich ein Dutzend neue.
> Wenn du nicht irrst, kommst du nicht zu Verstand.
> Willst du entstehn, entsteh auf eigne Hand!
>
> (7845–49)

In Act 3, similarly, there is no reason why in the stage-direction (9902+), we should plump for Byron in order to fix the identity of the figure we *think* we see in the dead Euphorion: "man glaubt in dem Toten eine bekannte Gestalt zu erblicken." We need not *exclude* Byron, of course; but it is far more in keeping with the diachronic temper of the play if we keep our mind open to any typical representation of that recurring sensibility we call Romantic, from Icarus to Scott Fitzgerald. A similarly diachronic reading is called for in the scene "Auf dem Vorgebirge" from Act 4, where Faust comes face-to-face with the brutal realities of warfare. This is, as Mephisto characteristically reminds his audience, an ever-recurring phenomenon (10770–73). And we hear age-old debates on battle-tactics (10345–74), the value of new methods of destruction (10425–54), the crucial role of leadership (10462–68), the aggression, greed, and endurance necessary for the conduct of war (10511–46), the employment of deception (10555–64), and the evaporation of morality in crisis (10705–6, 10709): in a word, the topics common to Julius Caesar's accounts of his campaigns, to Konrad Kyeser's *Bellifortis* (of 1405), and Clausewitz's *Vom Kriege* (see Gat). No less diachronic in appeal is Faust's final monologue (11559–86) in which he envisions his project of land reclamation as providing a Utopia for succeeding generations (11574–78). Faust's vision is the Western vision of a free society, founded on individual and collective responsibility:

> Eröffn' ich Räume vielen Millionen,
> Nicht sicher zwar, doch tätig-frei zu wohnen.
> [. . .]
> Solch ein Gewimmel möcht' ich sehn,
> Auf freiem Grund mit freiem Volke stehn.
>
> (11563–64, 11579–80)

In citing these lines in his 1936 lecture, "Freud und die Zukunft," in celebration of Freud's eightieth birthday, Thomas Mann claims that Freud was thinking of Faust's "cultural work" of land reclamation when he wrote: "Wo Es war, soll Ich werden. Es ist eine Kulturarbeit etwa wie die Trockenlegung der Zuydersee" (Freud, 86). But, since Faust's land reclamation is an amplification of the age-old topos of the benefits of self-limitation — of "cultivating one's garden," in Voltaire's famous phrase — it is a moot point whether Freud needed to think of Goethe in this connection at all. Reclamation is, after all, a paradigm of the engineering tradition of the West, from the Emperor Claudius's harbor at Ostia to Charles I's ordering in 1640 one of the greatest public works ever proposed in England — the draining of a vast area of low-lying marshland surrounding the Wash (which first brought Oliver Cromwell to national attention as a leading protester against the scheme). What is reflected in Faust's project is not the expression of Goethe's personal theory of how to combat modern hyperactivity (Wittkowski, 263); nor is it an instance of a "Dialektik der Aufklärung" (Borchmeyer, 561). What Faust is evoking, rather, is the typically Western application of science to the optimum conversion of the resources of nature to benefit humanity: such engineering feats have contributed, historically, to human welfare by providing the goods of shelter and comfort and by making human life as pleasant and satisfying as possible — precisely the objective Faust has in mind (see Mieth).

The fact that the opening lines of the play — the dedicatory poem, "Zueignung" — constitute "a prologue in a European theatrical tradition," one that participates in the ancient rhetorical gambit of the *Bescheidenheitstopos* (Atkins, 11), naturally opens up a diachronic vista which transcends the biographical context, which Goethe himself (in a letter to Reinhard of 22 June 1808) dismissed as irrelevant. Although lines 11–14 refer to the poet-as-persona they also refer to any ("implied") reader, for whom, "like any old-half-forgotten tale," *Faust* will evoke memories of a time and of feelings long since passed:

> Gleich einer alten, halbverklungnen Sage
> Kommt erste Lieb' und Freundschaft mit herauf;

Der Schmerz wird neu, es wiederholt die Klage
Des Lebens labyrinthisch irren Lauf.

(11–14)

And, by comparing his poem to the Aeolian Harp of ancient mythology (28), the poet makes clear that, just as the harp only makes music when the wind passes through it, so, too, this poem only has import when the inner life — of poet and reader/listener alike — are projected on to it. The result is an emotional release for both poet and reader, an externalization of feeling that is accompanied by a changed perception of the Past-in-the-Present and the Present-in the-Past:

Ein Schauer faßt mich, Träne folgt den Tränen,
Das strenge Herz, es fühlt sich mild und weich;
Was ich besitze, seh' ich wie im Weiten,
Und was verschwand, wird mir zu Wirklichkeiten.

(29–32)

Clearly, the past that becomes present is not restricted to the private life of feeling: by virtue of the diachronic perspective opened up here (the conception of poetry, for instance, as expressive of otherwise inexpressible feeling is as old as Pindar), what this prologue announces is a work of art to which the appropriate response is an aesthetic one, in the diachronic mode. Equally diachronic is the discussion in "Vorspiel auf dem Theater" between three figures, each of whom argues from a different, but equally traditional point of view (see Binder): the poet (who, the retention of the stanza-form suggests, is the persona of "Zueignung") — quite unrealistically — argues for art for art's sake (59–74); the Lustige Person, for sheer entertainment value (167–73); the Direktor, for box-office success (37–8, 41–2, 57–8). The reader, already prepared to take an aesthetic attitude, is now ready for the rhetorical devices that make for theatrical effect: a mixture of entertainment and art. In addition, the diachronic relevance of what is to come is sustained throughout the "Vorspiel." The point that the audience is well-informed is repeated (45–46; 116), as if to underline its awareness that all the positions taken in the "Vorspiel" about the relationship between the work of art and its recipients are commonplaces of Western aesthetic debate. In the third, and last, of the introductory prologues, the framework of the play as a whole is given: we move from the limitations of the *theatrum mundi* of "Vorspiel auf dem Theater" to limitless Heaven in the "Prolog im Himmel," from which life is seen not as an incomprehensible labyrinth, as the individual views it (as in "Zueignung," line 14), but as a harmonious whole. What we are about to witness as the play proper is to be seen *sub specie aeternitatis* — but only as the Western tradition has conceived it. The patently obvious allusion to the Book of Job in this scene, like the familiar theological doctrines enunciated (which are entirely consonant with orthodox Christian teaching [Atkins, 30]), makes the relevant diachronic context entirely clear. The world on to which the Archangels gaze is the (to the West) familiar *cosmos* of Greek metaphysics, bound by polarity:

> Und schnell und unbegreiflich schnelle
> Dreht sich umher der Erde Pracht;
> Es wechselt Paradieseshelle
> Mit tiefer, schauervoller Nacht.
>
> (251–53)

It is shown, too, as is entirely traditional, to be in process of Becoming:

> Das Werdende, das ewig wirkt und lebt,
> Umfass' euch mit der Liebe holden Schranken.
>
> (346–47)

And it evinces that beauty which the Greek word "cosmos" implies, as the Lord reminds his Archangels:

> Doch ihr, die echten Göttersöhne,
> Erfreut euch der lebendig reichen Schöne!
>
> (344–45)

Moreover, the anthropological views aired, respectively, by the Lord and Mephistopheles are equally traditional, and neatly encompass the opposed tendencies in the long history of the Western debate on Man: on the one hand, his capacity for development; on the other, his inclination to stasis:

> Ein guter Mensch in seinem dunklen Drange
> Ist sich des rechten Weges wohl bewußt.
>
> (328–9)

> Der kleine Gott der Welt bleibt stets von gleichem Schlag,
> Und ist so wunderlich als wie am ersten Tag.
>
> (281–2)

In reflecting in this prologue the close co-operation of God and Devil, of Good and Evil, Goethe is not deviating a jot from the Biblical tradition (Frye, 111; Scholem, 57). Rather he is opening up a long vista on what he called the still-problematic nature of Christian-Judaic theology in "die Geschichte des Worts Gottes" (HA 12, 232).

This same harmony with basic Judeo-Christian doctrines, if not with specific dogma, is evident, too, in what might be helpfully termed the "Epilogue" of the play, following Faust's death in Act 5. In the final two scenes of the play — "Grablegung" and "Bergschluchten" — in which Goethe draws on traditional images of the Day of Judgement taken from mystery-plays, Dante's *Paradiso,* and such painters as Cranach, we are afforded a peep in to the after-life *as Christian legend and iconography have envisaged it*: mountains, forest, hermits, and hovering angels (11844–53). In "Grablegung" we witness the struggle of Good and Evil over the soul, in which — as our religious tradition would have it — Good triumphs. Life and death are presented in Christian terms: life is a mere prelude (11604–11), death similarly. What we hear, from the Fathers, in the final scene, are traditional Western conceptions of ways of approaching God: through mortification of the flesh (11854–65), contemplation of nature (11866–89), love of one's fellow human beings (11890–93, 11898–909), and God's grace and forgiveness (11934–41, 12020–75). In a word, we are witness to the life of the spirit, *as the West has conceived it* (11922–25) — summed up in the mysterious *Chorus Mysticus*:

> Alles Vergängliche
> Ist nur ein Gleichnis;
> Das Unzulängliche,
> Hier wird's Ereignis;
> Das Unbeschreibliche,
> Hier ist's getan;
> Das Ewig-Weibliche
> Zieht uns hinan.
>
> (12104–11)

Here is the Western image of a loving God Who takes the initiative and saves us, the fallen and the sinful — a God in Whom "feminine" tenderness is so central a quality that the Mater Gloriosa co-exists with Him as co-redeemer:

> Blicket auf zum Retterblick,
> Alle reuig Zarten,
> Euch zu seligem Geschick
> Dankend umzuarten.
> Werde jeder beßre Sinn
> Dir zum Dienst erbötig;
> Jungfrau, Mutter, Königin,
> Göttin, bleibe gnädig!
>
> (12096–103)

The Doctor Marianus's "earnest tenderness," in the formulaic series of epithets that might well have been taken straight from the Kabbalistic *Zohar*'s attempt to describe the Shekhinah ("Virgin, Mother, Queen, Goddess"), opens up a long diachronic perspective that at once is Christian and transcends Christian dogma, by articulating the deeper religious roots from which it sprang and of which it bears the characteristic stamp. The religious discourse that accompanies Faust's ascent indeed parallels both medieval iconographic conceptions of Mariology and Dante, but the neo-Platonic notes sounded in it do not "demythologize" Catholicism in any way (*pace* Schmidt, 300 and 402). Rather, the blend of pagan and more familiarly Christian elements mirrors the West's long religious history. And that Faust is saved at the end does not simply reflect the fact that the legendary Faustus was often portrayed as escaping the terms of his pact with the devil, either by his own cunning or by the intervention of the Virgin Mary (Mason, 1). Its deeper significance lies in the fact that in the Western religious tradition, it is in God's nature to give salvation — it is "son métier," as Heine put it:

> The doctrine of grace in Christianity meant that there was no calculable road from moral effort to salvation; salvation lay beyond merit, and men's efforts, even their moral efforts, were not the measure of God's love. (Williams, 195)

Faust's salvation, then, in its traditional Christian orthodoxy, is entirely consonant with the diachronic modality of Goethe's drama.

In a letter to Zelter of 1 June 1831, written shortly before completing his *Faust*, Goethe, employing a variant of his much-used formula of the "open secret," confessed to the great difficulty he had encountered in giving "an inner skeleton" flesh and even clothing:

> [. . .] ein solches inneres, lebendiges Knochengeripp mit Sehnen, Fleisch und Oberhaupt zu bekleiden, auch wohl dem fertig Hingestellten, noch einige Mantelfalten umzuschlagen, damit alles zusammen ein offenes Rätsel bleibe, die Menschen fort und fort ergötze und ihnen zu schaffen mache.

In identifying this skeleton with the *Elementarhorizont* of the work (i.e., the limits of the kind of interpretation the work invites and will bear), Schadewaldt provided a useful orientation in *Faust* studies (165 and 204); and it might not be too bold, in view of what is argued above, to suggest that the fundamental organizing structure (the "skeleton") of *Faust* is precisely its doubled construction, both synchronic and diachronic. (That would seem to be what Goethe is getting at, at least, in another letter, written to Boisserée on 22 October 1826.)

In any case, "it is precisely in the quality of sophisticated introspection," as Barker Fairley put it in 1955, "that *Faust* comes nearest to the poetic writing of today" (108); and, it must be said, to that distracted, bewildered sensibility that is so routinely designated at the turn of the millennium as "post-modernist": that vague feeling of being at the fag-end of a long civilization, adopting a "retro-chic" style and winking ironically at earlier styles and modes. At a point in history when "time gallops withal" — indeed, to quote the sub-title of James Gleick's 1999 book, *Faster*, we seem to be caught up in "the Acceleration of Just About Everything" — it is perhaps salutary to recall that this twin anxiety about the relevance of past culture on the one hand and, on the other, what Goethe dubbed, in his own coining, the *"veloziferisch"* speeding-up of time (HA 12, 389), was shared, and much debated, in the eighteenth century. Goethe's own re-formulation of the problem is very much in tune with his clearly diachronic intent in *Faust*:

> Alles Gescheite ist schon gedacht worden, man muß nur versuchen, es noch einmal zu denken. (HA 12, 415)

Faust stands opposed, then, to the kind of temporal parochialism that, losing a sense of historical perspective, sees only change, never continuity; and to the kind of stupidity that the "Lemuren" represent in the final act: devoid of memory, they lack any sense of direction (or value). In its passionate re-formulation of the heritage of the West, Goethe's play is more than "modern" (though it is born of modern anxieties in respect of the past). In the solidity of its rootedness in the long, diachronic dimension of our shared cultural tradition, the play — for all its "romantic elements" — has that sound, "healthy" quality that Goethe famously dubbed the Classical.

My aim has been the limited one of corroboration; and, of course, corroboration is not confirmation, let alone "proof." For that degree of certainty a good deal more work needs to be done in the future. And, since one of the unique qualities claimed for Goethe's *Faust* is "the prospective open-endedness of Goethe's paradigms in respect of the future," allowing traditions with which Goethe himself may not have been familiar to be accommodated (Wilkinson 1972, 154), it is perhaps inevitable that such work will be undertaken, though never completed.

Works Cited

Atkins, Stuart. *Goethe's Faust: A Literary Analysis*. Cambridge, MA: Harvard UP, 1958.

Binder, Alwin. *Das Vorspiel auf dem Theater: Poetologische und geschichtsphilosophische Aspekte in Goethes Faust-Vorspiel*. Bonn: Bouvier, 1969.

Binswanger, Hans Christoph, Malte Faber, and Reiner Manstetten. "The Dilemma of Modern Man and Nature: An Exploration of the Faustian Imperative." *Ecological Economics*. 2 (1990). 197–223.

Borchmeyer, Dieter. *Weimarer Klassik: Portrait einer Epoche*. Weinheim: Beltz Athenäum, 1994.

Butler, E. M. *The Fortunes of Faust*. Cambridge: Cambridge UP, 1952.

———. *The Myth of the Magus*. Cambridge: Cambridge UP, 1948.

Destro, Alberto. "Faust, Johannes und die Geschichte." *Studii germanici*. NS 25 (1997). 7–23.

Durrani, Osman. "Biblical Borrowings in Goethe's *Faust*: A Historical Survey of their Interpretation." *The Modern Language Review*. 72 (1977). 829–44.

Fairley, Barker. *Goethe's "Faust": Six Essays*. Oxford: Clarendon P, 1953.

Freud, Sigmund. *Neue Folge der Vorlesungen zur Einführung in die Psychoanalyse*. No. 31. "Die Zerlegung der psychischen Persönlichkeit." In *Gesammelte Werke*, Vol. 15. London: Imago, 1940. 62–86.

Frye, Northrop. *The Great Code: The Bible and Literature*. London: Routledge and Kegan Paul, 1982.

Gaier, Ulrich. *Johann Wolfgang Goethe: Faust-Dichtungen*. Vol. 3 *Kommentar II*. Stuttgart: Reclam, 1999.

Gardner, Martin. *The Ambidextrous Universe: Mirror Asymmetry and Time-Reversed Worlds*. New York: Macmillan, 1979.

Gat, Azar. *Origins of Military Thought*. Oxford: Clarendon P, 1989.

Gray, Ronald. *Goethe the Alchemist: A Study of Alchemical Symbolism in Goethe's Literary and Scientific Works*. Cambridge: Cambridge UP, 1952.

Hallam, Anthony. *Great Geological Controversies*. Oxford: Oxford UP, 1983.

Holsovsky-Weill, Hanna. "Heinrich Faust: Zur Abweichung von der Tradition bei Goethe." *Jahrbuch des Freien Deutschen Hochstifts*. 1978. 165–72.

Humphrey, Nicholas. *Consciousness Regained: Chapters in the Development of Mind*. Oxford: Oxford UP, 1983.

Jantz, Harold. "Goethe, Faust, Alchemy, and Jung." *The German Quarterly*. 35. No.2 (1962). 129–41.

———. *The Form of Faust*. London: Johns Hopkins UP, 1978.

Kennedy, James. *Conversations on Religion with Lord Byron*. London: Murray, 1830.

Kruse, Jens. *Der Tanz der Zeichen: Poetische Struktur und Geschichte in Goethes Faust II*. Frankurt am Main: Suhrkamp, 1985.

Lamport, F. J. "Synchrony and Diachrony in *Faust*." *Oxford German Studies*. 15 (1984). 118–31.

Lukács, Georg. *Goethe und seine Zeit*. Berlin: de Gruyter, 1953.

Marlowe, Christopher. *Dr Faustus*. Ed. Roma Gill. London: A & C Black; New York: W. W. Norton. 1989.

Mason, Eudo C. *Goethe's Faust: Its Genesis and Purport*. Berkeley, CA: U of California P, 1967.

Mieth, Gunther. "Fausts letzter Monolog: Poetische Strukturen einer geschichtlichen Vision." *Goethe-Jahrbuch*. 97 (1980). 90–102.

Pelikan, Jaroslaw. *Faust — the Theologian*. New Haven: Yale UP, 1995.

Reed, T. J. *Goethe*. Oxford: Oxford UP, 1984.

Requadt, Paul. *Goethe's "Faust I": Leitmotivik und Architektur*. Munich: Fink, 1972.

Schadewaldt, Wolfgang. *Goethestudien*. Zurich: Artemis, 1962.

Schantz, Reinhard. "Goethes 'Urworte. Orphisch' in ihrer geschichtsphilosophischen Bedeutung." *Zeitschrift für Religions- und Geistesgeschichte*. 3 (1951). 38–53.

Schanze, Helmut. *Goethes Dramatik: Theater der Erinnerung*. Tübingen: Francke, 1989.

Schmidt, Jochen. *Goethes Faust, Erster und Zweiter Teil: Grundlagen — Werk — Wirkung*. Munich: Beck, 1999.

Scholem, G. G. *On the Mystical Shape of the Godhead: Basic Concepts in the Kabbalah*. New York: Schocken Books, 1991.

Simpson, James. *Goethe and Patriarchy: Faust and the Fates of Desire*. Oxford: Legenda, 1999.

Stephenson, R. H. "Die Aneignung des Fremden durch ästhetische Gestaltung anhand von Goethes 'Faust.'" In *Praxis interkultureller Germanistik*. Ed. Bernd Thum and Gonthier-Louis Fink. Munich: iudicium, 1993. 789–97.

———. *Goethe's Conception of Knowledge and Science*. Edinburgh: Edinburgh: UP, 1995.

Strich, Fritz. *Goethes Faust*. Berne, Munich: Francke, 1964.

Whitehead, A. N. *Adventures in Ideas*. 2nd ed. Toronto: Free Press, 1967.

Wilkinson, Elizabeth M. "The Theological Basis of Faust's *Credo*." *German Life and Letters*. NS 10 (1957). 229–39.

———. "Faust in der Logosszene." In *Dichtung, Sprache, Gesellschaft: Akten des IV. Internationalen Germanisten-Kongresses 1970 in Princeton*. Ed. Victor Lange and Hans-Gert Roloff. Frankfurt am Main: Suhrkamp, 1971. 115–24.

———. "Goethe's *Faust*: Tragedy in the Diachronic Mode." *Publications of the English Goethe Society*. NS 42 (1972). 116–74.

Williams, Bernard. *Ethics and the Limits of Philosophy*. London: Fontana, 1985.

Willoughby, L. A. "Goethe's *Faust*: A Morphological Approach." In L. A. Willoughby and E. M. Wilkinson. *Goethe: Poet and Thinker*. 2nd ed. London: Arnold, 1970. 95–117.

———. "On Editing and Commenting." *German Life and Letters*. NS 26 (1973). 93–111.

Wittkowksi, Wolfgang. "Goethe, Schopenhauer und Fausts Schlußvision." *Goethe Yearbook*. 5 (1990). 233–68.

Translating *Faust:*
A Personal Statement

David Luke

THIS CONTRIBUTION belonged in its original form to the context of
my own translation of *Faust: Part One* (1987). In the last few
pages of my introduction to that edition I tried to formulate the assumptions and priorities which, with hindsight, appeared to underlie
my version of the text. I was guided by the same general principles in
translating *Part Two* a few years later (1994), and I would not wish
now to retract any of my earlier brief manifesto or to make any substantial addition to it, beyond some appropriate updating. In what follows, I have quoted and analysed a few sample passages from one or
two of the numerous English versions, especially of Part One, which
have been attempted since the work originally appeared in 1808, not as
part of a systematic historical survey but rather for purposes of illustration and clarification. In any such assessment, as an interested party, it
would be hard for me to pretend to a decent degree of objectivity. For
the choices translators constantly have to make between different possibilities or impossibilities, the priorities they must constantly adopt or
renounce, are matters of personal judgement, of a kind that is almost
undiscussable.

In fact, paradoxically, I found the existence of so many predecessors
in the enterprise encouraging rather than daunting: when one actually
examines the other versions, the stimulus to try and do it differently is
nearly irresistible. We may hope that Faust himself, contemplating the
opening of St. John's Gospel, entertained no disrespect for his colleague and contemporary Martin Luther when he too felt this challenge
and decided "Ich muß es anders übersetzen" (1227). It is true that his
career as a translator was short-lived: having considered three alternative renderings of the first five words he was interrupted by the Devil
and promptly sold himself to him. In the beginning was the word, and
what have translators made of it? The intractability of the problem
arises, I would suggest, from the constant conflict between three absolute requirements: (1) that a poem such as *Faust*, having been written
almost entirely in rhymed or other stylised verse-forms, must be trans-

lated (even in the late twentieth century) into similarly rhymed or stylised verse-forms; (2) that it must nevertheless be translated into an English of the twentieth century, not of the nineteenth or earlier; and (3) that the essential elements of what can be perceived to be Goethe's meaning must be conveyed without significant distortion. My starting-point has been, rightly or wrongly, to treat all three of these propositions as self-evident, though they are perhaps in need of some further clarification.

On the first question, that of rhyme, I emphatically agree in principle with those translators (now, it seems, increasingly unfashionable) who have reproduced it throughout, and fundamentally disagree with those who have abandoned it altogether or used it only intermittently. If one is trying to offer something like an autonomous English "equivalent" of Goethe's text, and not merely the utilitarian reading-aid that may be appropriate to a bilingual edition, then one stands inescapably under formal demands similar — though they are less strict — to those imposed by Dante's *Divine Comedy* or Pushkin's *Eugene Onegin*. Dante has been put into English *terza rima* more than once with considerable virtuosity; as for Pushkin, Charles Johnston's prosodically meticulous and linguistically brilliant rendering of his relentlessly regular complex stanzas must surely stand as a model of what verse translation should and may rarely be. Goethe's schemes of rhyme and metre in most of *Faust* are more fluid and flexible, and some liberties may be taken with them, but they are still of the essence of the poem and must be imitated as closely as other considerations will allow. To use prose, or the kind of flat, rhymeless verse which is tantamount to prose, is simply a counsel of despair, an evasion of the main technical challenge. Half the point of what Goethe says is lost if it lacks the musical closure and neatness of the way he said it. As Walter Arndt succinctly puts it in an introductory essay to his strictly rhymed version: "[the rhyme] is part of the 'meaning' and the 'meaning' is part of it" (356), and "fidelity and prose are mutually exclusive goals" (360). Where one may differ is in some of the detailed applications of this fundamental principle. For example — given that English contains far fewer "feminine" word-endings than German or Russian, to say nothing of Italian — it seems to me neither possible nor desirable to conform to Goethe's regular alternation of masculine and feminine rhymes, even in a prosodically strict passage such as the *ottava rima* stanzas of "Dedication" (1–32). (A similar point is made by Walter Kaufmann, who also uses predominantly masculine rhyming.) In addition, I have used far fewer end-stopped lines than Goethe, and have not often (except, again, in a piece such as "Dedication") arranged the rhymes in exactly the same sequence as in the original or used exactly the same line-lengths. To es-chew these licences — that of fairly frequent overrunning, for exam-ple — seems to me to increase the difficulty of rhyming to a point at which too much else has to be sacrificed for the sake of it; rhyme be-comes, so to speak, too expensive.

This question of the cost of rhyme, of how expensive a luxury one is prepared to allow it to become, is one that constantly arises, and the answer must be a matter of personal judgement. The difficulty is cre-ated by the other two axiomatic constraints mentioned above, one of which is that of language and diction. Goethe's language was not ar-chaic to his contemporaries, and it is absurd to translate it today into poetic archaisms. The insidious pervasiveness of archaic sub-Shakespearean diction in English verse is even now very hard to resist altogether, but we should continue to try harder — asking ourselves, for instance, as a constant routine test: how would this word, or this phrase, sound to a present-day audience in the mouth of a present-day actor? If we answer that to either of them it would probably sound even slightly laughable, then like Faust himself we must try another word (or another phrase, another arrangement). Our imaginary actor should not only not be asked to say "methinks" as an equivalent of "mich dünkt," or to use "thou" and "ye" for the "du" and "ihr" which modern German has been fortunate enough to preserve: we should also not expect him to talk constantly in dustily poetic inversions (the ad-jective following the noun, for instance, or the negative following the verb). At the other extreme, however, we should avoid up-to-the-minute but rapidly dating colloquial jocularities and obtrusive neolo-gisms. The diction should be kept in a broad, quasi-timeless middle ground between the pallidly antiquated and the brashly modish. Worst of all is the incongruous mixture of the two. Better a discreet neutrality than the sudden jolt from one century to another, or from one register to another. Horace's dictum that art is the concealment of art must mean, in this context, that it should ideally be made impossible for the reader of a rhyme-pair to guess which word was chosen to rhyme with which. If he can guess this, then the chances are that the rhyme is too obtrusive, it has probably cost too much.

We come here to the problem of the third constraint, that of fidelity to the meaning — that is, to what I have advisedly called the essential meaning. Arndt, in this connection, is surely right in suggesting (361–62) that in the technical process of creating rhymed verse, many words or phrases are not so much primary ends in themselves as "acceptable fillers," co-opted into the poet's scheme for prosodic reasons. This seems to amount to a distinction between the primary semantic or expressive values in any given line or passage and its secondary or incidental details that have entered into combination with the main substance in one way or another. A translator's decision as to which elements are primary and which are secondary in any particular case will be a matter for his spontaneous aesthetic judgement. So will his decision on how much he can afford to pay for rhyme (and that is now to say, for suitable rhyming and suitable diction) in the currency of judicious paraphrase. His piety will incline him to treat every word of the German text as sacred, but he will find it necessary in practice to treat some as more sacred than others. He will also be compelled, in English, to use some degree of periphrasis or expansion, if only by the fact that his equivalent words are often several syllables shorter than their German originals (though the contrary can also be the case). How much can acceptably be modified, added, left out? Is not literalness, like rhymelessness, incompatible with fidelity in any sophisticated sense? What is the acceptable price for what effects and what fidelities? Translation is the art of the least intolerable sacrifice, of the instinctive choice between competing imperfections; it constantly exercises a kind of informed judgement which it is almost impossible to rationalize or to discuss with anyone else.

It follows, of course, that to compare other renderings with one's own is tedious as well as odious, but concrete examples are nevertheless the best way of making these general points clearer. For the main illustration I revert again to Walter Arndt, whose version starts from a sophisticated critical position and is particularly instructive as the most recent (1976) of a mere handful which seriously and thoroughgoingly attempt to reproduce Goethe's rhyming and metrical schemes in the unabridged whole of Parts One and Two. His translation of lines 315–35 is as follows:

THE LORD: As long as on the earth he lives,   315
     So long it shall not be forbidden.
     Man ever errs the while he strives.

MEPHISTOPHELES: My thanks to you; I've never hidden
     An old distaste for dealing with the dead.
     Give me a full-cheeked, fresh-faced lad!   320
     A corpse with me is just no dice,
     In this way I am like a cat with mice.

THE LORD: So be it; I shall not forbid it!
     Estrange this spirit from its primal source,
     Have licence, it you can but win it,   325

> To lead it down your path by shrewd resource;
> And stand ashamed when you must own perforce:
> A worthy soul through the dark urge within it
> Is well aware of the appointed course.

MEPHISTOPHELES: Maybe — but it has never lasted yet;   330
> I am by no means worried for my bet.
> And if I do achieve my stated perpent,
> You grant me the full triumph that I covet.
> Dust shall he swallow, aye, and love it,
> Like my old cousin, the illustrious serpent.   335

What I find unsatisfactory here are the archaisms ("ever," "the while," "aye," and the word-order in 315 and 334) and especially their incongruous combination with racy contemporary colloquialisms ("no dice") or bizarre quasi-Shakespearean inventions ("perpent"). In addition, "lad" and "worthy soul" have the wrong connotations, and "by no means worried for" is lame as well as colloquial. Imperfect rhyme, though almost wholly alien to Goethe, is difficult to avoid altogether, and to my ear "lad" rhyming with "dead" is at least tolerable as prosody if not as diction, but "he strives" rhyming with "he lives," in so famous and crucial a line, is not, and both these rhymes can be improved quite easily. Arndt gives unnecessarily high priority to ending his lines on the same word as Goethe, and to end-stopped lines generally; I should have preferred not only to avoid the imperfect rhymes but also to acknowledge, by simply shifting it from the rhyme-position, that there is no acceptable rhyme for "serpent." Moreover, although unlike Arndt I do not in general regard it as essential to preserve the exact order of Goethe's rhymes, it is particularly important in this passage to imitate the striking effect in 327–35 where he uses only two rhymes in nine lines (in the German the sound *-ust* recurs four times and *-ange* five; a similar rhyme-flow is achieved in Mephistopheles' later soliloquy, where the sound *-eben* is repeated six times in twelve lines, 1856–67). In my own version of the "Prologue in Heaven" passage (315–35) I have imitated this special effect and tried to steer round the other pitfalls, while also aiming at natural word-sequences and a broadly contemporary but suitable vocabulary. My rendering as "ancestress" of Goethe's now archaic word *Muhme* which in fact means cousin or aunt, is an instance of how an inessential detail of literal meaning may be sacrificed for what seems to be a more essential fidelity: in this case, to the nine-line flow of two rhymes.

One further short example is perhaps worth considering here. The first stanza of "Dedication" (a particularly intractable piece because of its prosodic strictness) ends with an instructive case of what Arndt calls the "filler" word. Goethe here (lines 7–8) writes:

> Mein Busen fühlt sich jugendlich erschüttert
> Vom Zauberhauch, der euren Zug umwittert.

Existing versions of this include the following:

> Deep stirs my heart, awakened, touched to song,
> As from a spell that flashes from your throng. (Wayne)

> My breast is stirred and feels with youthful pain
> The magic breath that hovers round your train. (Kaufmann)

> I feel youth's impulse grip my heart again
> At the enchantment wafting from your train. (Passage)

> What wafts about your train with magic glamour
> Is quickening my breast to youthful tremor. (Arndt)

My own rendering, I suppose, is based on (or can with hindsight be analysed into) the following judgements: (1) "umwittert" is probably the filler-word chosen to rhyme with "erschüttert." Its literal meaning suggests wind blowing about the "procession" of youthful memories which Goethe is apostrophizing, perhaps carrying their scent; but this literal meaning is of secondary importance, and "waft" is in any case a weak equivalent for it. (2) The literal meaning of "Zug" (procession, or less suitably "train") is also secondary; the memories are drifting back insistently towards him, an idea already twice suggested earlier in the stanza by "ihr naht euch" (you draw near) and "ihr drängt euch zu" (you throng upon me), and it should suffice to suggest this by some such word as "besiege." (3) The essential or primary elements in the sentence are "jugendlich erschüttert" (he feels rejuvenated and moved by deep nostalgia) and "Zauberhauch" (the memories come to him with magic force as if breathed into his heart by a gentle wind — a suggestion which "umwittert" merely reinforces. Accordingly my proposed version is:

> (you . . .) who so
> Besiege me, and with magic breath restore,
> Stirring my soul, lost youth to me once more.

This loses certain details, but the gains include a natural word-flow and a congruous diction.

In Part Two of *Faust*, the problems of translation are much the same as in Part One, with some added difficulties. My approach to it was based on the same assumptions and principles, including above all the dogma that readable prosodic correspondence must be allowed priority over referential literalness. In Act 3, the so-called "Helena Act," this priority gains added weight from the fact that Goethe here deliberately makes the prosody itself allegorically and dramatically significant. The whole point of his extraordinary treatment of the traditional theme of Faust's encounter with Helen, his whole original elaboration, in Acts 2 and 3, of this element in the legend, was that it should symbolize the "marriage," the fertile meeting and mingling, between the culture of classical Greece and that of modern Germany. This cultural synthesis is in its turn symbolized by a "marriage" of ancient and modern prosody: Faust teaches Helen to speak in rhymed verse. This Greek-German theme dominates the second and third Acts. Most of the second consists of the lengthy episode which Goethe ironically called the "Classical Walpurgis Night," a bizarre medley of themes and figures from classical and sub- or post-classical mythology, whimsically written in the rhymed verse unknown to the Greeks and more suggestive of modern opera libretto than of serious ancient drama. The third Act, on the other hand, with a remarkable stylistic shift, is composed predominantly in the metres and conventions of a classical Euripidean tragedy. The action takes place outside a palace, and the principal speaker (protagonist) Helen is supported by a "chorus" of attendant women. They are joined presently by the second main actor (deuteragonist) Mephistopheles, who has assumed the form of one of the hideous Phorcyads or Graiae. Helen and "Phorcyas" speak in the normal metre for dramatic dialogue, whether tragic or comic: the Greek iambic trimeter which became the Latin senarius. The chorus uses a complex pattern of lyric strophes. All the speakers, in some passages of high emotion, change to trochaic tetrameters. These are normal features of the Attic drama.

In his "classical" period Goethe enthusiastically and successfully, in *Hermann und Dorothea* and elsewhere, imitated the dactylic hexameter of the Homeric epic; in numerous other poems and epigrams he also adopted the "elegiac" style (hexameter-pentameter distichs). In fact, nearly all his poetry at this period was written in one or other of these two favourite dactylic verse-forms. This does not apply to *Faust*, to which important new material was added at the turn of the century, though it was not finished until the last five or six years of his life. The hexameter was an "epic" line and the pentameter belongs to the "elegiac" style; *Faust*, as a dramatic work, consequently made no use of either. On the other hand, it was in the "Helena Act" of Part Two (published separately in 1827, though its opening was sketched in about 1800) that Goethe introduced the classical dramatic metres, above all the iambic trimeter, to German drama. This had not been done before, though Lessing had considered using it in *Nathan der Weise* (1778) and Schiller, in *Die Jungfrau von Orleans* (1800), wrote some of the dialogue in trimeters, possibly under Goethe's influence and not with great success. But in the whole of Goethe's "Helen" episode, it is evident that the "Greek" metres have a special significance, and that imitation of them, as of the rhymed verse elsewhere in *Faust*, imposes itself as one of the essential aims of the translator of Part Two. A translation will in this case, of course, be at two removes from the ancient originals — an imitation of Goethe's imitation. The rules of Greek and Latin prosody were unlike those of anything that could purport to be a modern equivalent: for a Greek poet the syllables of the dactyls and spondees that composed his hexameter or pentameter line were not stressed or unstressed, but "long" or "short," their "quantity" being determined by special conventions. Although it is still quite uncertain how spoken ancient Greek sounded, we may take it that a "quantitative" hexameter recited by its author would have had a rhythm and intonation quite different from those of the same line spoken as an "accentual" hexameter by a German or English reader using modern pronunciation. Nevertheless, the requirements of Goethe's stylistic purpose oblige the translator to devise an approximation that will plausibly suggest something of the character of the ancient culture to which the Helena act was doing homage.

In his adaptations of ancient metres generally Goethe observed some of their conventions quite strictly, and this is not always noticed by English translators. The dactylic pentameter in his elegiac verse, for example, serves to illustrate this point. Firstly, it invariably obeys the rule of the central caesura, which divides the line into two symmetrical hemistichs, each of two-and-a-half metra, making five. The metra are in this case feet, either dactyls (/ U U) or spondees (/ /), though in practice the latter, especially in the modern imitation, tend to weaken into trochees (/ U). This symmetrical structure may be used in a pointed, emphatic way, as in lines such as "Sehe mit fühlendem Aug, fühle mit sehender Hand" or "Werd ich auch halb nur gelehrt, bin ich doch doppelt beglückt" (*Römische Elegien* VII), or it may be unobtrusive, but it should be possible to read the line aloud with an at least notional break in the middle, if it is to sound anything like a true pentameter. Secondly, no pentameter hemistich — and no hexameter for that matter — ever begins with an unstressed ("short") syllable. Thirdly, the pentameter's fourth foot is never a spondee, always a dactyl: that is, its second hemistich should always be (and in Goethe always is) / U U / U U /, not / U U / / / . These requirements are relatively straightforward, and the translator must devise an English equivalent conforming to them. In the case of the iambic trimeter, which is what we are chiefly concerned with in *Faust,* an attempt must also be made to convey, as Goethe does, something of its characteristic subtle rhythm. The trimeter is so called because it is supposed, in Greek at least, to consist of three metra, each of two iambic feet (the equivalent line in Latin drama has usually been regarded as simply a line of six iambic feet, hence its name "senarius"). The trimeter in its pure form (hardly ever found) would be U / U / U / U / U / U / . In practice, however, the first syllable of each metron is an "anceps" (X) which may be long or short, and the pattern for the line is therefore X / U / X / U / X / U / .

It is instructive to compare the rhythm of the trimeter to that of the "alexandrine," the standard line for German drama in the pre-classical period, when pre-Goethean German literature was dominated by French models. In *Faust II,* Goethe conveniently uses both these metres in Act 4, one in Faust's monologue at the beginning, the other in the ironic last scene in which the Emperor distributes ceremonial state offices, only to find himself helpless before the demands of the rapacious Church: here the archaic rhythms of the alexandrine pointedly evoke the empty formality of mediaeval imperial institutions. The alexandrine, like the iambic trimeter, has twelve syllables, but here the resemblance ends, and the translator's aim must be to distinguish the two metres as perceptibly as Goethe does. The rhymed couplets in which the French alexandrine and its German equivalent were always written are the first obvious point of difference. The next is the generally symmetrical structure of the line. There is a strict syllable-count, as in classical French verse generally, and the twelve syllables of the classical alexandrine invariably fall into two groups of six, with marked caesura between them. This is well suited to stately, ceremonious effects, as in the comic dialogue between the Emperor and the Archbishop (10977–11042):

> Mit welchem bittern Schmerz find' ich, in dieser Stunde,
> Dein hochgeheiligt Haupt mit Satanas im Bunde!
> Zwar, wie es scheinen will, gesichert auf dem Thron,
> Doch leider! Gott dem Herrn, dem Vater Papst zum Hohn.
> Wenn dieser es erfährt, schnell wird er sträflich richten,
> Mit heiligem Strahl dein Reich, das sündige, zu vernichten.

> I see with bitter sorrow, in this very hour,
> Your sacred Majesty enthralled to Satan's power.
> Your throne now seems assured, but by the means you used
> The Holy Father's mocked, God himself is abused.

When the Pope hears of it, a righteous doom will smash
Your sinful Empire with his sacred thunderflash.

I have tried to preserve the basic alexandrine pattern, but without
keeping strictly to the six-syllable half-lines, and without attempting to
obey the French and German rule of alternating masculine and feminine couplets. Goethe is stricter on both these points. His trimeters, on
the other hand, are more flexible, and not only because of the absence
of rhyme. In the first line of the example below (from Faust's opening
speech in Act 4) he even adds an extra iambus, making it a very acceptable septenarius:

Der Einsamkeiten tiefste schauend unter meinem Fuß,
Betret' ich wohlbedächtig dieser Gipfel Saum,
Entlassend meiner Wolke Tragewerk, die mich sanft
An klaren Tagen über Land und Meer geführt.

Gazing at those profoundest solitudes beneath my feet,
I tread with circumspection this high mountain-brink,
Dismissing now my cloudy vehicle, which has brought
Me gently through bright daylight over land and sea.

The occasional additional short syllables (Trag*e*werk, veh*i*cle) are also
in keeping with the character of the line, possibly as echoes of the
Greek practice of "resolving" a long syllable into two shorts. The caesura of the trimeter, moreover, unlike that of the alexandrine, was vari-
able in its position, occurring more or less unobtrusively just after the
first or just after the third syllable of the second metron. In the fourth
line of the above passage, for example, the notional caesura (||) comes
in the earlier position, after "Tagen" : (1)an klaren Ta-(2)gen || über
Land (3)und Meer geführt; in the English version it is in the later posi-
tion, after "daylight": (1)me gently through (2)bright daylight ||
o-(3)ver land and sea. It is in the later position again (after "wohlbedächtig" and "circumspection") in both the German and the English of
the second line. These conventions of Goethe's quasi-trimeters are unfamiliar to German verse and quite alien to English, but need to be
sufficiently suggested if a translation is to be plausible.

More laborious to imitate and describe are the patterns of the choric
odes. The first, beginning at line 8516, has three strophes separated by
Helen's trimeters but together forming one ode which recalls the
Greek "triadic" arrangement: strophe (8516–23), metrically parallel
antistrophe (8560–67), and metrically related epode (8591–603). In
8610–37 the three strophes are unseparated and similarly related to
each other, together constituting a second ode. In the rest of the scene,

the chorus varies this pattern but recognizably reverts to it from time to time, as in lines 8697–753, in which each of the second, fourth, seventh and ninth strophes fairly closely echoes the rhythm of the one preceding it. The same happens in lines 8887–902. I quote one passage (8728–43) in its English version as a relatively clear example of this rhythmical echoing or twinning of whole strophes:

> Which one are you among
> Phorcys's daughters?
> For I must liken you
> To that generation.
> Have you come here perhaps as one of the
> Grey-born hags, the Graiae, who take
> Turns, the three of them sharing
> One eye, one tooth, between them?
>
> Monster, how dare you be
> Seen beside beauty,
> Seen by the sun-god
> Whose gaze knows all things?
> Yet, step forth if you will; for indeed, he
> Himself can behold no hideous sight,
> Even as his sacred eye has
> Never yet looked upon shadow.

This attempts to meet, approximately at least, the metrical requirement of the German text.

Phorcyas enters the dialogue at 8754, and her confrontation with the chorus and Helen continues to 8881 in normal trimeters. These dominate the remainder of the scene but are intermittently replaced by trochaic tetrameters, lines appearing to contain eight trochees but officially consisting of four metra each of which is a double trochee ($/ \cup / \times$). The scene *Vor dem Palast des Menelas* culminates in Helen's acceptance, at Phorcyas-Mephistopheles' suggestion, of Faust's protection against her husband's threatening approach, and the transition to *Innerer Burghof* is marked by the solemn entry of Faust in the role of a mediaeval knight with his retinue. The symbolic change from Greek to mediaeval or modern metres begins here, unobtrusively at first with Faust's opening speech in Shakespearean blank verse which Helen has no difficulty in matching (9192–217). What first puzzles her are the speeches of Lynceus, who pays her homage in the rhymed stanzas of a mediaeval minnesänger. This leads to the remarkable exchange between Helen and Faust in which she learns to rhyme. The chorus follows with a strict triadic ode (9384–410), and the lovers then resume their duet, their music now fully enriched with internal rhymes as well (fern, gern; kaum, Traum; verlebt, verwebt; nicht, Pflicht). The delicate symbolism of the beloved "learning to rhyme" from her lover is exactly paralleled by Goethe's poem "Behramgur, sagt man, hat den Reim erfunden . . ." in the *Westöstlicher Divan*, which was based not only on a Persian legend but also on his sense of the emotional harmony between himself and Marianne von Willemer, the "Muse" of the *Divan*, whose contributions to the collection are, by some trick of loving imitation, written exactly in Goethe's style.

All these prosodic features, whether involving rhyme or not, are thus very much of the essence of this central scene, and the antique or quasi-antique metres of the Helena act are only slightly less demanding than the rhymed verse in which nearly all the rest of *Faust* is written. The invention of English equivalents for all these relatively strict styles involves the problems and dilemmas that have already been discussed. On the one hand, we cannot make literalness do duty for fidelity: they are not the same. On the other, we cannot be content with slavish metrical imitation at the expense of readability and speakability. Inescapably, throughout this enterprise, the scarcely analysable judgements have to be made and the near-impossible balances struck. In the end we have again to acknowledge the inherent hopelessness of our search for English equivalents of poetry of this order. *Faust* belongs to the German language as such, and to read its finest passages is to understand that no English will ever match the texture and flavour, the weight and density, the wit and magic of Goethe's native words. A translation must seek to stand by itself, but must also point beyond itself, back and on to the original miracle.

By permission of Oxford University Press.

Works Cited

Faust: Parts I and II. Trans. Philip Wayne. Harmondsworth: Penguin, 1949 and 1959.

Faust: Part I and Selections from Part II. Trans. Walter Kaufmann. New York: Garden City, 1961.

Faust: Parts I and II. Trans. Charles E. Passage. New York: Macmillan, 1965.

Faust: Parts I and II. Trans. Walter Arndt. Ed. Cyrus Hamlin. New York/London: W. W. Norton, 1976.

Faust: Part One. Trans. David Luke. Oxford UP: World's Classics, 1987.

Faust: Part Two. Trans. David Luke. Oxford UP: World's Classics, 1994.

Faust: The Play in Production

Robert David MacDonald

Editorial Note:

On 8 November 1985, the Citizens' Theatre in Glasgow staged, for the first time in the United Kingdom, Goethe's *Faust*, Parts I and II (Henry Irving's London production of 1895 staged only Part I). Of course, the work had to be greatly abbreviated, but the production met with great acclaim. Using the adaptation and translation prepared by Robert David MacDonald, who directed the play, the 1985 Glasgow production featured Mark Lewis as Faust and Andrew Wilde as Mephisto. Eighteenth months later, the Lyric Theatre, Hammersmith, in London decided to present a revised version of the play, under the direction of David Freeman, with a cast led by Simon Callow. This production was first performed on 28 March 1988, but whereas the Glasgow version had taken place on one evening (lasting three and a half hours), the Lyric, Hammersmith's version took place over two, and music (composed by Nigel Osborne) accompanied the production.

In the following essay, a revised version of his introduction to his performing version of Goethe's *Faust*,[1] Robert David MacDonald discusses the principles behind his stage adaptation and considers what he learnt about the play as director of the 1985 Glasgow production.

THE 1985 GLASGOW PRODUCTION OF *FAUST* sprang first from a suggestion of Dr. Georg Heuser, then director of the Goethe-Institut in Glasgow, which had helped to fund several productions at the Citizens' Theatre, including Goethe's *Torquato Tasso*, a lone salute in the British theatre to the 150th anniversary of the author's death. After the Citizens' had mounted Karl Kraus's monumental *The Last Days of Mankind* at the Edinburgh Film Festival in 1983, *Faust* seemed

---

[1] Johann Wolfgang Goethe. *Faust: A Tragedy: Parts One and Two.* Trans. Robert David MacDonald. Birmingham: Oberon Books, 1988.

a natural step to take in the direction of staging plays normally considered unperformable.

Two years later, the Citizens' Company performed a version of both parts of the play in one evening. The original intention was to perform the play over two evenings, with marathon performances of both parts at weekends; for various reasons, some fairly mundane, it was decided to try to stage the whole play, or as much of it as was feasible, on one evening. Not the least of these reasons was the feeling that the numberless inconsistencies between the two parts of the tragedy could most easily be reconciled if placed within the limits of a single evening in the theatre.

This decision made it necessary to cut roughly half of the translation as it stood, and to re-order the remainder to suit the available resources, material, financial, and human, as well as the production which was envisaged. This done, *Faust* hit the stage, with considerable success, on 8 November 1985.

To perform it on a single evening, it was clear that the main problem, as far as the text went, was one of selection. A further preoccupation was how to impart consistency to a whole which could otherwise appear inchoate. Emerson may have been right to say that "a foolish consistency is the hobgoblin of little minds [. . .] with consistency a great soul has nothing to do," but those lesser souls who sit in theatres like the evening to hang together in some way or other.

David Luke, in his admirable introduction to the most recent, and best, complete translation of Part One,[2] points out that *Faust* studies divide into two schools, the historical or genetic, which seeks to emphasize the discrepancies as being part of Goethe's continual development over the very long time it took to write *Faust*, and the unitarian, which insists that the whole work must be regarded as an integrated whole, springing from a single, unchanging conception, to be imposed on it at all costs. It would be good to avoid the lunacies of either of these two schools, but it must be said that while it is desirable to face the specifically theatrical problem as a unitarian, it is also mandatory to remember that the play was written, over a period of more than half a century, by the most enquiring mind in Europe during those sixty-odd years, whose own comments stress the fragmentariness of the work, but who, we must believe, built the later part of the great structure on the basis of what he had already published. (The time between his beginning and ending play is exactly equivalent to that between man's first

[2] Goethe, Johann Wolfgang. *Faust: Part One.* Trans. David Luke. Oxford: Oxford UP, 1987.

powered flight at Kitty Hawk, and the first man-made orbit of the earth in space.)

It will be clear that *Faust*, unlike Goethe's other plays, or almost any other play by any other author, was written with neither the neatly pre-conceived structure, nor the concentration of subject-matter and diction, which we conventionally assume to be essential to dramatic production. On the contrary, *Faust* grew like a wood, the new growth continually changing the aspect of the whole, fertilized by, yet not necessarily obscuring, what had gone before, and full of alien, variegated, often parasitic forms of life. Since it conforms to none of the rules, it must be considered independently of any such rules. In a poem called *Leavetaking*, written for an actor to speak as epilogue at the end of Part One, Goethe compares the poem to human life — "it certainly has a beginning and an end, it's just that it doesn't make a whole."[3] The ambiguity of his feelings for a work which was clearly of great personal importance to him, but which he was continually deprecating, particularly to Schiller, without whose encouragement it would never have been completed, indicates that he never really considered the work finished, but realized that its quasi-autobiographical nature was such that its final form would be at whatever stage it had reached at the time he died. His reluctance to publish Part Two, along with the reckless impracticality of the stage directions, possibly confirm this view. One could conclude, with Dr. Johnson's view of the Shakespearean history play — "as it had no plan, it had no limits."

The implications of all this for exegetists, commentators, interpreters, and, in the field that most concerns us here, theatrical directors, is that it will always be open season on *Faust*. It is like a huge stone quarry, from which people will hew out the play that interests them at the time, still leaving behind a quarry apparently undiminished, from which others will hack away according to their needs. What is excavated may be anything between a masterpiece and a shambles, but the elusiveness, as well as the toughness of the huge epic will absorb it all, brilliance along with ineptitude. Like *Hamlet* or America, the target is so big that we are all bound to hit it somewhere.

A yet further preoccupation in preparing a practical, performing script of the play was the need to marry up the two parts, so different in conception and indeed in diction, so that they hung together more closely than they in fact do. Here the Devil became, for once, the saviour. Faust himself changes markedly between the two parts, Mephi-

---

[3] "Abkündigung": "Des Menschen Leben ist ein ähnliches Gedicht / Es hat Anfang hat ein Ende. / Allein ein Ganzes ist es nicht" (WA 15.1, 344).

stopheles scarcely at all — hardly surprising, since it is Faust's character which develops, the Devil's being, by definition, already formed, even when he is finally, albeit briefly, thrown off balance by what H. C. Earwicker called the "fleshasplush cushionettes of some chubby boybold love of an angel." It was necessary, all the same, to bring some of the more ironic tone — not a common quality in German literature — of Part Two over into Part One. If Faust is seen as, to some extent, a self-portrait of his creator, his apparent inconsistencies no longer worry us; but it becomes yet more necessary to bear in mind that it is Faust's story we are telling, to the exclusion of all other distractions. The man who betrays Gretchen must be the same man who ends up draining the marshes: the Gretchen tragedy must be seen as the first, if the decisive, episode in a series of trials, and not as a separate play which, thanks to Gounod, it often becomes. It is the supreme irony of the play that the great scientist, when faced with infinite choice, chooses a love-affair which he conducts with all the egotistical inefficiency of an adolescent. When he has finally destroyed the object of his love, he proceeds, like many people who give up in that field — compare Alberich in Wagner's *Ring* — to the exercise of other less attractive passions: money, power, war and organising other people's lives.

Apart from the "torture of a thousand cuts," minute, and less minute, excisions, varying in length from a single word to over a hundred lines, in every scene that was preserved, nearly all the major omissions are there, or rather not there, to keep the story of Faust himself before the spectator. It is as surprising as it is clear how the purely dramatic interest of the play falls away when he is not on the stage: even Mephistopheles, a far showier part, cannot sustain the interest *on his own*. The main total or near-total casualties were the Student/Baccalaureus, a lot of the Walpurgis Night, the whole of the Walpurgis Night's Dream Intermezzo, the Carnival at the Emperor's palace in Part Two, huge chunks of the Classical Walpurgis Night, the scene of the Emperor after the battle and, of course, quantities of the final scene. To say "of course" about the excision of what must be the supreme poetic achievement of a world language sounds frivolous, but in the context of any production, the treatment of the final scene will be a sort of shorthand summing-up of the aims and ideals of the production itself and, as such, cannot be overextended without becoming over-emphatic and repetitive, telling the audience something they should already have a fair inkling of, after all the time they have spent in the theatre. Further, I transposed the scenes in Auerbach's Cellar and the Witch's Kitchen, as it seemed that the natural break should come between leaving the study and entering the world, and that Faust's rejuvenation was the best bridge between the two levels. Before the birth of Euphorion, I introduced a monologue of Mephistopheles, culled, as were several other less important and less noticeable lardings, from Goethe's early rejected sketches. This was partly to diffuse the rather high-falutin tone that begins to be established by the love scene of Faust and Helen, and which, if carried over unbroken into the Euphorion scene, would be, I felt, for British audiences at any rate, unendurably po-faced: it also had the real practical advantage of conveying the not entirely clear narrative in very few but vivid lines.

So much then, for the playing (and playable) text. The generosity of the Goethe-Institut enabled us to enlarge the Citizens' Company to some twenty actors. I had seen *Faust* twice before, in Germany, in each case with companies of nigh on 100 performers, so doubling of parts seemed inevitable. To me, however, this is unsatisfactory unless there is some consistency between the parts played, some creative connection, as in *King Lear*, where Cordelia was written to double with the Fool. This led me to conflate and concertina the roles to be played as single roles throughout the evening. So, for example, the Theatre Director of the prologue was (not became) God in the next prologue (in Heaven), and various divine apparitions, for example Proteus, at other times; the Emperor started life as a student, Gretchen as a waitress at Auerbach's, along with Martha, the Witch became a Sphinx, and so on. Exceptions were made in two cases, either when one character died (Valentine) or was so impenetrably disguised as not to be recognizable (for example, the Lamiae, though they were played by three leading politicians, giving a fairly familiar tone of corruption). A further cheating stratagem was the invention of a heavenly messenger who could pick up eccentric roles at will and be seen as some sort of supernatural messenger (Charioteer, Euphorion, Ariel, Homunculus, etc.).

This may sound neat enough and, by and large, worked, though in practice there was a certain amount of panic, redistribution of lines, having to wait for actors to change costume and the like, the theatre being, alas, a practical medium. But though there had to be some wrenching of the cloth to fit the dummy, the material gained some much-needed consistency.

The next question is: where is it happening? Goethe's Shakespearean high-handedness with location demands, or certainly deserves, a Shakespearean solution, a Globe-style "wooden O"; in more modern terms, an immobile, unchanging structure, anonymous enough to be acceptable as anywhere and handsome enough in repose. It is also important that we remember we are in a theatre: all the resources in the world will not convince us we are actually in Heaven, Hell or wherever — in such cases one is wiser not to try. Necessary are several levels on which action can take place; stairs, visible or hidden, to get from one level to another; and ways of revealing and concealing new actions. This was arrived at by taking the image of the stone quarry, from which all could hack the play they wanted — irregular blocks of stone, steps hewn from the rock, and gaps suitable for entering or leaving. The large block on the centre of the stage could revolve, to reveal where necessary, elements specifically, but temporarily, needed for the action of the moment, and afterwards discarded.

The opening, conveniently enough, takes place in a theatre. The three speakers (Director, Author, Actor) apart, the whole company came on to listen to the argument, dressed in whatever they had put on that morning — *not* things they fancied themselves in, unless they were prepared to wear them all day — and doing whatever they usually did at rehearsals, or at Equity meetings, knitting, drinking coffee, doing crosswords, arriving late, half in costume and the like: this was a theatre, after all, and neither could nor should be mistaken for anywhere or anything else. By the time the prologue became the prologue in Heaven, the company was fairly familiar to the audience, and the three archangels had, for example, become morning dress-suited ministers, with God, the Director (played, incidentally, by the director of the theatre, Giles Havergal) in his black director's suit, sitting in his director's chair, while Mephistopheles, hitherto indistinguishable from other stage hands, in dungarees with "Citizens' Theatre" stencilled on the back, detached himself from the crowd.

This procedure was reversed at the end of the evening. After the death of Faust, aged 100, looking as much like the aged Howard Hughes as possible, the company reassembled for the last scene, again in their day-clothes (after a long evening, a quick exit to the bar is appreciated by thirsty actors), speaking singly or in chorus the various farewell lines of the finale, while a ticker tape machine tapped out the last lines, read off by one or other of the main characters as a "message to the future."

I have been asked where the main emphases had to be placed in presenting *Faust* to a Scottish audience: the answer is that each audience will provide its own emphasis. I recall working on a production at the RSC of Dürrenmatt's *The Physicists*, in which the body of a murdered nurse lay on stage from the moment the audience came into the theatre, and for the half-hour before the play started. For one matinee, tickets were offered to, and accepted by some organisations of nurses, who more or less filled the house. They were less interested in the implications of the mad (or pseudo-mad) scientists in the asylum and their dangerous knowledge than they were the fate of the nurse (nurses, as it turned out later). The play became a play primarily about nurses, and only secondarily about their murderess: it would have required a totally perverse production to convince that particular audience to the contrary. So if there is anything in *Faust* that evokes a peculiarly Scottish reaction in a Scottish audience, it is up to that audience to find it. It was certainly not intended, although, as a Scot directing the play, it is possible that my contribution to the production may have contained, for instance, certain touches which a director of another nationality might not have thought of at all, or thought worthwhile if he had. The collective nature of a theatre audience will decide many things about the evening during which they collectively exist; this is of course, one of the things that differentiate the theatrical experience from television.

In the end, albeit ideally, directors work on a play because they want to — if enough people want to see what they make of this or that play, they will make it a success, regardless of the quality exposed, and that is that. The theatre is practical, fashionable, and has an enduring appetite for devouring its children. It also gives them the privilege of playing with the best toy yet unmarketed. Add one of the greatest works of imaginative literature in history, and your pleasure need know no limits, whichever end of the telescope, as spectator or participant, you are looking through.

Contributors

PAUL BISHOP is Senior Lecturer in the Department of German at the University of Glasgow. He is the author of various books and articles on C.G. Jung, Nietzsche, and Goethe, including *The World of Stoical Discourse in Goethe's "Die Wahlverwandtschaften"* (Mellen, 1999), *Synchronicity and Intellectual Intuition* (Mellen, 2000), and has edited *Jung in Contexts: A Reader* (Routledge, 1999) and (with R. H. Stephenson) *Goethe 2000: Intercultural Readings of his Work* (Northern Universities Press, 2000).

ALBERTO DESTRO is Professor of German at the University of Bologna. He is the author of numerous publications in the field of *Germanistik*, including studies of Rilke, Nestroy, Heine, and Goethe (with particular reference to *Faust*). He is one of the co-editors of the *Historisch-kritische Gesamtausgabe* (Hoffmann und Campe) of Heine's works, and he collaborated on the catalogue for the exhibition *Europa, wie Goethe es sah*, which was held in Düsseldorf in 1999.

OSMAN DURRANI is Professor of German at the University of Kent at Canterbury. His recent publications include *Fictions of Germany: Images of the German Nation in the Modern Novel* (Edinburgh UP, 1994), an edited volume on *The New Germany: Literature and Society after Unification* (Sheffield Academic P, 1995), and articles on numerous postwar authors, including Süskind, Westphalen, Schwanitz, Delius and Robert Schneider; a co-edited volume of conference papers on the German historical novel is forthcoming.

R. ELLIS DYE is DeWitt Wallace Professor of German at Macalester College in Saint Paul, Minnesota, where he teaches language, literature (especially Goethe and Romanticism) and philosophy (Nietzsche, Heidegger), and was Chair of German Studies and Russian. He has published widely on Goethe and related topics in a variety of journals, and he is the book review editor of the *Goethe Yearbook*. He is working on a book to be called *One and Double: Love and Death in Goethe*.

CYRUS HAMLIN is Professor of German and Comparative Literature at Yale University. He has published widely in the field of European Romanticism and hermeneutics, and his collected essays on these subjects appeared as *Hermeneutics of Form: Romantic Poetics in Theory and Practice* (Henry R. Schwab, 1998). He has recently completed a revised edition with commentary of Goethe's *Faust* for Norton Critical Editions (Norton, 2000), and is General Editor of the Suhrkamp Edition of Goethe in English (Princeton UP).

DAVID LUKE was a Student (Fellow) and Tutor in German at Christ Church, Oxford, until 1988. He has edited and translated Goethe's *Selected Verse* (Penguin, 1964), *Faust: Part One* (Oxford World's Classics, 1987) (which was awarded the European Poetry Translation Prize in 1989), *Faust: Part Two* (Oxford World's Classics, 1994), *Erotic Poems* (Oxford World's Classics, 1997), and *Selected Poetry* (Libris, 1999), as well as other works by Goethe, Kleist, the Brothers Grimm, and Thomas Mann.

ROBERT DAVID MACDONALD has been Co-Director of the Citizens' Company at the Citizens' Theatre in Glasgow since 1971, and has written fourteen plays for the company. As an actor with the Citizens' Company he has played numerous leading roles, and as a director with the Company he has directed fifty productions, including the premiere of Goethe's *Faust, I and II* (abridged) (1985). He has translated over sixty plays and operas from ten languages, including works by Goethe. In 1984 he was awarded the Goethe Medal.

ANTHONY PHELAN is a Faculty Lecturer in German and Fellow in German at Keble College, Oxford. His many articles reflect his interests in German literature and thought from 1760 to the present, and he edited *The Weimar Dilemma: German Intellectuals in the Weimar Republic* (Manchester UP, 1984). His books include a study of *Rilke: Neue Gedichte* (Grant & Cutler, 1992) and a series of papers on Brecht in the Thirties; he is completing a book on Heine's reception in the twentieth century.

RITCHIE ROBERTSON is Professor of German at Oxford University and a Fellow of St. John's College. As well as numerous articles on a wide range of subjects, his publications include *Kafka: Judaism, Politics, and Literature* (Clarendon Press, 1985), *Heine* (Peter Halban, 1988), *The "Jewish Question" in German Literature, 1749–1939* (Oxford UP, 1999), and he has recently edited *The German-Jewish Dialogue, 1749–1993* (Oxford World's Classics, 1999). He is the Germanic Editor of *The Modern Language Review*.

FRANZISKA SCHÖßLER is a Wissenschaftliche Assistentin at the Albert-Ludwigs-Universität in Freiburg im Breisgau. Her numerous articles include studies of contemporary drama and prose, gender studies, and studies of Goethe, Keller, Kafka, and Celan; and her postdoctoral thesis, *Goethes Lehr- und Wanderjahre als Romane der Epochenschwelle*, will soon be published. She has worked as assistant director and script writer for various theatres, including the Volksbühne Berlin.

PETER D. SMITH is a British Academy Postdoctoral Fellow in the German Department at University College London. He has published numerous articles on the relationship between German literature and science and on twentieth-century authors, and his most recent publication is *Metaphor and Materiality: German Literature and the World-View of Science, 1780–1955* (Legenda, 2000). He is currently writing on scientific ideas in American and European literature since 1600.

R. H. STEPHENSON is William Jacks Professor of German at the University of Glasgow, Director of its Centre for Intercultural Germanistics, and Head of its School of Modern Languages. He has published widely on various aspects of German literature and thought, including numerous articles, monographs on *Goethe's Wisdom Literature: A Study in Aesthetic Transmutation* (Lang, 1983) and *Goethe's Conception of Knowledge and Science* (Edinburgh UP, 1995), and a forthcoming study of the cultural theory of Weimar Classicism. He is co-editor (with Paul Bishop) of *Goethe 2000: Intercultural Readings of his Work* (Northern Universities Press, 2000).

MARTIN SWALES is Professor of German at University College London, and a Fellow of the British Academy. He has written widely on German literature of the eighteenth, nineteenth, and twentieth centuries, including book-length studies of Schnitzler, the German Novelle, the German Bildungsroman, Thomas Mann, Stifter, and realism; commentaries on works by Goethe and Thomas Mann; and he has also edited numerous books on these and other subjects. He was awarded the "Bundesverdienstkreuz" of the Federal Republic of Germany in 1994.

JOHN R. WILLIAMS was Senior Lecturer in German at the University of St. Andrews until 1993. He has published extensively in the field of Goethe studies, including numerous articles and reviews in a wide variety of journals, a book-length study of Goethe's *"Faust"* (Allen & Unwin, 1987), *The Life of Goethe: A Critical Biography* (Blackwell, 1998),

294 NOTES ON THE CONTRIBUTORS

and a translation of *Faust: The First Part of the Tragedy with the unpublished scenarios for the Walpurgis Night and the Urfaust* (Wordsworth Classics, 1999).

Index

Abeken, Bernhard Rudolf, 74
action/activism, xxiv, 29, 34–35,
  37, 48–49, 50–51, 114, 115,
  125, 183, 184, 185, 235, 248
  (*See also Faust*, themes; Faust, as
  man of action; Faust, *Streben*;
  Streben)
Addison, Joseph, 63–65, 70
Adelheid, von Walldorf, 105–6
Adler, Jeremy, 195
Adonis, xx
advertising, 174, 176, 255, 260
Aegean Sea, 159–60
Aeneas, 123
aesthetics, 178, 237, 239, 241
  aesthetic beauty, xxvi, 103, 238
African pagan tradition, xxiii
agricapitalism, xxxiii, 179–80
alchemy, xxii, 28, 137, 172, 173–
  74, 195, 206 (*See also* correspondences, doctrine of; Faust;
  Goethe; Wagner)
  alchemical symbolism, 125, 126
Alexander the Great, 147
Amrine, Frederick, 194
Anaxagoras, 159, 211, 260–61
androgyny, xxxi, 91, 97
angels, xxxi, 24, 41, 90, 91, 115,
  116
  archangels, 10, 34, 48
  hierarchies, 17, 77, 182
Antaeus, 25
anthropology, xxix, xxxiv–xxxv, 249,
  264
Antigone, 52
Aquinas, 249
Arabian Nights, 12, 126
Arcadia, evocations of, 15, 88, 165,
  174 (*See also* Faust, visions of
  utopia; Goethe, restorative
  utopias)

archaeology, 45
architecture, xxxii, 153, 163
Arens, Hans, 96, 123, 127, 130–31
aristocracy, 47, 68, 70
Aristotle, 17, 78, 179, 255
Arndt, Walter, xxxv, 272, 273–75,
  276
Arnold, Gottfried, 111–12
  *Unparteiische Kirchen- und
  Ketzergeschichte*, 243, 244
art, xxii, 88, 127, 189, 238, 244
  beauty in art, 238–39
artificial intelligence, xxxvii, 44,
  199–200 (*See also* Homunculus)
artificial needs, xxxiii, 170, 174,
  176, 177, 179, 181, 185
Astrologer (*Faust*), 153, 154, 173,
  186, 260
astrology, 172
Atkins, Stuart, xxvii, xxxv, 101,
  129–30, 131, 152, 247
atomic power, 205
Augustus, 249

Baccalaureus (*Faust*), 44, 112, 253–
  54, 255, 286
Bacon, Francis, 206
Bahr, Ehrhard, xxviii
Baioni, Giuliano, 65, 66, 68, 70
ballads, 95
Balsamo, Giuseppe. *See* Cagliostro
Baucis (*Faust*), 47, 51, 59, 62, 103,
  113, 203, 214, 246
Beauty, xxxiii, 87, 88, 186–87, 237,
  252, 264 (*See also* art; Helen of
  Troy)
Benjamin, Walter, 166
Bennett, Benjamin, xxviii
Berg, Alben, *Lulu*, 106
Berlin, xxxvi
  University of, 224

Samson and Delilah, 132
Sartorius, Georg, 170
Satan. *See* devil
satanic cults, 91
satire. *See Faust*
Schad, Wolfgang, 194
Schadewaldt, Wolfgang, 266
Schaffhausen, 205
Schaper, Rüdiger, xxxix
Schelling, Friedrich W. J. von, xxxiv,
    74, 144, 195, 226
    "Über Dante in philosophischer
        Beziehung," 222–24
    Philosophie der Kunst, 223
    Naturphilosophie, 229
    *System des tranzendentalen
        Idealismus,* 238
    *Über die Gottheiten von
        Samothrace,* 160
Schieb, Roswitha, *Peter Stein
    inszeniert Faust I und II: Das
    Programmbuch zur Inszenierung,*
    xxxvii
Schiller, Friedrich, xvi, xvii, xix, 1, 9,
    97, 222–23, 232, 239, 278, 285
    Der Geisterseher, 140
    Die Jungfrau von Orleans, 278
    Maria Stuart, 105–6
    *Über die ästhetische Erziehung des
        Menschen in einer Reihe von
        Briefen,* 232, 237–38
Schindler's List, 90
Schlaffer, Hannelore, 183–84, 186,
    187–88
Schlaffer, Heinz, 87, 125–26, 127,
    128–29, 141, 149
Schlegel, August William, xxxvi,
    221, 223
Schlegel, Friedrich, xxxvi, 23, 232,
    238
    "Über das Studium der
        griechischen Poesie," 221–22
    Gespräch über die Poesie, 164;
    Lucinde, 164
Schliemann, Heinrich, 45

Schlosser, Johann Georg, *Xenocrats
    oder über die Abgaben,* 170
Schmidt, Jochen, xxviii, 63–64, 70,
    183, 188
Schneider, Hans Ernst, 32, 56
Scholz, Rüdiger, 123, 124, 129
Schöne, Albrecht, xxviii, 86, 114–
    15, 117, 153, 198–99, 213, 214
Schopenhauer, Arthur, *Die Welt als
    Wille und Vorstellung,* 257
Schößler, Franziska, xxx, xxxiii,
    [169–90], 207
Schrepfer, Johann Georg, 137
Schrimpf, Hans Joachim, 66
Schubert, Franz, 9
    "Die schöne Müllerin," 109
Schweitzer, Christoph E., 115
Schwerte, Hans. *See* Schneider
science, xxx, 44–45, 194–95, 202,
    205, 211–12, 225 (*See also Faust,*
    science in; Goethe)
sea, 110–11, 159, 160, 200, 211,
    213, 214, 215
séances, 137, 138, 140
secularism, xxx
Segeberg, Harro, 211
Seidlin, Oskar, 82
Seismos, 159, 260
self-assertion, 51, 109
self-consciousness, 33, 34, 224–27,
    230–31, 236, 252
sensuality, 45, 57, 62, 86, 105
"Sermon on the Mount," perverse
    version, 85–86
Seven, 90
sexuality, xiv, xxii, 106, 112, 129,
    254
    sex, power of, 84, 85
Shaftesbury, Anthony Ashley
    Cooper, 3rd Earl of, theory of
    "inner form," 255
Shakespeare, xiii, xx, 5, 16, 19, 103,
    221, 287
    Anthony and Cleopatra, 7